Intellectual History

4

2015年3月

目錄

【論著】

敦化川流——論管東溟的判教思想及其時代關懷*

吳孟謙

國立臺灣大學中國文學研究所博士。主要關注領域為宋明理學、三教交涉。博士論文為《融貫與批判：晚明三教論者管東溟的思想及其時代》。另著有《默識天人之際——薛敬軒理學思想探微》、〈晚明心學成聖論述的變化——以羅近溪、管東溟為主要線索〉、〈晚明「身心性命」觀念的流行：一個思想史觀點的探討〉、〈管東溟《續原教論評》析探〉等。

* 本文初稿曾宣讀於中央研究院明清研究推動委員會主辦，「2013中央研究院明清研究國際學術研討會」（臺北：中央研究院，2013年12月5-6日）。承蒙評論人彭國翔教授和與會學者的指教，在修訂過程中，亦蒙鍾彩鈞、廖肇亨、楊祖漢、蔡振豐、鄧克銘諸先生暨本刊兩位匿名審查人惠賜寶貴意見，謹此致謝，一切文責由筆者自負。

敦化川流——
論管東溟的判教思想及其時代關懷

摘要

管東溟是晚明具有高度創造性的思想家之一，在朱子學、陽明學、禪學流弊俱顯的時代，他不爲一宗一派所拘限，透過《華嚴經》與《周易》的會通，解構前儒的道統論。在其「敦化川流」的判教論述中，管東溟一方面給予不同宗教學術一個共通的思想底盤，撤除三教的藩籬；另一方面也企圖衡定各種教説的淺深高下，勾畫其心目中理想的修行藍圖，爲當時學術尋求新的出路。

本文探究管東溟的判教思想，依次展開爲以下幾個面向：一、從宏觀的角度，釐清「三教合一」的幾個層次；二、分析晚明思想界價值多歧的時代氛圍，突顯管東溟判教論的形成背景；三、觀察管東溟如何會通《華嚴經》與《周易》，對理學的道統論述進行解構；四、討論管東溟「敦化川流」的判教思想，及其會通儒佛的見地；五、指出管東溟之所以判釋三教的時代關懷。最後，總結管東溟判教思想的理論特色與思想史意義。

關鍵詞：敦化川流、管東溟、判教、華嚴經、周易、三教

一、前言

判教，或稱教判或教相判釋，是中國佛教所發展出的觀念，意思是對不同教法的義理做出判析、闡釋與定位。狹義來說，它專指中國佛教諸宗派對大小乘各類教說的判釋；[1]推而廣之，也適用於跨學說乃至跨宗教的判釋，中國傳統的三教論者，乃至當代新儒學宗師牟宗三、唐君毅，都曾致意於此。[2]判教論本身的性格，看似重視分析與簡別，其背後實預設一綜合的、貫通的價值蘄向，足以將樣貌多端、甚至互相扞格的教法，統攝在同一個思想系統之中。專就佛教內部而言，大乘各宗進行判教的意義，主要在於整理卷帙浩繁的漢譯佛典，對立場雜多的各式教法，做一淺深高下的釐定，並藉由判教進行經典詮釋，闡發自宗所認識之究竟眞理——也即佛陀所開演的「一乘教」或「圓教」。如果依此反思中國儒、釋、道三教交涉的歷史，那麼最具統合三教之判教意識的時代，當屬晚明。

晚明三教思想互動之密切，邁越前代。荒木見悟曾經指出，晚明三教一致論的流行是受到陽明心學自由學風的影響，性格上是「心從三教中尋找其自我充足、自我開展的素材」，是「以心學爲基盤，不受限於三教各自的既成體系，而毋寧說一點一點地改變它，將之作爲

1 關於中國佛教判教思想的發展與內涵，可參藍日昌，《六朝判教論的發展與演變》（臺北：文津出版社，2003）、王仲堯，《隋唐佛教判教思想研究》（高雄：佛光山文教基金會，2001）。吳汝均近年更從當代的、國際的視野，檢討傳統佛教的判教論，而提出自身的判教體系，參見吳汝均，《佛教的當代判釋》（臺北：臺灣學生書局，2011）。

2 牟宗三判攝三教、融通康德之說，可參牟宗三，《現象與物自身》（臺北：臺灣學生書局，1975）一書；唐君毅則以「心靈九境」判釋世間、出世間之種種心靈境界，見唐君毅，《生命存在與心靈境界：生命存在之三向與心靈九境》（臺北：臺灣學生書局，1977）。

自家藥籠中之物而加以操作運用」。[3]並且強調：「三教一致不是串同三教，也不是湊集三教之長，而是超越三教，從根本源頭重新認識三教。」[4]此種追求超越三教之根本源頭的自覺，出於心學家對自身生命的高度內省，是純然的「尊德性」工夫。於此向內探求的尊德性工夫之外，若更加以「道問學」的思辯，在超越三教的同時還意圖總持之、衡定之，使支離矛盾的教法各安其位，藉以勾畫出清楚的修行藍圖，為學術找尋新的出路，就會產生集大成的、判教型的學者。晚明的三教論者管東溟（志道，1536-1608）即是箇中翹楚。

管東溟，南直隸太倉（今江蘇省崑山市）人，後遷居長洲（今江蘇省蘇州市），是晚明以會通三教著稱的思想家。他早年苦讀《性理大全》，鑽研宋儒理學；壯歲得耿天臺（定向，1524-1593）之啓發，於陽明心學有所悟入；其後旁通佛道、綜稽群籍，融攝多樣化的思想資源，重新詮釋孔學，成就了獨樹一幟的學問體系。管東溟著述宏富，但後世流傳不廣，至今學界識之者尚尠。[5]荒木見悟在所撰《明末宗教思想研究：管東溟の生涯とその思想》一書中，將管東溟視為認識晚明思想界不可忽略的要角，較全面地介紹其思想，明確指出管東溟「心中暗自抱持著想成為朱子、陽明之後，第三思潮之倡導者的悲願。」[6]然而該書除介紹管東溟的生涯及其與特定人物的關係以外，主

3　荒木見悟，《明末宗教思想研究：管東溟の生涯とその思想》（東京：創文社，1979），頁25。

4　荒木見悟著，廖肇亨譯，〈鄧豁渠的出現及其背景〉，收入荒木見悟《明末清初的思想與佛教》（臺北：聯經出版有限公司，2006），頁190。

5　關於管東溟的相關研究成果回顧，參見吳孟謙，〈融貫與批判——晚明三教論者管東溟的思想及其時代〉（臺北：臺灣大學中國文學系博士論文，2014），頁8-15。

6　參見荒木見悟，《明末宗教思想研究：管東溟の生涯とその思想》（東

要是以「時代思想觀」、「孔子觀」、「孟子觀」、「佛教觀」、「道教觀」……等範疇，論列管東溟的相關思想，未及統觀其判釋三教的洞見。管東溟之判教，蓋從《中庸》「萬物並育而不相害，道並行而不相悖，小德川流，大德敦化，此天地之所以爲大也」的經文中，拈出「敦化川流」四字作爲綱領，展開對三教傳統的重新詮釋與時代學風的批判反省。此種判教思想的內涵爲何？問題意識因何而發？所關懷與企圖解決的是何種問題？思想史上的特殊性何在？乃是本文所關注的重點。

本文的論述，將展開爲以下五個面向：一、從宏觀的角度，釐清「三教合一」的幾個層次；二、分析晚明思想界價值多歧的時代氛圍，突顯管東溟判教論的形成背景；三、觀察管東溟如何會通《華嚴經》與《周易》，對理學的道統論述進行解構；四、討論管東溟「敦化川流」的判教思想，及其會通儒佛的見地；五、指出管東溟之所以判釋三教的時代關懷。最後，總結管東溟判教論的特色與思想史意義。

二、「三教合一」的幾個層次

往昔學界描述晚明思想潮流時，「三教合一」是個被廣爲使用的概念，但其內涵卻並不明確。究竟「合一」是在什麼層次上合一？是有機一體、混合雜揉還是並行不悖？背後的動機爲何？對這些問題若

京：創文社，1979），頁1。荒木見悟在撰寫此書之前，另有一單篇論文介紹管東溟，亦可參照，見荒木見悟，〈管東溟——明末における一儒佛調合論者の思維構造〉收入荒木見悟，《明代思想研究：明代における儒教と佛教の交流》（東京：創文社，1972），頁149-185。

無自覺，而僅套用「三教合一」一詞來描述時代風潮，將不免含混籠統之弊。本文既欲討論三教論者管東溟的判教思想，自須對此問題加以反省，始能避免泛泛之談。[7]以下先製成一表，再加以說明：

交涉層次	思維模式	主要情境	關注面向
三教一致（體）	教異道同	菁英	眞理
三教會通（相）	融通判釋	菁英	學術
三教並用（用）	並行互補	帝王	政教
三教混融（用）	隨機取用	庶民	信仰

此表將「三教合一」這一寬泛的概念，大致析出四個層次：

（一）「三教一致」。這是從本體的層次，把握三教共通的眞理源頭，教雖爲三，理卻同源，此即教異道同的思維。主要出自於知識菁英對最高眞理的探求。

（二）「三教會通」。若說三教一致是對理體的契證；三教會通則

7　學界亦曾對此問題有過一些分析。例如錢新祖討論焦竑的思想時，指出三教的融合模式至晚明有從並存（coexist）到混融（intermix）的變化。參見Edward T. Ch'ien, *Chiao Hung and the Restructuring of Neo—Confucianism in Late Ming* (New York: Columbia University Press, 1986)一書。此外，卜正民（Timothy Brook）透過中西比較的視野，反省英語世界中syncretism一詞在中國宗教融合的適用性。他引用了Judith Berling對syncretism的定義：「一宗教傳統進入其他宗教傳統，透過選擇與調和的過程，在概念、象徵與實踐上之借鑒、肯認與整合。」卜氏透過分析後認爲，中國自元以來的三教交涉，並非嚴格的syncretism，而是一種三教共治的型態，亦即三教相當程度上和諧地共存，在理論與實用上皆平等，且透過多樣的方式自由地結合和交涉。參見Timothy Brook, "Rethinking Syncretism: The Unity of the Three Teachings and their Joint Worship in Late—Imperial China," *Journal of Chinese Religions*, 21 (1993), pp. 13-44. 這些觀點皆各有理致，本文則嘗試從新的角度加以分析。

涉及對事相的融通與判釋。換句話說，即是特別關注三教在具體理論與實踐上的異同，並可能因此產生判教思想。這雖然亦出於知識菁英對眞理的探求，但學術上的分析毋寧更爲細緻，如同前言中所說的，除了尊德性工夫外，更加以道問學的思辯。

（三）「三教並用」。這是從三教的作用上考量，認爲三教皆各有其長，能夠引導人們同歸於善道，故應當並行不悖、相輔相成。此種思維最常發生於並尊三教之帝王，而所關注的重點，則是維繫政教秩序的穩定。

（四）「三教混融」。這同樣是從三教的作用上考量，不在本體上統合，亦不在教相上會通，而是滲透到日常的宗教生活之中。民間的通俗宗教即是顯例，屬於庶民的信仰世界。

以上的分析，旨在釐清「三教合一」觀念中的不同層次，以利於更清楚的思想史論述。勞思光曾說：

> 明末流行的混合信仰……從未有一個比較可取的理論來支持它，因此，在哲學標準下，講「三教合一」或「儒佛合一」等等說法，就不能看作「哲學思想」。[8]

這不免將「三教合一」視爲只有「三教混融」這個層次，忽視了晚明知識菁英在「三教會通」方面的理論貢獻。又如饒宗頤描述三教合一思想：

> 只是一種初步的混合，不是高度具有創造性之思想。自然，他既缺乏概括原理之抽象性思考，又缺少莊嚴而凝固的宗教信念，只趨向於道德心靈的陶冶，及輔助政治力量

8 勞思光，《新編中國哲學史》（臺北：三民書局，2001），第3卷（下），〈後記〉，頁887。

的和諧。[9]

此處對「三教合一」的理解，也似僅包括「三教並用」與「三教混融」兩個層次。其所謂抽象性思考與宗教信念，在「三教一致」與「三教會通」之中實不曾缺席；至於高度具創造性的思想，更頻出於晚明，本文要討論的管東溟即是極佳的個案。

必須說明的是，上述四種交涉層次或思維模式，並非四條不相往來的平行線，相反地，它們可能交會於一人的觀念中。以管東溟爲例，他既追求三教一貫的眞理源頭，又致力於三教思想的會通判釋（詳見下文），並高度讚賞明太祖「主儒宗而賓仙佛」的三教政策，[10]此即兼具「教異道同」、「融通判釋」與「並行互補」的思維。思想史上的三教合一論，若依此詳加梳理與定位，當能更顯立體。

三、價值多歧的時代氛圍

晚明致力於會通三教的思想家，皆有其生命需求與時代需求。就生命需求的一面來說，當時不論儒者或方外之士，均致力於身心性命之學，管東溟亦不例外。此種學問以實踐受用爲導向，而非以知識興趣爲導向。換言之，三教論者並非純然爲了建立一理論體系而進行會通；毋寧說，他們是在自身的求道歷程中，展現出自身與三教思想資源相對話的成果。此中必然牽涉到思想家們獨特的人格情性、生命問題與證道體驗，因此，即使同樣從事於會通三教，不同思想家之間，

9 饒宗頤，〈三教論及其海外移植〉，收入饒宗頤，《選堂集林：史林新編》（香港：中華書局，2012），中冊，頁689-722。

10 參見管志道，《從先維俗議》，卷5，〈聖祖主賓三教大意〉，收入四庫全書存目叢書編纂委員會編，《四庫全書存目叢書》（臺南：莊嚴文化公司，1995），子部雜家類，第88冊，頁473。

立場與主張亦可能千差萬別。

另就時代需求的一面來說，陽明學流行以來，思想空氣日益自由，三教互動益發密切，學者很難如明初儒者一般，終身服膺程朱之教而不疑；[11]反之，他們必須面對價值多歧的挑戰，在其中自主思考，作出一己之判斷與抉擇。管東溟舉佛學的流行爲例，清楚指出這個時代現象：

> 居今之世，即使孔子持鐸，曾孟執轡以環天下，揭六經而家喻户曉之，能禁其不涉禪書乎？既涉禪書，能禁其不入佛氏之知見乎？既入佛氏之知見，能禁其不低昂於儒釋之際乎？[12]

晚明儒者對佛學的浸淫既遠邁前代，世間法與出世法的衝突與調和，就必然成爲思想界無可迴避的課題。世間法重在綱常秩序的建立，出世法則嚮往身心性命的解脫。兩者之間張力甚強，一旦失衡，將出現管東溟所謂「不以經世妨經世，則以經世濫出世」的流弊。[13]如何使之相輔相成、各得其所？遂不斷刺激學者的思考。趙大洲（貞吉，1507-1576）曾欲撰作《二通》一書，由〈內篇經世通〉與〈外篇出世通〉組成，[14]並說道：「經世者不礙於出世之體，出世者不忌於經世

---

11 明初大儒薛敬軒（瑄，1389-1464）曾謂「自考亭以還斯道已大明，無煩著作，直須躬行耳。」這一姿態與明代中期以後，「篤信程、朱，不遷異說者，無復幾人矣」的時代氛圍，已不可同日而語。參見張廷玉等編撰，《明史》（北京：中華書局，2011），卷282，〈儒林列傳一〉，頁7230、7222。

12 管志道，《問辨牘》（東京：尊經閣文庫藏，明萬曆二十六年[1598]序刊本），元集，〈答吳侍御安節丈書〉，頁50。

13 管志道，《問辨牘》，元集，〈答吳侍御安節丈書〉，頁47。

14 此書並未完稿，其內容概要參見趙貞吉，《趙文肅公文集》，卷23，〈史業二門都序〉，收入四庫全書存目叢書編纂委員會編，《四庫全書存目叢

之用，然後千聖一心，萬古一道，聖人憂世之念，可少慰矣。」[15]紫柏眞可（1544-1604）則云：「大丈夫處於大塊間，本分事元無多端，不過經世出世而已。」[16]又說：「蓋世法變極，不以出世法救之，則變終莫止；出世法變極，脫（按：此字疑衍）不以世法救之，則其變亦終不止。」[17]由此可知，身爲儒者的趙大洲並不以世間法自局，身爲僧人的達觀也不以出世法自限。博參廣涉、自由建構本身的思想，可謂晚明思想界的一大特色。但與此同時，各種教說之間的衝突與混濫，也更甚於往昔。管東溟感嘆道：

> 今世僧據禪案以訶仙，仙據玄案以訶禪，而腐儒則按程朱之舊說而兩訶之，皆所謂束於教而不可以語道者也。復有濫合三教之徒，不知其源之所以合而必分，流之所以分而必合，與應時立教之所以先後天而不違處，亂聒其間久矣，夫道術之乖裂也。[18]

又說：

> 蓋學路之多岐，未有甚於今日者也，吾安得執己之一條路，以閉諸人不一之路哉？亦安得任諸人之各路其路，而不齊之以歸元之一路哉？[19]

正因切身地感受到道術乖裂、學路多歧的時代問題，乃更增添管東溟

書》，集部別集類，第100冊，頁598-600。

15 趙貞吉，《趙文肅公文集》，卷23，〈祭古聖賢文〉，頁604。

16 眞可著，德清校閱，《紫柏尊者全集》，卷24，〈答于潤甫（二）〉，收入《卍新纂續藏經》（東京：國書刊行會，1975-1989），第73冊，頁350b。

17 眞可著，德清閱，《紫柏尊者全集》，卷23，〈與李君實〉，頁347c。

18 管志道，《惕若齋續集》（東京：尊經閣文庫藏，明萬曆刊本），卷2，〈追論曇仙昔年感通事〉，頁60。

19 管志道，《問辨牘》，亨集，〈續答南皋文書〉，頁99。

「應時立教」、「齊之以歸元之一路」的判教抱負。

自陽明學流行以來，學者固多半兼涉三教，[20]但卻未必具有此種判教抱負。王陽明（守仁，1472-1529）談三教一家、[21]王龍溪（畿，1498-1583）以良知爲範圍三教之樞，[22]其統合三教的方式，皆是以超越教相的「一心」來統合三教，在上文的分析中，偏重在「三教一致」的本體層次上。然而以一心統合三教，佛道中人亦不乏此說，如內丹學者云：「三教道同而名異，其實不離乎一心之妙也」、[23]禪僧云：「自心者，三教之源，三教皆從此心施設」。[24]此種統合三教之法，統的是三教之心，而非三教之所以爲教。即使在心性本體的層次上向三教開放，但對於三教教相系統的異同，卻並未認眞加以面對，因而未能眞正進入到「三教會通」的型態。[25]三教既然依舊隔別，則

20 《四庫提要》云：「蓋心學盛行之時，無不講三教歸一者也。」見永瑢等編纂，《四庫全書總目》，卷132，子部42，頁1124。

21 王陽明云：「心學純明時，天下同風，各求自盡，就如此廳事，元是統成一間。……其初只是一家，去其藩籬仍舊是一家，三教之分亦只似此。」見王守仁著，吳光等編校，《王陽明全集（新編本）》（杭州：浙江古籍出版社，2010），卷40，〈補錄二・稽山承語〉，頁1611。

22 王龍溪云：「良知者，性之靈，以天地萬物爲一體，範圍三教之樞。」見王畿著，吳震編校整理，《王畿集》（南京：鳳凰出版社，2007），卷17，〈三教堂記〉，頁486。

23 王道淵，《還眞集》，卷中，〈懲忿窒慾論〉，收入《正統道藏》（臺北：新文豐出版社，1985-1988），第40冊，頁565。

24 智旭，《靈峰蕅益大師宗論》，卷7，〈金陵三教祠重勸施棺疏〉，收入《嘉興大藏經》（臺北：新文豐出版社，1987），第36冊，頁386b。

25 當代學者鄭宗義也從不同角度指出這個問題：「對隱藏在一道三教與三教歸儒之間的理論張力，明末王學的三教合一論並未給予充分的注意，更遑論作出妥善的紓解。」。參見鄭宗義，〈明末王學的三教合一論及其現代迴響〉，收入吳根友主編，《多元範式下的明清研究》（北京：三聯書店，2011），頁212。

重視心地工夫、探求生命源頭、乃至關切生死問題的儒者，很容易向專長於此的佛教汲取思想資源，甚至轉而皈依之。譬如劉錫玄（1574-?）曾言「忠孝了不得生死……只念阿彌陀佛，一心不亂，便了生死」；[26]鄧豁渠（鶴，1498-1569）亦認爲良知「了不得生死」、「只與造化同體，不能出造化之外」；[27]甚至提倡講學不遺餘力的徐存齋（階，1503-1583），據說也曾有「龍谿（王畿）八十老翁，捨不得良知，終不濟事。欲了生死，須看話頭」的感慨。[28]如此一來，「三教一致」所導致的結果，很可能反而使得儒學教法的本來面目逐漸喪失。此種偏重在心性體證的三教觀，其特長是見地圓通，能在證悟心體的關懷下，廣泛接引三教資源；但其短處則在於「昧統類、無方法」，[29]缺乏進一步的教相判釋工作，很難成就統攝三教的一貫體系，反而助長學者的自由心證，使得學路多歧的現象日益擴大。

有鑑於此，管東溟感慨道：「不大爲之整頓一場，何以合人心之渙，定萬世之極？」[30]於是，他試圖從時代漩渦中跳脫出來，欲建立獨特的判教視野，以尋求學術的新出路。

26　劉錫玄雖爲積極入世的儒者，但仍至心皈依淨土法門，當其身陷圍城危機時，甚至曾說：「然被圍旬月來，任讀忠節諸傳、道學諸書，畢竟抹不倒怕死二字。一開禪藏，便不覺剝皮析骨，甘之如飴矣。」詳見何淑宜，〈時代危機與個人抉擇——以晚明士紳劉錫玄的宗教經驗爲例〉，《新史學》，23：2（臺北，2012），頁57-106。

27　鄧豁渠著，鄧紅校注，《南詢錄校注》（武漢：武漢理工大學出版社，2008），頁23。

28　張烈著，陸隴其敘評，《王學質疑》（臺北：廣文書局，1982），〈讀史質疑四〉，頁13。

29　此六字爲民初學者劉咸炘對陽明學的批評。參見劉咸炘，《推十書》（成都：成都古籍書店，1996），第1冊，〈流風〉，頁48。

30　管志道，《續問辨牘》（東京：尊經閣文庫藏，明萬曆二十七年[1599]序刊本），卷3，〈牘尾贅言〉，頁82。

四、「群龍無首」：理學道統論的解構

穆宗隆慶三年（1569），管東溟三十四歲時，曾遊訪北京西山碧雲寺，在寺中閱讀《華嚴經》時，產生了特殊的悟道體驗：

> 隆慶己巳，應選入供北京，閱《華嚴經》於西山碧雲寺，至〈世主妙嚴品〉，頓悟《周易》「乾元統天，用九無首」之旨，與《華嚴》性海，渾無差別。豁然若亡其身，與太虛合。照見古往今來，一切聖賢，出世經世，乘願乘力，與時變化之妙用。[31]

〈世主妙嚴品〉共有五卷，是《華嚴經》的第一品，列舉出前來參與、莊嚴此華嚴法會的無量「世間主」，亦即在世間教化一切眾生的諸大菩薩。這些大菩薩有的化身爲天龍鬼神，部類、形貌、稱號及修習的法門皆不同，然而無不悟入佛陀功德智慧之大海。此品的結尾這樣寫道：

> 一切世界中，悉有如來坐於道場；一一世主，各各信解，各各所緣，各各三昧方便門，各各修習助道法，各各成就，各各歡喜，各各趣入，各各悟解諸法門，各各入如來神通境界，各各入如來力境界，各各入如來解脫門。如於此華藏世界海，十方盡法界、虛空界、一切世界海中，悉亦如是。[32]

《華嚴經》所開展的境界，乃是一爲無量、無量爲一、重重無盡、事

---

31 錢謙益，《牧齋初學集》（上海：上海古籍出版社，1985），卷49，〈管公行狀〉，頁1258。

32 實叉難陀譯，《大方廣佛華嚴經》，卷5，〈世主妙嚴品第一之五〉，收入《大正新修大藏經》（東京：大正一切經刊行會，1924-1935），第10冊，頁25c。

事無礙的世界海。管東溟由此經文所示境界的觸發，產生一飛躍性的領悟，從而與《周易》乾卦彖傳「大哉乾元，萬物資始，乃統天」與爻辭「用九，見群龍無首，吉」的義理相互會通。簡要言之，管東溟所體悟的「乾元」即是事事無礙的華嚴性海；而所謂「群龍」，即是上述引文中，在十方世界隱顯出沒、自行化他的世界主。這些聖賢在世間現身的姿態不同，但同樣出入於乾元性海之中，無需強分高下，正所謂「種種出沒，種種張弛，各有條理，難可思議。此無他，龍德不可爲首也。」[33]於是，「群龍無首」，遂形成他看待古往今來一切聖賢的根本見地。[34]

荒木見悟在解釋這一事件時，認爲管東溟當時在碧雲寺所讀的，乃是李通玄（635-730）的《華嚴合論》，並深受其華嚴解釋學的影響。[35]然而考諸管東溟平生對此悟道經驗的多次回憶，皆只說閱讀《華嚴經》，並無一字提及李通玄，例如：「暇索《華嚴經》閱之」、「偶取《華嚴經》閱之」、「偶揭《華嚴．世主妙嚴品》數卷」……等。[36]乃至在其自傳詩中亦曰：「龍藏尊經出海濱，大千眼界一時新，

33 管志道，《惕若齋集》（東京：尊經閣文庫藏，明萬曆二十四年［1596］序刊本），卷1，〈奉復先生見咎音問稀濶書〉，頁38。

34 依據管東溟在他處的記載，他對「群龍無首」的體會，最早可以追溯到二十九歲之時。他說：「余從甲子（1564）冬，從耿師處省及群龍無首大意；又從己巳（1569）夏，於碧雲寺省及《華嚴經》中權實大意。沉繹有年，深悟乾元統天，即是毘盧法界；群龍無首，即是普賢行門。」參見管志道，《步朱吟》（東京：尊經閣文庫藏，明萬曆三十一年〔1603〕序刊本），頁39。

35 荒木見悟，〈管東溟——明末における一儒佛調合論者の思維構造〉，頁155-158。

36 此事件相關文獻之匯集，參見魏珮玲，〈管志道年譜〉（臺南：臺南大學國語文學系碩士論文，2010），頁38-41。

〈妙嚴〉數卷驚餘夢，恍惚天開萬象春。」[37]由此可見，管東溟的悟境是直接來自於《華嚴經》本文的啓發，而非透過任何後人的註釋，其體悟方式亦是冥契的、直覺的，而非論理的、思辨的。

如同王陽明龍場之悟一般，管東溟在碧雲寺會通《華嚴》與《周易》的冥契經驗，對其畢生的思想格局與方向有著決定性的影響。他「群龍無首」的聖賢觀，與宋儒以來的道統論極爲不同，[38]管東溟亦由此展開對理學的批判。他說：

> 大槩宋儒之張皇絕學，酷似五花開後禪流之張皇宗學，雖能動學者向上之思，不能遏學者虛驕之氣。[39]
>
> 先儒……進退古今，表裡人物之有失衡處，則皆爲「群龍無首」之義不明也。……群龍無一可以爲首，而隨時隨地，則群龍無一不可以爲首。[40]

管東溟批評宋儒標舉道統，酷似禪門之高揚燈統，此說頗爲有見。從歷史上看來，宋儒的道統論頗受韓昌黎（愈，768-824）啓發。而韓昌黎之標榜道統，表面上雖承繼自孟子，實際上確實深受禪宗「教外別傳」之說所影響。[41]道統論述的基本性格，自始即因欲樹立權威而

37 管志道，《步朱吟》，頁7。

38 道統論是宋明理學史上的核心論域之一，允許哪些人物進入到傳道的系譜之中，相當程度上反映出理學家對道的理解與詮釋。關於由宋到清儒學道統論述之發展，可參考荒木見悟，〈道統論の衰退と新儒林傳の展开〉，收入荒木見悟，《明清思想論考》（東京：研文出版，1992），頁1-83。另土田健次郎曾整理道統論的相關研究成果，參見土田健次郎著，朱剛譯，《道學的形成》（上海：上海古籍出版社，2010），頁465-466，註1。

39 管志道，《從先維俗議》，卷4，〈明道四語〉，頁387。

40 管志道，《從先維俗議》，卷4，〈群龍無首〉，頁390。

41 陳寅恪，〈論韓愈〉，收入陳寅恪，《金明館叢稿初編》（北京：三聯書

具有排他色彩，被排除在道統系譜外的，不僅僅是佛老，還有道學家所不認同的儒者。針對此點，管東溟認爲，道統論昧於「群龍無首」之義，因而在評價歷史人物之際陷於主觀，亦長養後學的「虛驕之氣」。[42]於是，他試圖上溯先秦儒學，拈出「群龍無首」一義，藉以衡定先哲學問：

> 見「群龍無首」之學，此孔子一生大欛柄也。顏子、子貢步趨焉。……曾子不無有首意在，而志亦向於無首。……子思敏達不下子貢，弘毅不下曾子，豈無纖毫首意在？而《中庸》一篇，則宛然群龍無首之家學也。……至孟子而龍首全現矣。既以孔子爲千古群龍之首，亦以自己爲戰國人龍之首。

此處所謂「首意」，即是對道的認識帶有學派相，從而奮身擔當或高度標榜。依管東溟看來，由孔子至子思，學風大抵皆寬大平和，而曾子「士不可以不弘毅」（《論語・泰伯》）的形象，稍帶首意；至孟子高抬孔子於諸聖之上，又秉持著「如欲平治天下，當今之世，舍我其誰也」（《孟子・公孫丑下》）的自負，即已「龍首全現」，是後世有首之學的發端。他接著說：

店，2009），頁321。

42 朱子的論敵陳龍川（亮，1143-1194）對理學家自我標榜之弊有如下描述：「二十年之閒，道德性命之說一興，迭相唱和，不知其所從來。後生小子讀書未成句讀，執筆未免手顫者，已能拾其遺說，高自譽道，非議前輩以爲不足學矣。世之爲高者，得其機而乘之，以聖人之道爲盡在我，以天下之事爲無所不能，能麾其後生以自爲高而本無有者，使惟己之向，而後欲盡天下之說一取而教之，頑然以人師自命。」陳龍川所論或不無誇飾之處，但亦非空穴來風。參見陳亮著，鄧廣銘點校，《陳亮集》（北京：中華書局，1987），卷24，〈送王仲德序〉，頁270。

> 周元公……《太極》一圖，雖標聖人主靜立極，而以無極爲究竟，無首之旨躍然。二程得其傳而未竟，從樂處認得本體，遂脱卸六經，以興起斯文爲己任。伊川且欲自出聖宗，駕元公之上，渾身是首。而明道亦欲繼孟子而出首，其言曰：「顏子陋巷自樂，以有孔子在焉；若孟子，世既無人，安可不以道自任？」無乃道統爲儒家之私物哉？匹夫任道，顯是天子無道矣，孔子又何以有中庸遁世之說？程學走作孔門一線，正在於此。孔子但以學之不講爲憂，而未嘗以道自任也。與人爲善，取友輔仁，乃儒者家常茶飯耳。如曰有道可任，卻是於庸德庸言上，多添一分意思，此子貢之所謂我加諸人也。紫陽夫子，益申道統之說，而以上古聖神繼天立極之說，盡屬諸三代後之匹夫，君相無一與焉。……姚江翻其格物，而不翻其道統。其徒泰州王氏，且以一竈丁舉身於堯舜伊尹之上，自任帝王師、萬世師，於是潛龍之跡削，而飛龍之格卑，而群龍之首，全屬於見龍矣。孟子後，唯禪家有蓋天蓋地、無君無師之話頭，而今乃淫於儒家，則泰州倡之也。是故一失則狂，再失則僞，又再失則狂僞兩合，而成無忌憚之小人，皆從有首之端起。[43]

管東溟此段思想史見解頗爲獨到。在理學家中，他僅肯定周濂溪（敦頤，1017-1073）能通於「無首」之旨；二程（顥，1032-1085；頤，1033-1107）則不免任道之意過盛，以爲眞儒不出於世則天下無道，

43 以上兩段，見於管志道，《從先維俗議》，卷4，〈曾孟程朱有首〉，頁393-394。

隱隱以道爲儒家之私物；朱子（熹，1130-1200）於〈中庸章句序〉更以「上古聖神繼天立極」論道統之傳，在孟子以後，獨推許二程能上繼此千載不傳之緒，將三代以後的在位者悉皆排除在外。在管東溟看來，這都是「於庸德庸言上，多添一分意思」，此意發展至極，便成爲王心齋（艮，1483-1541）泰州一派的隻手擎天、赤身擔當，往往因自視過高而產生狂僞交雜的流弊。蓋管東溟平生對泰州學派獨首「見龍」之意多所批判，並由此檢討「君道」與「師道」的關係，指出就龍德而言，群龍無一可以爲首；而就其位分而言，「見龍」不得不遜於「飛龍」。換句話說，道統應歸於在位之聖王，而非由在野的師儒、庶人所承擔。此觀點與管東溟「君師道合」的政教理想有關，雖是「群龍無首」論的一部分，但非本文關注的焦點，爲免夾纏，茲僅就其解構儒家本位主義的思考脈絡加以討論。[44]

依管東溟之見，龍德既不可以爲首，則參與道脈之流行的人物，就不會僅止於講學的理學家，而是以多重的姿態出沒於歷史長河之中。他說：

> 後儒專以見龍高孔子之品，而謂龍德必在理學家，皆不知無首之義者。如漢之蕭酇侯（蕭何）、諸葛武侯（諸葛亮），唐之狄梁公（狄仁傑）、郭汾陽王（郭子儀），宋之李文靖公（李沆）、王沂公（王曾），國朝之中山武寧王（徐達）、于忠肅（于謙）、劉忠宣公（劉大夏）等，皆龍德中人也。……安可以學術事功囿龍德？即方術家，如伶倫之於音，大撓之於曆，扁鵲之於醫，鬼谷之於卜，管輅

44　關於管東溟「君師道合」思想的討論，參見吳孟謙，〈融貫與批判——晚明三教論者管東溟的思想及其時代〉，頁153-166。

之於數，張道陵、許遜之於玄，詎知其非乘龍而來者耶？儒則姑舍是，而所宗在孔耳。悟此可以得群龍無首之說。[45]

管東溟指出，身爲儒者，學問雖不可無宗主，卻不應以單一的標準侷囿龍德。因此歷代建立事功的將相，乃至方技、道術諸方面有遺德於世的人物，皆可同列於群龍，與講學的儒者不相軒輊。又云：

周元公作《太極圖說》，而一貫之宗顯；程朱又分一以爲一，便不能貫釋老性命之宗，而於蘇子瞻、陸子靜之學，若對壘然。諸如文潞公（文彥博）、趙清獻（趙抃）、富鄭公（富弼）之晚向佛學，劉元城（劉安世）、馮濟川（馮楫）、張無垢（張九成）之早入禪宗，且等之於夷狄外道矣。然而數君子者，皆宇宙內不可少之人物也，其道亦不在孔子一貫外也。以爲在一貫外，則程朱之所謂一貫，不但不通出世，亦不通於用世矣。[46]

程朱雖主「理一分殊」，但其所謂一，排他性卻極強，歷來學者稍染禪學、甚至皈心向佛者，不論其出世、用世之具體德行如何，皆一律擯除於道統之外。管東溟認爲，程朱所謂一貫，持道太孤、論人太嚴，實與孔學眞正的一貫精神不同。

管東溟既從《華嚴經》發悟，則其世界觀亦從此方此世，拓寬至十方三世，在此背景下，展開一條無盡時空的修行道路。就空間上來說，世界無盡，因此經世與出世並非兩相扞格，管東溟云：

蓋世之論者，漫曰「儒學經世、佛學出世」云爾，實未嘗

45 管志道，《師門求正牘》（東京：尊經閣文庫藏，明萬曆二十四年序刊本），卷下，〈續答天臺先生教劄〉，頁10-11。

46 管志道，《問辨牘》，亨集，〈續答南皋丈書〉，頁98。

> 究世出世間之實也。經世不待言已，所謂出世者，豈謂三界之外，別有一等沖虛寂滅之場，去形骸而留神識，爲諸佛藏身之地耶？非也。世界之外，皆世界也。諸佛現身，不越四生六道中。出一世界，還復入一世界，何世可出？出世云者，不過謂其性體純淨之極，形神俱妙，出入三界而無障礙也。[47]

依據佛教的世界觀，未出三界（欲界、色界、無色界）者爲輪轉生死之凡夫，超出三界者爲了脫生死之聖人。大乘菩薩則是既出生死而還入生死，既出一世界又還入一世界，世界無窮、願力無盡。修行既不限於一方國土，則所謂出世，僅是就超出三界煩惱而言，而非經世的對立面。此外，就時間上來說，生命無盡，因此聖人的修行姿態亦是多元顯現，管東溟云：

> 蓋以一生而論，則孔不濫釋、釋不濫孔。安得既修庸德庸言之教，而猶顯釋氏之神通；既提不生不滅之宗，而猶建帝王之功業？以多生而論，則得道眞人出入於三教中，改形而不改性，易地而不易心。透出世之宗者，必累功於經世；累經世之功者，必歸根於出世。……孟子曰：「禹、稷、顏子，易地則皆然。」使孔與釋而易地，亦然也。載考《仁王》、《報恩》諸經，則釋迦之爲國王而行正法，爲孝子而報親恩，俱從多生歷過；而此生以一大事因緣出現，故辭金輪而成正覺耳。設使端冕垂裳，操三重以王天下，其於唐虞三代之治何有哉？[48]

47 管志道，《問辨牘》，亨集，〈答周符卿二魯丈書〉，頁26-28。
48 管志道，《問辨牘》，亨集，〈答周符卿二魯丈書〉，頁33-34。

若僅將眼界局於一生，經世立功業與出世了生死，自然是相異的生命追求；但是若將修行的歷程延展向無盡的生命，出世與經世便只是不同階段的修行課題。例如今生現出家相的釋迦，過去生曾爲國王、爲孝子，與堯舜無異。以此推之，今生現經世之相的聖人，在他生也顯現出家求道之相。這就是所謂「易地則皆然」。

在這樣的眼界下，固守儒家本位的理學道統觀不能不被解構，甚至禪家也不應自負得佛心印而貶抑儒者。管東溟云：

> 以孔子差等百王之道眼，合如來豎窮三際之佛眼參照之，則一切訶佛罵祖之徒，顚倒豪傑，單傳之龍象者，未必不是行未起、解未絕，新發意之衆生；而宰官居士中，或有忠孝性生，寬仁天植，德慧術智，迥出凡流者，即不參禪、不修玄、不講聖學，未必不是行起解絕之大士也。論世者不開此眼，而以一生建立，判百代天挺人豪，可乎哉？[49]

管東溟依據《華嚴經．十地品》，認爲大乘菩薩十地階位中，二地以上的菩薩是從「見道位」入「修道位」，也就是由「解」入「行」。「行起解絕」一詞，本是華嚴宗用以討論法界觀的用語，管東溟此處則借用來發揮自身思想，他認爲氣概沖天的禪門宗師，未必越過見道位；而闇然日彰的儒行君子，卻可能已入修道位，「出沒於三祇劫中，隨分隨力行菩薩道。」[50]由此看來，理學的執儒闢佛固不可取，禪門的揚禪抑儒同樣是佛眼未開，見地都只侷限於此生。管東溟云：

---

49 管志道，《從先維俗議》，卷5，〈參釋門行起解絕之義以定儒家論世權衡〉，頁508。

50 管志道，《從先維俗議》，卷5，〈參釋門行起解絕之義以定儒家論世權衡〉，頁507。

> 聖賢出沒三祇劫中，亦何定相之有？安知孔子再來之不現祖師相，馬祖再來之不現儒宗相乎？……吾儕不具佛眼，則姑以群龍無首一案收之可矣。[51]

正因聖賢觀被置放在無盡時空、無盡生命的修行歷程裡，因此群龍不必有首，聖賢可以「無定相」。在此，理學家嚴格的儒釋之辨與道統論述，遂無用武之地矣。

晚明思想界因心學的流行，追求聖賢之道者，對生命本原（「心體」）的契悟高度重視，使之相對容易從歷史、文化、社會、學派等後天身份中超脫出來。此外，佛教義學的發達，也使學者便於借鑒大乘佛典廣大的時空觀與修道次第，尋求三教的會通。管東溟上述的思想，雖是本於自身的證悟經驗，實亦與當世學風密切相關。例如紫柏眞可云：「自古群龍無首吉，門墻雖異本相同。」[52]袁小修（中道，1570-1623）言：「道不通於三教，非道也；學不通於三世，非學也。積習之弊必遡之於多生之前，而後其旨明；盡性之功必極之於多生之後，而後其量滿。」[53]方密之（以智，1611-1671）亦言：「尼山、鷲峰皆藏身於一切法、一切物中，而人不能以一法一物限量之。藏身無跡，無跡莫藏。」[54]凡此種種論述，皆可看出當時性命之學的廣大圓通。而在各種支持三教會通的理論資源中，《華嚴經》無疑扮演著關

51　管志道，《從先維俗議》，卷5，〈儒釋兩家詖辭〉，頁511。

52　眞可著，錢謙益纂閱，《紫柏老人別集》，卷1，〈題三教圖〉，收入《卍新纂續藏經》，第73冊，頁406c。

53　袁中道，《珂雪齋近集》，卷10，〈示學人〉，收入續修四庫全書編纂委員會編，《續修四庫全書》（上海：上海古籍出版社，2002），集部別集類，第1376冊，頁690。

54　方以智著，龐樸注釋，《東西均注釋》（北京：中華書局，2001），〈茲燚黈〉，頁289。

鍵角色。

《華嚴經》在三藏教典之中號稱「經王」，文辭燦美，義理豐贍，華嚴宗四祖清涼澄觀（738-838）曾云：「交映千門，融冶萬有，廣大悉備，盡法界之術，唯《大華嚴》。」[55]宋代以來，理學家談心論性，雖多能涉獵佛教而吸收其養分，但究其實際，往往得於禪宗者多、深入教門者寡。程朱理一分殊之說，雖似有得於華嚴學的月印萬川，卻也是間接從禪宗得來。[56]程伊川更有「看一部《華嚴經》，不如看一艮卦」的貶抑之詞，[57]在此傳統下，儒者罕能深入佛學義海，自是可想而知。但近世以來，不受理學闢佛思維所限囿的三教合一思想家，深受《華嚴經》啓發者卻所在多有。在管東溟之前，金儒李屏山（純甫，1177-1223）已曾言：

> 吾讀《首楞嚴經》，知儒在佛之下。又讀《阿含》等經，知佛似在儒下。至讀《華嚴經》，無佛無儒，無大無小，能佛能儒，能大能小，存泯自在矣！[58]

管東溟的同門焦澹園（竑，1540-1620）在其〈刻大方廣佛華嚴經序〉中也說：

> 餘以謂能讀此經，然後知六經、論語、孟子無非禪，堯、

55 續法輯，《法界宗五祖略記》，卷1，〈篇名〉，收入《嘉興大藏經》，第77冊，頁622c。

56 呂澂曾指出，理學所受華嚴學說的影響，乃是「通過禪學特別是所謂華嚴禪而間接受到的影響，並非是直接研究而得之華嚴的。」見呂澂，《中國佛學源流略講》（臺北：天華出版社，1986），頁274。

57 程顥、程頤著，王孝魚點校，《二程集》（北京：中華書局，2004），卷6，頁81。

58 李純甫著，荒木見悟解題，《鳴道集說》（京都：中文出版社，1977），卷5，頁135。

舜、周、孔即爲佛，可以破沈空之妄見，糾執相之謬心。[59]

下至清代中葉，著名的居士彭際清（紹升，1740-1796）亦曰：

予讀孔氏書，得其密意。以《易繫》無方，《中庸》無修之旨，遊於《華嚴》藏海，世出世間，圓融無礙。始知此土聖人，多是大權菩薩，方便示現。[60]

這些華嚴學式的會通思維，都與管東溟的「群龍無首」之旨交互輝映。晚明高僧蕅益智旭（1599-1655）更曾指出，讀《華嚴經》之〈世主妙嚴品〉與〈入法界品〉，將能體會世法、佛法貫通不二的如來境界。[61]管東溟讀〈世主妙嚴品〉而悟入乾元性海，正與智旭所言不謀而合。

五、「敦化川流」：判教思想的開展

管東溟既以「群龍無首」說解構了理學的道統論述，則三教已可被安放在一個更廣大的思想底盤上，不相違礙。但如何將各個具體的思想教說給予恰當的定位，將涉及更爲複雜的判教問題。管東溟對於不同學說教派的義理衝突，每抱持著超然的立場，並試圖同情理解立說者的用意。以下這段設問，可以略窺他對此類問題的思考：

釋迦，人天師也，豈其身不從父母胞生？而忍於滅絕天倫如是，必有箇大根由在。則又虛心爲尼父想曰：尼父，萬

59 焦竑著，李劍雄整理，《澹園集》（北京：中華書局，1999），卷16，〈刻大方廣佛華嚴經序〉，頁183。

60 彭紹升，《一乘決疑論》，卷1，收入《卍新纂續藏經》，第58冊，頁704b。

61 智旭，《靈峰蕅益大師宗論》，卷2之4，〈法語四．示朝徹〉，頁290a。

世師也，豈其道果出於釋迦之下？乃不以一大事顯，而局於名教如是，必有箇大機括在。則又虛心而爲達磨想曰：達磨，逆流之古佛也，名利之根已斷，何所需於中國？乃泛重溟而忍五毒，九年冷坐，守一神光，其艱辛如是，必有箇大功行在。則又虛心而爲程朱想曰：程朱，命世之上賢也，天果以達磨操道印，何不亦以此印印程朱之心？而故使操戈入室，其相左如是，必有箇大肯綮在。則又虛心而爲我高皇想曰：高皇，不世出之堯舜湯文也，既尊尼父爲萬世師，翼以程朱之註，何不盡用其說，人二氏之人，火二氏之書，廬二氏之居，其時三重在我，孰能撓之？而乃並尊三教之祖，至於註《道德》而序《心經》，若以身爲二氏之程朱者，其總括包羅又如是，必有箇大經綸在。[62]

一旦不從特定學派的道統論看待思想史上的學說時，就沒有任一學說會被貼上外道或異端的標籤，而是道在不同時節因緣下的展現，思想家亦各自抱持著不同的使命而來。此種思考，一如佛教的判教論，不將某一經典的教說做爲定論，以排斥其餘，而是將所有經典皆視爲佛陀的契機施度，各有不同層次的意義與價值。但究竟各學說的意義與價值如何衡定？這是管東溟所關注的核心問題。他在爲老師耿天臺寫的祭文中，自澆塊壘地說道：

風會滔滔，孰遏其勢？三教呶呶，孰持其衡？……安得起（天臺）先生於九原，與三大聖人陟降一堂之上，進海內之英才而陶鑄之，相與溯函三之太極，窮用九之乾元，交

62 管志道，《續問辨牘》，卷4，〈答張儀部文石丈書〉，頁46-47。

攝互入，以持大德敦化之統。因而觀根逗機，起一代之時教，志必通諸《春秋》，行必本諸《孝經》，出方矩於圓宗之中，而俟諸百世永無惑也。捧爲衣鉢而守之，以衍小德川流之宗。[63]

這段文字提到了兩個足以挽救「風會滔滔」、「三教呶呶」之世風的重點：一是「持大德敦化之統」，二是「衍小德川流之宗」。前者即是上溯乾元性海，在此制高點上融貫三教；後者則是於圓融中加以析別，對不同思想流派的定位加以檢討，並指示一條適合時代的道路。

「大德敦化」、「小德川流」之語，源於《中庸》「萬物並育而不相害，道並行而不相悖，小德川流，大德敦化，此天地之所以爲大也」的經文。管東溟特拈出「敦化川流」四字，以做爲判釋三教的總綱。「敦化」與「川流」，即是江海與百川，對應的是總與別、一與多、體與用的關係。除了《中庸》以外，在思想史上，此一修辭最早可追溯到《淮南子．氾論訓》的「百川異源，而皆歸於海」，《易經．繫辭傳》「天下同歸而殊途，一致而百慮」的語意亦與此相通。但後世運用此隱喻而發揮精微義理的，則出於佛門。如華嚴宗三祖賢首法藏（643-712）云：

事雖宛然，恒無所有，是故用即體也，如會百川以歸於海；理雖一味，恒自隨緣，是故體即用也，如舉大海以明百川。由理事互融，故體用自在。[64]

法藏使用大海與百川之喻，發揮不變隨緣的法性，闡發理事、體用不二之義。而在中國近世佛教史上影響力極大的永明延壽（904-975），

63 管志道，《師門求正牘》，卷下，〈祭天臺先生文〉，頁47。

64 法藏述，《華嚴經義海百門》，卷1，〈體用開合門第九〉，收入《大正新修大藏經》，第45冊，頁635。

更將此喻落實到判教上，他說：

> 三教雖殊，若法界收之，則無別原矣。若孔老二教，百氏九流，總而言之，不離法界，其猶百川歸於大海；若佛教圓宗，一乘妙旨，別而言之，百家猶若螢光，寧齊巨照？如大海不歸百川也。[65]

延壽以法界爲大海，各種教說如百川，百川同歸於大海，猶如三教歸一；但佛教所開闡的究竟成佛之道，非孔老百家所及，因此大海不歸百川。這一論斷，體現出延壽以佛教收攝儒道的判教觀。

管東溟使用同一隱喻，雖未必不受前人影響，但其判教內涵卻別具理路。他自云：

> 程伯淳有言曰：「吾學固有所受，然天理二字，卻是自家體貼出來。」余敢曰：「吾學固有所受，然敦化川流四字，亦是自家體貼出來也。」[66]

在《周易》、《華嚴》相會通的見地下，管東溟所謂大德敦化，指的是《周易》之「大哉乾元」，通於《華嚴》之「毘盧性海」，[67]乃是超越一切宗派學說的眞理源頭；而其所謂小德川流，即是《周易》之「乾卦用九」，通於《華嚴》之「普賢行海」，[68]乃是由敦化之源分出的

65 延壽集，《宗鏡錄》，卷33，收入《大正新修大藏經》，第48冊，頁608。

66 管志道，《師門求正牘．引》，頁3。

67 毘盧，梵名Vairocana，意譯遍一切處、遍照、光明遍照，爲法身如來。毘盧遮那佛之體性廣大無限，猶如大海，故稱毘盧性海。參考佛光大辭典編修委員會編，《佛光大辭典》（高雄：佛光出版社，1988），冊4，「毘盧性海」、「毘盧遮那」條，頁3858-3859。

68 普賢，梵名Samantabhadra，此菩薩之身相及功德遍一切處，純一妙善，故稱普賢。華嚴宗將斷絕一切言語思慮之佛境界，稱爲「性海果分」，即毘盧遮那佛之法門；相對於此，應眾生機緣而說教之「緣起因分」，即普賢菩薩之法門。參閱佛光大辭典編修委員會編，《佛光大辭典》，冊

各種教說。

「大哉乾元，萬物資始，乃統天」，此三言者，括盡毘盧法界矣。又曰：「乾元用九，乃見天則」，此兩言者，括盡普賢行海矣。雖佛書未入中國，而佛理何嘗不在儒門？特華梵之音文異耳。然孔子不以乾元統天之心法顯，而以坤元承天之身法顯。庸言庸行，若無若虛，臣道然也，亦此方之教體宜爾也。蓋隱其全智，而現身為儒教分流之祖矣。孔子未生，老聃蓋以藏用之乾元，待之於柱下；釋迦實以顯仁之乾元，開之於竺方，是為後世禪玄二學之祖。分禪分玄，亦屬川流，吾道則一以貫之也。子思贊之曰：「小德川流，大德敦化」，至矣。[69]

管東溟認為，三教教主皆同證乾元本體，但教化的姿態各異。孔子雖知天命，立教卻偏重於世間的倫理德行，屬「坤元承天之身法」；老子雖闡無為之天道，卻並不直顯出世之實相，故判為「藏用之乾元」；釋迦則以一大事因緣出現於世，揭明自行化他的究竟解脫之道，乃是「顯仁之乾元」。教分為三，故屬川流；其道一以貫之，故為敦化。於此，管東溟對三教主是平等視之的。[70]但其中亦不妨再加分梳：

以命制性，仙學也，分老氏之一宗而未全也；以性制命，

5，「普賢」、「普賢菩薩」條，頁5000-5002。

69 管志道，《問辨牘》，元集，〈答屠儀部赤水丈書〉，頁68-69。

70 管東溟曰：「釋迦聖之聖者，老聃聖之智者，孔子聖之仁者……智仁聖義中和，周所稱六德也，有何高下，高下自在人所造耳。」參見管志道，《理要酬諮錄》（東京：尊經閣文庫藏，明萬曆三十年［1602］序刊本），卷下，〈倣孟子文句三條表憲章〉，頁69。

> 禪學也，印佛乘之初地而非證也；盡性至命，孔子之學也，越仙與禪而行三祇劫中菩薩之道，此分身之佛而非全體也；性還無始，命還無始，佛地之果也，是謂無極而太極，太極本無極，聖學於此究竟焉。故仙階易陟，而禪宗難透；禪宗易透，而孔矩難成；孔矩易成，而佛果難證。證佛果者，窮未來際，能隨順眾生入生死。[71]

仙學、禪學、孔學、佛學，雖皆是通往乾元性海的性命之學，但若判其淺深次第，則後後勝於前前，以佛果最爲究竟，因爲「不問三教中人，未有不以成等正覺爲究竟者。」[72]孔子之學則屬三祇劫中的菩薩道，是過程而非終點。但若據此而斷定管東溟揚佛抑孔，又不免以偏概全，忽略了他「群龍無首」的思維方式。[73]

管東溟大抵認爲，仙學不足以盡老學、禪學不足以盡佛學，理學亦不足以盡孔學，如果說儒釋道聖人之各自立教，相較於乾元性海，已屬敦化中的川流；那麼理學、禪學、仙學等三教後學，則更是川流中之川流。故說：

> 元公實通孔子並育並行之化，融三教於《太極圖》中，而不得不以斯文之脈發川流於兩程；達磨實遊釋氏毘盧遮那之海，融五法於《楞伽經》中，而不得不以單傳之宗，衍

71 管志道，《惕若齋集》，卷3，〈性命説書楚客扇頭〉，頁70。

72 管志道，《從先維俗議》，卷5，〈儒釋禁戒異同〉，頁519。

73 管東溟曰：「現相必隨願力，願力又從因緣，釋迦以一大事因緣而出，孔子以整三五之頹綱因緣而出，安得同？然而龍德不可爲首也。……繼天立極之至聖，多從古佛逆流而來，又不必首釋迦於群聖之上矣。《經》云：『不可以三十二相見如來。』則亦胡可以三十二相之不完具見諸聖？」參見管志道，《從先維俗議》，卷5，〈剖儒釋現悟修證境界〉，頁506。

川流於五派。應時立極，天命然也。傳派既久，則必執川流之小宗，掩敦化之大宗，至並其川流之初意而傷之，此則爲之徒者之罪，而於初祖何尤焉？[74]

管東溟對理學開山周濂溪與禪門初祖菩提達磨（?-535）的評價皆高，認爲其自身造境皆能上接三教一貫之大宗。而周濂溪開理學一脈、達磨開教外別傳一脈，是由敦化發爲川流，在當時皆各有其天命。但後世儒禪傳人各執門戶、相互排擠，就不免以川流掩敦化，遂失其初祖之眞意。

管東溟又常論及大乘佛典中的菩薩修證行位，認爲就聖賢等第的判位而言，佛經所提供的思想資源最爲豐富。

《魯論》中有聖人、君子、善人、有恆之四稱；《七篇》中有善、信、美、大、聖、神之六號；《大學篇》有格、致、誠、正、修之五階；《中庸篇》有誠、形、著、明、動、變、化之七級，皆有賢聖次第，寓於其間。然未有如佛經之行布森嚴者，其大義見於《華嚴》、《楞嚴》、《瓔珞》三經中，賢分十住、十行、十回向，聖分十地，開爲四十心。三賢之前，復有十信初心，而發端於三漸次，十聖之後，復有十一地等覺，而究竟於如來。……儒聖闕多生之因果，而從一生論進修，其判位自略；釋聖略一生之事業，而從三祇論修證，其判位自詳，各有攸當也。如欲窮乾元之道岸乎？畢竟儒之所判是權，釋之所判是實也。……唯《易》道必與《華嚴》之旨相合，故可會而通之。《易傳》略而釋經詳，儒者何嫌以釋經參《易傳》？

74　管志道，《惕若齋集》，卷3，〈題知儒編〉，頁28-29。

然而日用工夫，則亦自足於《易》道中。[75]

這段文字條理清楚，毋須多做說明。正因佛經所提供的聖賢等第甚爲詳密，管東溟便常借用之以判定三教聖賢的修證階位。例如他認爲禪門中，達磨居於初地位，馬祖道一（709-788）則爲十住位，五宗分派以後爲十信位，禪者的根器日薄。而在儒門中，管東溟判定顏回爲初地位，曾子爲初住位。[76]此外，在〈仿蓮經文句評儒門聖賢〉一文，管東溟更列舉古今三教人物，並判其造詣之淺深：最上一層是已證成佛果的釋迦；其次則孔子、老子、西天傳燈諸祖並列，皆爲應時而生的權佛；再次則儒家的周元公，道家的陳希夷（摶，871-989）、王重陽（1113-1170），佛家的馬祖道一與禪門五宗祖師；再其次則程明道，程伊川與朱子又下之；當朝的薛敬軒、王陽明是「伯仲之間見程朱」；王陽明以後，管東溟特別推舉羅念菴（洪先，1504-1564）、羅近溪（汝芳，1515-1588），但以爲不出於薛敬軒、王陽明之範圍。而管東溟的自我定位，則是願學孔子。[77]

上述對三教學說與人物所做的判釋，源於管東溟總攝三教的見地，他意圖將不同學術整合在同一系譜之中。由於同屬一系譜，彼此之間便無須妄設藩籬，執「川流」而掩「敦化」；但也由於清楚定位了各個教說在此系譜中的位置，因此亦能避免混濫、籠統之弊。管東溟此種判教論，與當時的心學家相比，頗具個人特色。茲引陽明後學

75 管志道，《從先維俗議》，卷5，〈儒釋家賢位聖位淺深權實之辨〉，頁501。

76 管志道，《從先維俗議》，卷5，〈剖儒釋現悟修證境界〉，頁504-507。

77 該文參見管志道，《理要酬諮錄》，卷下，頁71。管東溟晚年更著〈聖學或問十三篇〉，判定三教聖人之品地、道脈之遞嬗、修證之次第亦頗具理致，詳參管志道，《諴餘音》（東京：尊經閣文庫藏，明萬曆三十四年[1606]序刊本），卷下，頁22-76。

周海門（汝登，1547-1629）對儒釋異同的討論做爲對照：

> 儒與禪合乎？曰不可合也。儒與禪分乎？曰不可分也。……不可合者，因緣之應跡難齊；而不可分者，心性之根宗無二。……孔子之旨，闡在濂洛以後諸儒；如來之旨，闡在曹溪以下諸師。嗟乎！人而有悟於此，則儒自儒、禪自禪，不見其分；儒即禪，禪即儒，不見其合。[78]

周海門承繼王陽明、王龍溪一路，以「心性之根宗」會通儒佛，將其異同僅付諸個人的心性體悟。與此相較，管東溟「敦化川流」的思想史觀則更具層次條理，具有欲令理學、孔學、禪學、佛學各安其位的判教意識。

晚明的三教論衡，主要的議題還是集中在儒佛兩家，管東溟對儒佛的融通與判釋，亦用力特深。[79]除了上述綱領式的判教以外，還可通過本體論與工夫論兩方面，做更詳悉的闡釋。管東溟曾以「以西來之意合聖宗，而以東魯之矩收二氏」二語，[80]概括其生平三教論述的旨趣，前一句可視爲本體論上的會通原則，後一句則是工夫論上的會通原則。

首先，就本體論而言，管東溟認爲，儒佛二家聖人的言教雖異，意旨實相互貫通，他說：

> 大哉乾元，即諸佛敦化之海；塵沙諸佛，即乾元川流之淵

78　周汝登，《東越證學錄》，卷7，〈佛法正輪序〉，收入《四庫全書存目叢書》（臺南：莊嚴文化，1997），集部別集類，第165冊，頁550。

79　管東溟自謂其「綜核三宗，多及儒釋而罕及道」，是因宋儒以來闢老不如闢佛之甚，而當時究心於性命之學者，耽老學亦不如耽禪學之甚。因此往往「舉釋以該道」。參見管志道，《問辨牘》，亨集，〈續答二魯丈書〉，頁77-78。

80　管志道，《問辨牘》，元集，〈答王太常塘南先生書〉，頁7。

> 也。謂孔傳不盡佛法之纖悉，則可；謂乾元不該諸佛之因果，則不可。蓋《周易》一書，正與釋藏中之《華嚴》相表裡，是《大學》、《中庸》之鼻祖，亦三藏十二部之經王也。[81]

又說：

> 眾生必從乾元因海中流出，實無一人不分身於塵點劫前之佛者；眾生必歸乾元果海中示寂，亦無一人不合體於塵點劫前之佛者。[82]

前文曾提及，管東溟會通《華嚴》之毘盧性海與《周易》之乾元，做爲一切教法的敦化之源，在管東溟的體證中，此二者名異而實同，不但毘盧性海可收攝儒家聖賢、乾元性海亦可收攝釋家諸佛。此本體是一切眾生生命的源頭（「因海」），而同時也是其修行的歸宿（「果海」）。宋代理學家每以「聖人本天，釋氏本心」[83]做儒釋之辨，對此，管東溟提出反對意見：

> 宋儒有言：「吾儒本天，釋氏本心」，本既二矣，焉得同？曰：此非究竟語也，爲其歧心與天而二之也。苟究其極，則儒亦本心，釋亦本天，何者？天有乾元，有乾儀；心有眞覺，有妄覺。本天者，必本乎乾元，即釋氏所謂毘盧性海耳；本心者，必本乎眞覺，即夫子所謂乾元統天耳。[84]

---

81 管志道，《從先維俗議》，卷5，〈儒書含攝八識四智三身義理」，頁500。

82 管志道，《從先維俗議》，卷5，〈究孔子上達道岸〉，頁522。

83 此說發自程伊川，參見程顥、程頤著，王孝魚點校，《二程集》，卷21下，〈附師說後〉，頁274。

84 管志道，《師門求正牘》，卷上，〈攻乎異端斯害也已訓義〉，頁7。

宋儒本天，背後是三才並立的宇宙觀；禪門本心，背後則是萬法唯心的宇宙觀。兩者本難會通。管東溟則將「乾元」與「乾儀」做了區分，乾儀是三才中的天，乾元則是貫通世間與出世間的毘盧性海，與如來藏思想中的常住眞心相通。這即是他會通儒釋二家本體論的方式。客觀言之，管東溟在本體論上的會通，偏向「以佛（華嚴學）解儒（易學）」，故云「以西來之意合聖宗」。

另在工夫論方面，管東溟也進行儒佛之會通，將孔學定位爲悟後起修、隱悟顯修的大乘菩薩道。

> 釋氏有六度圓修之說，一曰布施，二曰持戒，三曰忍辱，四曰精進，五曰禪定，六曰智慧，謂之六波羅密（蜜）。梵語波羅密（蜜），華言彼岸到，即《大學》止至善之義也。儒家以爲異端之教而排之，禪宗亦以爲漸修之階而掃之，然六度如之何其可掃？「理須頓悟，事以漸除」，漸除非六度不可。五常百行，三百三千之儀，無一而非六度也。[85]

管東溟認爲儒者以佛說爲異端，禪家重頓悟而輕漸修，皆不免忽視菩薩道的六波羅蜜（六度）。他則將儒家綱常倫理，通貫於六波羅蜜的內容。但在會通中亦有所析別，對具體的實踐方法提出解釋。例如其論「持戒」云：

> 持儒之戒，又不在區區戒酒、戒殺間也，儒以齊家治國平天下爲分內事，即不飲不殺，曾何以當普賢行之萬一？而一言足以僨事，一念足以殺人，雖有小因，詎贖重垢？即使言寡尤、行寡悔，而出謀發慮不爲天下萬世起念，僅爲

85 管志道，《從先維俗議》，卷5，〈儒者兼修六度〉，頁488-489。

> 一身一家起念，如大乘之戒何？儒者之戒經，備在禮儀三百、威儀三千中，而大要則蔽於《易傳》見龍一爻中。曰：「庸言之信」，口戒也；「庸行之謹」，身戒也；「閑邪存其誠」，意戒也。斯之謂大乘菩薩戒。[86]

以儒禮、《易》爻做爲大乘菩薩戒，在思想史上殆不多見。管東溟又論「忍辱」云：

> 聖賢所乘願力不同，乘絜矩以平天下之願力耶？道在稱物平施。以直報怨，以德報德，其施乃平。當其情理兩迫，父母兄弟之仇亦報，四凶之罪亦誅，唯藏身必以恕而已，此儒家之所以克己復禮也。成慈悲修出世之願力耶？道在難忍能忍。觀彼冤仇，如己父母，其忍乃眞，當其機緣所至，雖歌利王割截身體，亦誓道成首度，雖調達累劫作仇，亦與授記作佛，然亦度之於報盡罪滅之日而已。此釋家之所以克己復禮也。在聖人易地則皆然，學者胡得執此議彼？唯吾儕既立身於冠裳中，則亦守孔子之矩而已矣。[87]

此處將儒釋二家聖人的願力以及相配合的應世原則，做了清楚的分析，並認爲兩者不相衝突，但身爲儒者自當堅守儒矩。大體而言，管東溟在工夫論上會通儒佛，頗運用「以儒（名教倫理）攝佛（菩薩道）」之法，故云「以東魯之矩收二氏」。

管東溟從本體、工夫上全面會通儒釋，並將孔學判爲悟後起修的大乘菩薩道，揚其地位於禪學之上，此種說法在思想史上甚具特色。

86 管志道，《從先維俗議》，卷5，〈儒者兼修六度〉，頁490-491。
87 管志道，《從先維俗議》，卷5，〈儒者兼修六度〉，頁491。

一般儒者於佛典涉獵不深，固未論及於此；即令佛門高僧，也往往以佛攝儒，判儒學爲世間法、人天乘，抑揚之意顯然。如天臺智顗（538-597）云：

> 施法藥凡愚本自不知，皆是聖人託跡同凡，出無佛世誘誨童蒙。《大經》（按：《大般涅槃經》）云：「一切世間外道經書皆是佛說，非外道說。」《光明》（按：《金光明經》）云：「一切世間所有善論，皆因此經，若深識世法，即是佛法。」何以故？束於十善即是五戒，深知五常五行義亦似五戒。……周孔立此五常爲世間法藥，救治人病。……然世法藥非畢竟治，屈步移足，雖垂盡三有，當復退還。故云：凡夫雖修有漏禪，其心行穿如漏器，雖生非想當復退還。[88]

智者大師認爲大乘菩薩「託跡同凡」，以各種方便法門化導眾生，因此一切世間法若究實而論，亦即是佛法，如周孔五常之教，即與佛法相通。但他最終仍將儒說視爲不究竟的法藥。此外，圭峰宗密（784-841）一方面說「孔老釋迦皆是至聖」；一方面卻仍強調「策萬行，懲惡勸善，同歸於治，則三教皆可遵行。推萬法，窮理盡性，至於本源，則佛教方爲決了。」[89]永明延壽亦然，雖主張「儒道先宗，皆是菩薩，示劣揚化，同讚佛乘」；但論及儒道二家教法，仍認爲「未逾俗杜，猶局塵籠，豈能洞法界之玄宗，運無邊之妙行乎？」[90]在在可見

88 釋智顗，《摩訶止觀》，卷6，收入《大正新修大藏經》，第46冊，頁77a。

89 釋宗密，《原人論．序》，收入《大正新修大藏經》，第45冊，頁708a。

90 延壽，《萬善同歸集》，卷3，收入《大正新修大藏經》，第48冊，頁987c-988a。

佛門高僧以佛攝儒、佛勝儒劣的立場。管東溟則將儒家的名教倫理等同於普賢行門，將孔門師弟視爲行起解絕、隱悟顯修的大士。他如此抬高「孔矩」的地位，除卻其個人主觀上的信念以外，也有著時代的針對性，即希望透過篤實的儒行，救正晚明狂禪之弊，下節將對此做進一步申論。

綜合來看，管東溟一方面欲將儒佛置放在一貫的修行道路上，一方面又欲對其教法的偏重給予不同定位。以下這段文字對此有清楚的說明：

> 孔釋原無二修，亦無二證，在多劫互爲隱顯，而一生之教體，則各有攸重焉。儒聖重悟後之修，修至於高禪所不能修，修乃圓，此吾儕之所以奉爲矩者也，安得以禪悟壓之？佛聖重修後之證，證至於大聖之所不能證，證乃竟，是吾儕之所望以爲歸者也，安得以儒矩圍之？[91]

「頓悟、漸修、圓證」是管東溟心目中的成聖次第，在其著作中一再提及。他將孔學的長處定位在悟後之修，強調其大乘菩薩道的地位非禪悟所能取代；又將佛法的重心定位在修後之證，認爲佛經揭示了出世間的究竟果位，此果位也是儒者修行的最後歸宿，因此不當因執守儒矩而排斥出世法。由於其說不偏於一家一派，因此也不易爲時人所理解，管東溟云：

> 昔陽明在龍場衡困中，發悟機於枕席之上，蓋嘗中夜號其僮僕，欲有所拈而口復噤。忽然湧出「良知」二字，遂乃橫說豎說而不可窮，蓋從苦心中流出也。愚所拈「敦化川

91　管志道，《酬諮續錄》（東京：尊經閣文庫藏，明萬曆三十三年［1605］序刊本），卷2，〈柬劉大司成雲嶠丈〉，頁30。

流」之旨，自謂苦心近之。第宋儒止窮孔子之學於儒典中；而愚兼窮孔子之學於釋典中。近儒之拂孔矩也，以濫於禪；而愚之尊孔矩也，以通於釋。此則舉世高賢之所難信者。[92]

時人難信，正顯現出管東溟「敦化川流」思想的超學派性格。端就對孔學的詮釋而言，其說既不同於宋儒（程朱學），也有別於近儒（陽明學）。管東溟即是在此獨特的學問基礎上，展開他對思想史的反省與對時代的批判。

六、道脈自覺與時代批判

管東溟開展判教論的良工苦心，並非單純出自理論思辯的興趣，而是本於對古今道脈遞嬗轉移的自覺，從而思考學術的新方向。他自稱對《禮記》中「言必慮其所終，行必稽其所敝」二語時時體貼，因此對歷代三教學人所遺留的下弊端深自警惕。[93]他如此分析有明一代的學風：

蓋自聖祖垂統以來，道風無慮三變：初但轉胡風之穢濁，入程朱之行門，則革除之節義爭先，而河東以復性收之；繼乃轉俗學之支離，入周、邵之性境，則江門之致虛立本，而浙東以良知暢之；今其當轉三教濫觴之弊，入孔門一貫之淵，則儒標不得矜絕學，而禪鋒不得侈無上矣。[94]

管東溟認爲明代學術發展有三階段，明初以程朱理學爲官學，儒者謹

92 管志道，《問辨牘》，亨集，〈答周符卿二魯文書〉，頁56-57。
93 管志道，《酬諮續錄》，卷3，〈再答段幻然輝縣來書〉，頁43。
94 管志道，《問辨牘》元集，〈答王太常塘南先生書〉，頁7。

尊程朱教說，重視綱常，代表人物有方正學（孝孺，1358-1402）的氣節與薛敬軒的復性；其後，理學因科舉考試而逐漸僵滯化、支離化，乃有陳白沙（獻章，1428-1500）、王陽明先後發明爲學大本，使學者回歸周濂溪、邵康節（雍，1011-1077）的灑落境界；王陽明以後，三教交涉頻繁，但也流弊各出，管東溟認爲此時學術的要務，是發明孔門一以貫之的精神，會通三教，以導正各家的流弊。何以要回歸孔子？因爲在管東溟看來，朱子學、陽明學皆不足以擔負此新時代的任務。他說：

> 五宗濫觴之餘，天下知有禪宗，不知有聖學，故天以程朱挽之。然程朱但能以道行奪二氏，豈能以性宗奪二氏？久而理障日增，澆風轉盛，天下知有名利辭章，不知有性眞之學，故天又以文成挽之，然文成但知禪宗之逼聖學，而不知聖學之必究於佛果，故以自私自利之根疑二氏，而擯之於孔矩之外，曾不思聖賢經世事業，槩從多劫見性中來，佛所稱爲行菩薩道者。特以隱實顯權，而不以出離生死爲教耳。文成蓋以良知蔽禪宗，因以禪宗蔽佛道，疎矣。……程朱重孔矩，而矩未必其從心；文成重從心之矩，畢竟矩有踰處，其不能收二氏均也。[95]

管東溟認爲道脈由禪學轉爲程朱理學、又由程朱理學轉爲陽明心學，皆有天命，後出者亦能救先行者之弊。然而在他看來，程朱之學在行持上固然謹嚴，對心體的透悟卻顯不足，難使佛道門徒心服；而陽明學回歸本心良知，所悟雖能與禪學較量，但禪學只重當下一念而少談三祇修證，王陽明亦僅從世間法的角度考慮儒學，因此亦難以眞正會

95 管志道，《問辨牘》，元集，〈答吳侍御安節文書書〉，頁50-51。

通儒佛。此外，程朱學雖強調理的規範作用，但心與理不免判而為二；陽明學雖主張心即是理，卻容易認情識為良知，可謂各有其短。若要收攝佛道而重振儒門，必須回歸「孔矩」。管東溟云：

> 當此之時，不患三教之不合，而患合之不以其矩。合之不以其矩，則儒不儒、禪不禪、玄不玄，而世教且斁，不如各執本宗之為愈也。[96]

晚明三教合一風氣甚盛，但倘使毫無方法與規範，最終只成三教混濫而已。他之「以東魯之矩收二氏」，目的即在防止流弊。又曰：

> 蓋不言收二氏，是儒者止有經世之道，而無與於出世之宗，將謂身死則神隨形滅，所不朽者惟名而已矣，名豈足以絆上乘之豪傑？然收二氏之而不言矩，則宗風峻而皇綱卑，匪但狂禪無所檢束，而士之希慕上乘者，必且裂冠毀冕以為高矣。其敝也，不以出世妨經世，則以經世濫出世。……以孔矩收二氏，言以從心不踰之矩，範圍二氏之化而不過也。蓋不但通其本來出世之宗，亦挽其末流誣世之弊焉。及其至也，豈直孔矩能收二氏，二氏之矩亦足以收孔子，蓋龍德不可為首矣。吾儕，孔氏之徒也，必贊皇綱以治二氏之徒，是以特拈孔矩云。[97]

經世與出世相扞格，是三教衝突最關鍵的問題之一，若僅從心性論上談「三教一致」（如陽明學以良知範圍三教），依舊無法徹底解決此問題。管東溟透過判教進行「三教會通」，使儒學向出世法延伸（收二氏）、禪學向世間法收攝（以孔矩），這是他「剖藩籬，標正鵠」

96 管志道，《從先維俗議》，卷5，〈儒先論三教得失〉，頁533。
97 管志道，《問辨牘》，元集，〈答吳侍御安節丈書〉，頁47。

的方法。[98]

管東溟又將當時學術的流弊歸納爲「狂」與「僞」，他指出：「今日所當拒者，不在楊墨，而在僞儒之亂眞儒；今日所當闢者，不在佛老，而在狂儒之濫狂禪。」[99]大體而言，陽明學的流弊偏於狂，朱子學的流弊偏於僞，若進一步分析，又可分爲以下幾種流弊：

> 世有毀儒行以從禪者，爲拂經；執儒言以排佛者，爲局見；以此合彼，而未免有依違揀擇者，爲無權之中；以此望彼，而不能無所歆羨畔援者，爲二本之學。皆不合於孔子之矩，愚無取也。[100]

此處所說的「拂經」爲狂儒、狂禪之弊；「局見」爲程朱理學之弊；「無權之中」、「二本之學」則爲當世兼涉三教者常犯的毛病。在管東溟看來，無論何者皆非孔子一貫之眞諦。[101]底下這段文字，非常明確地表達出他會通三教的宗旨與蘄嚮：

> 志在祖述仲尼，憲章聖祖，上參氣運，下合群機，體乾元而血脈之以敦其化，核三教而主賓之以川其流。見欲圓，即以仲尼之圓，圓宋儒之方，而使儒不礙釋，釋不礙儒，極而至於事事無礙，以通並育並行之轍；矩欲方，亦以仲

98 管志道，《問辨牘》，元集，〈答吳侍御安節丈書〉，頁48-49。

99 管志道，《從先維俗議》，卷4，〈知命論世〉，頁413。

100 管志道，《問辨牘》，元集，〈答王太常塘南先生書〉，頁5-6。

101 管東溟曾言：「孔庭之一，必貫佛氏之一，與老氏之一。一也者，中也，天下之大本也。立天下之大本，自能以敦化起川流，而何所不貫？……洛閩諸儒之一，大類子莫所執之一；而今之出入三教，影響立宗者，又類夷子二本之一，其失孔庭之一則均矣。本不二，一不執，是謂孔庭之眞一。」與此可相參照。參見管志道，《問辨牘》，亨集，〈答周符卿二魯丈書〉，頁25。

> 尼之方，方近儒之圓，推而極於法法不濫，以持不害不悖之衡。[102]

其中「祖述仲尼，憲章聖祖」二語，化用自《中庸》所稱「祖述堯舜，憲章文武」的孔子志願，在管東溟的著作中經常提及。蓋晚明時期以羅近溪爲首的儒者群中，曾吹起一股明太祖崇拜的風氣，[103]管東溟也受此影響。他對明太祖的推崇，偏重在其並尊三教、主孔教而賓二氏的宗教政策。[104]當然，明太祖的三教觀重在「三教並用」，未若管東溟進行「三教會通」的義理判釋，但管東溟依舊深信太祖的三教觀，爲後世整頓三教奠定了基礎，應當引以爲楷模。在上述引文中，他重新發揮了「敦化川流」的判教思想，認爲三教皆從乾元性海中流出，理體不二，當合而不當分，這是「敦其化」；但三教之教體各異，事用各別，當分而不當合，這是「川其流」。就「敦化」的一面而言，重在事事無礙，因此必須以孔學的一貫之宗，矯正程朱的排斥異端，這是「圓宋儒之方」；就「川流」的一面而言，重在法法不濫，因此必須以孔學的名教矩矱，矯正王學末流的籠統良知，這是「方近儒之圓」。[105]如此，三教學者之間方能如《中庸》所云：「道並

102 管志道，《師門求正牘》，卷中，〈奉答天臺先生測易蠡言〉，頁24。

103 龔鵬程曾留意到此現象：「以明太祖作爲當代的聖人典型，乃羅近溪以下，李贄、焦竑、楊復所、袁宗道等這一批思想家共有的特徵。」見龔鵬程，《晚明思潮》（北京：商務印書館，2005），頁34。

104 關於太祖三教政策的簡要介紹，可參見酒井忠夫著，劉岳兵、何英鶯譯，《中國善書研究（增補版）》（南京：江蘇人民出版社，2010），上冊，頁207-214。大體而言，太祖的主張是「天下無二道，聖人無兩心」，以儒教爲主、佛道二教爲輔來共助王綱。

105 「圓宗方矩論」亦是管東溟的重要論述。大體而言，此論以圓宗配屬悟門、方矩配屬行門，主張學者所悟之道理需圓融、而所行之矩矱需方正，恰與管東溟「頓悟漸修論」的工夫論取向相配合。較詳盡的討論參

行而不相悖，萬物並育而不相害」。管東溟又從另一角度申述此意：

> 以孔子之一，貫二氏之一，是曰「大德敦化」；以孔子之矩，別二氏之矩，是曰「小德川流」。用程朱之方而去其偏，則無執一之弊；用陽明之圓而防其濫，則無二本之嫌。通性命之宗於無極，以蕩儒家名利之根，則毋敢飾儒行以藏偷，而朝聞夕可之脈正；稽菩薩之行於三祇，以遏禪家我慢之氣，則毋敢影禪宗以踰矩，而盡性至命之學深。蓋不但使孔氏之徒，知有因果之說，不得不素位而行，求所以爲究竟者；亦使二氏之徒，知儒宗行大乘菩薩之道，不得不小心畏法，助皇綱以化頑。[106]

這段文字言敦化川流之意、執一二本之弊，大體與前一段引文相同。但此處更進一義，強調了挽救儒弊與禪弊的苦心。管東溟認爲，後世儒者之弊在於不通三世因果，故奉行名教之際，不免藏有貪圖令聞之偷心，他藉由出世法，發明孔學「朝聞道，夕死可矣」的生死學見地，意在洗滌儒者的名利之根；另一方面，禪門之弊則在於不講究三祇漸修的菩薩道，故高抬悟門、忽略行門，使學者滅裂世間名教、卑視皇綱法網，管東溟特別會通孔學與菩薩道，即在約束禪者的我慢之氣。

管東溟對三教的融通判釋，除顧及各學派的流弊，也考慮到不同根機的對象，他並不打算如陽明學者一般，拈定一講學宗旨；也不打算如三一教主林兆恩（1517-1598）一般，將三教論做爲一宗教學說來推行。他主張契理還需契機，不同根機的對象，應該採取不同的實

見吳孟謙，〈融貫與批判——晚明三教論者管東溟的思想及其時代〉，頁95-109。

106 管志道，《問辨牘》，亨集，〈答周符卿二魯文書〉，頁38。

踐立場。管東溟云：

> 愚以毘盧法界印乾元，以普賢行海印孔矩，意有在也。……通乎此義，而後孔子下學上達之實際可窮已。愚特拈之以爲越孔躐佛，重解輕行者戒焉。然亦斷不敢以普賢行海，槩責三教中人，恐其未入大乘之路，而先喪成佛之因；亦不敢以毘盧法界，槩喻儒門中人，恐其未悟涅槃之因，先染禪狂之見。則亦儒而儒之，禪而禪之，玄而玄之，不相爭而亦不相濫，其可矣。日用不知之百姓又何從焉？齊以聖訓之六條，而導以蓮臺之九品，可也。此所謂以人治人，而其道，亦徹上徹下之道也。竊意孔子生於今日，其憲章亦如是矣。[107]

管東溟晚年發明孔學，特重「下學上達」四字，下學即是行孔矩（通於普賢行海），上達即是悟乾元（通於毘盧性海），可說是一條悟修並重、儒佛會通的成聖之路。但從普賢行海（修門）來說，其路迢遙，三教中急於了脫生死者必不能領受；而從毘盧性海（悟門）來說，其境玄遠，儒門中根器不及者參之，容易濡染狂禪見解。對這些人而言，倒不如隨自身法緣，於三教門中各自修行，較無流弊。換句話說，對其不必深論「三教一致」與「三教會通」，採取「三教並用」之法即可。而對於一般庶民百姓，亦不妨並用，既以明太祖的聖諭六言（「孝順父母，尊敬長上。和睦鄉裡，教訓子孫。各安生理，毋作非爲」）安頓其倫常世界，復以淨土宗的念佛往生安頓其信仰世界，蓋聖諭與淨土法門皆爲簡易通俗之教，在庶民中最易收效。管東溟又云：

107　管志道，《問辨牘》，元集，〈答屠儀部赤水文書〉，頁70-71。

> 愚究孔子之上達，而通諸出世之宗，此亦爲上士言也。上士將經大經，立大本，以知化育，不究斯道之全，何以贊高皇之九疇，定彝教於萬世？若中下之士，則亦閑之以程朱之繩墨而已。但聖人重三畏，程朱之撥因果，近於不知天命，其排佛老之書，近於侮聖人之言，亦當爲儒流戒之。至於日用不知之百姓，則六經之義難通，而程朱之訓難入，不以禍福報應惕之則奚懼？不以念佛往生導之則奚歸？蓋孔子之矩誠足以範圍二氏，而二氏之教，亦能齊孔矩之不齊而使之齊也。[108]

此處明確將學者分爲三等：上士當會通三教，方能窮究大道之全體；中下之士根機稍淺，應謹守程朱理學，較無流弊，但於程朱闢佛之論亦不應盲從；一般百姓則應該用禍福因果、念佛往生之教導之。此等觀點皆從教化層面上考慮，頗爲務實。

此外，針對晚明儒者普遍參究佛學的風氣，管東溟也有自己獨到的看法：

> 佛道能發君子之正智，亦能發小人之狂心也。儒者果負顏子聞一知十之資乎，聞易道，即知佛道，聞佛道，亦知易道，參固有助於博文，不參亦無損於約禮。若聞一知二如子貢，及聞一知一如柴愚、參魯、師辟、由喭諸賢，則以一貫爲正因，亦以多學而識爲助因，生今之世，苟不得言性與天道之夫子而師之，釋典其不厭參也已矣。其下者，舉一隅不以三隅反，此則聞一不能知一者也。多聞適足亂心，不若專守下學一路，而以往生西方之因助之。又其劣

108 管志道，《問辨牘》，元集，〈答王太常塘南先生書〉，頁9。

者，啓明嚚訟如丹朱，智足拒諫、言足飾非如殷紂，其資未必不在聞一知一之上，而根頑性拗，一入佛教之圓通，適足以滋其僞而長其狂耳，何如不參之爲愈哉。[109]

這段文字的說法，與前段引文稍有差別，但亦不矛盾。管東溟將儒者分爲數等：上根如顏回，一通百通，學儒知佛，因此於佛學可參可不參；中根如子貢以下諸賢，應多學而識，兼參佛學；下根者智淺，不宜多聞，應當重視下學，兼修淨土。至於才智高而德行薄者，更不當參，以免錯用圓通之教，反滋流弊。管東溟做此議論，一方面是有感於狂學、僞學交作的時代風氣；另一方面在自己的長子身上，見證到錯學佛法之弊端。[110]因此他自己「雖參儒釋異同，而對子姓眷屬，絕不談及出世密旨，惟以庸言庸行率之而已」。[111]他復用以下的比喻，爲兼學佛法的儒者提出建議：

此有二喻，可以定儒釋之綱紀也，論行門之分派，當以父執之交爲喻。孔子以經世之家法師儒流，吾道中之父也，釋氏以出世之家法師緇流，吾道中之父執也。孝子雖以事父之禮事父執，然未有不承父祧而承父執之祧者，繼別之宗有在也。論性海之同源，當以祖父之脈爲喻。孔子以三綱五常之教含一大事，儒門中之父脈也；釋氏以一大事之教含綱常，儒門中之祖脈也。仁人雖以嚴父之心嚴祖，然

109 管志道，《從先維俗議》，卷5，〈剖儒釋現悟修證境界〉，頁506。

110 管東溟六十九歲時，長子士珩病逝，他感嘆道：「此子一獵竺墳，便起尊三寶而薄五常之思，視過庭之《詩》、《禮》，土苴耳……故拙刻中言及狂禪之引狂儒，每每痛心疾首，不啻口出，豈專爲李卓吾及達觀僧之屬？大半有激於家庭耳。」對自我的剖析甚爲直白。見管志道，《酬諮續錄》，卷4，〈再答茹翁書〉，頁67。

111 管志道，《從先維俗議》，卷5，〈教子孫敦實行〉，頁456-457。

> 未有不禰其父而上禰其祖者，世及之統有在也。執此以定紀綱，而心師身師之義較然矣。[112]

這裡將儒釋關係分爲「行門之分派」與「性海之同源」兩方面，實通於「川流」與「敦化」之義。就「川流」一面而言，儒釋之教體有別，身爲儒者，應以孔門爲父、釋門爲父執，敬佛而守儒矩；而就「敦化」一面而言，儒釋之教理相通，但所側重者亦有經世、出世之別，儒者應以孔門爲父、釋門爲祖，不能越過綱常而別求出世解脫。總而言之，學者之心量固可廣大，儒佛兼師而無礙；立身則須謹嚴，儒佛有別而不濫。管東溟以此態度自修，亦力圖爲當世儒者訂定修行的準則。

從以上這些論述可知，管東溟對自己提出判教主張的意義與目的，始終保持著高度的自覺。在他看來，泛泛地融通三教並不難，難的是「酌量時緣，通聖人之作用」。[113]易言之，即是對所處時代的問題有深刻的反省，在辨章學術的同時應病投藥、去短集長。晚明史家朱平涵（國禎，1558-1632）云：「三教互相攻 ，此低秀才、潑和尚、癡道士識見。儒者能容之、用之，暗禁末流，方見廣大。」[114]此語恰可做爲管東溟判教論述的註腳。

七、結論

晚明時期，思想界空氣相對自由，三教互動日益密切，求道者一

112 管志道，《從先維俗議》，卷5，〈儒流參求二氏法度〉，頁478。

113 管志道，《續問辨牘》，卷1，〈答馮大司成具區丈書〉，頁69-70。

114 朱國禎，《湧幢小品》，卷28，〈篇名〉，收入續修四庫全書編纂委員會編，《續修四庫全書》（上海：上海古籍出版社，1997），子部雜家類，第1173冊，頁384。

方面得以透過多樣化的理論資源，對身心性命的源頭進行深刻的探索；另一方面也面臨了價值多歧、思想混雜的時代問題。求道意識與時代關懷均極強烈的管東溟，不爲一宗一派所拘限，透過自身的體悟，以「群龍無首」之說解構前儒的道統論，進一步別開生面地展開「敦化川流」的判教論述，既給予不同宗教學術一個共通的思想底盤，試圖止息三教爭端；也同時衡定各種教說的淺深高下，勾畫其心目中理想的修行藍圖，爲當時學術找尋新的出路。綜合來說，管東溟的判教思想具有以下幾個特點：

（一）體相用兼具

本文一開始曾將「三教合一」的層次析而爲四，「三教一致」關注本體、「三教會通」闡發教相、「三教並用」與「三教混融」則涉及現實作用。晚明學者的三教合一思想，較常見的是以一心統攝三教的「三教一致」之論，管東溟的三教論則兼具體相用三層：乾元性海與毘盧法界的貫通屬於「體」；學派、人物、義理的定位與判釋屬於「相」；重視孔矩、因機施教以維繫世風則屬於「用」。如果將王陽明良知教的簡易學風類比於禪學；則管東溟「敦化川流」思想的判教性格，毋寧較近於天臺、華嚴學。

（二）儒佛相融攝

思想史上，儒者判釋佛教之法，向來是「以儒攝佛」，如宋明理學家認爲儒者下學而上達，佛教則務上達而遺下學；至於佛門中人判釋儒學，則莫不「以佛攝儒」，如宗密、延壽皆以佛法通於世間、出世間，儒學則侷限於世間。平心而論，「以儒攝佛」者關注的是世間倫理；「以佛攝儒」者則偏重出世解脫，故皆以己之長判人之短。管東溟的判教與此兩種立場皆不同，他同時關注世間倫理與出世解脫，可說是「儒佛相攝」的型態。從敦化的本體而言，是乾元性海與毘盧法界相攝；從川流的行門而言，則是儒門禮教與普賢行門相攝。單就一時一方論之，雖可說儒學是權、佛學是實；但擴展至無盡時空的見地中，儒佛聖人皆無定相，皆往來於同一條修行道路上。管東溟這一世界觀與生命觀，自是源於大乘佛學；但就其所採取的立場而言，眞理並非佛學所專屬，《周易》之中同樣揭示此理，儒佛畢竟相互融攝、無有高下。

（三）華嚴式的孔學詮釋

宋明理學諸家雖莫不涉獵佛教而吸收其養分，但卻是得自禪門者多、深入教門者寡。管東溟則具有較深厚的華嚴學根底，其解構道統與判釋三教的思維，受華嚴意境的啓發亦最大。故而他對孔學的創造性詮釋，與理學諸儒自不能不面貌迥別。他之所以有「寧學孔子而未至，不欲向世人腳根下盤旋，既補程朱之闕，復拾陽明之遺」的自信，[115]原因也在於此。

（四）回歸儒行的菩薩道

心學流行的晚明，儒者特別關注生死問題，同時藉由講學經世，希望救拔蒼生出離利欲的苦海，共證一體之心源。這與大乘菩薩道兼

115 管志道，《問辨牘》，亨集，〈答周符卿二魯文書〉，頁38-39。

重出離心與菩提心的精神，可謂若合符節。[116]管東溟乘此風會，融合儒佛，使儒學與菩薩道不僅在胸懷上相通，更在修證階位上相通，孔學因而被定位爲行起解絕的普賢行。在儒學史上，儒者若非世間之儒，即爲通禪之儒，罕有以大乘教法爲實踐藍圖者；而在佛教史上，佛門多視儒學爲人天權教，亦罕有將儒學視爲普賢行門者。管東溟以大乘菩薩道恢拓儒學之規模，意在使儒者可以進窺出世之法，不落於深閉固拒的排佛窠臼；又以儒行落實普賢行，則懷抱出世追求者，亦將不礙於篤實入世，避免滅裂倫常的狂禪弊端。

關於三教的融合會通，熊十力曾有以下看法：

> 言三家合一者，自己無有根據，無有統類，比附雜揉而談合一，是混亂也。會通之旨則異是。體眞極而辨眾義，辨眾義而會眞極，根據強而統類明，是故謂之會通。[117]

錢穆則云：

> 夫範圍三教，融通歸一，豈非學術界一大業，思想界一大事。唯其言思意境，必能卓乎有以超乎三家之上，乃始可以包絡乎三家之外，而後三家之異同乃可融會消攝於我範圍之內，而俱以爲我之用。否然者，隨順含糊，管攝不住，終必決裂以去。抑且自亂本宗，精微昧失，粗跡流傳，其害不可勝言矣。故君子之學，別異尤審於會同。[118]

116　呂妙芬曾指出晚明儒者的聖人觀與佛教的大乘菩薩有相似之處，同時也密切關注生死議題。參見呂妙芬，〈儒釋交融的聖人觀：從晚明儒家聖人與菩薩形象相似處及對生死議題的關注談起〉，《中央研究院近代史研究所集刊》，32（臺北，1999），頁165-207。

117　熊十力，《新唯識論（語體文本）》，收入蕭萐父主編，《熊十力全集》（武漢：湖北教育出版社，2001），冊7，頁202-203。

118　錢穆，〈說良知四句教與三教合一〉，收入錢穆，《中國學術思想史論叢》

平心而論，管東溟對三教的融通與判釋，開宗創派、自居教主之意少；而辨章學術、匡正時弊之意多，其判教論述「統類」甚明，且兼有「別異」與「會同」，在宋明思想史乃至三教交涉史上，均有獨特的意義與價值。

（臺北：東大圖書公司，1986），冊7，頁152。

Of Great and Small Beneficence:
Guan Dongming's Re-evaluation of the Intellectual Tradition and his Contemporary Concerns

Abstract

Guan Dongming is one of the most original thinkers in his time. By deconstructing the legacy of moral legitimacy justification (道統論) propagated by the Neo-Confucians through a synthesis of the *Avatamsaka Sutra* and the *Book of Changes*, he avoided limiting himself to any single school of thought at a time when the deficiencies of the Zhuxi and Yangming schools, as well as Chan Buddhism were manifest. Through his discernment between philosophies of great and small beneficence in the intellectual tradition, Guan not only provided a syncretic basis on which the three teachings of Confucianism, Daoism and Buddhism can be integrated, but also sought to find the ideal guide to spiritual practice to renew the intellectual tradition.

This essay examines Guan's re-evaluation of the intellectual tradition by way of: (a) analyzing the different levels of syncretism on a macro scale; (b) revealing the background in which Guan's strategies of philosophical discernment are formed; (c) observing how Guan deconstructs the justifications of moral legitimacy through a synthesis of the *Avatamsaka Sutra* and the *Book of Changes*; (d) discussing Guan's discernment of philosophies and his insights into the syncretic relationship between Confucianism and Buddhism; (e) pointing out Guan's concerns over contemporary issues which guided his re-evaluation of the intellectual tradition. Finally, I shall conclude by highlighting the distinguishing features of Guan's discernment of philosophies and its significance in intellectual history.

Keywords: beneficence, Guan Dongming, discernment of philosophies, *Avatamsaka Sutra, Book of Changes*, three teachings.

徵引文獻

一、傳統文獻

方以智著，龐樸注釋，《東西均注釋》，北京：中華書局，2001。
王守仁著，吳光等編校，《王陽明全集（新編本）》，杭州：浙江古籍出版社，2010。
王道淵，《還眞集》，收入《正統道藏》，臺北：新文豐出版社，第40冊，1985-1988。
王畿著，吳震編校整理，《王畿集》，南京：鳳凰出版社，2007。
永瑢等編纂，《四庫全書總目》，北京：中華書局，2003。
朱國禎，《湧幢小品》，收入續修四庫全書編纂委員會編，《續修四庫全書》，子部雜家類，第1173冊，上海：上海古籍出版社，1997，據復旦大學圖書館藏明天啓二年（1622）刻本影印。
李純甫著，荒木見悟解題，《鳴道集説》，京都：中文出版社，1977。
周汝登，《東越證學錄》，收入四庫全書存目叢書編纂委員會編，《四庫全書存目叢書》，集部別集類，第165冊，臺南：莊嚴文化，1997，據清華大學圖書館藏明萬曆刻本印。
宗密，《原人論》，收入《大正新修大藏經》，第45冊，東京：大正一切經刊行會，1924-1935。
延壽，《萬善同歸集》，收入《大正新修大藏經》，第48冊，東京：大正一切經刊行會，1924-1935。
______集，《宗鏡錄》，收入《大正新修大藏經》，第48冊，東京：大正一切經刊行會，1924-1935。
法藏述，《華嚴經義海百門》，收入《大正新修大藏經》，第45冊，東京：大正一切經刊行會，1924-1935。
眞可著，德清校閱，《紫柏尊者全集》，收入《卍新纂續藏經》，第73冊，東京：國書刊行會，1975-1989。
______，錢謙益纂閱，《紫柏老人別集》，收入《卍新纂續藏經》，第73冊，東京：國書刊行會，1975-1989。
袁中道，《珂雪齋近集》，收入續修四庫全書編纂委員會編，《續修四庫全書》，集部別集類，第1376冊，上海：上海古籍出版社，2002，據明書林唐國達刻本影印。
張廷玉等編撰，《明史》，北京：中華書局，2011。

張烈著，陸隴其敘評，《王學質疑》，臺北：廣文書局，1982。
陳亮著，鄧廣銘點校，《陳亮集》，北京：中華書局，1987。
彭紹升，《一乘決疑論》，收入《卍新纂續藏經》，第58冊，東京：國書刊行會，1975-1989。
智旭，《靈峰蕅益大師宗論》，收入《嘉興大藏經》，第36冊，臺北：新文豐出版社，1987。
智顗，《摩訶止觀》，收入《大正新修大藏經》，第46冊，東京：大正一切經刊行會，1924-1935。
焦竑著，李劍雄整理，《澹園集》，北京：中華書局，1999。
程顥、程頤著，王孝魚點校，《二程集》，北京：中華書局，2004。
實叉難陀譯，《大方廣佛華嚴經》，收入《大正新修大藏經》，第10冊，東京：大正一切經刊行會，1924-1935。
管志道，《步朱吟》，東京：尊經閣文庫藏，明萬曆三十一年（1603）序刊本。
______，《師門求正牘》，東京：尊經閣文庫藏，明萬曆二十四年（1596）序刊本。
______，《問辨牘》，東京：尊經閣文庫藏，明萬曆二十六年（1598）序刊本。
______，《從先維俗議》，收入四庫全書存目叢書編纂委員會編，《四庫全書存目叢書》，子部雜家類，第88冊，臺南：莊嚴文化公司，1995，據天津圖書館藏明萬曆三十年（1602）徐文學刻本影印。
______，《惕若齋集》，東京：尊經閣文庫藏，明萬曆二十四年（1596）序刊本。
______，《惕若齋續集》，東京：尊經閣文庫藏，明萬曆刊本。
______，《理要酬諮錄》，東京：尊經閣文庫藏，明萬曆三十年（1602）序刊本。
______，《酬諮續錄》，東京：尊經閣文庫藏，明萬曆三十三年（1605）序刊本。
______，《謔餘音》，東京：尊經閣文庫藏，明萬曆三十四年（1606）序刊本。
______，《續問辨牘》，東京：尊經閣文庫藏，明萬曆二十七年（1599）序刊本。
趙貞吉，《趙文肅公文集》，收入四庫全書存目叢書編纂委員會編，《四庫全書存目叢書》，集部別集類，第100冊，臺南：莊嚴文化公司，1995，據杭州大學圖書館藏明萬曆十三年（1585）趙德仲刻本影印。
德清著，福善日錄，通炯編輯，《憨山老人夢遊集》，收入《卍新纂續藏經》，第73冊，東京：國書刊行會，1975-1989。
鄧豁渠著，鄧紅校注，《南詢錄》，武漢：武漢理工大學出版社，2008。
黎靖德編，王星賢點校，《朱子語類》，北京：中華書局，1999。
續法輯，《法界宗五祖略記》，收入《嘉興大藏經》，第77冊，臺北：新文豐出版社，1987。
錢謙益，錢曾箋注，錢仲聯標校，《牧齋初學集》，上海：上海古籍出版社，1985。

二、近人論著

土田健次郎著，朱剛譯，《道學的形成》，上海：上海古籍出版社，2010。
王仲堯，《隋唐佛教判教思想研究》，高雄：佛光山文教基金會，2001。
牟宗三，《現象與物自身》，臺北：臺灣學生書局，1975。
何淑宜，〈時代危機與個人抉擇——以晚明士紳劉錫玄的宗教經驗爲例〉，《新史學》，23：2（臺北，2012），頁57-106。
佛光大辭典編修委員會編，《佛光大辭典》，高雄：佛光出版社，1988。
吳汝均，《佛教的當代判釋》，臺北：臺灣學生書局，2011。
吳孟謙，〈融貫與批判——晚明三教論者管東溟的思想及其時代〉，臺北：臺灣大學中國文學系博士論文，2014。
呂妙芬，〈儒釋交融的聖人觀：從晚明儒家聖人與菩薩形象相似處及對生死議題的關注談起〉，《中央研究院近代史研究所集刊》，32（臺北，1999），頁165-207。
呂澂，《中國佛學源流略講》，臺北：天華出版社，1986。
林義正，〈儒佛會通方法研議〉，《佛學研究中心學報》，7（臺北，2002），頁185-211。
唐君毅，《生命存在與心靈境界：生命存在之三向與心靈九境》，臺北：臺灣學生書局，1977。
荒木見悟，〈道統論の衰退と新儒林傳の展开〉，收入荒木見悟，《明清思想論考》，東京：研文出版，1992，頁1-83。
________，〈管東溟——明末における一儒佛調合論者の思維構造〉，收入荒木見悟，《明代思想研究：明代における儒教と佛教の交流》，東京：創文社，1972，頁149-185。
________，《明末宗教思想研究：管東溟の生涯とその思想》，東京：創文社，1979。
________著，廖肇亨譯，〈鄧豁渠的出現及其背景〉，收入荒木見悟《明末清初的思想與佛教》，臺北：聯經出版社，2006。

酒井忠夫著，劉岳兵、何英鶯譯，《中國善書研究（增補版）》，南京：江蘇人民出版社，2010。
陳寅恪，〈論韓愈〉，收入陳寅恪，《金明館叢稿初編》，北京：三聯書店，2009，頁319-332。
勞思光，《新編中國哲學史》，第3卷（下），臺北：三民書局，2001。
熊十力，《新唯識論（語體文本）》，收入蕭萐父主編，《熊十力全集》，冊7，武漢：湖北教育出版社，2001。
劉咸炘，《推十書》，三冊，成都：成都古籍書店，1996。
鄭宗義，〈明末王學的三教合一論及其現代迴響〉，收入吳根友主編，《多元範式下的明清研究》，北京：三聯書店，2011，頁181-233。
錢穆，〈說良知四句教與三教合一〉，收入錢穆，《中國學術思想史論叢（七）》，臺北：東大圖書公司，1986，頁121-147。
藍日昌，《六朝判教論的發展與演變》，臺北：文津出版社，2003。
魏珮玲，〈管志道年譜〉，臺南：臺南大學國語文學系碩士論文，2010。
饒宗頤，〈三教論及其海外移植〉，收入饒宗頤，《選堂集林：史林新編（中）》，香港：中華書局，2012，頁689-722。
龔鵬程，《晚明思潮》，北京：商務印書館，2005。
Brook Timothy. "Rethinking Syncretism: The Unity of the Three Teachings and their Joint Worship in Late-Imperial China," *Journal of Chinese Religions*, 21 (1993), pp. 13-44.
Ch'ien Edward T. *Chiao Hung and the Restructuring of Neo-Confucianism in Late Ming*, New York: Columbia University Press, 1986.

【論著】

從宗族到民族——「東亞民族主義」的形成與原理

蔡孟翰

日本千葉大學地球環境福祉研究中心特任准教授，研究興趣爲東亞政治思想史、政治經濟學，業餘興趣爲西洋政治思想、日本研究、國際關係。《騰訊·大家》專欄作家：http://dajia.qq.com/user/nishinotoin#af。近著論文：〈思考《易經》在現代社會的意義〉收於《八卦城談易——第三屆中國·特克斯世界周易論壇文集》，2015年中出版。〈21世紀的中日大戰？東亞國際秩序中的「日本問題」〉，《思想》第25期2014年5月。〈東亞的過去是西方的現在與未來——現代性與現代政治論述之商榷〉收於《普遍與特殊的辯證：政治思想的探掘》，2012年。"This Culture of Ours: Politics, Confucianism, and East Asian identities," *Journal of Political Science and Sociology*, 15 (September 2011), pp. 1-20.

從宗族到民族——「東亞民族主義」的形成與原理

摘要

本文試圖回答東亞的各國（中日朝越）是否有一個共同的民族主義建構，亦或是各有各的民族主義。從東亞政治思想史切入，考察「民族」一詞的由來，東亞各國皆用「民族」一詞，發現「民族」一詞雖爲歐語nation的新造譯語，但是「民族」概念的構成，實出自宋代以來之宗族論。宗族論則又出自於郡縣封建論爭之脈絡。文中復討論宗族論中宗統君統合一或二分與大宗小宗之辨，大宗宗法至明末清初，業已被視爲統合人民、保衛國家之道，但尚未有一國所有人民皆爲一族之想像。郡縣封建論爭飄洋過海，在日本江户時期伊始綿綿不休，至19世紀會澤正志齋面對西方威脅，在封建郡縣的脈絡裡，以大宗宗法建構「國體」論與「始祖」論，奠定「東亞民族主義」之基礎。「東亞民族主義」則完成於明治時期穗積八束之憲法理論。中越朝於19世紀末自日本襲取「民族」一詞與民族主義理論。文中進而討論東亞之「始祖」論與歐洲之「始祖」論，由此證明歐洲民族主義，在思想上對「東亞民族主義」之建構無甚影響。東亞之「民族」源於宗族論，「東亞民族主義」則是世俗化宗統君統合一的大宗宗法，亦是一種政治神學。這種民族主義實則爲國家民族主義，有別於市民民族主義或族群民族主義。

關鍵詞：民族主義、宗族、封建、大宗、朱熹、張載、會澤正志齋、穗積八束、國體、政治思想

"Patriotism is the last refuge of a scoundrel" ——Samuel Johnson[1]

愛國主義是惡棍最終的避難所 ——塞繆爾·強森

"If I should die, think only this of me:
That there's some corner of a foreign field
That is for ever England". From the Soldier, Rupert Brooke[2]

如果我將死去——請念我如斯
在異國異土的某個角落，
有永遠的英格蘭。 出自魯伯特·布魯克〈士兵〉一詩（作者譯）

1 Susan Ratcliffe, *Oxford Dictionary of Thematic Quotations*,（Oxford: Oxford University Press, 2000）, p. 280.

2 Rupert Brooke, edited by Geoffrey Keynes, *The Poetical Works*,（London: Faber and Faber, 1970）, p. 23.

一、前言

進入21世紀以來，東亞國際政治最大的不安，有別於美國或歐盟，不是政府債務或民間大量不良債務所引發的金融危機，而是民族主義或國族主義的再度高漲。[3]日韓、中日可以爲了幾個沒人居住的小島鬧到元首外交中斷，中日甚至爲此而使得雙方關係時時處於緊張狀況，乃至雙方都已有備戰的心態，情勢十分險峻。雖然如此，東西學術界對東亞民族主義的研究卻極其貧乏，此非因無人研究東亞各國的民族主義，只是在汗牛充棟的研究中，直到今日仍極少對東亞民族主義進行全面的瞭解與對比，東亞各國的民族主義研究仍然處於一個分裂割據，直到老死互不往來的現狀。即使有些掛名東亞民族主義合著的書，翻開細看仍多是將各國的篇章集合編爲一書，並沒有系統性的比較考究。[4]如果東亞各國的民族主義眞的互不相干，那麼各自埋頭自

3 「國族主義」一詞的使用與取代「民族主義」一詞主要在臺灣的學術界，但兩岸三地中文社會仍普遍使用「民族」一詞，而非「國族」。「國族主義」一詞可能是來依據Ernest Gellner, *Nations and Nationalism* (Oxford: Blackwell, 1983), p. 1的定義，「nationalism基本上是一個認爲政治單位與民族單位應該吻合的政治原則」（作者譯）。本文因「民族」是歷史上與今天仍使用的字眼，所以「nationalism」的翻譯整齊起見採「民族主義」。今日「國族」一詞早見於清末民初章太炎之〈社會通詮商兌〉章太炎，《章氏叢書》（臺北：世界書局，1982），頁829，一文中與孫中山，《三民主義》（臺北：三民書局，1965［1924］），〈民族主義第五講〉，頁57。又，國族兩字合而言之則最早見於《禮記・檀弓下》：「美哉輪焉，美哉奐焉，歌於斯，哭於斯，聚國族於斯」，見孫希旦，《禮記集解》（北京：中華書局，1989），上，卷11，〈檀弓下〉，頁299。

4 可以參看米原謙、金鳳珍、區建英，《東アジアのナショナリズムと近代——なぜ対立するのか》（大阪：大阪大学出版会，2011），書中各章對中日韓三國的民族主義做了簡潔扼要的敘述分析，十分值得參考，但對於三國民族主義的共同性或有無共通性等相關問題，沒有提出任何理

己圈內的研究，雖非最佳情況，但亦無可厚非。

此外在一般的民族主義研究裡，東亞的民族主義的案例一直在理論建設中可說沒有任何重要性或建樹。比如說在莉亞．格林菲德（Liah Greenfeld）民族主義研究中五個案例，東亞一個也沒有。[5]現代主義的艾尼斯特．葛爾納（Ernest Gellner）與主張族群歷史性的安東尼．史密斯（Anthony D. Smith）也最多蜻蜓點水，對東亞的民族主義幾筆帶過而已，主要還是以歐洲或歐洲殖民地爲案例。[6] 不消說，一個占有全球人口近4分之1人口的中日韓越等地區，占有世界經濟體排名第二與第三的中日兩國，在目前的研究中只有近乎微不足道的份量，不得不說是民族主義研究中很大的缺陷。但這個問題並不能完全搪塞給東亞地區以外的研究者，東亞地區的學者其實亦要承擔相當

論亦無討論。以英文的研究文獻來看，情況並無顯著不同，Frank Dikötter, ed., *The Construction of Racial Identities in China and Japan*，（London: Hurst & Company, 1997），此書導論還坦誠道來，雖然書是關於中國與日本，但「它並不假裝提出統一有整合的視角，它也沒有系統地比較東亞的各種種族認同形成」（p. 11）。書中分成兩部分，前半部關於中國，後半部關於日本，沒有作者間的整合，只是論文的分類排比而已。Kai-wing Chow（周啓榮），Kevin M. Doak and Poshek Fu, eds., *Constructing Nationhood in Modern East Asia*,（Michigan: The University of Michigan Press, 2001），而此書亦是如此，且行文之際，已經認定東亞的民族主義是不同的複數（nationalisms）（p. 2），非源自共同的分母。整本書各章中國的寫中國，日本的寫日本，或看日本如何談中國等，亦是一本書中“同床異夢”。

5 Liah Greenfeld, *Nationalism: Five Roads to Modernity*（Massachusetts: Harvard University Press, 1992）.

6 Ernest Gellner, *Nations and Nationalism*. Anthony D. Smith, *The Nation in History: Historiographical Debates about Ethnicity and Nationalism*（Cambridge: Polity Press, 2000）與 Anthony D. Smith, *The Cultural Foundations of Nations: Hierarchy, Covenant, and Republic*（Oxford: Blackwell Publishing, 2008）.

的責任。自己對所處的地區的民族主義都說不出個所以然來，怎能期待遠在歐美的學者越俎代庖呢？東亞民族主義的特色反而是艾瑞克．霍斯班（Eric Hobsbawm）獨具慧眼早已點出，以他來看，這個特色即使中日朝三國在民族主義興起以前，政治單位中同一民族的比例極高是鮮見的例子，但卻無深入挖掘，整合到他對民族主義的分析中。[7]職是之故，本文試圖針對這個學術研究的空白，提出一些初步的觀察與分析。

在此文中，東亞各國指歷史上的中國、日本、朝鮮與越南，偶爾觸及已經亡國的琉球。時間下限至1910年代，主要理由是各國政治在1910年代均告一段落，展開新的一頁。1911年中國爆發辛亥革命，結束兩千年的帝制，亦可謂是漢族民族主義在現代政治的里程碑。日本1912年明治時代結束。朝鮮則在1910受到日本併吞亡國。越南在1884年全國淪爲法國殖民地後到了1910年代，殖民地政權已經相當穩固，一些由殖民地化後社會上的新興勢力也已經儼然成形，加上越南受到中國與日本影響在此段時間達到最後的高峰。[8]但最主要的理由還是，到1910年代東亞各國的民族主義可謂先後陸續形成，這裡有一個共時性，本文以下會詳細敘述。

同時必須聲明本文並非處理歷史上的「族群意識／認同」（ethnic identity）亦或是「我者」與「他者」的分辨，例如「漢人」意識、「滿人」意識、「中國人」意識、「朝鮮人」意識、「日本人」意識，

7 Eric Hobsbawm, *Nations and Nationalism since 1780: Programme, Myth, Reality*（Cambridge: Cambridge University Press 1991）, p. 66.

8 參看今井昭夫，〈二〇世紀初頭のベトナムにおける開明的儒学者たちの国民国家構想〉，收入 久留島浩、趙景達編，《アジアの国民国家構想——近代への投企と葛藤》（東京：青木書店，2008），頁155-164。

所以並不討論「眞正」的中國人或日本民族意識實際上始於何時或所指爲何，當然亦不深入考察族群文化如何或歷史上某個族群形成的經緯。本文所關注的是在思想史的滾滾長流中，在過往的一千年，面對外來的威脅與侵略，回溯東亞既有的典籍與政治經驗，東亞的人們如何使用西方文化進入東亞以前的語言概念來組織人民，進而構築一個擬血緣的命運共同體，這套語言又如何接上後來所謂的「民族」與「民族主義」。這區別是相當重要的，這正是「族群意識／認同」本身不等於「民族」，亦不等於「民族主義」的理由，例如漢人的意識可能可上推到南北朝，但「漢人」族群或「胡人」族群意識與其伴隨的「漢化」、「胡化」等現象，[9]雖然不能斷言在政治上毫無影響，甚至必須承認是政治史與社會史上非常重要的話題，儘管如此，卻沒有「民族」與「民族主義」的論述來組織成爲一個有目的有宗旨的政治力量與群眾運動。

以下會分爲三大部分討論。首先，稍微釐清東亞民族主義或東亞型民族主義與既有民族主義研究的文獻理論的關係，凸顯東亞地區民族主義與既有民族主義的範式異同。第二，敘述東亞地區「民族」一詞出現的經緯，同時從政治思想史的角度，在歷史的長鏡頭中（longue durée）解釋東亞民族主義形成的緣由。最後，排比東亞各國民族主義之共同處，集中討論東亞民族主義中的始祖論，接著與歐洲政治思想中「始祖論」（progenitor or founding father）一併討論。結論則提出東亞型民族主義是「國家（statist）民族主義」，有別於所謂以西歐與央格魯薩克遜國家爲主的「市民／公民（civic）民族主義」

9 請參考許倬雲，《我者與他者——中國歷史上的內外分際》（臺北：時報出版，2009），頁79-93。

與中歐東歐及其他地區爲主所謂的「族群（ethnic）民族主義」。

二、民族主義研究與東亞民族主義

（一）單一東亞民族主義亦或是多個東亞民族主義？

從思想史角度研究民族主義，在日本乃至整個東亞最精彩的仍爲戰後日本政治學泰斗丸山眞男（1914-1996）的日本民族主義論。丸山的說法是從日本江戶時期（1603-1868）開始，而非從19世紀與西方大量接觸後著眼。[10]這個說法高超的地方即在尚未經歷過美國戰後費正清（John K. Fairbank, 1907-1991）、賴謝和（Edwin O. Reischauer, 1910-1990）對東亞近現代史提出「挑戰與回應」的敘事模式以前，老早已經推出一個超越這個模式的觀點，丸山眞男的敘事模式已經預告排演後來不少試圖突破「挑戰與回應」模式的劇本，比如說近來汪暉的《現代中國思想的興起》或葛兆光的《宅茲中國》。

所以，丸山眞男不從19世紀下手，日本民族主義的興起則要上推到江戶初期（17世紀），在如同西方中古世紀自然法的朱子學君臨日本的思想社會狀況來說。這個背景在丸山眞男來看是日本與東亞各國共有的，不過，丸山眞男卻又認爲日本民族主義是特殊的，與東亞其他各國不同。其中一個原因自然是，丸山眞男認爲其他東亞各國並沒有獨自發展出打破此種中世紀思想文化的歷史過程，毋寧是停滯的，有待西方或他者刺激改變。這在他的《日本政治思想史研究》一

10　丸山眞男，《日本政治思想史研究》（東京：東京大学出版会，1999［1952］）。

書，[11]開門見山立刻引用黑格爾（1770-1831）《歷史哲學》一書說明中國的停滯性即可看到。可是，日本卻有獨特的歷史進展，這個突破來自於日本儒學古學派荻生徂徠（1666-1728）對朱子學的分解改造，進而風靡全日本，成爲一代顯學，簡單的說，荻生徂徠把「自然」的秩序觀之朱子學／儒學轉化爲「作爲」的制度觀之儒學，建構政治與道德分開的儒學思維，達成可類比歐洲馬基維利（1469-1527），霍布斯（1588-1679）所開創出的政治思路。爾後產生一連貫走向現代的發展，只是這個展開並不順利，而在途中受到挫折，[12]導致日後日本逐漸走向「超國家主義」（ウルトラ・ナショナリズム ultra-nationalism／エクストリーム・ナショナリズム extreme nationalism）或軍國主義之道。[13]

丸山眞男的日本民族主義論述，雖然從東亞的共同思想背景出發，最後卻走到否定東亞有相同的民族主義，這除了上述的理由以外，最關鍵的是在他對戰前日本的反思裡，認爲日本的民族主義與法西斯主義息息相關，日本的民族主義引導日本侵略亞洲各國，在國內則摧殘自由民主，與此相對，現實中亞洲其他各國的民族主義沒有造成侵略他國的事實，故日本民族主義與其他東亞各國自然不同。[14]

丸山眞男的歷史論述，無需他人批判。他退休前的入門弟子，亦是後來接了他在東京大學法學院東亞政治思想史講座的渡邊浩即認爲

11 丸山眞男，《日本政治思想史研究》，頁3-139。

12 丸山眞男，《日本政治思想史研究》，頁195-239。

13 丸山眞男，《現代政治の思想と行動》（東京：未来社，2006［1964］），頁11。

14 丸山眞男，《現代政治の思想と行動》，第一部、第1章，〈超国家主義の論理と心理〉，頁11-28、第5章〈日本におけるナショナリズム〉，頁152-170。

丸山眞男的說法在歷史上站不住腳，而且一開始便錯。渡邊浩的研究指出，在江戶初期的儒學，特別是朱子學根本沒有君臨日本，也不是官學，朱子學在日本社會的普及與在政治上的抬頭，需要等到18世紀中葉以後才逐漸成形。[15]更核心的問題是，東亞各國政治社會制度上的差異極大，日本尤其不同，所以就算18世紀中葉以後朱子學取得官學地位，逐漸深入日本社會政治，日本與東亞各國的差異並沒有因此消失。[16]渡邊浩的修正主義歷史論述在1980年代以來日本思想史學界內已經廣爲接受，連丸山眞男在《日本政治思想史研究》一書的英文版內也承認他對江戶初期思想的描述失眞，而接受渡邊浩的修正。[17]儘管如此，渡邊浩並沒有眞正提出新的日本民族主義詮釋取代丸山眞男的說法。

在渡邊浩歷史論述的籠罩下，日本思想史研究者則愈傾向強調日本思想與社會的獨特性，其末流則是令人覺得日本思想史彷彿與其他東亞各國了無瓜葛，甚至與民族主義也不太有關係，誇張點說，就是

---

15 渡辺浩，《近世日本社会と宋学》（東京：東京大学出版会，1985），第1章「徳川前期における宋学の位置」，頁6-32。

16 渡辺浩，《東アジアの王権と思想》（東京：東京大学出版，1997），頁142-145。書中將東亞各國的差異有更細膩全面的描述，且表列出政治社會制度上種種的異同，可以一目了然。這個問題在日本一直爭辯不休，辻本雅史指出：「寛正異學之禁（1790），才使得朱子學成爲武士教育的一部分而遍及日本，這形成了『日本近代國民教化的原型』」，見辻本雅史，《思想と教育のメディア史——近世日本の知の伝達》（東京：ぺりかん社，2011），頁203。最近小倉紀蔵則是主張日本社會眞正朱子學化要等到明治時期才普及完成，見小倉紀蔵，《朱子学化する日本近代》（東京：藤原書店，2012），特別是第1章〈朱子学化する日本近代〉，頁10-41，與第9章〈明治の『天皇づくり』と〈朱子学的思惟〉——元田永孚の思想〉，頁251-272。

17 丸山眞男，《日本政治思想史研究》，（日譯）英文版序言，頁400-403。

一般所以爲的日本民族主義論述都可以不放在民族主義的框架裡處理，造成一種最極端的一國主義思想史研究。這樣當然影響日本近來對民族主義的研究，以2013年兩本相當有代表性的論文集爲例，《日本思想史講座4-近代》與《日本の外交──外交思想》。兩本書中的多數作者皆爲1960、1970年代出生，換句話說就是日本現在青壯輩的學者。這兩本共計22章，且附帶5個小專欄裡頭，沒有一章是以民族主義爲主題或副題，只有一篇3頁的小專欄正面談到民族主義。在前一本一般認爲的日本民族主義是以「日本主義」與「皇國史觀」來掌握，[18]後一本則是以「國體」爲中心考察日本民族主義。[19]兩篇完全沒有正面透過民族主義此一概念來理解日本的民族主義，實在令人咋舌。

熟知使用歷史語言情境中的語彙固然可喜可嘉，但完全不理會已經是全球人文社會學科內共有的概念，則是對現在主義（presentism）的矯枉過正。更何況民族主義不是與今日完全無關的歷史語彙，而是近兩三百年來世界政治的一股洪流，豈可輕易不理不睬。在此種走到極端內向的研究思路中，東亞有無單一共通的民族主義這樣的問題意識不但是天方夜譚，連東亞是否有多種形態的民族主義探討都可能了無意義，只剩下日本有無民族主義這樣把他者相對化，自我特殊化與絕對化的想法。此外在日本過去歷史語言情境中的語彙，很多其實是無法支持「日本特殊觀」（「日本人論」，*Nihonjinron*），甚至是可以拆穿「日本特殊觀」的幌子。

---

18 苅部直、黒住眞、佐藤弘夫、末木文美士、田尻祐一郎編，《日本思想史講座4-近代》（東京：ぺりかん社，2013）。

19 井上寿一、波多野澄雄、酒井哲哉、国分良成、大芝亮編，《日本の外交 第3巻──外交思想》（東京：岩波書店，2013）。

如果東亞各國有民族主義，那麼值得追問的是，各國的共通點是來自民族主義這個共同分母而已，還是來自各國過去以宋明儒學、漢字等共有的文化基礎上，以及在各國歷史的互相連鎖關係裡形成的呢？反言之，各國的相異處是來自不同形態（市民或族群）的民族主義，亦或是來自相同的民族主義在之後在各國不同的內外政治社會狀況因而呈現的差異？

（二）東亞民族主義是「自古有之」的（primordial）還是「現代」的產物？

在民族主義研究裡，早已成爲老生常談的不外是，到底民族主義是「自古有之」，還是因應工業化，商業社會或印刷資本主義等18世紀中葉以來的種種新現象而產生或發明的。這個就是「自古有之」（primordialism）與「現代主義」（modernism）難分難解的爭議，但在近二三十年來的切磋琢磨後，兩造的爭論可能業已平分秋色。這裡面可以細分爲兩方面，其一：民族主義，其二，民族形成與民族意識。若以本文起頭提起艾尼斯特·葛爾納對民族主義的定義，那麼堅持民族主義「自古有之」的人今日可謂微乎其微，連主張民族／族群「自古有之」的安東尼·史密斯也同意民族主義是相當晚近才出現的。[20]但是在民族形成與民族意識／認同方面，愈來愈多人同意安東尼·史密斯的觀點，認爲不少民族的形成與民族意識出現遠遠早於現代主義者所宣稱的18世紀19世紀，而是可以上推到中古晚期至16世

20 Anthony D. Smith, *The Nation in History: Historiographical Debates about Ethnicity and Nationalism*, pp. 27-28.

紀。[21]王明珂以黃帝爲例，說明中國的民族建構可以上溯到從戰國至漢初而一路緩慢發展到19世紀末，並非突然出現在清末而已。[22]

阿薩・哥特（Azar Gat）在2013年出版的新書《民族》，成爲少數還主張民族主義淵源久遠，在歐洲以外，很多地方自古以來多數的政治單位都可說是「民族的國家」（national state，請注意尚非nation-state民族國家）。[23]他也提到本文前述霍斯班注意到中日韓三國民族與國家高度整合的現象，[24]強調中國的案例應早該爲關於民族辯論的核心，只是整個論爭仍極爲歐洲中心論。故此，阿薩・哥特花費更多的篇幅處理中國日本，只不過審視他的討論，中日韓的例子對他而言並非如霍斯班所言罕見，而是眾多例子中的佼佼者而已，連19世紀的非洲的祖魯（Zulu）在毫無現代性影響下亦出現「民族國家」建構的過程，最早的「民族的國家」還可上推到古埃及。[25]在他的書中，中日韓雖然受到重視，不過因爲中日韓乃是較爲出色「民族的國家」例

21 Anthony D. Smith, *The Cultural Foundations of Nations: Hierarchy, Covenant, and Republics*, Chapter 3-5, pp. 48-134.

22 王明珂，〈論攀附：近代炎黃子孫國族建構的古代基礎〉，收入《中央研究院歷史語言研究所集刊》，73：3（臺北，2002），頁583-624。

23 Azar Gat, *Nations: The Long History and Deep Roots of Political Ethnicity and Nationalism*（Cambridge: Cambridge University Press, 2013), pp. 83-110.

24 關於這一點，東南亞史大師Anthony Reid從與東南亞比較的角度觀察，亦承認東北亞的中日韓在民族主義抬頭以前，早已有「永續的國家」（enduring state），見Anthony Reid, *Imperial Alchemy: Nationalism and Political Identity in Southeast Asia*（Cambridge: Cambridge University Press, 2009），pp. 15-17。三谷博對比歐洲的經驗，強調日本與朝鮮很長的一段時間領土範圍與住民的構成沒有變動，見三谷博，《明治維新を考える》（東京：岩波書店，2012），頁31-32。

25 Azar Gat, *Nations: The Long History and Deep Roots of Political Ethnicity and Nationalism*, pp. 52-97.

子而已，中日韓的民族主義與民族成立過程有無特色，與其「內在發展」的理路遂掩埋其中。

現代主義對於民族主義的解釋如同艾尼斯特．葛爾納所言，農業社會的組織是不利於民族主義的運作，民族主義須待工業社會興起後才能成長茁壯。[26]班納迪克．安德森（Benedict Anderson）對何以工業社會有利於民族主義發展，提出更令人信服的理由；他的主要解釋是印刷資本主義（print capitalism）的出現，使得民族情緒可以傳遞千里之外，在互不認識的陌生人之間渲染想像出一種共同的歸屬感，在一個人容易產生失落感的現代社會裡，在基督教沒落後，提供一種替代的、工具性的宗教信仰與團體。[27]艾瑞克．霍斯班則強調民族主義在19世紀的功能在建立一個較為民主的市民國家，只要政府能控制利用民族主義，成為官方愛國主義的一部分，民族主義為政府所帶來的紅利極為龐大。[28]然而，非官方的民族主義一旦與政府的愛國主義結合以後，不是沒有風險，其中最嚴重即是造成國內某些民族／族群覺得受到排擠，進而形成分裂／反國家的民族主義。[29]

東亞的民族主義面對這個主要建構在歐洲案例的民族主義論爭中到底比較傾向那一邊呢？再以丸山眞男對日本民族主義的詮釋作為討論。丸山早年對日本民族主義的分析，從本文先前的分析來看，的確是極為現代主義式的，不過到了1972年晚期的丸山眞男卻有新的看

26　Ernest Gellner, *Nations and Nationalism*, Chapter 2-3, pp. 8-38.

27　Benedict Anderson, *Imagined Communities: Reflections on the Origin and Spread of Nationalism*（Revised Edition）（London: Verso, 1991）.

28　Hobsbawm, *Nations and Nationalism since 1780: Programme, Myth, Reality*, pp. 86-91.

29　Hobsbawm, *Nations and Nationalism since 1780: Programme, Myth, Reality*, pp. 93-100.

法：古層說。丸山眞男認爲江戶時期日本思想史是兩條主軸：「現代化」與「古層的隆起」交互影響抵抗編織而成的，[30]似乎已經淡化原來的現代主義，整篇文章即在描述他所謂執拗的持續低音是什麼，雖無正面觸及或修正他早年對日本民族主義的詮釋，但可以確定在他的「文化原始主義轉向」（the primordial turn）中，他肯定日本原始文化的存在與其持續的影響。

另一方面，清末梁啓超（1873-1929）曾說中國人沒有國家觀念，只有「天下」的觀念，這樣相當危言聳聽的說法，在現代中國以來卻成了金科玉律。在戰後美國學者列文森（1920-1969）即順著梁啓超的斷言，勾勒出儒家在現代中國必然凋落的命運，一言以蔽之，中國民族主義的政治認同摧毀了中國原來具有普世精神的文化主義。[31]羅志田接著暢敘此意，重申中國民族主義的盛行與中國傳統的崩壞有關，這個過程也是中國由文化的天下觀走向中國民族主義的歷程。[32]孫隆基經由對黃帝崇拜的研究，也斷定是現代的舶來品，只是這個舶來品與日本無甚關係，而是來自西方的一個全球政治社會現象。[33]另一位研究中國民族主義的大家沈松僑亦持有相同的觀點，他

30　丸山眞男，〈歷史意識の古層〉，頁293-351，收入丸山眞男，《忠誠と反逆——転形期日本の精神史的位相》（東京：筑摩書房，1992［1972］）。認爲「江户時期歷史的動態，不僅是現代化這一方面而已，更是「現代化」與「『古層』的隆起」這兩個契機之間相剋相乘複雜多聲中進行（作者譯）」，同書，頁337。

31　Joseph R. Levenson, *Confucius China and Its Modern Fate: A Trilogy* (Berkeley: University of California Press, 1965).

32　羅志田，《民族主義與近代中國思想》（臺北：東大圖書公司，1998），第3章，〈夷夏之辨與道治之分〉，頁61-91。

33　孫隆基，〈清季民族主義與黃帝崇拜之發明〉，《歷史研究》，3（北京，2000），http://www.douban.com/note/223028101/（2015/02/16）。

說：「毫無疑問，近代中國在進行民族的建構時，其所師法的楷模，當然是近代的西方」。[34]但是20世紀以前中國眞的沒有民族主義言論的蠢動，眞的沒有政治化的族群/民族意識嗎？

且看明末清初王夫之（1619-1692）《黃書》（1656）中激烈排滿的觀點，可說是帶有種族歧視的政治化「民族」觀，亦可稱爲漢族民族主義的一種雛形（prototype）。書中言及漢族與非漢族常用「族類」一詞，這個用法與以前的使用不同。《左傳》成公四年「非我族類，其心必異」，這裡的族類指的是有共同血緣的氏族，而不是漢族與非漢族的意思。但是，「族類」在《黃書》中卻帶有今日民族的意思，比如他說「治軒轅之天下，族類強植」，[35]於此，王夫之已經將「中國」視爲黃帝以來的「領域」，這「領域」中的「族類」需要強化，又說「今族類之不能自固，而何他仁義之云云也哉」，[36]在此把「族類」的重要性放在「道」或是儒家價値之上，孫隆基在〈清季民族主義與黃帝崇拜之發明〉文中也將此點詮釋的非常精湛，他說：「《黃書》之獨特，在異於儒家話語之言必宗堯舜與三代，而以孔子爲聖道之集大成者。儒家思想裡固然也有嚴『夷夏之防』的春秋大義，但黃帝從來不是攘夷的典範。黃帝剿滅蚩尤並不被理解爲種族戰爭，而被解做平定作亂的諸侯，肇文明之始基」。[37]

王夫之的觀點可說與前述晚清民族主義的主張同仇氣概。與他同

34 沈松僑，〈近代中國民族主義的發展：兼論民族主義的兩個問題〉，收入林毓生主編，《公民社會基本觀念》（臺北：中央研究院人文社會研究中心，2014），下卷，頁593。

35 王夫之，〈黃書〉，收入《梨洲船山五書》，（臺北：世界書局，1988［1656］），頁25。

36 王夫之，〈黃書〉，收入《梨洲船山五書》，頁37。

37 孫隆基，〈清季民族主義與黃帝崇拜之發明〉。

時的顧炎武（1613-1682）面對滿人入關，便有有亡國亡天下之辨：「易姓改號，謂之亡國，仁義充塞，而至率獸食人，人將相食，謂之亡天下」，結論是「保國者，其君其臣，肉食者謀之，保天下，匹夫之賤，與有責焉耳矣」，[38]一個強調文化價值與社會秩序高於一個國家或政權存亡的觀點，簡直與王夫之的觀點爭鋒相對；日本漢學京都學派的開山祖師爺內藤湖南（1866-1934）就曾畫龍點睛評道：「清初三子，船山憂種類，梨洲憂生民，亭林憂道心」。[39]可是從歷史來看，王夫之民族主義式的號召在當時不但沒有廣為流傳，激發出漢族民眾的反滿政治運動，甚至在士大夫中也少有知音，反而從清初直到同治光緒初期士大夫的言行來看，顧炎武的觀點具有絕對優勢。[40]

約翰・布勿立（John Breuilly）說：「民族主義政治一定是群眾政治（mass politics）（作者譯）」，[41]認為動員群眾投入民族主義政治需要有政治經濟文化等條件配合，這些條件的成熟則要等到18世紀末

38 顧炎武，〈正始〉，《日知錄》（臺北：世界書局，1991）上，卷13，頁306-308。

39 內藤湖南，《內藤湖南漢詩文集》（廣西：廣西師範大學出版社，2009），頁139。

40 類似王夫之民族主義的不遇或消沉，可見余英時，《中國思想傳統的現代詮釋》（臺北：聯經出版公司，1987），特別是在〈清代學術思想史重要觀念通釋〉一文從思想史的「內在理路」立論，解釋清初學風轉變，主要非由外因造成，而是學術思想內在理路的要求所致。然而，清初學風轉變亦可理解滿人政權對思想文化的控制摧殘，導致明末以來的思潮遭遇挫折與變相；近來王汎森與楊念群在此有精湛的分析，見王汎森，《權力的毛細管作用——清代的思想、學術與心態》（臺北：聯經出版公司，2013），與楊念群，《何處是江南？清朝正統觀的確立與士林精神的異變》，（北京：三聯書店，2010）。本文於此無法進入此清代思想史之一大公案，僅能略記之，以待他日。

41 John Breuilly, *Nationalism and the State* (second edition), (Manchester: Manchester University Press, 1993), p. 19.

以後才出現。由此觀之，東亞在19世紀以前就算有民族主義的思想，並沒有因此形成民族主義的政治。但19世紀以前，在尚未受到西方影響下的東亞是否有發展出民族主義思想的走向與脈絡，則是本文所欲追求探討的首要問題。以目前學術界對東亞的民族主義研究情況而言，比照既有民族主義研究的理論文獻，亦難遽然下定論，歷史的實際情況亦不能以非此即彼的二分法處理理解，對東亞的民族主義研究需要拉長歷史的焦距，放寬視野，從全球思想史角度，以東亞地區爲單位，在諸多脈絡（contexts）中進行對比考察。

三、從「宗族」到「民族」[42]

（一）「民族」一詞的出現與勝出

「民族」兩字連用的一詞，在19世紀以前東亞各國文獻，最早見

42　在英文研究中國民族主義文獻裡，最早注意到宗族與中國民族主義的關聯應爲Frank Dikötter（馮客）的*The Discourse of Race in Modern China*,（Hong Kong: Hong Kong University Press, 1992），隨後Prasenjit Duara（杜贊奇）在其名著*Rescuing History from the Nation: Questioning Narratives of Modern China*,（Chicago: The University of Chicago Press, 1995), pp. 75-79，立即採用馮客的說法，踵事增華，闡述的更加流暢。接著，Kai-wing Chou（周啓榮）在一篇文章裡，同樣演繹馮客的說法，在史料上補充馮客與杜贊奇的不足，列舉清末革命黨人中以宗族論語言論述中國民族與主張黃帝爲中國民族始祖之例子，詳論章太炎以宗子論顛覆清廷的合法性，見Kai-wing Chou, "Imagining Boundaries of Blood: Zhang Binglin and the Invention of the Han'Race'in Modern China" in Frank Dikötter, ed., *The Construction of Racial Identities in China and Japan*, pp. 34-52. 之後周啓榮在另一篇文章點出清初以來的古典研究（classical scholarship）與清末的宗族論關聯性，但無深入談論，見氏著，"Narrating Nation, Race, and National Culture: Imagining the Hanzu Identity in Modern China", pp.

成書於南梁的《南齊書》，其中有一段提到民族兩字連用：「今諸華士女，民族弗革，而露首偏踞，濫用夷禮，雲於翦落之徒，全是胡人，國有舊風，法不可變」。[43]不過，方維規認爲，最接近今日「民族」一詞意義的出現，比日本明治翻譯西書的時期還早，最早可見於清道光17年（1837）《東西洋每月統記傳》文中有提及「民族」一詞：「昔以色列民族如行陸路渡約耳旦河也」，而且意思等同後來的使用，因此方維規認爲這毫無疑問證明「民族」一詞非源自日本。[44]此外，根據郝時遠的研究，在《南齊書》之後，「民族」一詞從唐到

53-63，特別是p. 61, in Kai-wing Chow, Kevin M. Doak, Poshek Fu, eds., *Constructing Nationhood in Modern East Asia*。上述的研究基本上認爲宗族論充當接受來自西方民族主義的媒介（medium），經由宗族論語言論述中國民族，實有啓迪新觀點之功勞，不過對宗族論與民族主義的關係尚停留在初步片面的理解。此外不像中文與日文的研究文獻，對日本在此歷史過程所扮演的角色幾乎沒有討論，乃是一個很大的缺憾。另外，周啓榮稍早在自己的專著裡，已經處理過清初的宗族論，雖然有討論大宗小宗，不過與本文的分析看法有不少出入，其中尤其顯著的差異，便是在周啓榮書中並沒有從「宗族」走向「民族」的論點，加上周啓榮繼承Patricia Ebrey的觀點，認爲宋代理學諸儒如張載與程頤均是小宗論者，周氏更進一步主張宋代新儒家（the Sung neo-Confucians）沒人支持大宗制，（很令人納悶的是周氏做此斷定時，竟然引用清代的御用學者李光地與北宋蘇軾的小宗論；又，蘇軾不是一般認知的宋代新儒家），見 Kai-Wing Chow, *The Rise of Confucian Ritualism in Late imperial China: Ethics, Classics, and Lineage Discourse*（California: Stanford University Press, 1994), pp. 100-102. 本文不同意這些說法，在以下將會提出分析詮釋，以示不同。

43 邱永君，〈「民族」一詞見於《南齊書》〉，《民族研究》，3（北京，2004），http://big.hi138.com/wenxueyishu/hanyuwenxue/200808/72386.asp#.VOKgELv9mpo（2015/2/16）。

44 方維規，〈論近代思想史上的「民族」、「Nation」與「中國」〉，《21世紀》，4（香港，2002），頁33-43。

清中葉，使用的例子亦尚有9次，所以《南齊書》的「民族」，絕非孤例，而且非常可能在1870年代以前經由日本翻譯爲數不少的中文書籍過程中，甚至影響到日本後來使用「民族」對譯nation。儘管如此，他並不主張今日中文「民族」一詞的使用，是直接源自《南齊書》，而認爲仍是受到明治日本日譯西書的影響。[45]

王柯亦認爲方維規所指摘的「民族」，因爲沒有「國民」的意思包涵其內，所以不算是現代意義的「民族」。[46]王柯應是受到現在日本將nation翻成「國民」影響所致，比如說nation-state在今天日文常見的翻譯就是「國民國家」，而非「民族國家」。[47]石塚正英與柴田隆行合編的《哲學．思想翻譯語事典》最新版仍將nation翻爲「國民」，而且「民族」只對應德語的volk，可以看出現在一般日本學術界對nation理解的偏頗。[48]王柯對nation的理解，與此書的「國民」與「民族」兩條接近。然而，「民族」是英語中nation的對應詞與翻譯詞，nation可上溯到拉丁語的natio，其衍生語在歐語系統的是沒有必然包涵「國民」（civis/citizen）的意思，現代民族主義的英文文獻裡的nation多數亦沒有內涵此意。而且「民族」（nation）在西方政治思想史脈絡裡，其實比「國民」「人民」更爲現代、晚近。[49]所以，現代使

45 郝時遠，〈中文民族一詞源流考辨〉，2010年1月20日發布，共識網：http://www.21ccom.net/plus/wapview.php?aid=2812（2015/2/16）。

46 王柯，《20世紀中国の国家建設と「民族」》（東京：東京大学出版会，2006），頁61。

47 王柯，《20世紀中国の国家建設と「民族」》，頁55-60。可以看到他對nation一詞的討論本於日譯與今日日本學術界的理解，因爲對此nation歐語與歐洲例子的討論沒有引用任何研究此歐語與歐洲的例子。

48 石塚正英、柴田隆行監修，《哲學．思想翻譯語事典》（東京：論創社，2013）。

49 詳見蔡英文，〈民族主義、人民主權與西方現代性〉，收入林毓生主編，

用的「民族」，以時間先後順序而言，仍以方維規所言為近乎是。

雖然如此，「民族」一詞在1837年以後，僅散見於郭嵩燾，王韜，薛福成零零星星幾個例子，除此之外，有半世紀之久為人罕用，[50]不過，日本早在1876出版由明六社的成員加藤弘之翻譯伯倫知理（Johann Kaspar Bluntschli）的《國法泛論》（*Algemeines Staatsrecht*）時，將書中的nation很明確地翻譯為「民族」一詞。梁啓超寫過一篇談伯倫知理的文章〈政治學大家伯倫知理之學說〉，也讀過加藤弘之的翻譯。[51]加藤弘之將nation對應為「民族」的翻譯是目前為止最早的確證。「民族」在日本廣泛的使用，還是得歸於在1890年前後由《日本人》雜誌與《日本》報紙提倡國粹主義時使用「民族」一詞，推波助瀾使得「民族」在短短一兩年內遂在日本成為日常用語。[52] 1892年從德國留學回日，日本明治時期憲法學的重鎮，在1897年成為東京帝國大學法學院院長的穗積八束（1860-1912），他將「民族」與國體結合起來，並將「民族」一詞提到憲法學層次討論，再以「民族」一詞為解釋明治憲法的核心概念，因而確定「民族」一詞在日本政治社會的軸心地位。[53]

甲午戰爭（1894）後，中國、朝鮮乃至於越南士人來日本學習西

《公民社會基本觀念》（臺北：中央研究院人文社會研究中心，2014），上卷，, 頁32-48。

50 金觀濤、劉青峰，《觀念史研究——中国現代重要政治術語的形成》（北京：法律出版社，2009），頁560-561。

51 參見Andre Schmid, *Korea Between Empires*, 1815-1919 (New York: Columbia University Press, 2002), Chapter 5, Endnote 3, p. 348.

52 安田浩，《近代天皇制国家の歴史的位置——普遍性と特殊性を読みとく視座》（東京：大月書店，2011），頁30-32。

53 安田浩，《近代天皇制国家の歴史的位置——普遍性と特殊性を読みとく視座》，頁33-39。在此前後，日本已經有不少人使用民族一詞。

學與日本成功的原因，進而使得「民族」一詞一併其他眾多日製漢語、日譯漢語遂廣爲東亞其他國家使用。王柯便指出梁啓超著作中多處引用穗積八束的著作，他同時考察「民族」一詞在中國使用普及的時間點與流傳管道，發現亦與在1896年創刊的《時務報》中經常出現大大有關，而且《時務報》中的文章提起「民族」一詞多在〈東文報譯〉專欄裡，這個專欄的負責人是日本熊本縣出身的日本人：古城貞吉。[54]

此外，金觀濤、劉青峰提到1898年康有爲上書中提到「民族」一詞，與其弟子梁啓超同年翻譯日文小說《佳人奇遇》明確將「民族」一詞對應nation。[55]這個時間點也符合支持王柯的說法與本文的考察。在他們的的統計數據裡，「民族」一詞的使用從幾乎無人使用到1900年以後突然飆升，乃至在1903中國的文獻中出現幾乎2500次，遠遠高於約1500次的「天下」一詞。[56]光從數據統計的結果與兩人所引用康梁兩人的例子，更是令人無可置疑——「民族」一詞在中國流行的日本淵源。

若放眼東亞各國，即可發現「民族」一詞在朝鮮、越南皆有之，同樣的漢字，只是發音不同，在日語是minzoku，在中文是minzu，朝鮮語是minjok，在越南語是dân tộc，前三者發音非常類似，四處用

54 王柯，《20世紀中国の国家建設と「民族」》，頁61。

55 金觀濤、劉青峰，《觀念史研究——中国現代重要政治術語的形成》，頁241-242、562。必須要強調的是作者在書中並不介入或處理民族一詞是否源自日本，甚至也沒提起梁啓超「翻譯」的《佳人奇遇》，其實原來是日文，而且是漢文味極重的書下文（書き下し文）。原來的標題即是《佳人之奇遇》，原日文書中凡名詞幾乎皆用漢字，包括民族一詞。

56 金觀濤、劉青峰，《觀念史研究——中国現代重要政治術語的形成》，頁242。

法也大同小異。如果追問朝鮮、越南兩國的「民族」一詞從何而來，立刻可以看到日本在其中的軸心角色。以越南爲例; 在1895年越南出版極爲重要的越南字典《大南國音字彙》，其中尚無「民族」或「國民」一詞。「民族」進入越南的語彙則要在1905年，越南興起所謂的「東遊運動」，在日本接觸到「民族」一詞以後才有。其中最著名的不外是越南儒學者潘佩珠。潘佩珠抵日後不久，即與梁啓超結識，鼓勵越南士子到日本留學。潘佩珠旅日時，以漢文撰寫《越南亡國史》，後來在朝鮮還被翻成漢文與諺文混合的朝鮮文，廣受注意。前段提到梁啓超翻譯的《佳人奇遇》，則由另一位越南學者潘周楨在留法時，以梁啓超的版本再改寫爲韻文小說，[57]而「民族」一詞便隨著改寫本一起進入越南。

簡單整理上面的討論，與今日用法相同的「民族」一詞最早見於1837年的中國，爾後50年少有人用，1876年，在日本加藤弘之正式將德文的nation翻譯爲「民族」，自1890年前後，日本兩份刊物《日本人》與《日本》推廣使用「民族」一詞後，到了1892年在日本的使用於是普遍定著。1894年後，中國官宦士子對日本興趣大增，旅日人數劇增，日本對「民族」一詞的使用，遂在中國傳開。朝鮮與越南兩國亦是經由日本傳回本國或經由在日本以漢文爲溝通基礎的東亞國際網絡中輾轉傳回本國，這些現象即是山室信一所云的「知之迴廊」。[58]

57 今井昭夫，〈二〇世紀初頭のベトナムにおける開明的儒学者たちの国民国家構想〉，收入久留島浩、趙景達編，《アジアの国民国家構想——近代への投企と葛藤》（東京：青木書店，2008），頁153、157-159。

58 參看山室信一，《思想課題としてのアジア——基軸・連鎖・投企》（東京：岩波書店，2001）。書中對東亞在19世紀20世紀連鎖關係做了一個詳盡深入的探討，並全面檢討日譯漢詞對東亞的影響。

以下將從政治思想史的角度敘述說明「民族」一詞何以勝出，同時進一步詮釋東亞民族主義的性質與原理。

（二）「民族」成立以前：「宗族」

1. 從「族類」到「民族」

「民族」一詞是由「民」與「族」兩個漢字合成的，這個組合的勝出，不完全是偶然的，在東亞政治思想史上，這兩個字都占有極爲核心的地位，其實不瞭解這兩字從中唐以來，在過去一千多年的歷史，就很難眞正掌握到東亞政治思想史的脈絡。[59]現在使用的「民族」一詞，簡單說就是一群民是屬於同一族，或者說住在某國的人民都是同一族。在19世紀末以前，在東亞思想史一般的認知裡，很難想像所有的民是同一族，因爲，民有百姓，既然有百姓就是不同族。

連王夫之可能也難以想像所有的民爲一族，在他使用的字眼是「族類」與「種類」。他對「族類」的理解其實是由政治地理決定的，《黃書》第1章〈原極〉，他說「水耕宜南，霜耕宜北，是非忍於其泮散而析其大宗也，亦勢之不能相救而絕其禍也，是故聖人審物之皆然而自畛其類」又說「華夏不自畛以絕夷，則地維裂矣」又說「保其類者爲之長」，接著又有強調「故聖人先號萬姓而示之以獨貴，保

59　與「族」息息相關的政治思想，則有「祖宗之法」，請參見鄧小南，《祖宗之法——北宋前期政治述略》（北京：三聯書店，2006）。針對日本江户時期「祖宗之法」在政治史與政治思想史的考察，參看藤田寛，《近世後期政治史と対外関係》（東京：東京大学出版会，2005）；眞壁仁，《德川後期の学問と政治——昌平坂学問所儒者と幕末外交　容》（名古屋：名古屋大学出版会，2007）。關於「民」在中國宋代以來思想史的最經典研究則屬溝口雄三，《中国前近代思想の屈折と展開》（東京：東京大学出版会，1980）。

其所貴，匡其終亂，施於子孫，須於後聖，可禪，可繼，可革，而不可使夷類間之」。[60]

王夫之的意思很清楚，他認爲聖人原來應該是要保護所有的人，但人生在不同的地理環境中，進而有不同的生活，聖人無法同時照顧所有人，只好將人依地理風土分開，只有先照顧一部分的人，分開後也可以預防衝突。分開以後人就各有其族類，不同族類的人各自保護與自己同一族類的人，在華夏或是中區，能保其族類的人就是君，在其內政治上不管是革命也好，逼君「禪讓」也好，也就是種種一般政治倫理所不贊同的政治行爲，在王夫之來看都好過於讓夷類的人統治中國。所以華夏的族類，並非是有同一血緣同族的人，而是住在華夏地區的萬姓，久而久之便爲「同類」（不是同族），不住在此的就叫「夷類」。這點非常關鍵，雖然王夫之早已高舉軒轅之大纛，然而這與後來東亞民族主義內容中的大宗制及其始祖論沒有什麼關聯，這也間接說明儘管清末讀王夫之的人眾多，且「族類」或「種類」的使用亦相當多，可是王夫之的「族類」「種類」最終仍被「民族」一詞取代。

雖然如此，王夫之的「族類」觀卻與「民族」以前的宗族論出現的背景原因相同——如何在華夏地區組織「民」對抗華夏以外的外患外夷與防止華夏內部動盪渙散。在王夫之的「族類」論裡，「族類」如何鞏固，答案竟是模糊的，到最後他的理論仰賴的是能保住華夏，使得華夏免於外患的聖人或君，這樣的聖人或君主出乎意外與馬基維利的君王論（Principe/Prince）是類似的——「維持自己的地位／國

60 王夫之，〈黃書〉，收入《梨洲船山五書》，頁1-3。

家」（mantenere lo stato），[61]換成王夫之的說法就是，爲君者要能保住自己的「畛域」，只要能保住自己的「畛域」，不管手段爲何，誰就是君主。相對的，在宗族論辦法很多，條路也清晰可循，而且出自儒家一貫重視宗族／家族的思想，更不依賴王夫之式的君主觀。況且，王夫之的君主觀不得不說，與宋明以來儒家主流之君主觀大相徑庭。

日本漢學京都學派的開山大師內藤湖南之後繼者——宮崎市定，曾說中國在近代初期民族主義是回應受到中國北方遊牧民族的民族主義壓迫應運而生的，[62]這個說法除了僅僅用語（民族主義）不妥以外，確實很有見地。王夫之的「族類」論與宋代以來的宗族論，的確皆是面對內外在挑戰，困知苦思後回應發展而出。再回到上面的問題；一個地方所有的民如何能想像與論述成同一族人呢？這個可能性就出自宗族論，特別是宗族論裡關於「大宗」、「小宗」的區別與爭論。

宗族是過去東亞各國組織家族的概念與理論，雖然學界一般認爲日本與儒家的宗族沒有關係。儘管如此，實有共通處，最大的相異處爲在日本已經老生常談的異姓養子許可，以及沒有祖祠的祭拜與嚴整的族譜……等等。日本的「家」（ie）雖與中國（特別是唐朝）以來的家愈來愈不同，然而與唐以前，特別是先秦以前的家本質上有相通相同之處，也就是家有家業，在先秦家業就是以政治爲業，[63]宋代以

---

61 Quentin Skinner, "A Genealogy of the Modern State," *Proceedings of the British Academy*, 162 (2009), pp. 325-370.

62 宮崎市定，《アジア史概説》（東京：中公文庫，1987），頁239-250。

63 中國家族的世業或家業，不但先秦有之，即使在西漢仍相當常見。詳見邢義田，《天下一家：皇帝、官僚與社會》（北京：中華書局，2011），〈從戰國至西漢的族居、族葬、世業論中國古代宗族社會的延續〉，頁414-435。

下，中國的家均是以血緣爲主，沒有家業的家，但有意思的是宗法宗族的原理應用到中國社會上的組織則不少見，如江西詩社。[64]在日本則是後來逐漸從政治的家業延伸到各行各業的家業。家業的繼承就是長子或一子繼承，在英國就是所謂的長子繼承制（primogeniture），[65]在英格蘭的貴族制內至今仍是如此。

在日本，家（ie）制度中所謂的「本家」（honke）即類似大宗，亦是由長子或一子繼承。日本從江戶到戰前結束則基本上是推行本家（大宗）制。家（ie）與封建的關係，在明治5年（1872）日本討論起草新民法時，有一段十分令人矚目的對話，當時的法國人顧問提問司法卿江藤新平（約略）說現在日本從封建編變爲郡縣，家是否亦如郡縣而諸子平分呢？江藤新平的回答是若如郡縣分家分產則家產減少，不易國富，故不分家產，代代相續爲善。[66]這段話十分有洞見，首先注意到不分家產亦即資本累積（capital accumulation）與資本主義的關係，再來亦可以看到受到《近思錄》中關於宗族的言論，特別是來自程頤關於不析產的言論，詳見於以下討論。

2. 宗統與君統──宗族的政治安排

在儒家的宗族論裡，日本「本家」制度的情況實質上接近大宗

64 龔鵬程，《江西詩社宗派研究》，（臺北：文史哲出版社，1983）。

65 自2010年在英國ITV電視台播出的電視連續劇《唐頓莊園》（Downton Abbey）前三季故事的主軸就是繞著在英格蘭一個貴族家庭因領主膝下無男丁，但貴族須執行長子繼承制（primogeniture），於是引發種種問題的家庭劇。這部連續劇轟動到沒有貴族制的美國。

66 出自福島正夫，《日本資本主義と家》（東京：東京大學出版會，1967），頁11。在此書中詳細討論這種「本家」制的家如何落實在明治民法兼論及「本家」與資本主義發展的關係。

制，但宗族論的大宗不僅僅侷限於財產、家業與宗子地位的繼承而已。大宗之宗子須祭拜始祖，百世不遷，嫡長子以外，其他的諸子可爲小宗，但小宗皆須受制於大宗。小宗不能僭越祭拜始祖，小宗祭祀只能上溯四代，祭拜到高祖考，所以五世而斬。[67]大宗制宗族在先秦以前是政治社會的核心組織原理，與先秦的封建制一體兩面，亦是周代制定之禮制。

如《禮記．大傳》所載：

> 別子爲祖，繼別爲宗，繼禰爲小宗。有百世不遷之宗，有五世則遷之宗。百世不遷者，別子之後也。宗其繼別子之所自出者，百世不遷者也。宗其繼高祖者，五世則遷者也。尊祖故敬宗，敬宗，尊祖之義也。[68]

《禮記．喪服小記》亦有類似的記載：

> 王者禘其祖之所自出，以其祖配之，而立四廟。庶子王，亦如之。別子爲祖，繼別爲宗，繼禰者爲小宗。有五世而遷之宗，其繼高祖者也。是故，祖遷於上，宗易於下。尊祖故敬宗，敬宗所以尊祖禰也。庶子不祭祖者，明其宗也。庶子不爲長子斬，不繼祖與禰故也。庶子不祭殤與無

---

67 百世不遷者是大宗，五世則遷者是小宗。杜正勝是將宗法與封建放在一起討論的，且將大小宗的關係解釋的很清楚：「凡祭祀能上及始祖皆是大宗，相對與大宗的祖廟是小宗，只祭與寢的士庶人則無廟，嚴格說是無宗，此皆就主祭之族而言。每一祭祀除主祭之族長以外都有族群成員與祭，可以一起祭祀者謂之同宗，視所祭之祖而與祭族群之範圍有所不同。這套分別宗族成員的方法叫做宗法，所以大小宗制是周人在昭穆制以外收族的另種方式」。見杜正勝，《古代社會與國家》（臺北：允晨文化，1992），頁406。

68 孫希旦，《禮記集解》，卷34，〈大傳〉，頁914。

後者，殤與無後者從祖祔食。庶子不祭禰者，明其宗也。」[69]

以上這兩段《禮記》的記載雖然闡明宗族宗法大義，可是關於大小宗的說明卻留下不少疑義，使得歷代對於天子與不同姓的諸侯是否爲其族之大宗宗子則有重大分歧。換言之，即是君統（政治權力）與宗統（宗族權力）是否二而合一的問題，因此宗統與君統在歷史上的周代與在儒家理論上是否一致向來聚訟紛紜，直至今日，尙未定讞。以時間順序，先以《毛詩傳箋》的《毛傳》爲例：《詩．大雅．文王》：「本支百世」，《毛傳》解爲：「本，本宗也，支。支子也」；[70]《詩．大雅．公劉》：「君之宗之」，《毛傳》解爲：「爲之君爲之大宗」；[71]《詩．大雅．板》：「大宗維翰」，《毛傳》解爲：「王者，天下之大宗」。[72]

由此可以看到《毛傳》中的王者是合君統（政治權力）與宗統（宗族權力）於一身。清代馬瑞辰（1782-1853）對《詩．大雅．公劉》「君之宗之」的解釋是：「《傳》云：爲之大宗，《正義》引板《傳》：王者，天下之大宗。此與天子諸侯以母弟爲別子，繼別者爲大宗異義。蓋天子諸侯皆得爲大宗，自爲天地、宗廟、社稷、臣民之宗主，而非五宗之所得擬（按：五宗乃別子爲祖之後的一大宗四小宗是爲五宗之謂）」。[73]這段話很有意思，馬瑞辰認爲君統是天下之大宗，

69 孫希旦，《禮記集解》，卷32，〈喪服小記〉，頁866-896。

70 毛亨注，鄭玄箋，《毛詩傳箋》，〈大雅．文王〉，收入《漢魏古注十三經附四書章句集注》（北京：中華書局，1998），上，頁117。

71 毛亨注，鄭玄箋，《毛詩傳箋》，〈大雅．公劉〉，頁131。

72 毛亨注，鄭玄箋，《毛詩傳箋》，〈大雅．板〉，頁135。

73 馬瑞辰，《毛詩傳箋通釋》，（北京：中華書局，1989），頁909。

可是天子的大宗乃天地、宗廟、社稷、臣民大宗，並非他的宗族裡的大宗，他的宗族大宗仍是繼承別子（他的同母弟弟）的嫡系才是大宗。這個說法與後來王國維（1877-1927）對宗統君統的解釋異曲同工。王國維在《殷周制度論》中將宗法起源與君統宗統關係有鞭辟入裡的解釋。他認為殷代無宗法，因傳位於弟於子皆可，傳子之制始於周代，有傳子之制，才有嫡庶之別，「由嫡庶之制，而宗法與服術二者生焉」。在天子、諸侯則君統與宗統合，雖無大宗之名，而實為大宗之大宗，大夫、士以下，宗統自成一獨立系統，無關於君統、世卿。[74]

然而，歷代卻有不少反對將宗統與君統合一的詮釋，從鄭玄（127-200）為《毛傳》作箋時，在上面《詩．大雅》的三個例子，就沒有謹守「疏不破注」，而與《毛傳》唱反調。[75]

《詩．大雅．文王》「本支百世」，鄭玄箋解為「故天下君之，子孫適為天子，庶為諸侯，皆百世」。[76]鄭玄在此將原來《毛傳》君統宗統合一的解釋轉為強調君統。

《詩．大雅．公劉》「君之宗之」，鄭玄箋解為「宗，尊也，公劉雖去邰國來遷，群臣從而君之，尊之猶在邰也」。[77]鄭玄在此一同對《詩．大雅．文王》詮釋，將「宗之」解釋為「群臣從而君之尊之」，取消族人「宗之」的宗統義，混同君統宗統，將原來《毛傳》

74 王國維，《王國維手定 觀堂集林》，（杭州：浙江教育出版社，2014），頁247-261。

75 馬瑞辰亦說：「鄭君箋詩，自云宗毛為主，其間有與毛不同者，多本三家詩」。馬瑞辰，《毛詩傳箋通釋》，頁20。

76 毛亨注，鄭玄箋，《毛詩傳箋》，〈大雅．文王〉，頁117。

77 毛亨注，鄭玄箋，《毛詩傳箋》，〈大雅．公劉〉，頁131-132。

君統宗統合一的解釋轉爲僅有君統；關於這點馬瑞辰亦有指摘：「《傳》意蓋以宗爲主、爲長，與《箋》訓尊異也」。[78]但這兩例子本身仍無法完全確認鄭玄主張君統宗統二分，而是參看以下的例子，才可觀察到其君統宗統二分說法的來龍去脈。

《詩．大雅．板》「大宗維翰」，[79]鄭玄箋解爲「大宗，王者同姓世適子也」。鄭玄對大宗的解釋遵從「別子爲祖，繼別爲宗（大宗）」將君統與宗統二分。鄭玄雖然主張君統宗統二分，但不免晦澀，須與鄭玄對《禮記．大傳》中「別子爲祖，繼別爲宗」的解釋：「別子，謂公子，若始來在此國者，後世以爲祖也。別子之世適也，族人尊之，謂之大宗」，[80]以及對《禮記．喪服小記》「別子爲祖」的解釋：「諸侯之庶子，別爲後世爲始祖也，謂之別子者」，[81]兩者合看，才能比較看得明白鄭玄事實上主張君統宗統二分。

後人如清初萬斯大（1633-1683），在《學禮質疑》中就更明確提出宗統宗法有別於君統，他在〈宗法一〉開宗明義說：「宗法何昉乎？諸侯之適長爲世子，嗣爲諸侯，其支庶之後，族類繁多，懼其散而無統，因制爲大宗小宗之法」，[82]接著在〈宗法四〉他解釋「宗法由別子而生，鄭康成注《小記》。指別子爲諸侯之支子。注《大傳》則兼言來自他國之臣」。[83]他在〈公子宗道圖說〉中再舉例闡述宗統有別

78 馬瑞辰，《毛詩傳箋通釋》，頁909。

79 毛亨注，鄭玄箋，《毛詩傳箋》，〈大雅．板〉，頁135。

80 鄭玄注，《禮記》，〈大傳〉，收入《漢魏古注十三經 附四書章句集注》（北京：中華書局，1998），上，頁124。

81 鄭玄注，《禮記》，〈喪服小記〉，頁119。

82 萬斯大撰，溫顯貴校注，《經學五書》（上海：華東師範大學出版社，2012），卷2，〈宗法一〉，頁46。

83 萬斯大撰，溫顯貴校注，《經學五書》，卷2，〈宗法四〉，頁56。

於君統之義：「滕人於魯曰：吾宗國，《左傳》魯以邢、凡、蔣、茅、胙、祭爲同宗。是知周之先，文王之諸子以周公爲宗，周公之諸子，以魯公爲宗」。[84]在此，萬斯大直言周公是姬氏的大宗，因爲他是別子，周王不是姬氏的大宗。在他所繪製〈大宗百世不遷之圖〉中，可以看得更清楚諸侯的嗣君不爲大宗，大宗則由諸侯的支子／庶子爲大夫者爲大宗，不爲大夫者則爲小宗。[85]後來梁啓超在《先秦政治思想史》中對君統宗統的解釋全面採取萬斯大的說法，他說：「國君之外，更有唯一之百世不遷的大宗，有無數五世則遷的小宗」。[86]

中國在秦漢以來，除了皇帝與孔家是大宗制以外，其餘皆僅能實行小宗制，值得注意的是皇帝與孔家則是宗統君統合一的大宗宗法。萬斯大的詮釋在現存經文上或許說的通，但在歷史上與實踐上恐怕是不免疑竇叢生。就以萬斯大的例子而言，「文王之諸子以周公爲宗」，固然聲稱天下之君統與宗統不爲一，但「周公之諸子，以魯公爲宗」，不是反而證明在魯國之中君統與宗統合一嗎？這豈非自我矛盾？因爲，如果周公其他諸子皆在魯國之內，而以魯公爲大宗宗子，那萬斯大所說「國君以外，別子爲大宗」的說法不就難以成立？如果周公諸子爲其他國國君而宗魯國國君爲大宗，不就是說明魯國國君爲周公一系之大宗，而非姬氏之大宗，更遑論爲天下之大宗。

於是，評騭兩造說法優劣，以歷史、思想爲準繩，本文現下無法

84　萬斯大撰，溫顯貴校注，《經學五書》，卷2，〈公子宗道圖說〉，頁52。

85　萬斯大撰，溫顯貴校注，《經學五書》，卷2，〈大宗百世不遷之圖〉，頁53。

86　梁啓超，《先秦政治思想史》（長沙：岳麓書社，2010），第4章，〈政治與倫理的結合〉，頁46。又，頁47之〈宗法表〉亦取自萬斯大之〈大宗百世不遷之圖〉。

深入討論，僅能以上略記之，待來日詳論。不過，在政治思想史上，宗統君統合一或二分的認識對宋代以來大小宗之辨與相關的政治論述，卻有不言而喻的影響，固不必汲汲於此是彼非，而是須知其影響何在。先簡言之，言復大宗者多傾向《毛傳》「王者天下之大宗」的宗統君統合一，小宗論者多不免如《鄭箋》力主「別子爲祖」的宗統君統二分。君統宗統合一，抑或君統宗統二分，這個經學禮學上看似不著邊際的古董問題，其實攸關君統（政治權力）的性質，權力與合法性問題，而且自明代大禮議以降，愈發緊要，最後在19世紀中葉後影響東亞各國政局至深且巨，至今仍乏人探賾，本文稍後借解析會澤正志齋之政治思想與穗積八束之憲法理論，略論日本君統宗統合一政治之大概。

言歸正傳，不管是大宗制，還是小宗制，主要目的是合族之道，其差異只是將同族之人結合起來的原理形態意義有所不同。[87]實行大宗制的社會中間組織容易長久，組織日久則龐大，因此中間組織對個人的整合約束力亦大，與國家或中央政權抗衡的力量也愈大；行小宗制的社會，中間組織會不斷分化，雖然可以整合同族之人，規模不易變大，容易落入一句俗話「富不過三代」，因此對中央集權的皇權不容易形成威脅，對個人的約束力亦相對微弱，易成孫中山所說的「一盤散沙」。[88]

3.「封建與大宗」對抗「郡縣與小宗」——從北宋到清初

正因普遍實行大宗制對皇權／權力集中容易形成挑戰，宋代以來

87 參考溝口雄三、丸山松幸、池田知久，《中国思想文化事典》（東京：東京大学出版会，2001），「宗法」條，頁180-183。

88 孫中山，《三民主義》，頁56。

主張郡縣制的人，很多都是反對大宗制。以朱子為例，在《朱子語類》中常見，他反對封建制，他甚至斬釘截鐵地說「封建實是不可行」，[89]他與呂祖謙合編的《近思錄》卷八〈治體〉，卷九〈治法〉中贊成封建的言論無有，僅僅摘錄張載一句言及井田與封建的因果關係：「井田卒歸於封建，乃定」，[90]可是這句原出於《經學理窟．周禮》，通篇是主張復井田封建，其立論是「治天下不由井地，終無由得平。周道止是均平」。後來接上「井田卒歸於封建，乃定」。簡單說，即是治理天下不推行井田就無法均平，欲推行井田須恢復封建，這是周朝之道。朱子對此卻故意斷章取義，無非是誘導讀者從復井田須要復封建來判斷兩者究竟可不可行，朱子的想法是自然認為在柳子厚寫出〈封建論〉提出「封建，非聖人之意也」以後，[91]多數讀者必打退堂鼓，因為恢復封建若不可行，恢復井田自然亦不可行。[92]

正因為朱子將封建與大宗的關係看得很透徹，他亦擺明他在大宗小宗之間的立場，他說：「大宗法既立不得、亦當立小宗法」。[93]所以，《近思錄》仍摘錄了一些支持宗族（雖然是主張大宗）的言論，如程頤：「管攝天下人心，收宗族，厚風俗，使人不忘本，須是明譜

89 朱熹著，黎靖德編，《朱子語錄》（北京：中華書局，1994），卷108，〈朱子五 論治道〉，頁2679。

90 朱熹、呂祖謙編纂，《近思錄》（臺北：金楓出版，1987），卷9，〈治法〉，頁102。

91 柳宗元，《柳河東全集（第二版）》（臺北：世界書局，1999），上，卷3，〈封建論〉，頁58。

92 朱子完全贊同柳宗元的〈封建論〉。他說：「封建只是歷代循襲，勢不容已，柳子厚亦說得是」，朱熹著，黎靖德編，《朱子語錄》，卷108，〈朱子五 論治道〉，頁2679。

93 朱熹著，黎靖德編，《朱子語錄》卷90，〈禮七 祭〉，頁2308。

系，收世族立宗子法」，[94]宗子法就是大宗制的核心制度，在此爲大宗制宗子。故有宗子法，自然會形成世族。又引程頤所言：「宗子法壞，則人不自知來處，以致流轉四方往往親未絕，不相識，今且試以一二巨公之家行之，其術要得拘守得，須是如唐時立廟院，仍不得隔分了祖業，使一人主之」，[95]程頤認爲先從不分割祖業家產著手，不必立即推行宗子法。

最後，程頤將大宗制看成是不行封建時的替代，並且將宗子法提到天理的高度，同時說出宗族使人尊祖重本，因而鞏固朝廷。他說：「今無宗子，故朝廷無世臣，若立宗子法，則人知尊祖重本，人既重本，則朝廷之勢自尊。古者子弟從父兄，今者父兄從子弟，由不知其本也。且如漢高祖欲下沛時，只是以帛書與沛父老，其父兄便能率子弟從之；又如相如使蜀亦移書責父老，然後子弟皆聽其命而從之。只有一個尊卑上下之分，然後順從而不亂也，若無法以聯屬之，安可？且立宗子法，亦是天理，譬如木必有從根直上一幹，亦必有旁支；又如水雖遠必有正源，亦必有分派處，自然之勢也，然而又有旁支達而爲幹者，故曰古者天子建國，諸侯奪宗」。[96]

何爲宗子？《說文解字義證》曰：「主宗廟祭祀者，曰宗子」，[97]於此可推論在行大宗宗法下，大宗有宗子，小宗無宗子，有大宗宗廟，無小宗宗廟，小宗便是以宗人身份參與大宗宗子主持的廟祭，這

94　朱熹、呂祖謙編纂，《近思錄》，卷9，〈治法〉，頁99。

95　朱熹、呂祖謙編纂，《近思錄》，卷9，〈治法〉，頁99。

96　朱熹、呂祖謙編纂，《近思錄》，卷9，〈治法〉，頁100。

97　桂馥，《說文解字義證》（濟南：齊魯書社，1987），卷22，〈宗〉，頁636。

即是《禮記・大傳》所云:「有大宗而無小宗者」,[98]因爲若小宗有宗子則必有小宗之廟,既有小宗宗廟,則與大宗不同廟矣,可乎?在行小宗宗法下,無大宗,因而小宗有宗子,便有小宗宗廟,這即是《禮記・大傳》所云:「有小宗而無大宗者」。[99]程頤的宗子是大宗宗子,非小宗宗子。何以知道程頤的宗子爲大宗宗子呢?因爲通觀程頤的宗子論,他既要有世臣(爵位),要不分祖業,由一人主之(土地),又要立廟院(宗廟),更要宗子能統領族人,族人聽其命(人民);這正如以禮學馳名的清儒淩廷堪(1757-1809)所言:「有宗廟,土地,爵位,人民,方謂之大宗」。[100]是故,程頤談論宗子法,結語即以天下之大宗的天子與一國之大宗的諸侯爲學習榜樣,而不是去提君統宗統二分論中別子爲祖的大宗。同理,程頤的理想最終是恢復大宗制,絕非小宗制。

但朱子在《近思錄》卻刻意忽略在宗族論上影響程頤至深,[101]宋代大宗宗族論的開先者——張載;在《近思錄》中完全沒有收錄張載對宗族的看法,這點即令人尋味。張載的大宗宗族論,不但是他的宇宙本體論的基礎,[102]更是奠定大宗宗族論以後發展的格局與可能性,

98 孫希旦,《禮記集解》,卷34,〈大傳〉,頁915。

99 孫希旦,《禮記集解》,卷34,〈大傳〉,頁915。

100 淩廷堪,《禮經釋例》(臺北:中央研究院中國文哲研究所,2012),卷8,〈附 封建尊尊服制考一篇〉,頁442。

101 程頤關於宗族的發言受到張載影響,見張載,《張載集》(北京:中華書局,1978)《經學理窟・宗法》,頁258-261,其中有一些說法高度雷同,如張載「宗子之法不立,則朝廷無世臣」與正文所引用程頤「今無宗子,故朝廷無世臣,若立宗子法,則人知尊祖重本」,朱熹、呂祖謙編纂,《近思錄》,卷9,〈治法〉,頁100。

102 何炳棣認爲由儒家宗法模式構成張載的宇宙本體論,此說極有洞見,但同時認爲「兩千年來負載儒家思維的框架是宗法模式的」,則言過其

並且一手翻新從西周以下宗族論的理論語言。總之沒有張載的宗族論，很難想像後來大宗宗族論的發展。在此之前的宗族論，無論是包含廣大人群的大宗論或範圍受限的小宗論，畢竟都是建立在有眞正血脈或血緣關係上的人群組織。張載一方面繼承血脈基礎的宗族論，例如，他在《經學理窟．宗法》裡便反覆此意，並無脫逸，開宗明義即說：「管攝天下人心，收宗族，厚風俗，使人不忘本，須是明譜系世族與立宗子法。宗法不立，則人不知統系來處。古人亦鮮有不知來處者，宗子法廢，後世尚譜牒，猶有遺風。譜牒又廢，人家不知來處，無百年之家，骨肉無統，雖至親，恩亦薄」。[103]

另一方面，張載在《正蒙．乾稱篇》（西銘）突破宗族論的血緣基礎，引進「氣」的觀念重新論述宗族論。他說：「凡可狀，皆有也，凡可象，皆氣也」。[104]從這裡才推得出在〈乾稱篇〉開始的著名的幾段：「乾稱父，坤稱母；予茲藐焉，乃混然中處。故天地之塞，吾其體；天地之帥，吾其性。民，吾同胞；物，吾與也。大君者，吾父母宗子；其大臣，宗子之家相也。尊高年，所以長其長；慈孤弱，所以幼其幼；聖，其合德；賢，其秀也。凡天下疲癃、殘疾、惸獨、鰥寡，皆吾兄弟之顚連而無告者也」。[105]所有「可狀可象皆是氣」的觀點，便導出「民，吾同胞；物，吾與也」，因爲民已是我的同胞，自然可以套用大宗宗族論組織同胞，同時，張載很明顯的持有宗統君

實，流於泛泛。見何炳棣，《思想制度史論》（臺北：聯經出版公司，2013），第12章，〈儒家宗法模式的宇宙本體論：從張載的〈西銘〉談起〉，頁396。

103 張載，《張載集》，〈經學理窟．宗法〉，頁258-259。

104 張載，《張載集》，〈正蒙．乾稱〉，頁63。

105 張載，《張載集》，〈正蒙．乾稱〉，頁62-63。

統合一的觀點，故他說：「大君者，吾父母宗子；其大臣，宗子之家相也」。至此，張載將「血脈觀」的宗族論轉化爲「血氣觀」的宗族論，這是張載在整個宗族論中最有創意的思想發展。[106]

朱子當然察覺張載血氣觀宗族論的新穎與挑戰，而試圖淡化整合張載血氣觀宗族論回到血脈觀的宗族論裡，他說：「蓋以乾爲父，以坤爲母，有生之類，無物不然，所謂理一也。而人物之生，血脈之屬，各親其親，各子其子，則其分亦安得而不殊哉！一統而萬殊，則雖天下一家，中國一人，而不流於兼愛之弊；萬殊而一貫，則雖親疏異情，貴賤異等，而不牿於爲我之私。此西銘之大指也」。[107]朱子這段評論大有深意。首先，他先點出張載血氣宗族論最大的問題是「流於兼愛之弊」，那麼如何避免呢？他用「理」統攝萬物，取代張載的「氣」，所以萬物有同理，但不同氣，然後再從人物之生，只能從「血脈之屬」而出，所以萬物（包括人）只能「各親其親，各子其子」而已，將張載擴大的宗族範圍拉回到小宗宗族論認可的範圍的「親」、「子」關係。這樣的親子關係自然有萬種的不同，但這萬種的不同卻又有同理——親子關係，所謂「一統而萬殊」，「萬殊而一貫」。但又有親情等差，所以並非楊朱爲我之私。最後朱子很狡猾地說這就是西銘的大意。朱子明尊暗貶〈西銘〉，又用己意詮釋曲解張載原意，試圖將已經跳出的精靈塞回到瓶子裡，同時調解與張載一系

106 王夫之的族類觀是受到張載「血氣觀」的宗族論影響，不過他卻拒絕宗族論模式，而將「血氣觀」與「領域」結合起來；這點立刻證明何炳棣的說法「兩千年來負載儒家思維的框架是宗法模式的」有疑義。見何炳棣，《思想制度史論》（臺北：聯經出版公司，2013），第12章，〈儒家宗法模式的宇宙本體論：從張載的〈西銘〉談起〉，頁396。

107 張載，《張載集》，〈附錄．朱熹西銘論〉，頁410。

在思想上的衝突。[108]朱子使勁降伏〈西銘〉的苦心孤詣直到19世紀中葉以前沒有枉費，但自19世紀末朱子深深恐懼的精靈（「流於兼愛之弊」）已經逐漸成爲反噬主人（儒家）的巨獸（民族國家／民族主義），此詳見於後論。

雖然從宋代以來，支持大宗制的言論此起彼落，[109]但歷代的朝廷深知大宗制與封建的密切關係，所以並不積極恢復大宗制，只是大力鼓勵小宗制的宗族組織，[110]一同朱子所給的建議。蘇洵在《嘉佑集》第17卷，申述其對宗族、族譜、大小宗的看法。他的結論見於〈族譜後錄上篇〉，即是：「獨小宗之法，猶可以施於天下，故爲族譜，其法皆從小宗」，於此可見，從北宋歐陽修，蘇洵以來所提倡的譜法；皆是與朱子同樣主張小宗宗法，反對大宗宗法。[111]因此，宋代以來雖然修族譜之風盛行，宗族逐漸成爲地方社會之中流砥柱，這裡的宗族不是大宗制的宗族，而是小宗制的宗族。再來從《四庫全書》輯錄成兩冊的《明人譜牒序跋輯略》中，[112]可以看到明代譜牒的序跋絕

108 朱子的〈西銘論〉亦回應二程學生楊時對〈西銘〉的批判。

109 關於宗法與宋學的密切關係，參考龔鵬程，《思想與文化》（臺北：業強出版，1986），第5章，〈唐宋族譜之變遷〉、第6章，〈宋代的族譜與理學〉，頁179-304。

110 參考溝口雄三、丸山松幸、池田知久，《中国思想文化事典》，「宗法」條，頁185-188。按：此條（頁186）認爲明清士大夫支持大宗制的人很多，只是朝廷不支持，這個看法並不完全符實。支持小宗法的絕非少數，且有朝廷背書。此外，明清兩代其實在明世宗嘉靖十五年時，曾因夏言奏疏，而開放民間在冬至祭祀始祖，但未爲常制，僅一時政策，詳見常建華，〈明代宗族祠廟禮制及其演變〉，《南開學報》，3（天津，2001），頁64-66。

111 蘇洵，《嘉佑集》，卷17，〈族譜後錄上篇〉，收入《三蘇全集》（京都：中文出版社，1986），上，頁106。

112 吳宣德、宗韻編，《明人譜牒序跋輯略》（上海：上海古籍出版社，2013）。

大多數不以復大宗制爲目的，均以小宗制爲前提或主張小宗制，如王衡（1561-1609）寫的〈吳氏族譜序〉：

> 族之有譜也，以敬宗而收族，夫人而知之。雖然，至於五世，而祖且祧，服且盡矣（按：此言小宗）。遙遙遠胄，貴賤貧富殊量，嗜欲殊趨，居不同裡門，食不同井爨，強而聯之曰同，即序以燕齒，班以燕毛，而其中有途人之心，目瞪瞪相對，按譜而始識其字號。如此，郵吏之數過賓，過而不有，於睦族何居焉？……吾甚怪張公藝之書忍也，彼所與同居者何人，而必忍而後同乎？忍而後同，可謂同乎？
>
> 物不可以強同，人必有所自生，所自生者同，勢不容受以異。人知髮膚之皆父母，而後知愛髮膚；知疾痛之呼父母，而後知謹疾痛。不然，情欲之所不至，一身之外，且視之若委土聚沫然，欲強途人而爲兄弟，其亦難矣。[113]

認爲大宗制違反人情，因爲五世以後，即使同出一祖，貴賤貧富差距大，生活習慣亦不同，大家平時互不往來，不住在一起，也互相不認識，如果欲以大宗宗法強制聯合諸小宗，對睦族（收族）一事完全無補。從人所生自不同，所能關切的不外是自己的父母而已，此外皆爲路人，大宗制不顧及這個親情的自然範圍，當然難以實行。這兩段發揮蘇洵〈蘇氏族譜〉中主張小宗法，反對大宗法的理由：「無服則親盡，親盡則情盡，情盡則喜不慶，憂不弔，喜不慶憂不弔則塗人也」。[114]

---

113 吳宣德、宗韻編，《明人譜牒序跋輯略》，下冊，〈吳氏族譜序〉，頁1290。

114 蘇洵，《嘉佑集》，卷17，〈蘇氏族譜〉，頁104。

值得一提的是，他用「忍」來批評大宗制是非常嚴厲的譴責，這出於《孟子》〈公孫丑上〉：「孟子曰：人皆有不忍人之心。先王有不忍人之心，斯有不忍人之政矣。以不忍人之心，行不忍人之政，治天下，可運之掌上。所以謂人皆有不忍人之心，今，人乍見孺子將入於井，皆有怵惕惻隱之心」。他的意思即是大宗制在今日已經絕非先王之政，因爲要「忍」才能行大宗制，「忍」便無「怵惕惻隱」，亦即不仁。

更多的譜牒序跋完全不言及大小宗或對大小宗之辨茫然，[115]明末清初的錢謙益（1582-1664）在〈王氏杕蔭堂祠堂記〉一劈頭便感嘆這個現象：「宗法之亡也，以近世士大夫不講先王大宗小宗之義」。不過，錢謙益卻非因此而主張大宗制，他如同前引的朱子與王衡，認爲小宗制可行，大宗制不可行。以錢謙益在明末清初的官場身份與文壇地位，他對小宗制的支持是很具代表性的，同時須注意即便在封建論大盛的明末清初，反對封建反對大宗制的大有人在。他的理由即是沒有封建，大宗制亦不可行，他解釋爲：「蓋封建既廢，古今之禮典懸矣！」，他接著舉例說明爲何大宗制於今日難行，比如兄是平民，弟爲士大夫，如果令兄主祭，以宗子立廟，作爲弟弟的士大夫陪祭，供牲物，也並不符合禮，因爲禮是要大夫主祭，平民爲介子常事。所以他得到的結論是：「時異殊俗，禮之窮而不得不變也久矣。眉山蘇氏，知禮之變者也，謂先王制禮，獨小宗之法，猶可施於天下。故爲族譜，其法皆從小宗，後世論宗法者，莫善於此，而世亦莫之宗

115 呂妙芬，《孝治天下：《孝經》與近世中國的政治與文化》（臺北：聯經出版公司，2011）。此書對明清孝經的研究無一語觸及大小宗的論爭即是間接證據，此與孝經在明清基本上爲輔翼小宗制宗族的教化有關。

也」。[116]

這裡錢謙益暗中搬出《禮記．禮器》中「禮，時爲大」做爲反對實行大宗制的理由，[117]稱讚蘇洵提倡小宗族譜的主張，並且斷言先王的禮只剩下小宗宗法還可以推行。然而，錢謙益所舉的例子，其實就是反駁拒絕《禮記．曾子問》中已經面對的類似案例及其應對的辦法：「曾子問曰:宗子爲士，庶子爲大夫，其祭也如何？孔子曰：以上牲祭於宗子之家，祝曰：孝子某，爲介子某薦其常事」。[118]錢謙益認爲《禮記．曾子問》「孔子曰：以上牲祭於宗子之家，祝曰：孝子某，爲介子某薦其常事」，這段假孔子之口的權宜做法不符合禮，在淩廷堪來看，並沒有不符合禮，他說：「若士之庶子有爲大夫者，當其在時，則以上牲祭於宗子之家，至卒後，則其子孫別立廟，以是人爲祖，不祖士之宗子」。[119]當庶子爲大夫，位高於宗子時，在庶子在世時，仍循《禮記．曾子問》假孔子之口所言，到宗子家，仍由宗子主祭，自己爲副祭，但死後庶子的子孫脫離宗子，形成別子爲祖，自立爲大宗。淩廷堪的說法就是一個君統宗統合一的大宗宗法支持者，相對之下，錢謙益便是徹底的小宗論者。由此觀之，宋代以來反對大宗制不必然僅僅爲了鞏固皇權，更不須立刻提到可能相當時代倒置（anachronistic）的「儒法對峙」或「儒表法裡」層次上的解釋，而是可以從儒家內部的理論與經典相互辯難來反駁或贊同大宗制。

越南阮朝的阮文超（1799-1872）在《方亭隨筆錄》中〈品家及

116 錢謙益，《牧齋有學集》（上海：上海古籍出版社，1996），頁1029-1030。

117 孫希旦，《禮記集解》，卷23，〈禮器〉，頁627。

118 孫希旦，《禮記集解》，卷19，〈曾子問〉，頁537-538。

119 淩廷堪，《禮經釋例》，卷8，〈附 封建尊尊服制考一篇〉，頁452。

士庶家祠禮〉一文，重申錢謙益所指出實行大宗制的困難，亦同意在封建廢除後，因無世祿，所以大宗制難行，只有天子與孔府可以實行，因為封建廢除以後，公卿皆不能保證其後世一定或貴或賢：「封建廢，世祿不行，惟天子得立尊人府，其在臣下惟衍聖公近之，若公卿以下，皆不能立尊子（按：尊子即宗子），而乃欲自始祖以下，並以長子之子孫為尊子，抑不知能保其比貴比賢否」。[120]但是阮文超接下來的討論，相當有意思，他認為與其執意於大宗小宗之辨，不如在現實上，吸取范仲淹的義田之法，才能眞正尊祖收族。他說：「不有范文正公義田之法存乎？蓋祠堂者敬尊也，義田者收族也。祖宗之神依於主，無祠堂無以安亡者，子孫之生依於食，無義田則無以保其生，兩者當並重而不可偏廢」。[121]他最後結論說：「如宗子能行，則當念及支庶之貧者以慰其先，若出於支子，則尤宜留意，以不失宗子之法焉」。[122]也就是如果現實上能行大宗制的家族，則行之，但勿忘支庶的生計問題，如果，現實上，是支子（非宗子一長子）主導，勿忘宗子法的用意，一種非常務實折中的態度，有效回應錢謙益拋出的難題，但卻缺乏從大宗延伸到更大的共同體想像，於此，又要回到中國宋明以來對實踐大宗制的思考。

在明神宗萬曆（1573-1620）以前，諸多族譜序跋中僅有數篇論及大宗或宗子之重要，且主要仍是解釋譜牒的興起，出於宗法盪然無存，如，〈姚氏譜後序〉一語道盡：「蓋自宗法既廢，而譜學行」，

120 阮文超，《方亭隨筆錄》（臺北：國立臺灣大學出版中心，2013），卷3，〈品家及士庶家祠禮〉，頁221-222。

121 阮文超，《方亭隨筆錄》，卷3，〈品家及士庶家祠禮〉，頁224。

122 阮文超，《方亭隨筆錄》，卷3，〈品家及士庶家祠禮〉，頁225。

〈東陽丁氏族譜序〉同樣簡潔：「夫自宗法廢，而君子始講譜牒」。[123] 其中少數佼佼者如，〈題三舍劉氏族譜後〉便引《近思錄》中程頤對宗子法的支持表示對大宗制的嚮往。[124]〈黃巖蔡氏族譜序〉更將大宗小宗之法之功用有很簡潔的交代，明確指出大宗制之宗法在於統合人民，人民的統合與祭祀息息相關：「古者諸侯自適子而次，有大宗以重其本，有小宗以聯其枝而四時之祭於廟，則子姓昆弟無不在焉，所以統宗合族，周且詳如此，故其知親親之重本。後世宗法廢，祭法不明，民使離析渙散，無所統一」。[125]

從封建，井田的立場重視宗族宗法，試圖重建大宗制組織人民，進而強化國家來對抗外敵，在萬曆以後，就又不罕見，例如〈文江蕭氏族譜序〉：「三代而上，諸侯士大夫皆世其爵土，故宗法大行於朝，而有世家」。[126] 湯賓尹在〈方氏族譜序〉詳細勾勒出宗法、封建與井田三者緊扣相聯：「井田也，封建也，宗法也，古制之相爲用者也。井田之制既廢，民不得各有其土，而侯王之家焉得各有其民，故

123 吳宣德、宗韻，《明人譜牒序跋輯略》，上冊，〈姚氏譜後序〉，頁479、〈東陽丁氏族譜序〉，頁489。此外可參見上冊，〈廖氏族譜序〉：「自古宗子之法廢，而世之人類不知所自來，往往親未盡而相視如楚越者有焉」，頁404；上冊，〈劉氏重修族譜序〉：「自三代以降，有大宗小宗之法，而秦漢唐宋以來，宗法既廢，衣冠之家各自爲譜」，頁461；上冊，〈四明月湖陸氏宗族譜〉：「自大小宗之法廢，而尊尊親親之道賴以不墜著，惟譜牒存焉耳」，頁467。

124 吳宣德、宗韻，《明人譜牒序跋輯略》，上冊，〈題三舍劉氏族譜後〉，頁473。

125 吳宣德、宗韻，《明人譜牒序跋輯略》，上冊，〈黃巖蔡氏族譜序〉，頁488-489。

126 吳宣德、宗韻，《明人譜牒序跋輯略》，下冊，〈文江蕭氏族譜序〉，頁1329。

封建無所行也。無世業，故無世官。無世官，故無世族」。[127]接著反駁如上述主張的小宗制，他同意在當時的中國宗族已經渙散，同樣從人性立論，但理由不是王衡所謂的人只是對其所生的父母有親，此外皆爲路人，而是封建井田瓦解後，人性皆保護自己的生命與追求利益，當無固有的田地可以養活自己時，人們自然四處流離，導致互不認識，但本來是同根：

> 均是人也，趣生走利之性，不學而能。產無常授，土之毛不贍以活，欲其勿散而四方，其可得乎？散而之四方矣，反所自始，爲同爲異，非職見於眉面也。塗之人過而相誰，其中有一本者矣。草木之無知也。手其西柯，東條驚，本同故也。[128]

他接著反駁：「人則相誰而不問，忍乎哉？於乎！族之合也，其終復井田乎？田不可井，族不可聚，所由來非一日矣」。[129]他譬喻，即使草木無知，用手搖草木西邊的枝幹，東邊的枝幹則爲驚動，因爲根幹是相同的，他以此說明同族之人休戚與共。[130]王衡認爲大宗制強人所難，人要「忍」（不仁）才能合在一起，這裡湯賓尹反過來責問本來同根的人們互不相識，這可以「忍」嗎？這不是眞正的不仁嗎？最後，恢復大宗制的根本在恢復井田，有了井田聚族才有基礎。湯賓尹的論點作爲歷史分析言之有理，做爲政治實踐，則缺乏彈性，條件太

127 吳宣德、宗韻，《明人譜牒序跋輯略》，下冊，〈方氏族譜序〉，頁1315。
128 吳宣德、宗韻，《明人譜牒序跋輯略》，下冊，〈方氏族譜序〉，頁1315-1316。
129 吳宣德、宗韻，《明人譜牒序跋輯略》，下冊，〈方氏族譜序〉，頁1316。
130 這個樹枝樹幹譬喻自然是來自主張恢復大宗制的張載程頤，詳見於前正文。

高，窒礙難行，因爲若是井田無法恢復，那大宗制亦無法恢復，在近兩千沒有井田制的中國，欲恢復井田，豈非比登天還難？

這個立論的缺失，後來經由顧炎武在理論上才有較爲妥善務實的處理。當然，湯賓尹的說法也不必看得太僵硬，他所謂的井田可以理解或轉換爲宗族共同的財產，換句話說就是程子所提倡的不析產，更可以詮釋爲前述提及越南阮文超引范仲淹的義田爲例。盛清時的方苞（1668-1749）在〈柏村吳氏宗祠記〉中提到「惟吳郡范氏，七百餘年宗法常行，而無或敢犯，爲有義田以養其族故也」，[131]亦正是此意。

由大宗制的宗族論推到更大的群體／共同體想像（尚非「民族」）也同時逐漸趨於明朗，金鉉（1610-1644）在〈蔣氏族譜序〉中指出大宗制瓦解後，人心渙散，不像王衡那些小宗論者所說，就算父子兄弟也不親，只有行大宗制，才有可能挽回人心，從一個人到千萬人，從一家到四海皆融洽，甚至宇宙間充滿太和。他說：「治天下莫先管人心。宗子法者，則人心之所管也。人之情其渙也久，各私其身，即父子兄弟間，雖強結於所敘，而無以極其性之所不忍欺，是以誠愈漓而俗愈戾，泯泯棼棼，蓋取諸此。惟宗法行，大者千百世，小者四三世，皆敦其仁之盡而各稱其義之宜，一人至千萬人，家至四海，皆此愷悌以相蒸格，太和其在宇宙間乎！」[132]他序文結論說：「宗法者，家本所萃，而治天下實不外焉」。[133]在這樣的論述中，大宗

131　方苞，《方苞集》（上海：上海古籍出版社，2012），下冊，集外文，卷8，〈柏村吳氏宗祠記〉，頁762。

132　吳宣德、宗韻，《明人譜牒序跋輯略》，下冊，〈蔣氏族譜序〉，頁1389。「太和」在此應來自張載，《正蒙》首章便是〈太和〉，可見張載「血氣觀宗族論」對此文主張大宗進而推及千萬人四海的影響。這裡亦有宗統君統合一的觀點。

133　吳宣德、宗韻，《明人譜牒序跋輯略》，下冊，〈蔣氏族譜序〉，頁1390。

宗法竟可從一人推到千萬人，乃至於四海，成爲治理天下，連結千萬人的核心制度。

所以，從宋代以來，郡縣與小宗爲一組，封建與大宗爲一組，大宗小宗之辨，亦即是在封建郡縣之爭論中進行。誠然在宋代尚有不少人公開支持恢復封建，但整體來看郡縣論畢竟占上風，一方面固然是宋代以來君王不願意行封建，連唐太宗一番假惺惺的欲恢復封建，聆聽百臣意見的故事，[134]竟也沒人敷衍了事；另一方面，主張郡縣反對封建的朱子學在元明清三代皆是官學，因此，註定封建論在中國、朝鮮、越南三國的在野性質。到了清初顧炎武於其膾炙人口的〈郡縣論〉中提出「寓封建之意於郡縣之中」的說法時，[135]就宣告了在中國欲以封建全面取代郡縣的政治想法已經大勢已去，但這並非完全放棄封建或與其關聯的一些理念，如本文所處理宗族論中的大宗宗法。恰恰相反，支持封建的人於是更務實的思考如何在不全盤推翻既有的郡縣政治體制裡，推動符合三代封建的理念與政策。在顧炎武的看法，唯有如此，「兩千年以來之敝可以復振」。[136]

而「寓封建之意於郡縣之中」的實際做法，顧炎武所孜孜著意的即在宗族，在〈華陰王氏宗祠記〉，他將宗族看爲國家政事之本，這裡的次序不是《大學》裡的「修身齊家治國平天下」的次序，這裡的次序是顧炎武自己的論述，他說：「是故有人倫，然後有風俗，有風俗然後有政事，有政事然後有國家，先王之於民，其生也，爲之九族

134 吳競撰，謝保成集校，《貞觀政要集校》（臺北：中華書局），卷3，第8章，〈論封建〉，頁172-180。

135 顧炎武，《顧亭林詩文集》（香港：中華書局，1976），卷1，〈郡縣論一〉，頁12-13。

136 顧炎武，《顧亭林詩文集》，卷1，〈郡縣論一〉，頁13。

九紀，大宗小宗之屬以聯之」。[137]在〈斐村記〉中他又進一步痛論大宗制的宗族對國家存亡何等重要，他說：「嗚呼！自治道愈下而國無疆宗（按：讀爲大宗），無疆宗，是以無立國，無立國，是以內潰外畔而卒至於亡，然則宗法之存，非所以扶人紀而張國勢乎！」。[138]文末三復其旨，他語重心長地說：「夫不能復封建之治，而欲藉士大夫之勢以立其國者，其在重氏族哉！其在重氏族哉！」。[139]時至晚清，洋務運動的先鋒馮桂芬（1809-1874）在《校邠廬抗議．復宗法議》開門見山便說：「三代之法，井田封建一廢不可復，後人頗有議復之者，竊以爲復井田封建，不如復宗法」，[140]就是承襲顧炎武的說法。與顧炎武同時的幾社領袖陳子龍（1608-1647）在〈江南氏族論〉一文，雖非立足從大宗制的宗族論，同樣肯定世家大族在治國的功用，而且還替六朝的世家歷史評價翻案，說：「當時論其塞路，後史嘆其靡忠，指弊實多，稱美未覩。以余論之，誠馭世之良風，建賢之次策也」。[141]

宋代以來的大宗制的宗族論，跨洋過海，在17世紀的琉球王國竟然有了最全面的落實。1609年日本德川幕府允許薩摩藩（今鹿兒島縣）出兵侵略受明朝冊封的琉球王國，同年3月6日從鹿兒島出發，7日即登陸在琉球王國北部的奄美群島，之後勢如破竹，不到一

137 顧炎武，《顧亭林詩文集》，卷5，〈華陰王氏宗祠記〉，頁114。

138 顧炎武，《顧亭林詩文集》，卷5，〈斐村記〉，頁106。

139 顧炎武，《顧亭林詩文集》，卷5，〈斐村記〉，頁107。

140 馮桂芬，《校邠廬抗議》（鄭州：中州古籍出版社，1998），下篇，〈復宗法議〉，頁166。

141 陳子龍著，王英志輯校，《陳子龍全集》（北京：人民文學出版社，2011），卷22，〈江南氏族論〉，頁708。

個月就打到沖繩本島攻破首里城。[142]之後琉球國政實際上遂多受薩摩藩箝制，成爲中日「兩屬」的狀況，在這麼嚴峻的內外局勢，琉球王國採取加速中國化的策略，以固國本，以示與日本不同，[143]當然，日本亦因不同的原因而默認甚至鼓勵此一發展。在這中國化的過程中最值得一提的就是，琉球王國王府與士族在1650年以後全面選擇以大宗制重寫族譜，琉球士族族譜編寫完成後，須上呈琉球王府，批准後重新謄寫兩份，一份交上給王府。[144]所有的族譜第一頁就會宣示這是大宗的族譜亦或是小宗的族譜，琉球的大宗制族譜至今尙存留三千多份。[145]因此，琉球的族譜實際上是建立在大宗小宗宗法的譜牒，在東亞這應該絕無僅有，只此一家，爲琉球一絕。

（三）「東亞民族主義」理論的形成與日本

1. 從嚮往三代的封建論到國學派對抗中國的日本想像

令人尋思的是封建郡縣論爭在17世紀的日本江戶伊始遂即展開，由於日本德川的幕藩體制與封建制有相通之處，整體外在環境有別於郡縣制的中國，相當有利於贊成封建制的言論，這樣的言論與擁護現實的政治體制亦常結合。比如18世紀初日本第一大儒荻生徂徠

142 上里隆史，《琉日戦争一六〇九——島津氏の琉球侵攻》（沖繩：ボーダーインク，2009），第5章，〈島津軍、琉球へ侵攻〉，頁222-284。

143 赤嶺守，《琉球王國》（東京：講談社，2004），第5章，〈王国の改革と中国化〉，頁122-124。

144 木村淳也，〈琉球史書の特質と問題——東アジア国際関係を軸として〉，收入《交響する東方の知——漢文文化圏の輪郭》（東京：明治書院，2014），頁180-182。

145 2013年2月底作者赴沖繩開會考察時，到那霸市市立博物館看到所有的族譜都明言大宗小宗，無一例外。

（1666-1728）的高徒太宰春台（1680-1747）在其〈封建論〉序就將此種關聯一表無遺，他說：「神祖受命，奮其英武，統一海內，於是以其地降者，因封之，且又侯子弟功臣於要地，以藩屏王室，凡三百諸侯，宛然三代之制，於乎美哉！」。[146]其實，說贊成封建的言論是江戶時期的主流，一點也無言過其實。

接著太宰春台讚揚封建制的好處：「先王以建萬國親諸侯，夫封建者，聖人之制也，不徒所以推恩報功，親親賢賢，外以防禦夷狄，內以藩屏王室，天下之利，莫大於斯，邦家之守，莫要於斯」。[147]通觀全篇卻無一語及宗族，與中國的情況大異，這最基本的差異還是在於，日本已經實行封建，宗族論遂無關緊要，更何況日本統治階層均行近乎大宗的家制度，宗族在日本的封建論中遂無甚地位。然而，封建論的霸權，受到最嚴重的挑戰，並非來自主張郡縣制的觀點，而是先出自於與太宰春台同時京都的儒學者伊藤東涯（1670-1736）。

伊藤東涯的做法，不同於柳宗元對封建激烈的批判，對伊藤而言，封建郡縣沒有本質的優劣之分，只有古今中日的不同而已。他批評贊成封建論者，「經生晚達，專狃聞三代，而謂秦漢以還無如上世，不知封建革而郡縣興……布壞而為泉鈔……牘便而為紙帛，椅而不席，騎而不乘，今之中夏，非古之中夏」。[148]這個序言寫在他一部名為《制度通》的和文書，其中主要考究中國從三代以來至宋明政治

146　太宰春台，《春台先生紫芝園稿》（東京：ぺりかん社，1986），前稿卷5，〈封建論〉，頁80。

147　文中「親親賢賢」的「親親」，其實就是宗族的理念，不過將全文與日本其他支持封建的理論併看時，便知親親在此僅為套語，因為宗族論幾乎不見於支持封建的論述。

148　伊藤東涯，《制度通》（京都：中文出版社，1993），〈序〉，頁6-8。

經濟制度的變遷，同時略談與日本的異同。他的處理使得封建郡縣皆為相對的、沒有絕對的優劣。這不但相對化三代的崇高價值，也進而相對化中國作為在江戶日本的先進地位。當然他本人的用意應非如此，他只是試圖說明理解制度本身之重要性，而非如許多人不懂制度的古今和漢差異，便貿貿然辯論封建郡縣之優劣。儘管如此，伊藤東涯的價值中立研究比較古今中日的政治社會體制，提供往後日本民族論從封建郡縣論爭中解放出來的基礎，使得民族論可以不與任何一種特定的政治體制或政治價值掛勾這一點很重要，因為這解釋東亞的民族主義者為何封建可，郡縣亦可，可以支援君主制，亦可以主張共和，既可以是自由主義者，更可以是社會主義或共產主義者。

但是，伊藤東涯並沒有參與從宗族到「民族」之道的論述，這是18世紀中葉以後，日本國學派諸位思想家的工作。國學派崛起的背景是一個非常崇拜中國的江戶社會，一個企圖建立日本主體性的反動。雖然從江戶初期直到18世紀末為止（1790），朱子學誠如渡邊浩指出並非官學，而儒學，特別是儒學學者在政治上的影響力相當有限，日本社會同時與中國，朝鮮存在著相當大的差異。但無可否認的，到了18世紀初，日本社會充滿所謂中華崇拜的風氣，不少日本人都有三個字中華風的姓名。漢詩的唱和也極為普遍，學術界的主流也幾乎清一色是儒學，連幕府本身也大量搜購中國的圖書，並聘請學者研究中國，[149]前述的荻生徂徠與他的弟弟荻生北溪（1673-1754）都參與此太平盛事，其中最有影響力的莫過荻生徂徠在1723年刊行的《明律國字解》，這本書影響深遠，後來明治維新初期的法律制定都

149 大庭脩，《徳川吉宗と康熙帝——鎖国化での日中交流》（東京：大修館書店，1999），第6章，〈吉宗と漢籍〉，頁181-232。

與此有關。[150]

國學派理論建構最重要的則是本居宣長（1730-1801），他經由對《古事記》與《源氏物語》的研究，發展出兩個重要的面向。其一，則是在語言論。他的語言論不但受到荻生徂徠古文辭學的影響，更吸收了清朝訓詁考證學。例如，他對讀音語音的重視，與顧炎武重視讀音因而著述《音學五書》一樣。但他更進一步強調音先於字，即「ことば（kotoba）」（言葉・語）高於「ふみ（fumi）」（文）。是故，他認爲日本在接受漢字漢語以前，有一個沒有受到中國污染的「やまとことば（Yamato kotoba）」（大和語言）與一個「やまとこころ（Yamato kokoro）」（大和心），他主張日本需要重新發現這個沒受到「漢意」陰霾的日本。這樣一個原始日本的情緒，則是「もののあはれ（mono no aware）」（物之哀），一種中國沒有纖細優美的美感。[151]

這樣的纖細優美的美感後來則呈現於對櫻花的喜好。在此之前，日本喜好的花樹與中國幾乎相同，君子三友的松竹梅、重九的菊花、華麗的牡丹、芍藥等，此外。日本明治以前的庭園幾乎不種植櫻花。今天，櫻花無疑是日本美感的象徵，這個轉變可解釋爲來自本居宣長的「もののあはれ」（物之哀）的體現，但這個這個舉世皆知的象徵不過是19世紀以來才被發明的，絕大部分櫻花種植在野外山里或19世紀以來的公共空間如公園、河邊等。

其二，他基於日本神話演繹的宇宙論與歷史觀。他從閱讀《古事

150 Paul Heng-chao Ch'en, *The Formation of the Early Meiji Legal Order: The Japanese Code of the 1871 and its Chinese Foundation*（New York: Oxford University Press, 1981）, p. 10.

151 小森陽一，《日本語の近代》（東京：岩波書店，2000），第1章，〈「日本語」の発見〉，頁1-30。

記》演繹出一個三層世界的宇宙生成論：天，地，與黃泉三層世界，分別爲「高天原」、「葦原中國」、「黃泉國」，從此三層世界證成日本作爲一個「國」的特殊性。簡單的說，「高天原」是諸天神住的、潔淨的，「黃泉國」是死人的前往的居國，而「葦原中國」則是兩者之間，淨穢夾雜的（人間）地方。產出萬物的是「產靈（Takamimusubi）」（タカミムスビ），「日之神」爲「皇祖神」，皇國（日本）之神爲「天照大神」，天照大神所管轄的即是位居三者之上的「高天原」，一個有「國」的意識，本居宣長對「國」的理解是有「界限之義」，他也引用賀茂眞淵對「國」的解釋——告知界限的地方（限りてしらするところ），「國」亦須有統治者 此後天照大神的兒子忍穗耳命的兒子邇邇藝命（即天孫）降臨到位居「高天原」與「黃泉國」之間的「葦原中國」成爲其君主。「葦原中國」即是後來的日本。[152]

在此，本居宣長並沒有直指天照大神爲日本人的始祖，而且他也沒有認爲日本之人皆爲一個民族想法，此外，始祖論的神話原型應須上溯到司馬遷的《史記‧五帝本紀》。儘管如此，他卻爲「大和語言」與「大和心」找到了「天照大神」庇護，發明出一個神話、美感的日本，一個對抗、相對、脫離中國有「界限」的想像共同體。雖然，國學派日後修正發展他的觀點，這個想像的共同體基本上仍是文化主義的，而非政治的。[153]政治化的想像共同體則需待19世紀20年

152 東（宮沢）より子，〈宣長神学のコスモロジー：「国」概念の発見〉，《下関女子短期大学紀要》，14：15（山口，1996），頁1-13。

153 Susan L. Burns, *Before the Nation: Kokugaku and the Imagining of Community in Early Modern Japan* (Durham: Duke University Press, 2003), pp. 224-226.

代以後，所謂的後期水戶學，將本居宣長等的國學派理論融入儒家的政治思想裡，才有所突破。

2. 宗統君統合一的大宗宗族論——會澤正志齋的「國體」

水戶藩（今茨城縣水戶市）爲收容明末朱舜水流亡日本，編纂大日本史著名的德川「禦三家」之一的雄藩。在日本江戶後期與所謂的幕末的政治扮演極其重要的角色，德川幕府最後的將軍原來是水戶藩主德川齊昭的兒子德川慶喜，許多政治事件都有水戶藩的影子，比如轟動一時、流風波及清末中國、朝鮮的「櫻田門外之變」。這個事件就是由水戶藩與薩摩藩脫藩的浪士在幕府將軍的住所（今皇宮）的櫻田門外暗殺彼時幕府大老（似清朝軍機處領班大臣）井伊直弼，開啓了後來東亞各國的政治暗殺事件風氣。

後期水戶學影響日本以及東亞各國最深遠的首推水戶藩藩校弘道館教頭會澤正志齋（1782-1863），他在1825年上呈水戶藩藩主德川齊修他撰寫的《新論》。這本書，一言以蔽之，將國學派文化的想像共同體完全政治化、儒家化，業已十分清楚的想像出一個民族國家，爲迎接19世紀萬國爭雄，西方入侵東亞的新局面做出一個政治、理論、心理的準備，[154]他書中的國體論完成東亞民族論與民族主義的原型，提供東亞民族主義日後發展的藍圖，往後的發展常常只是引進西方的政治詞彙取代、補充、強化原有的政治論述與理路。這本書證明瞭他的先知先覺，也是日本在19世紀以來思想上以及其他方面能領導超越東亞其他各國的見證。

---

154 米原謙，《日本政治思想》（東京：ミネルヴァ書房，2007），頁29，將水户學稱之爲「危機的政治學」。

《新論》這本書是以典雅的漢文寫成的，有〈國體〉（上中下三章），〈形勢〉，〈虜情〉，〈守禦〉，〈長計〉五論，共7章。[155]雖說是漢文撰寫，裡面如「中國」、「天朝」兩詞指的是日本，不是中國。在〈國體上〉，他批判日本的陋儒俗學，說：「昧於名義，稱明清爲華夏中國，以汙辱國體」。江戶線裝本文中凡遇到「天朝」、「朝廷」等皆有抬頭，這當然也不是對中國的抬頭。此外，一些日本當時用通用的名詞稱呼，在書中多換成儒家或中國詞彙，比如，「侍」改爲「武士」，「公儀」改爲「幕府」，「大名」改成「邦主」或「諸侯」等，當然這些語言轉換從江戶伊始，日本儒學學者就不斷進行，只是成效一直有限，到了幕末如會澤正志齋的《新論》等著作才是將此前和制漢語的名詞完全轉化爲儒家或中國詞彙，所以到了1970年代，很多人甚至包括專業的歷史學學者，都忘了在幕末以前的江戶時期「幕府」被稱爲「公儀」一詞，而且，「幕府」一詞官方文書幾乎不使用。

討論這點主要的原因並非僅僅提醒閱讀日本漢文著作如《新論》時須有的警戒與知識，更重要的是，說明幕末很多儒學如水戶學雖然容納國學派的一些理論，但是他們卻拒絕了國學派的語言論，這不但反應在他們拒絕和制漢語，反而以儒家或中國詞彙取代，更呈現在他們書寫的文體——漢文（文言文）。但這個勝利不是全面的，明治維新以後朝廷的敕語檔，並非使用漢文，而是典雅帶有尙書體的「書下文」，這就是與國學派的一種妥協。「書下文」基本上是文言文改成日文文法，明治時期著作很多都是「書下文」。會澤正志齋一方面拒

155 會澤正志齋，《新論》（江户／東京：玉山堂，安政四年［1857］版，線裝本）。

絕國學派的語言論，另一方面卻又引進國學派的神話歷史觀，[156]這形成《新論》一書中最重要的理論創見——「國體」。

國體論出現的背景從書中也有很清楚的線索——感受到即將到來的西方入侵與企圖脫離中國中心觀進而建構日本的主體性。《新論・序》一開始就先指出西方入侵的危機，[157]這在鴉片戰爭爆發的15年前，他說：「今西荒蠻夷，以脛足之賤，奔走四海，蹂躪諸國，眇視跛履，欲淩駕 上國，何其驕也！」[158]他十分警覺到未來局勢的險惡，在〈序言〉的結尾，他說：「是五論者，皆所以祈天之定而復勝人也，臣之自誓而以身殉天地者」，[159] 言之剴切，豈不動容？日本江戶明治三百年文章學問義理可觀者，亦復如是。

「國體」到底爲何呢？由於書中對「國體」並沒有簡潔的定義，日本思想史研究已故碩學尾藤正英在其研究國體思想一書中，亦指出

156 關於國學與儒學在會澤正志齋思想的關係與本文分析接近的，可參考藍弘岳，〈「神州」、「中國」、「帝國」——會澤正志齋的國家想像與十九世紀日本之亞洲論述〉，《新史學》，22：3（臺北，2011），頁78、81。藍弘岳也同樣強調會澤引進國學派的皇國觀，但乃是置於儒家的觀點來論述的，同時也站在儒家的立場批判國學，此外，文中對會澤如何使用「中國」此一概念與對中國的理解有周到的分析交代。

157 辻本雅史，《近世教育思想史の研究——日本における「公教育」思想の源流——》（京都：思文閣出版，1990），第6章，〈国家主義的教育思想の源流——後期水戸学の国家意識と統合論——〉，頁270-271，討論後期水户學時，即以所謂的常陸大津濱事件——1824年英國船突然到水户藩一事爲發展的背景。當時，會澤正志齋奉命前往與上陸的英國人交涉，他警覺這些不是來捕鯨的俄羅斯人，英國人有侵略的目的。會澤的《新論》一書即在在此事件的隔年寫作。辻本說：「會澤的《新論》受到此事件的觸發而執筆毫無疑問。在這個意義上，大津濱事件對水户學是一個里程碑」。

158 會澤正志齋，《新論》，頁1。

159 會澤正志齋，《新論》，頁2。

歷來對於何謂「國體」亦莫衷一是，恍如在五裡霧中。[160]近來小島毅以《全譯 漢辭海（第二版）》中提到「國體」一詞有四個意思，1：作爲國君手足最受信賴之大臣（《春秋穀梁傳・昭公15年》），2：國家的典章制度（《漢書・成帝紀》），3：國家的體面（《後漢書・孔融傳》），4：國家的統治體制。[161]前三種皆出於中國古典，而第四種，不列出處，小島毅判斷第四種最接近明治時期以來「國體」一詞的意思，而這個用法的出處究竟昉於何書或成於何人之手呢？小島毅一同尾藤正英斷定出於江戶後期會澤正志齋《新論》一書，雖宋代有近乎第四種用法之例，但終究不是。這個判斷大約無誤，小島毅雖然詳盡解說會澤的「國體」爲何與其時代背景的關係，不過並無繼續追溯會澤的「國體」出典爲何。[162]追根究底，「國體」其實不能解爲「國家的統治體制」，以下詳論。

通觀全書旨意，「國體」，一言以蔽之，應即出於《公羊傳》之「國君一體」，「國」與「君」爲一體是爲「國體」。在《會澤正志齋文稿》（以下簡稱《文稿》）〈復讐紀事跋〉中有云：「夫復讐之義大矣，齊襄公報九世之讐，春秋義之」，[163]此處「齊襄公報九世之讐」，所指爲何呢？此則須上溯到《春秋》莊公四年「紀侯大去其國」，即是齊國滅掉紀國一事。會澤不採《左傳》、《穀梁》兩傳在此事件對

160 尾藤正英，《日本の国家主義──「国体」思想の形成》（東京：岩波書局，2014），頁3。

161 小島毅，《增補 靖國史觀──日本思想を読みなおす》（東京：筑摩書房，2014）頁23-24。

162 小島毅，《增補 靖國史觀──日本思想を読みなおす》，頁27-55。

163 會澤正志齋著，名越時正編，《會澤正志齋文稿》（東京：国書刊行会，2002），頁226。

齊國批判的觀點；如《穀梁》就指責齊襄公爲小人，[164]而是承襲《公羊傳》的說法，所以他才會說「春秋義之」，因爲春秋三傳只有《公羊傳》認同齊襄公的復仇，這亦即是「國體」出自《公羊傳》的鐵證。《公羊傳》對此事件的看法爲何呢？《公羊傳》認爲齊襄公滅紀爲遠祖齊哀公復仇是正義，因爲紀侯的先世曾經在周夷王面前散布讒言，導致齊哀公被處死，[165]所以不以爲非。[166]《公羊傳》如此議論：

> 九世猶可以復讎乎？雖百世可也。家亦可乎？曰 不可。國何以可？國君一體也。先君之恥也，猶今君之恥。今君

164 《春秋穀梁傳》：「紀侯賢而齊侯滅之，不言滅而曰大去其國者，不使小人加乎君子」。於此，紀侯是君子，齊襄公則是小人。見穀梁赤撰，范寧注，《春秋穀梁傳》收於《漢魏古注十三經 附四書章句集注》，下，（北京：中華書局，1998），莊公四年，頁31。《左傳》：「紀侯不能下齊，以與紀季。夏，紀侯大去其國，違齊難也」。見左丘明撰，杜預注，《春秋經傳集解（左傳）》收於《漢魏古注十三經 附四書章句集注》，下，（北京：中華書局，1998），莊公四年，頁74。《左傳》在此暗批齊國霸道，且綜觀全書，可以斷定《左傳》並不支持復仇，詳見於李隆獻，〈復仇觀的省察與詮釋——以《春秋》三傳爲重心〉，《臺大中文學報》，22：6（臺北，2005），頁99-150。

165 可參見司馬遷，《史記》（北京：中華書局，1982），卷32，〈齊太公世家〉，頁1481。

166 會澤採《公羊傳》之說，乃極有深意，並非孤例，而是一以貫之。後世反對《公羊傳》對此事的斷案綦繁，不勝枚舉，如清末廖平（1852-1932）在《穀梁古義疏》就說：「九世復仇之說，非常可駭」。見廖平，《穀梁古義疏》（北京 中華書局，2012），頁133。越南吳時任（1746-1803）在其《春秋管見》反對《穀梁傳》的詮釋，嚴厲批判紀侯，他說：「禮，國君出奔，曰：何爲其亡社稷也？故有死社稷，未有去而不顧，若是之甚也」。又接著批評《公羊傳》的經解「不相關」與「殊甚迂闊」，他說：「若夫九世復讐之說，與此義尤不相關。賢襄公而諱其滅紀，殊甚迂闊」。見吳時任，《春秋管見》，收入北京大學儒藏編纂與研究中心編，《儒藏 精華編 越南之部一冊》，（北京，北京大學出版社，2013），頁289。

之恥也，猶先君之恥。國君何以爲一體？國君以國爲體，諸侯世，故國君爲一體也。[167]

這段主要是論復仇，討論爲何「國」就算過了百世，仍可以復仇。理由是「國」與「君」一體。「國君一體」，是故以前君主的恥辱即是現在君主的恥辱，現在君主的恥辱也會成爲先前君主的恥辱。爲何「國」與「君」能一體呢？其一是「國君以國爲體」，這是「君」爲首(頭腦)，「國」爲其身體，所以「國」與「君」自然爲一體，[168]由於只有「國」之君才可以復仇，「家」之君則不行，所以「君」若不以「國」爲體，「君」亦不能復仇，所以，「國」在此有恆久之意。其二是「諸侯世」，王建文對此有精湛的說明，「不同時代的國君之所以能爲一體，百世不絕，正因爲諸侯以上是百世不遷的大宗，這樣一體可以永遠以其大祖廟作爲仲介，宗族成員尊祖敬宗，宗子收族。」[169]在此事先強調由於國君一體，百世不絕，因此已經帶有所謂「法人」性格，稍後在討論穗積八束會論及「國體」有「法人」的性質。

格外值得矚目的是「國君一體」的「一體」，出於《儀禮．喪服傳》的「一體」。因此，「一體」此一概念與祭祀、宗法密不可分，「一體」特別指涉「父子一體」。由於「一體」，所以在大宗制裡世世

167 公羊高撰，何休注，《公羊傳》收於《漢魏古注十三經 附四書章句集注》，下，(北京：中華書局，1998)，莊公四年，頁39。

168 王建文對「國君以國爲體」的解釋爲一個空間的關係，即「國家（或謂天下）的空間是一永恆不變的空間」，就算統治者換人，同樣的空間仍在，只要新的統治者有天命，「統治者家族的空間與國家的空間重又取得了特殊的聯繫」，值得商榷。見王建文，《奉天承運——古代中國的「國家」概念及其正當性基礎》（臺北：東大圖書，1995），頁116。

169 王建文，《奉天承運——古代中國的「國家」概念及其正當性基礎》，頁110。

代代的宗子皆可以連爲「一體」，[170] 這其實就可以解釋何以「國君」百世仍可以復仇，因爲現在的「國君」與百世前的「國君」仍爲「一體」。唐代賈公彥在《儀禮注疏》中如此解釋「父子一體」，「云父子一體也者，謂子與父骨血同爲體，因其父與祖亦爲一體，又見世叔與祖亦爲一體也」。[171] 這個「一體」的觀念貫穿於《新論》的日本創建歷史敘述之中，在《文稿・三器集說序》他將「一體」的意思說比在《新論》中明白，他說「聖子神孫，莫非天祖遺體」，[172] 這樣的論述就是依據「父子一體」的說法。後來1937年日本文部省頒發的《國體之本義》〈聖德〉一章中再三強調天皇與皇祖皇宗「御一體」，〈臣節〉一章有「祖孫一體」，「君臣一體」的說法，皆可以清楚看到《公羊傳》「國君一體」的思想痕跡。

雖然《新論》裡的「國體」出於「國君一體」，但已非僅僅「國君一體」，在「國君一體」中，「國」與「君」雖可以連爲一體，仍卻保有其獨立性，而「國體」則是兩者結合後產出之「物」。於是「國體」，簡單的說就是政治化的想像共同體之大本，亦是「國家」的別名，一個有大宗直系，即所謂的「萬世一系」，連貫歷史生命不可割裂的國家，因此，所謂天皇「萬世一系」的說法，說穿了即是會澤正志齋從《春秋公羊傳》「國君一體」，基於儒家大宗宗族論，發展而出的「國體」思想下之論述系譜。[173] 同時，國體論亦成爲面對西

170 王建文，《奉天承運——古代中國的「國家」概念及其正當性基礎》，頁98-107。

171 鄭玄注，賈公彥疏，《儀禮注疏》（上海：上海古籍出版社，2008），卷30，〈喪服第十一〉，頁911。

172 會澤正志齋著，名越時正編，《會澤正志齋文稿》，〈三器集説序〉，頁93。

173 辻本雅史亦認爲國體論「應説是面對西方侵略來臨而產生有一種國家論的性格」，但在文中未從「國君一體」與「宗族論」的角度分析「國

方侵略，特別是作爲西方意識形態的前衛尖兵——基督教的挑戰，一種對抗防衛的「意識形態戰略」。[174]

這個「國體」——日本，是富有內容的「國體」。這個內容即是引進國學派的神話歷史觀後轉換爲儒家的大宗宗法論述，一個有歷史生命、有歷史精神的共同體。這個共同體還有天寵，這個天寵將日本這個國體提升到有宇宙論面向的存有論。國體的起源來自於天祖，即是天照大神，值得注意的是他於《新論》通篇使用「天祖」一詞，[175]目的就在加強「天照大神」爲「國體」之祖的印象。「天祖」以後將天位交給「天孫」，這裡如同「天祖」，「天孫」另有他稱，在《古事記》爲「天邇岐志國邇岐志天津日高日子番能邇邇芸命」，在《日本書記》中亦即「瓊瓊杵尊」。如果他寫「天照大神」將大位交給「瓊瓊杵尊」，這樣就回到神話的世界，爲了彰顯「天祖」作爲「國體」始祖，之後「天孫」繼位，由祖至孫，由孫再一直往下傳這樣的歷史生命，[176]這些大和語言則必須轉換成宋明以來宗族論的語言。

體」，亦未直言「國體」爲何。見辻本雅史，《近世教育思想史の研究——日本における「公教育」思想の源流——》，第6章，〈国家主義的教育思想の源流——後期水戶学の国家意識と統合論——〉，頁286。

174 米原謙，《日本政治思想》，頁33-34。

175 子安宣邦認爲「天祖」一詞雖不見於中國典籍，但這無礙於天祖一詞源於中國儒家的天觀與祖考觀，詳見於子安宣邦，《日本ナショナリズムの解読》，（東京：白澤社，2009），頁59-62。此外，子安宣邦非常強調「天祖」一詞在《新論》整個理論架構中的核心地位，這個說法與拙文有同調之處，不過他並沒觸及大宗宗法與《新論》的關係。

176 其實，由祖至孫，非由祖至父再傳至孫，這樣的系譜述模式亦帶有中國昭穆制的痕跡，宗廟中央爲太祖（始祖）其右2世4世6世爲昭，其左3世5世7世爲穆，就是父子不同昭穆，祖孫同一昭穆。

會澤正志齋說：「群臣也者，亦皆神明之冑，其先事 天祖 天孫，有功德於民，列在祀典，而宗子糾緝族人以主其祭」，他在此句下麵，注有小字，「古者故家名族，爲國造縣主者，各統其族人而祭其先」。[177]這即是宗族論的大宗制、祭祀與宗族論密不可分，[178]這也是不能只單單論祭祀，而忽略宗族論的理由，[179]張載在《經學理窟．祭祀》就說得很透徹：「今既宗法不正，則無緣得祭祀正」，[180]即是沒有釐清宗法關係，祭祀不可能正當正確。職是之故，會澤的祭祀論實亦建立在他的宗族論之上，他的說法有意思的地方，即是繼承轉化張載《正蒙．乾稱》的「大君者，吾父母宗子；其大臣，宗子之家相」，[181]即在於一起祭祀天祖天孫，各群臣之後各自祭拜其祖，「其政教有奉天報祖之義」，即能有「億兆一心」與「天人之合」。

在前述「億兆一心」與「天人之合」一段以下有段小字的註腳，即引易經〈觀卦〉的彖詞「觀，盥而不薦，有孚顒若，下觀而化也。

177　會澤正志齋，《新論》〈國體．上〉，頁5。

178　參見龔鵬程，《思想與文化》（臺北：業強出版社，1986），第4章，〈宗廟制度論略〉，頁122-196。文中詳論宗廟、宗法與政治密切的關係，其中簡潔而要地說明：「廟制尤與宗法不分。有廟，即須大致依宗法來辦」，（頁153）。

179　高山大毅，〈「遅れてきた「古学」者——会沢正志斎の位置」〉，收入《日本思想史》，79．［特集］儒教の解釈学的可能性（東京，2012），頁104-130。其主張會澤正志齋的祭祀論須放在荻生徂徠的祭政一致的延長線理解，本文不否定荻生徂徠對會澤正志齋的影響，但極力主張須先將會澤定位於宋代以來封建論與郡縣論對立中大宗小宗宗法論的大脈絡之中，之後再處理荻生徂徠對會澤的影響。在東亞各國各地不少研究者如高山氏的說法陷於一國主義的思想史，對所謂宋學的理解亦太狹窄偏頗。又，荻生徂徠的祭政論實亦無脫離此論爭系譜的藩籬。高山氏的論文由交通大學藍弘岳副教授提示。

180　張載，《經學理窟．祭祀》，收於《張載集》，頁292。

181　此乃宗統君統合一的大宗宗法宗族論。

觀天之神道，四時不忒，聖人以神道設教，而天下服矣」。引這段的用意不僅僅在提示「聖人以神道設教」而已，其深意可從王弼的《周易注》對這段彖詞的詮釋得知，王弼說：「王道之可觀者，莫盛乎宗廟；宗廟之可觀者，莫盛乎『盥』也」，[182]宗廟即是大宗制宗族論與政治（「王道」）結合體現的場所。[183]會澤正志齋這種祭祀（祭政一致）的構想，正是一種國家統合的政治目的，富有國家宗教體系的性格。[184]

會澤正志齋以大宗宗法在其《新論》中建構「國體」論是有跡可尋的。他在《文稿》〈作洛論〉上中下三篇以周代制禮爲典範，將政事祭祀宗族三者合論，便是另一個極爲有力的佐證。在〈作洛論〉

---

182 王弼著，樓宇烈校釋《王弼集》，（北京：中華書局，1980），上冊，《周易注》上經，〈觀卦〉，頁315。

183 龔鵬程於《思想與文化》，第4章，〈宗廟制度論略〉，文中提到宗法是從屬於宗廟祭祀，「宗法當屬一種廟祭秩序法或宗族組成法，用以架設並鞏固宗廟制度，因此它所能達成的作用，幾乎全是宗廟制度的具體功能（如尊祖，敬宗，合族）」，見龔鵬程，《思想與文化》，第4章，〈宗廟制度論略〉，頁141。由此可知祭政一致絕非荻生徂徠獨有的觀點。按：知道宗廟的重要性，即可知爲何在明治以來伊勢神宮即被日本政府指定爲國家最高神社，因爲伊勢神宮的神主就是天祖——天照大神，也就是日本天皇的宗廟，至今每年伊始，日本總理皆率領其他內閣大臣到伊勢神宮參拜。

184 辻本雅史，《近世教育思想史の研究——日本における「公教育」思想の源流——》，第6章，〈国家主義的教育思想の源流——後期水戶学の国家意識と統合論——〉，頁308-311。又，他強調會澤的構想可以追溯到水户藩伊始以來，前期水户學對儒教的理解，即引進儒式的葬禮排斥日本常用的佛葬的儒教實踐，所以會澤的祭祀構想並非突然無中生有。而田世民以兩個《喪祭儀略》的版本流傳爲中心，考察水户藩前期的儒禮在後期水户學諸儒中的接受反應。見田世民，〈水戶藩の儒禮受容—— 喪祭儀略を中心に〉，《京都大學大學院教育學研究科紀要》，53（京都，2007），頁137-149。

下，他整篇繞著宗族立論，並將宗族論定位爲宗禮，宗禮定於周公，亦引用《周禮》的「九兩繫邦國之民，其五曰宗以族得民」支撐其論述。他接著解說宗禮的效用，宗禮是聖人所制，「能入政令所不能入」，因此能繫民。那麼，宗禮爲何呢？他直言：

「所謂宗禮者，宗子緝族以祭祖（這句亦見於《新論》〈國體上〉），稱之禮也。禮有五宗之法。大宗率小宗，小宗率群弟，長其和睦，通其有無，疾病相扶，患難相恤，以統理族人，同祭其祖於宗子之家，以致其孝敬，念祖德之心，油然而生」。[185]

由此佐證可見會澤正志齋熟知，並且運用大宗宗族論，至此業已毫無疑問，「大宗率小宗」一句更是點出他「國體」論立論的根本——宗統君統合一的大宗宗法宗族論。文中「大宗率小宗，小宗率群弟，長其和睦，通其有無，疾病相扶，患難相恤，以統理族人」實出於東漢班固（32-92）《白虎通義．宗族》「大宗能率小宗，小宗能率群弟，通於有無，所以紀理族人者也」。《白虎通義》於此句之後，接著說明大小宗之別，「宗其爲始祖後者爲大宗，此百世之所宗也。宗其爲高祖後者，五世而遷者也，高祖遷於上，宗則易於下。宗其爲曾祖後者爲曾祖宗，宗其爲祖後者爲祖宗，宗其爲父後者爲父宗。以上至高祖皆爲小宗，以其轉遷，別於大宗也。別子者，自爲其子孫爲祖，繼別也，各自爲宗」。[186]由此可斷定會澤絕不可能不熟悉大宗宗族論，[187]而且再次證明大宗宗法塑造會澤正志齋政治思想的骨

185　會澤正志齋著，名越時正編，《會澤正志齋文稿》，〈作洛論．下〉，頁74。

186　班固著，陳立注，《白虎通疏證》（北京：中華書局，1994），頁394。

187　另見會澤正志齋以宋英宗爲宋仁宗「人後」的例子，討論「爲人後」的問題，不懂大宗小宗宗法的人，根本無法在理論上討論「爲人後」的問題，暫舉一例，在「爲人後」的討論裡，一般認爲只有大宗無後須要有

幹，特別是其「國體」論述。他文章結論讚美周公定宗禮，「以長親親之恩，化民成俗，能推其所爲而功德所暨，維持人心至於八百年之久，盛哉！」[188]

會澤在《新論》中是怎麼談宗族的形而上呢？他對宗族成員的認定是建立在血脈觀之上？抑或是建在血氣觀之上呢？他娓娓道來：

> 夫萬物原於天，人本於祖，承體於父祖，稟氣於天地，故言苟及天地鬼神。雖愚夫愚婦，不能無怵動於其心，而政教禁令一出於奉天報祖之義，則民心安得不一乎，人者天地之心，心專則氣壯，故億兆一心，則天地之心專，而其氣以壯，其氣壯，而人所以稟元氣者得其全，天下之人，生而皆稟全氣，則國之風氣賴以厚，是謂天人之合也，是以民不忘古，而其俗淳厚，能報其本反其始，久而不變。[189]

這段與張載《正蒙．乾稱》關係匪淺，對比之下，從文字概念結構來看，可見會澤一方面確實承襲張載血氣觀的宗族論，又可以進一步看到對血氣觀宗族論的修改完善，使得他的宗族論與治天下更加緊密結

「人後」，小宗則否，見鄭玄注，賈公彥疏，《儀禮注疏》，卷30，〈喪服第十一〉，頁917，即云：「爲人後者，孰後？後大宗也。曷爲後大宗也？大宗者，尊之統也」。另外，會澤文中提及「司馬光謂爲人後者，不得顧私親」，他非常首肯地說：「是實萬世之公論也」。他的觀點於此亦可看出是宗統君統合一，而且君統統攝宗統的政治或國家主導宗族論。見會澤正志齋著，名越時正編，《會澤正志齋文稿》，〈宋濮議論〉，頁86-89。關於濮議與類似事件如明代大禮議等的研究，首推張壽安，《禮學考證的思想活力》，（臺北：中央研究院近代史研究所，2001），第3章〈「爲人後」：清儒論君統之獨立〉，頁215-335。

188 會澤正志齋著，名越時正編，《會澤正志齋文稿》，〈作洛論．下〉，頁75。

189 會澤正志齋，《新論》，〈國體．上〉，頁5-6。

合。在《正蒙．乾稱》「天」、「天地」、「父母」、「氣」、「萬物」、「民」等但散見於各處，仍是語錄體，並非首尾一貫的議論文體，因而需要讀者自己去串聯。在《新論》中「父祖」取代「父母」，採取一個回歸《禮記》、《儀禮》、更加純粹的男系大宗宗族論，削弱《正蒙．乾稱》中母親女性的地位，所以是「人本於祖」。在《正蒙．乾稱》萬物皆氣，但是被「天」包載其中，《新論》中的「天」被突出，而且不但是一個如同《正蒙．乾稱》中超越性的「天」，同時亦是賜予日本建國的「天」。在《新論》萬物則是「源於天」，萬物仍然是氣，但「稟氣於天地」而已，接著他接受朱子《西銘論》對張載《西銘》的修正，最後仍需「承體於父祖」。於是，會澤的宗族論是富有歷史性的血氣觀宗族論。

張載的血氣觀宗族論在政治上導向一個博愛、互助、相親、皆吾兄弟的社會，如《正蒙．乾稱》所說：「尊高年，所以長其長；慈孤弱，所以幼其幼；聖，其合德；賢，其秀也。凡天下疲癃、殘疾、惸獨、鰥寡，皆吾兄弟之顛連而無告者也」。[190]會澤正志齋有歷史的血氣觀宗族論在政治上則是導向在一個億兆一心、奉天報祖、風俗淳美、報本反始、高度團結一致的國家。這樣的國家才能應付即將到來的西方侵略。張載提出血氣觀的宗族論使得不同族的人們可以連結一起，有若一家人，突破血脈觀宗族論的局限，同時在理論上解釋何以實際上不同血脈血緣的人們可以是一家人。然而張載的這一家人的範圍卻無法清楚界定穩定下來，而可以無限擴張，甚至延伸到萬物——動物，植物等，這樣宏大博愛普遍的構思與情懷，在當時的世界的社會條件，實踐上可能就陳義過高，無從實行，即便今天全球化科技發

190　張載，《張載集》，〈正蒙．乾稱〉，頁62。

達生產條件大幅提升的世界，如此的政治願景的實現仍然遙不可及。反之，會澤正志齋的宗統君統合一的大宗宗族論切實地將宗族的範圍鎖定在天祖建國的一國之內，而這一國之內的政治，不似張載的政治願景相當平等互愛，進而容易背離周代的政治理念與範疇；會澤以「奉天報祖」爲主，上下「億兆一心」，一個君子德風，小人德草，風吹草偃而接近孔子「從周」理念的新古典中國政治願景。

他的「國體」論與封建郡縣的關係爲何呢？他基本上採取了前述伊藤東涯的看法，封建郡縣均爲因時因勢的政體制度，但「國體」的規格高於封建郡縣。這樣的看法貫穿《新論》的歷史論述。在他看來封建郡縣皆能致治，但之後皆有流弊，所以郡縣有流弊就轉而成封建，封建有流弊就轉而行郡縣，這裡郡縣封建猶如正反關係，[191]亦即《易經．繫辭上》第五章所說「一陰一陽之謂道，繼之者善也。成之者性也」，[192]乃歷史中的變與不變，唯有順應其變才是。這是他在封建郡縣論中很獨具一格的說法。後期水戶學非常器重《易經》，藩主德川齊昭撰寫的《弘道館記》，碑文就在弘道館完全中國建築式樣的八卦堂裡。[193]文中亦提起「國體」一詞，而「國體」所依據的即是「天地位焉，萬物育焉」，[194]雖說是出自《中庸》的「致中和，天地位

191 會澤正志齋，《新論》，〈國體．中〉，頁17-24。

192 伊藤東涯，《周易經翼通解》收於《漢文大系16．周易．傳習錄》，（臺北：新文豐，1978），卷17，頁8-9。

193 名越時正，《水户藩弘道館とその教育》（茨城：茨城縣教師會，1972），頁9。

194 德川齊昭在《弘道館記》中說到：「弘道之館何爲而設也。恭惟上古神聖、立極垂統、天地位焉、萬物育焉。其所以照臨六合、統御宇 者、未曾不由斯道也。寶祚以之無窮，國體以之尊嚴、蒼生以之安寧、蠻夷戎狄以之率服」。見瀨谷義彥、今井三郎、尾藤正英，《日本思想大系53．水戶学》（東京：岩波書店，1973），頁422-426。

焉，萬物育焉」，在此更是源自《易經》繫辭、說卦等中演繹的宇宙論，[195]緊密呼應上面《新論》所言及的「天人相合」，同時解釋水戶藩為何會刻意築八卦堂供奉「弘道館記」的碑文。

在《新論．國體上》，他設問「保四海長安久治天下不動搖」要依賴什麼呢？他說就在「億兆一心，皆親其上而不忍離之實」。換句話說即是所有人都有「共同的心理，認同執政者或國家」。[196]這個「共同的心理與認同國家」不就是民族主義所欲塑造的認同嗎？實在這裡固有虛實之實意，更有實體，實物，果實之實意，是故，「國體」的不能只讀成體用之體，而是實有其物。這國體維持的原理為何呢？就是要有「君臣之義，父子之親」，這乍看之下可能很像一般儒家的教忠教孝，但細看則非，其一，君臣他沒說忠，他只說義，而義是天地之大義，父子他也沒說孝，他僅強調親，親則是天下之至恩。所以，維持國體在於做到「大義」與「至恩」；其二，之後他又對忠孝有新解，他說：「忠以貴貴，孝以親親」。這是很有意思的說法，忠不再是忠君而已，而是要寶貴尊貴或值得寶貴的事物，孝亦非聽從父親，而是與該親熱親近的人親近親熱。這就是何以他提到日本的武士時如此批評他們，「能為其主死，而名義不明，其忠非忠，其孝非孝」；其三，這樣的忠孝觀頓時從儒家的五倫中解放出來，進而投向想像的公共空間——「國體」。

195 參看伊藤東涯，《周易經翼通解》〈繫辭〉，卷17，第7章「天地設位，而易行乎其中矣，成性存存，道義之門」，頁12-13。卷18，〈序卦〉，頁36，其中有「有天地然後萬物生焉」，又，卷18〈序卦下篇〉，頁38，從天地萬物言及父子君臣上下。通觀德川齊昭《弘道館記》全文收於《日本思想大系53．水戸学》，頁422-426，亦未提及中和中庸，便知其意更近於易經。

196 會澤正志齋，《新論》，〈國體．上〉，頁2。

會澤正志齋想像的公共空間或新日本實際上到底爲何？德川幕府在此新的想像共同體內的地位爲何呢？會澤正志齋畢竟是德川幕府下德川「御三家」的家臣，所以，雖然他相對化封建與郡縣，他並不主張推倒幕府建立郡縣制，直接由天皇親政。他的想法毋寧是一個代表天祖之天皇家爲所有大宗之首，再由其代理德川幕府領導他諸侯，各諸侯帶領其管轄下人民之各大宗，一個試圖在現實與理念見取得平衡的一個方案。但是，從他對封建與郡縣的討論，他在理論上卻又有非常開放的態度。他可以接受一個沒有封建制的新日本，換句話說，即是一個沒有德川幕府與沒有他所屬水戶藩的日本。會澤正志齋在《新論》中對現實德川幕藩體制的曖昧兩義，造成後來水戶藩裡分裂爲兩派，以水戶藩藩校弘道館爲中心掌權的「諸生門閥黨」與以水戶藩諸多鄉校爲據點的尊皇攘夷「天狗黨」，兩黨的出現，可以詮釋爲對《新論》兩個解讀的對峙。[197]這個對峙最後在1864年爆發了所謂的天狗黨之亂，天狗黨在築波山（今茨城縣築波市）興師，此後幾年兩黨廝殺慘烈，到了明治維新，水戶藩人才消耗殆盡，難怪明治政府領導層無水戶人。[198]

---

197 星山京子亦強調後期水户學，特別是會澤正志齋思想的「多義性」，並不能僅從尊王攘夷的角度來掌握，會澤的開明與對西學的興趣不可輕估。見星山京子，〈後期水户學と近代——會澤正志齋を中心に〉，《大航海》，67（東京：2008），頁58-65。此說與本文對會澤正志齋《新論》的詮釋互通。

198 J. Victor Koschmann以「保守」形容諸生黨，以「激進」形容天狗黨。參見此章對兩黨從1864至1869年間的衝突有詳盡的敘述分析，幕末沒有一個藩內部的衝突激烈過於水户藩。見J. Victor Koschmann, *The Mito Ideology: Discourse, Reform, and Insurrection in Late Tokugawa Japan, 1790-1864*（Berkeley: University of California Press, 1987）, Chapter 5, pp. 152-172.

行文至此，無論如何閱讀《新論》，會澤正志齋的「國體」論中一個有始祖的想像政治共同體已然形成，一個共同的民族想像已經幾乎呼應而出，只剩下「所有民皆爲一族」的「民族」與「天照大神爲萬民之始祖」兩項而已。東亞民族主義與民族想像的理論輪廓已經勾勒而出，這是一個相當漫長的歷史過程，從宋代迤邐而至日本文政年間／清道光年間，跨越中日兩國，起於中國大陸，成於日本列島，後從明治日本經由滯日東亞各國士人，再流向中國、朝鮮與越南，引發現代東亞史上的巨大海嘯，因而物換星移，面目全非。不過，這個輪廓還需再度上妝才會隆重面世。這就要等到明治後期，日本公布明治憲法前後了。

3.「民族」的誕生——從穗積八束到東亞

明治22年（1889）日本政府頒布「大日本帝國憲法」，同年不到30歲的穗積八束（1860-1912）從德國回日本到（東京）帝國大學法學院任教，不久即對明治憲法提出一系列的詮釋，在日本影響至巨，其憲法學中的「民族論」與「國體論」承襲轉化會澤正志齋的「國體論」，成爲從明治到戰前日本擁護天皇中心政治體制主要的憲法解釋與政治理論，[199]更是完成了東亞民族主義與民族論，使得在上下幾百年，橫跨中日兩國的封建郡縣爭議中發展的大宗制宗族論中的「宗

199　穗積八束的憲法理論雖然擁護體制，但與日本官方的關係一直微妙，直到1937年日本文部省印行《國體之本義》，才可說是成爲官方的御用理論。另一方面，在憲法學界的地位，自大正時期（1912-1926）始，便爲東大法學部同事美濃部達吉的「天皇機關說」憲法理論所取代，到了1935年日本政府發布「國體明徵聲明」，「天皇機關說」在政治上淪爲異端，穗積八束的憲法理論才又在憲法學界取回主導之位。

族」與「宗法」正式搖身一變爲「民族」與「民族主義」，籠罩此後東亞各國的政治，至今欲罷不能。

他的憲法論核心即爲「民族」與「國體」，在1896年出版的《憲政大意》，他開宗明義說「國家」是「民族的團體」，並非如多數學者以爲爲獨立平等的個人結合的團體，他極力否認國家建立在個人與個人間的契約，他甚至痛詆由契約而產生憲法是爲了限制國家權力，以伸張個人權利的主張，他認爲這種主張不啻以野生禽獸爲人生的生活目的。[200]他接著點出統治的主權即在「國體」，「國體」出於國民相信「主權所在」的歷史，他又說明主權乃國家之意思。「國家意思」自然與「人」有意思是一樣的，「國家意思」如何形成的歷史遂區分「國體」爲兩類，其一爲「君主國體」，其二則爲「民主國體」。他說「以特定一個人的意思權力爲國家的意思權力即爲「君主國體」，以人民眾多之意思權力爲國家之意思權力則爲「民主國體」（作者譯，以下譯文皆是）」。[201]

這個區別的判斷在主權成立的形態。他的說法有意思的地方在於「國體」以下，他又有「政體」的區別。他定義「所謂政體乃爲涉指統治主權之行動形式」。[202]他的「君主國體」「民主國體」，不是亞里士多德以來西方政治思想思考模式的「君主制」、「貴族制」、「民主制」或「一位」、「少數」、「多數」三種政治形態意義的區分，亞里士多德的區分對他而言是所謂的「政體」，這裡他的思考模式依然亦步亦趨伊藤東涯以來，特別是會澤正志齋的模式：「國體」之下有

200 穗積八束，《憲法大意》，（日本：穗積八束博士遺稿憲政大意發行所，1917［1896］），第1章，〈國家ノ觀念〉，頁1-17。

201 穗積八束，《憲法大意》，第2章，〈國體政體ノ辨〉，頁18。

202 穗積八束，《憲法大意》，第2章，〈國體政體ノ辨〉，頁19。

「封建」「郡縣」。蓋「國體」之形成乃歷史過程之結晶，爲不可變革之物；「政體」則是因時可遷。所以同樣的「國體」可以有不同的「政體」，不同的「國體」可以有相同的「政體」。他指出歷來政治討論混同「國體」「政體」是造成政治禍機的原因，所以他強調「變革國體是革命，變革政體是改正」，立憲政治是針對「政體」而言，非對「國體」。[203]他區分政體有兩大類，其一權力分立，其二專制。他指出很多西人混同民主主義與權力分立，民主主義由來已久，並非嶄新。他分析19世紀上半歐洲政治動盪不安原因在皆爲混同「國體」與「政體」與沒有區分「民主主義」與「權力分立」而導致的。[204]

對穗積八束而言，日本的「國體」爲何呢？他基本上只是將會澤正志齋深奧語言轉成淺顯易懂以及與西方接軌的法律政治術語，同時直截了當將會澤正志齋原來隱而未發或言猶未盡的論點，推到邏輯上可有的結論。他說：「大日本帝國乃萬世一系天皇之統治。此天壤無窮之國體，經數千年之歷史，其根底愈深，因民族一致確信之，而愈加鞏固，政體雖有變遷而未嘗動搖其基礎之毫末。抑我建國之根本乃在於我固有之家制，我固有之家制乃以祖先崇拜統一血族團體之謂也」。[205]此段表明民族出於日本「家」制——大宗制。同時三言兩語將國學派的歷史神話與會澤正志齋的儒學化歷史交代的很清楚了當。日本憲法學學者長尾龍一從卡爾·施密特（Carl Schmitt）理論將穗積八束的「國體」論爲詮釋一種「政治神學」（political theology），[206]的

203 穗積八束，《憲法大意》，第2章，〈國體政體ノ辨〉，頁19-20。
204 穗積八束，《憲法大意》，第2章，〈國體政體ノ辨〉，頁20-23。
205 穗積八束，《憲法大意》，第3章，〈我カ國體〉，頁24。
206 長尾龍一，《日本国家思想史研究》（東京：創文社，1982）。特別是第一部的第1、2章。

確是極為敏銳透徹的見解，其實，依此觀之，會澤正志齋的「國體」論已經是「政治神學」。只是長尾龍一的「政治神學」所指的是國學派日本歷史神話的世俗化（secularisation）與政治化，更加確切精準無誤的理解應是儒家大宗宗法的始祖崇拜，這才是會澤正志齋與穗積八束的「政治神學」的本質。[207]

接下來的展開如同畫龍點睛，他說：「民族乃是有共同祖先之人民之義。統治民族者即是保護民族始祖之子孫之威靈，萬世一系之皇位。」[208]他又說：「皇位乃神聖不可侵犯，此乃天祖之靈位為國家主權之本位，世世代代之天皇為代天祖之位而居之，天皇以其遺愛統治此民族，若皇位為神聖，則主權亦為神聖，視此崇敬之意惟我國體有之。」[209]在此，「民族」是所有人民有「一個共同的始祖」，所由人民皆為一族，天祖是日本始祖，居其位者的天皇是民族之祖之大宗。後來在1900年〈憲法の精神〉一文，他又重申此意，他說：「我民族乃同族之血類，追想我萬世一系之皇位乃民族始祖天祖之靈位也」。[210]同一篇中又不厭其煩申明「天賦之主權者為民族之共同始祖，我萬世

207 長尾龍一的斷定出於Carl Schmitt（施密特）, trans by George Schwab, *Political Theology: Four Chapters on the Concept of Sovereignty*（Chicago: University of Chicago Press, 2005）, Chapter 3, p. 36，特別是第一句「所有顯著的現代國家理論概念全都是世俗化的神學概念（作者譯）」，至此本文已經很詳細的分析「民族」與「國體」兩個現代東亞重要的政治概念都是源自儒家的大宗宗族論，與日本國學派的關係很次要表面，不過卻部分說明何以「國體」在東亞其他國家不具有在日本政治的地位，有效解釋日本與東亞其他各國最大不同之處。

208 穗積八束，《憲法大意》，第3章，〈我カ國體〉，頁25。

209 穗積八束，《憲法大意》，第3章，〈我カ國體〉，頁28-29。

210 穗積八束，〈憲法の精神〉，收入長尾龍一編，《穗積八束集》（東京：信山社，2001［1900］），頁19。

之皇位爲我民族始祖天祖之靈位，其直系之皇統繼承此位，代表天祖之威靈，以天祖之慈愛臨其子孫」。[211]這裡反復致意的正是會澤正志齋所謂的「天地之大義」與「天地之大恩」。總而言之，穗積八束這樣的政治想像，實乃宗統君統合一大宗宗法的政治構想。

似穗積八束如此論述「民族」與「始祖」在當時日本不乏其人，如磯部武者五郎《國體述義》（1892）中就有「我日本人民爲四千萬人之一大族，其先祖爲一」、「我王室爲四千萬人之宗家」，或井上了圓在《日本倫理學案》（1893）說「億兆人民皆是皇室之臣下，同時亦是皇室皇族之末裔」或中西牛郎《教育宗教衝突斷案》（1893）中有「我邦皇統爲天孫，日本國民皆同其祖先，皆同一祖先之分派」。[212]宗族論於是蛻變爲民族論，在早一兩百年前尚難以想像的所有人皆爲同一族人，霎時間遂變得十分自然普遍的「事實」。後來1937年日本政府文部省編一了本《國體之本義》當成學校必修教材，其中就通俗化穗積八束的論述，[213]頻頻強調日本皇室是「國民的宗家」，[214]這就是擴大到全日本民族的大宗制說法，但是對日本起源的敘述，卻回到使用國學派的語言——大和語，例如天祖改回天照大神等，這可以看出國學派的語言論在彼時日本已經取得上風。

日本對「民族」的想像論述自然感染到當時滯留過日本的許多東亞士人，不過日本的「國體」論則是往往橘逾淮爲枳，雖不若在二次

211 穗積八束，〈憲法の精神〉，頁24。

212 以上皆出於安田浩，《近代天皇制国家の歴史的位置——普遍性と特殊性を読みとく視座》，（東京：大月書店，2011），頁36-37。

213 文部省，《国体の本義》，（東京：文部省，1937）。

214 「國民的宗家」可上溯到張載〈正蒙‧乾始〉「大君者，吾父母之宗子，其大臣，宗子之家相也」。見張載，《張載集》，〈正蒙‧乾始〉，頁62。

世界大戰前日本舉足輕重的地位，卻竟亦影響毛澤東的憲法思想，而成爲中國人民共和國憲法實踐與理論的一部分。[215]但是中國朝鮮越南的民族主義不同於日本的民族主義其中最突出的一點，即是沒有照單全收日本的「國體」論，且「國體」一詞在中朝越三國的政治與政治思想史中亦不占有如「國體」在日本的重要性。米原謙形容日本的民族主義爲「國體民族主義」，雖無法涵蓋中日朝越的民族主義，勾勒東亞的共同處，但用以凸顯日本與中朝越的差異，亦甚有獨到之見，況且國體一詞本出自大宗論，因此「國體民族主義」可說是「東亞民族主義」下的細目或從屬概念（sub-category）。[216]

「國體」在中國的使用往往等同「政體」，例如《清帝遜位詔書》中有而「徒以國體一日不決」一句，此處的「國體」即近於「政體」。不過在明治以來日本的政治思想脈絡，「國體」則最有兩種常見的用法。其一則是以穗積八束爲代表，視「國體」與「政體」有別。其二則是以美濃部達吉爲代表，將「國體」等同「政體」，同時不認爲「國體」是憲法學上的概念，僅僅是倫理社會的概念。[217]

---

215 林來梵深入淺出的概觀，考察「國體」此一概念在古今日本與中國的流變，文中提起穗積八束在中國的影響，主要在清末學部右侍郎達壽與梁啓超兩人。見林來梵，〈國體概念史〉，《中國社會科學》，3（北京，2013），頁73-78。

216 米原謙、金鳳珍、區建英，《東アジアのナショナリズムと近代——なぜ対立するのか》（大阪：大阪大学出版会，2011），第1章，〈「国体」の創造——日本（1）〉，頁19-49。

217 藤井隆將「國體」與「政體」的使用分爲三類，第一類與第二類最大的差別在於第一類認爲一個「國體」不可變，「政體」可變，第二類認爲一個「國體」可變，「政體」可變。此外，第二類的「國體」與「政體」爲德語「staatsform」與「regierungsform」的對照翻譯日語。第三類則是美濃部達吉的用法。其中第二類用法最爲常見。見藤井隆，〈政体論から「開明専制論」を読む〉，《修道法学》34：2（広島，2012），頁25-

不過，「民族」卻非如「國體」，而是相當完完整整在東亞各處傳播接受，其中最主要的原因乃是中國日本朝鮮越南在「民族」論形成以前，都已經有宋代以來共同的思想基礎與方向，特別是封建郡縣之辨下的大宗小宗宗族論。著名的民族主義者章太炎在〈社會通詮商兌〉通篇「民族主義」一詞到處可見，其中也有「復我民族之國家」，[218]以「民族」爲主體發揮政治主張。這種近似鸚鵡學舌的呼籲，在清末民初革命黨人中比比皆是。[219]在文中他最有意思的看法即是，他肯定中國宗族（文中用宗法社會一詞）在過去的功能，但現在則需「以四百兆人爲一族，而無問其氏姓世系」，[220]再來演繹立足「民族主義」的組織如會黨如何可以消解「宗法社會」，進而說明爲何「宗法社會」已經完成其歷史功能，而需要被淘汰，這個過程彷彿由戰國諸國林立走向大一統的帝國。[221]章太炎的說法扼要地道盡從「宗族」是如何走向「民族」，這也註定「宗族」功成身退，掩埋在歷史的洪流

81。按：第一類與第二類皆認爲有「國體」、「政體」二分，其實可以歸爲一類，故兩類而非三類。此外，亦有朱子學學者、後改信基督教的中村正直（1832-1891）在〈審國體〉一文，將會澤源自《公羊傳》的國體改爲朱子學的國體，他說：「國體者何，理直之謂也，治內者理直，則域內之民，莫不服從，治外者理直，則域外之國，莫敢干犯……理直則名正言順。可以事神，可以治民，是之謂國體」。轉引自河野有理編，《近代日本政治思想史——荻生徂徠から網野善彦まで》，（京都：ナカニシヤ出版，2014），頁117。此處的直要做「直內方外」的「直」解。

218 章太炎，《章氏叢書》（臺北：世界書局，1982），下，頁828。

219 例如：劍南〈私心說〉：「我四百兆民族，皆我同胞，而爲我黃祖黃帝軒轅之子孫，雖散處於莽莽神州，而究竟不失爲同一血胤」。轉引自黃克武，〈從追求正道到認同國族：明末至清末中國公私觀念的重整〉，收入黃克武、張哲嘉主編，《公與私：近代中國個體與群體之重建》，（臺北：中央研究院近代史研究所，2000），頁106。

220 章太炎，《章氏叢書》，下，頁829。

221 章太炎，《章氏叢書》，下，頁830。

裡。

稍後，孫中山在《三民主義》〈民族主義第五講〉裡是如何論述民族主義呢？其實，同出一轍。他說：「中國人對於家族與宗族的觀念是很深的。譬如有兩個中國人在路上遇見了，交談之後，請問貴姓大名，只要彼此知道是同宗，便是非常親熱，都是認爲同姓的伯叔兄弟。由這種好觀念推廣出來，便可由宗族主義擴充到民族主義」，[222] 接著他又敘述這個擴充的過程與目的，他說：「用宗族的小基礎，來做擴充國族的功夫」，又說「把各姓的宗族團體，先聯合起來，更由宗族團體，結合成一個民族的大團體，要抵抗外國人，積極上自然有辦法」。職是之故，雖然清末民初宗族間的聯宗活動熱鬧一時，但宗族的聯宗在此只是一個促成民族主義的工具，摶合中華民族過渡期的階段，而非新時代的重要組成制度。[223]

回顧宗族論從先秦一路蜿蜒曲折迤邐到20世紀的民族主義；先有漢代《毛傳》「王者天下之大宗」的宗統君統合一與《鄭箋》「別子爲祖」之宗統君統二分的對立，中間經過封建郡縣爭論復出下的宋代，由心儀周道的張載，高舉建立在血氣觀的「民吾同胞」宗統君統合一之大宗宗族論。反對封建的朱子立足在血脈觀，倡導宗統君統二

222 孫中山，《三民主義》，〈民族主義第五講〉，頁56。

223 山田賢對聯宗運動情況有詳細的討論，他亦提到聯宗之所以成立是建立在中華民族有共同祖先的歷史觀（文中沒有用始祖一詞）。見山田賢，〈「宗族」から「民族」へ——近代中国における「国民国家」と忠誠のゆくえ〉，收入久留島浩、趙景達編，《国民国家の比較史》（東京：有志舍，2010），頁115-136。本文的標題與山田賢的論文標題相同〈從宗族到民族〉，兩篇論文從截然不同的角度切入，山田賢由中國地域社會史，本文則是東亞思想史，而達到類似的結論，亦是相互佐證。然山田賢的論文先出，於此識之，不敢掠美。

分之小宗宗族論，兩系遂爭鋒相對，脈絡分明；一系是試圖恢復封建／井田／大宗／宗統君統合一／血氣觀，另一系則是大力護持郡縣／阡陌／小宗／宗統君統二分／血脈觀，這個東亞政治思想史上，唐宋以來旗幟鮮明的對峙，直到19世紀中葉東亞在日本除外的中國，朝鮮，越南皆由朱子代表的系統取得上風，成爲體制內的官學，廣爲服膺。最後跨過一衣帶水到江戶日本——東亞唯一接近周代封建的政治社會體制。日本的封建體制提供封建／井田／大宗／宗統君統合一／血氣觀一系繼續發展茁壯的空間，從江戶伊始，封建郡縣之爭論即在缺乏觸犯皇權的危險以及不存在挑戰體制禁忌之下展開，於是封建論便大行於日本，後由會澤正志齋化解封建郡縣之爭，整合張載朱子之歧義，繼承荻生徂徠之政治儒學或儒學的政治轉向（political turn），[224]提出「億兆一心」的國體論，進而創造出一個宗統君統合一的大宗宗族政治想像，一個實際上幾乎是「民族」國家（nation-state）的願景。

明治日本眾多的士人學者，特別是穗積八束，將此水到渠成的世俗化政治化大宗宗族思想發展，受到西方民族主義政治經驗啓示之後，套上一些18世紀以來西方法政的術語，遂很輕易地轉換爲民族主義與民族國家的藍圖。甲午戰爭後，由於中國慘敗，中日在東亞國際政治中正式易位，日本立刻成爲東亞政治文化的新中心，中國、朝鮮、越南士人大量湧入日本東京等地，很快就駕輕就熟掌握到這套源自儒家宗統君統合一大宗宗法的民族主義，各自回國後便大力宣揚民族大義，遂在東亞澎湃展開，但是一開始並非一帆風順，而是與東亞

224　荻生徂徠的政治儒學博大精深，爲朱子、王陽明暨清初三子之後東亞第一大儒，但非系出公羊學，徂徠先生經學經世義理文章皆臻上上乘，更有高徒濟濟，扶翼發揚師說。

體制內既有的傳統有一番驚濤駭浪的格鬥後，才脫穎而出，以下會做更詳細的交代。

四、東亞民族主義的「始祖論」

(一)「始祖論」獨霸以前

在東亞民族主義出籠以後，一開始並非立刻席捲東亞各國，各國抵抗排斥民族主義的力量其實不可小覷，這股反對民族主義的力量來自既有的知識統治階層以外，亦有令人想不到的「東亞主義」。東亞各國既有的知識統治階層不支持民族主義的理由大概與歐洲舊體制內反民族主義的理由相差無幾，因爲民族主義往往要求政治改革與新的社會制度安排，舊體制不覺得對己有利，但這只是一種守舊守成的抗拒。眞正能挑戰東亞民族主義還是「東亞主義」而已。[225]

在17世紀至19世紀的東亞，有一點與歐洲截然不同——即是區域內的（古典）「通用語文」（lingua franca）完全不同的地位。在歐洲這段時間是作爲「通用文」的拉丁文逐漸被各國的本國語取代，知識界從17世紀開始，拉丁文的著作愈來愈少。霍布斯就是一個有象徵性的例子，他在早年寫《市民論》（*De Cive*）時用拉丁文，到後來寫《列維坦》（*Leviathan*）時改爲英文，雖然後來他又將《列維坦》翻成拉丁文，但後來在英國像他這樣主要的思想家就再也沒人用拉丁文寫作。歐洲的情況與一般民族主義研究指出的情況相當符合——即是各國白話文的興盛促進民族意識的浮起，民族主義的推動有助於本

225 在本文中的「東亞主義」有別於「亞洲主義」（Asianism），「東亞主義」以同文爲基礎，「亞洲主義」以同黃種爲出發點。

國文體的推廣。[226]

東亞的情況恰恰相反，在17世紀時日本用漢文寫作的並不多，而且文章多帶有和語氣息（有語病），就連中華崇拜者，許多人認爲日本第一大儒荻生徂徠的漢文也有語病，他的著作大約只有一半左右是以漢文寫的。一個世紀後，19世紀的前半部，以《日本外史》、《日本政記》等發揮天皇中心史觀而風靡全日本的賴山陽，除了私人信件以外，所有著作清一色皆以漢文寫作。[227]從文章的寫作水準來看19世紀日本漢文的清通流暢遠遠高於18世紀，即使今天18世紀儒者的著作比較受到重視，一般也認爲比較有創見，18世紀日本的漢文寫作水準是比不上19世紀的日本。試想一本奠定日本／東亞民族主義的著作——《新論》竟是用漢文撰寫的，設若放到歐洲的歷史脈絡，實在很難想像費希特（Johann Gottlieb Fichte）用拉丁文或法語寫《告我德意志民族》（*Reden an die deutsche Nation*）。

所以，19世紀雖是東亞民族主義奠定之刻，一個從「宗族走到民族」的過程，同時，東亞各國共同漢文圈文化的純熟與著作交流亦達到歷史高峰。這是東亞民族主義興起時所須直接面對的現實。這兩個潛在相對抗的力量就在東亞民族主義隨著「民族」一詞傳播開後的1890年代到1911年，在中國與朝鮮展開了激烈的廝殺。在朝鮮，根據史丹佛大學Gi-Wook Shin的研究，在1895至1905朝鮮報紙的社論

226 Peter Burke主張歐洲各國白話文興起的時間要上推到15世紀，而非先前現代主義者的民族主義研究這所説的1800爲分水嶺。見Peter Burke, "Nationalisms and Vernaculars, 1500-1800", in John Breuilly ed., *The Oxford Handbook of the History of Nationalism*（Oxford: Oxford University Press, 2013), pp. 21-35.

227 請參看木崎愛吉、賴成一共編，《賴山陽全書》，（東京：国書刊行会，1983［1932］）。

評論支持「東亞主義」亦即「中日朝同盟論」，居然比支持民族主義的言論多了不少。[228]

同樣的情況在清末中國亦可看到。沈松僑很細膩地考察黃帝在清末如何成爲中華民族的始祖，其中不少例子皆可爲本文佐證，這個經緯亦可說是在一個文化主義與民族主義互相激盪中，兩個不同的想像共同體藉由「孔子紀年」與「黃帝紀年」的論爭中呈現，之後又轉爲「國民主義」對抗「種族革命」，在持續的兩股勢力僵持中，民族主義最後的勝出也並非必然，沈松僑認爲清廷不積極才使得民族主義最後站上風。[229]無論是孔子紀年的文化主義亦或是後來的國民主義，兩者皆與東亞主義聲氣相通，亦即是不採取以保衛所謂「民族」爲第一義的方式來建構一個對付外在威脅，西方挑戰的現代國家。由中國朝鮮兩國的例子來看，民族主義均在與「東亞主義」一番生死格鬥後才贏取各國政治的主導權。

（二）東亞各國的「始祖」

在東亞各國接納了東亞民族主義與民族觀以後，皆不約而同的高舉各國「始祖」，發明出形形色色的新文化政治象徵。先以日本爲例，早在室町時期僧人巖圓月就提出日本天皇的祖先是吳泰伯，泰伯

---

228 Gi-Wook Shin, *Ethnic Nationalism in Korea: Genealogy, Politics, and Legacy* (California: Stanford University Press, 2006), pp. 25-40.

229 沈松僑，〈我以我血薦軒轅——黃帝神話與晚清的國族建構〉，《臺灣社會研究季刊》28：12（臺北，1997），頁1-77。又，參看山室信一，《思想課題としてのアジア——基軸・連鎖・投企》（東京：岩波書店，2001），頁404-407。書中提到中國的黃帝紀年與朝鮮的檀君紀元皆取法自日本的神武紀元。

之後從吳渡海到日本，成爲天皇的祖先。在江戶時期，這所謂的泰伯皇祖說在儒者間頗爲風行，而且自江戶儒學開山祖師爺藤原惺窩與林羅山就倡導此說，[230]林羅山以泰伯附會神道傳說，以泰伯爲天照大神，但是在參與官方著述時，林羅山並不採取泰伯皇祖說。之後其子林鵞峰、其孫林鳳岡紹述、闡揚泰伯皇祖說，門下之中亦不少，當然，反對意見在儒者間亦不少。[231]且自國學派提出天照大神爲皇祖以後，水戶學如會澤正志齋的接納，即表示到19世紀中葉，泰伯皇祖說已經是過往雲煙。

朝鮮的情況相當有啓發性，在20世紀以前，朝鮮尊崇向來是箕子，原因很簡單，因爲箕子是商朝貴冑，後來到朝鮮半島建國朝鮮延續至今。尊崇箕子不只是尊崇中國而已，更是強調朝鮮系出中國，而非蠻夷。不過，甲午戰爭後，中國大敗，中國在朝鮮的威信一落千丈，加上朝鮮逐漸已經從日本接受東亞型的民族主義，祭祀尊崇的對象遂開始從箕子轉移到檀君，檀君於是被被認爲是朝鮮的始祖。申采浩（1880-1936）在其《讀史新論》（1908）中將朝鮮歷史上推到檀君建國，即西元前2333年前，此書亦是很清楚的將自己定位爲大韓民族史，也是試圖將中國去中心化的里程碑。[232]只是檀君第一次在文獻上出現，則是在高麗時期13世紀末，目前也沒有任何考古證據支持檀君的存在。不過，這一點也不重要，「始祖」的創出，本來就是一種神話／迷思的創出，一個信者恆信，不信者恆不信的情況，民族主

230 前田勉，《兵学と朱子学・蘭学・国学——近代日本思想史の構図》（東京：平凡社，2006），頁119-120。

231 吳偉明，〈日本德川前期吳太伯論的思想史意義〉，《新史學》，25：3（臺北, 2014），頁143-169。

232 Andre Schmid, *Korea Between Empires*, 1815-1919, pp. 180-187.

義就是要達成一國之中，絕大多數的人相信「民族」神話／迷思。這點在日本的始祖論中是最誇張的，因爲日本的始祖是具有神格的。

越南的情況亦大同小異；根據奇思・泰勒（Keith Taylor），現代越南歷史的敘述，均無一言談及炎帝，而是從越南民族的「始祖」雒龍君說起。[233]這也很有意思，因爲常常被認爲是越南民族主義的源頭的《大越史記全書》，從15世紀末黎朝開始一直陸續編纂到19世紀最後的阮朝。這本書對抗中國的意識極強，但並非兩個民族間的對立，毋寧是兩個政治體的對立，進而從歷史上尋求越南政治體的獨立與合法性。書中凡例中說：「其記始於吳王者，王我越人，當南北（讀爲越南中國，作者注）分爭之時，能撥亂興邦，以繼雄王趙武之統故也」。也有提到「北朝歷代主皆書帝，與我各帝一方也」，[234]明顯有分庭抗禮之意。在這本書中，越南的建國則上推到炎帝。書中越南始於涇陽王，涇陽王是炎帝三世孫帝明到五嶺時與當地的女子生了涇陽王，涇陽王同父異母的哥哥是帝宜，帝明則「立帝宜爲嗣，治北方」。帝明封涇陽王於南，治南方。涇陽王的兒子就是雒龍君。[235]所以，在「東亞型民族主義」進入越南以前，就算與中國有抗衡之意的《大越史記全書》仍然強調越南爲炎帝之後，全書中越關係皆放在南北關係中理解，就是前述所謂「各帝一方」。可是現代越南史的敘述卻切斷與中國的關係，這與朝鮮末期，當代韓國不是異曲同工嗎？

中國的情況，論之者眾，此處僅強調少有人提及的黃帝成爲中

233 Keith Weller Taylor, *The Birth of Vietnam* (Berkeley: University of California Press, 1983), pp. 1-7.

234 陳荊和編校，《大越史記全書》，（東京：東京大学東洋文化研究所，1986，校合本），頁67。

235 陳荊和編校，《大越史記全書》，頁84、97。

國，中華民族的始祖這個想法到底從何而來。本文已經很清楚說明來源，不過還借當時當事者劉師培之口，在其〈黃帝紀年說〉一文有很坦白的交代，他說：「故中國之有黃帝、猶日本之有神武天皇也、取法日本、擇善而從」。[236]還有在黃帝變成中華民族的始祖以前，東亞各國包括中國，所最尊崇為孔子，周公，周文王，商湯，堯舜等，這些在黃帝為始祖的中華人民共和國與中華民國都淪為只是歷史上著名或惡名昭彰的人物而已。但是，有始祖的民族主義的確是兩岸不少人的共同情懷，黃帝也成為一個超越性的效忠對象。兩岸支持統一或傾向統一的人很多皆訴諸「中華民族」與「黃帝」。[237]臺灣歌手李建復的「黃山」，馬森寫的歌詞，就是將此民族主義感情演繹得淋漓盡致。歌詞中「黃帝子孫凝聚在一起，凝聚在一起，大鵬的翼，大鵬的翼，飛翔在故國山河的高空裡」道盡不少人的心聲。

東亞的始祖論於是有脫離政治的中國中心主義（以中國為中心的朝貢冊封體系），也有打破文化中國中心論（東亞共同文化教養的孔子儒學漢字漢文等），換取的是一個嶄新的效忠對象，一個有「始祖」的「民族」本位國家觀與歷史觀，一個遠離孔子的國度。然而，

236 劉師培著，李妙根編，《劉師培辛亥前文選》（北京：三聯書店，1998），〈黃帝紀年說〉，頁3。

237 馬英九在2013年雙十國慶大會的致詞裡，就提到「兩岸人民同屬中華民族，兩岸關係不是國與國的關係」。見中華民國總統府官網：http://www.president.gov.tw/Default.aspx?tabid=131&itemid=30931&rmid=514（2014/2/16）。還有連戰七次到中國大陸，卻從來沒有到過曲阜，只有去黃帝陵祭拜黃帝，至少兩次。另一位國民黨前主席吳伯雄也只有去黃帝陵祭拜。這比起日本總理福田康夫2007年12月到中國正式官方訪問時，特地抽空到曲阜孔廟致敬形成鮮明對比，有趣的是，日本網上網友普遍譴責福田康夫罵他賣國，不是又值得令人深省嗎。2012年習近平就任中國共產黨總書記時的講話裡中華民族一詞出現約23次。

弔詭的是，「東亞型民族主義」其實是宋明儒學宗族論在封建郡縣難分難捨之爭下展開，明末清初，東移日本，爾後發展而出的集大成，這豈非宋明清諸大儒始料所不及之也乎！

（三）東亞始祖論與西洋政治思想中的「始祖」

穗積八束在憲法學中對「國體」的分類與討論乍看的確令人覺得他似乎對西方政治思想有很大的誤解，只要稍微細讀便知，他「國體」論中所謂的「民主國體」，其實指的就是以社會契約做爲政原論或說是政治權力與政治社會來源的基礎，接近斯金納所謂「人民」（populist）的國家論，[238]這也是他大力反對的對象，他的「君主國體」一方面是支持天皇制（他沒主張天皇親政），一方面則是欲以歷史證成君主國體的絕對性，有機性，接近斯金納所謂的「絕對主義」（absolutist）的國家論。另一方面，穗積八束的「國體」是一個「擬制的身體」（corpus fictum），其實近乎斯金納所謂「虛擬」（fictional）的國家論，也就是不管是「君主」（absolutist）國體，還是「民主」（populist）國體都是法人意義下的區別。受過19世紀德國法學訓練的穗積八束如此整理提煉原來在會澤正志齋裡就有的區別，[239]一點也不令人意外。

理查．米尼爾（Richard H Minear）發現穗積八束所受到的19世紀德國法學影響，主要是保羅．拉班德（Paul Laband）的法律實證主

238 Quentin Skinner, "A Genealogy of the Modern State," *Proceedings of the British Academy*, 162 (2009), pp. 325-370.

239 會澤正志齋的《新論》裡頭，是國體在上，封建郡縣在下，兩層很清楚的關係。

義（legal positivism），特別是拉班德的「國家法人論」（the legal personality of the state/the state as legal person），米尼爾指出後來穗積八束雖然觀點有轉變，但從未完全排斥法律實證主義。[240]另外，列奧·施特勞斯（Leo Strauss）也指出法律實證主義雖然不能等同歷史主義（historicism），但其說服力主要是來自歷史主義的前提，[241]換句話說即是歷史主義與法律實證主義並非不可相容（incommensurable），而是有共存的餘地。因此斷定穗積八束憲法理論的性格即是法律實證主義與歷史主義的折衷，亦極爲合理符實。綜合這兩點可以反駁日本不少學者皆以爲穗積八束的「國體」論是沒有法人性格的看法，這大概是從穗積八束的學生上杉愼吉與主張「天皇機關論」的美濃部達吉之間關於日本憲法的辯論，逕而認爲穗積八束的「國體」論是反對或缺乏國家法人性格。

一個可以質疑的是既然穗積八束已經受到德國法學的影響，那麼他的日本君主國體與始祖論到底有無受到歐洲的影響呢？換句話說，「東亞民族主義」在本文目前一直舉證立論其發展之東亞內在理路，「東亞民族主義」之獨立發展昭然可見。然而，以穗積八束來看，追問「東亞民族主義」中的始祖論是否有受到西方政治思想的影響極爲合情合理。更何況處理19世紀20世紀東亞政治思想史或一般而言的東亞史，皆不能避開西方與東亞各國的種種關聯，如何更進一步瞭解這個極其盤根錯節的過程，比較東亞與西方的「始祖論」則極有意

240 Richard H. Minear, *Japanese Tradition and Western Law: Emperor, State, and Law in the Thought of Hozumi Yatsuka*（Cambridge Massachusetts: Harvard University Press, 1970）, pp. 32-55.

241 Leo Strauss, *Natural Right and History*（Chicago: University of Chicago Press, 1965）, p. 10.

義。

西方政治思想裡，其實有兩種「始祖論」，其一根據爲基督教《聖經》創世紀上帝創造亞當，上帝再由亞當的肋骨一根創造出夏娃，[242]亞當遂爲人類的始祖。其二則是來自羅馬創建的羅馬之父或羅馬建國者，羅慕路斯（Romulus）之事蹟。羅慕路斯有羅馬時期史家李維（Livy, 59B.C.-17A.D.）的《羅馬早期史》第一卷，[243]與稍後希臘人普魯塔克（Plutarch, 46-120A.D.）《比較列傳》的第一列傳，[244]兩者都對羅馬建國國父羅慕路斯有所記載。這兩種「始祖論」在西方政治思想史的出現則是較爲晚近的事。

政治思想裡的亞當始祖論，以羅伯特．飛莫爵士（Sir Robert Filmer，1588-1653）的*Patriarcha*爲代表。在這本書裡，他很有系統地論證爲何君主的權力非來自人民的同意，他主要的依據則是所有君主／國王的權力來自人類始祖的亞當。因爲，亞當管他的小孩並不異於管他的王國，所有的人皆是他的子孫，所有子孫的子孫，同時也是臣服於他。因此，小孩服從父親是「所有君主權威」（all regal authority）的根源。君主權力來自於他們是亞當的後代，決定生死，宣戰，與和約皆爲主要的君主權力。他接著解釋世界上很多講不同語言的人，怎麼可能都是亞當的後代，他以諾亞方舟爲例子，在大洪水以後，諾亞帶著他的兒子在地中海環海十年，讓他的兒子在亞細亞，非洲與歐洲下船定居。這些到處定居下的兒子也成爲他們後代的家長

242 Robert Carroll ed., *The Bible:Authorized King James version*, (Oxford: Oxford University Press, 1997 [1611]), pp. 1-64.

243 Livy, *The Early History of Rome* (New York: Penguin Classics, 1960).

244 Plutarch, *Parallel Lives in Complete Works of Plutarch* (Delphi Classics, 2013).

與君主，繼而形成各式各樣的語言與文化。[245]

他反駁薩拉曼卡學派（Salamanca School）的法蘭西斯科．蘇亞雷斯（Francisco Suárez, 1548-1617）的主張十分重要，因爲只要這點他的論證成功，接下來反對君王權力來自亞當始祖的阻力將可迎刃而解。他對蘇亞雷斯認爲亞當並沒有「政治權力」（political power），只有「經濟權力」（economical power）（按：家戶權力，英文的economical來自希臘語的oikos，即家戶的意思）是來自對家父權力錯誤的認識。蘇亞雷斯確實承認亞當對他家裡的妻子小孩有家父權力，但人類的家庭增加以後，分散四方，每家每戶的家長也都有家父權力，所以，政治權利始於各家各戶聚集起來形成一個社群，這樣的社群當然便非亞當所創始，也非因他的意志而出現，而是經過各家各戶同意，所以沒有理由相信「始祖」（progenitor）便是他的「子孫後代的國王」（King of his posterity）。[246]

飛莫舉例在亞當時，他有很多子孫，但不是所有的子孫都能住在同一屋簷下，有些要住遠一點。如果承認亞當對他的子孫有家父權力，那麼爲什麼只有住在亞當屋簷下的小孩才需聽他的，而不住在一起的就不用。他接著推測以亞當活了930年，起碼生了七八代，他的子孫口數恐怕都多於許多「小國家」（commonwealths）或「王國」（kingdoms）。所以，他認爲亞當的家庭就是個「國家」（commonwealth）。如果，同意飛莫的這個論證，那麼則必須同意亞當的「家父權力」與「政治權力」是一體兩面。[247]他接著再駁亞當非

245 Robert Filmer, *Patriarcha and Other Writings*（Cambridge: Cambridge University Press, 1991）, pp. 6-8.

246 Robert Filmer, *Patriarcha and Other Writings*, p. 15.

247 Robert Filmer, *Patriarcha and Other Writings*, pp. 15-16.

政治共同體創始者，他說共同體當然不始於亞當，因爲，除了亞當以外，根本沒有其他的人。社群的出現正是因有了亞當以後，因爲「亞當的創造」（his creation）與「他的意志」（his will）決定他的兒子們該有什麼。他總結「如是，良善的財產與共同體的確始於亞當，這也是做父親的義務要照顧他的小孩共同福祉（good）以及個別情況」。[248]

這段討論西方政治思想中亞當始祖論之所以稍微冗長的原因，在於亞當始祖論與東亞民族主義的始祖論（特別是日本的原型）的立場最爲相似，兩者皆爲絕對主義的政源論，可是細讀其論述即可知兩者乃互不相干，亞當始祖論是繞著《聖經》創世紀一章發展而出，這裡面沒有大宗小宗，也沒有國學派的語言論與反中國論，更何況東亞在20世紀以前少有學者因或依基督教聖經立論，所謂影響，若有亦是無足輕重。不過，亞當始祖論，在洛克批駁後，[249]在經過18世紀歐洲世俗化，在西方的民族主義運動中並沒有亞當始祖論的影子，也沒有受到亞當始祖論啓發的例子。

另一個始祖論則是來自一個完全不同的傳統——「羅馬政治」與「羅馬政治思想」。從李維對羅慕路斯的敘述，就可以看到羅慕路斯在羅馬創建之時所占有的地位，等到羅慕路斯走了以後，他做爲在羅馬「始祖」/「國父」的地位已經確立。李維在《早期羅馬史》序，非常簡潔扼要的道盡羅慕路斯的「始祖」地位，他如此寫來：「羅慕路斯建立羅馬，組成參議院，討伐薩比你，獻最高榮耀給朱庇特神，

248 Robert Filmer, *Patriarcha and Other Writings*, p. 19.

249 請參看Peter Laslett, ed., *Two Treatises of Government* by John Locke（Cambridge：Cambridge University Press,1988), pp. 67-71. 書中討論洛克《政府二論》與飛莫此書的關係。

分給人民議事會，他的勝利是神聖的」（作者譯）。不過，細讀羅慕路斯一生值得非議或疑問之處甚多，但這無妨後代的羅馬史家對羅慕路斯的讚美。

李維對羅慕路斯描述隨著文藝復興在歐洲各地逐漸廣爲人讀，亦給現代早期的馬基維利留下深刻的印象，所以，馬基維利在1513/14年寫完《君主論》（*The Prince*）意猶未盡，再接再厲寫了《李維論》（*The Discourse on the First Ten Books of Titus Livius*）。他有一個很重要的觀點，一個城市／國（city/civitas）的命運取決於建立之初，建立之時，「創建者」（the founder）的資質很關鍵，從何看出他的資質？其一，擇地，其二，立法。他認爲羅馬兩次創建均符合這兩點，而且羅馬有一個不仰賴他人自由的開始（dipendenza），加上羅慕路斯——羅馬國父，努馬（Numa）等使得羅馬能避開諸多問題而且持久不腐敗。[250]

從這裡馬基維利看到在建國之刻，最好只有一個人作爲建國者或始祖，[251]像羅慕路斯一樣的國父，因此，整本書爲羅慕路斯辯解之處甚多，在第一書第九論中他替羅慕路斯辯護爲何無需指責羅慕路斯殺死自己的弟弟與薩比你人的國王台提烏斯（Titus Tatius）這樣的惡行，他提醒大家需注意羅慕路斯的目的爲何。他爲羅慕路斯辯護主要

250 Niccolò Machiavelli, translated with an introduction and notes by Julia Conaway Bondanella and Peter Bondanella, *Discourses on Livy*（Oxford: Oxford University Press, 1997), Book 1 Discourse 1, pp. 19-22.在第一書第二論中他再度提到羅慕路斯與其他的先王立了不少適合活於自由的良法。

251 蕭高彥亦提到「一個人」（或創建人）「在馬基維利公民共和主義論中樞紐地位」，但劍橋學派的波考克刻意略過不提，轉而專注闡揚「共和社群的存在意義」，並且「強調公民自治的自我創造」。見蕭高彥，《西方共和主義思想史論》，（臺北：聯經出版公司，2013），頁164-165。

有兩點：其一，如果一個共和國或王國要有良政，他就強調建國時或維新之刻均需只有一個人。其二，則是結果決定評價，如果有像羅慕路斯那樣的好結果，那自然可以脫罪。他又說羅慕路斯的惡行無需受到譴責，因爲他的行爲是爲公而非爲己，因爲之後他設立參議院，廣採眾議而治。在第二書第一論，他解釋羅馬如何成爲一個偉大的帝國，他就說源自羅馬軍隊的強大，何以如此，則歸功於羅馬第一位立法者──羅慕路斯的制度。此外，書中馬基維利對羅慕路斯的讚美眞是不下二三十次，他說像努馬是守成之君，一切只能聽時機與「命運」（fortuna），像羅慕路斯這樣的君主隨時隨地皆可以保「國」（keep his state 或 mantenere lo stato）。[252]

馬基維利的始祖論自然影響到後來不少人，其中最著名的有英國哈林頓（James Harrington 1611-1677）的《大洋國》（*The Commonwealth of Oceana*），裡頭就有一位類似建國國父的 Olphaus Megaletor，之後，盧梭的《社會契約論》一書也有一位立法者（lawgiver/legislator）在其理論中。[253]當然，馬基維利時就認識到一個偉大的國家，不能只靠一個人，所以他也花了一些篇幅討論創始人之後的君主如何重要，[254]這自然也影響到後來的態度。所以，美國認定開國有功者爲國父，而且國父是複數而非單數，反映馬基維利以來對開國國父，換句話說，就是對「始祖」的重視。

這個濫觴於羅馬的共和主義系譜中的「創建者」（始祖論）與東亞民族主義更是風馬牛不相及，不過，由於美國獨立革命與19世紀

252 Niccolò Machiavelli, *Discourses on Livy*, Book 1, Discourse 19, p. 72.

253 Alan Ryan, *On Politics: A History of Political Thought from Herodotus to the Present*, (New York: Liveright, 2012), p. 501.

254 Niccolò Machiavelli, *Discourses on Livy*, Book 1, Discourse 19-20, pp.72-73.

末20世紀初美國日益壯大，使得美國成爲更令人嚮往的國家，因此這套系譜裡的某些象徵與語言確實影響到東亞民族主義在政治上的一些做法與論述，例如：「獨立」這個概念，越南的獨立宣言來看受美國獨立宣言影響甚大，以及中國與1918-1919大韓獨立萬歲等也有美國因素，[255]而「獨立」這個概念則可上溯到新羅馬（Neo-Roman）的自由觀。[256]再者「國父」這個概念，就是來自羅馬—馬基維利—哈林頓—美國這個系譜而非宗族論，所以沒人尊稱孫中山國祖，只有稱呼他國父，這就是中國受到此影響的確證。[257]孫中山何時被尊稱爲「國父」呢？根據李恭忠的研究，[258]「國父」初見於民國14年（1925）各處追悼孫中山的活動，其中有稱孫中山爲「國父」時，亦言及華盛頓的例子。儘管如此，孫中山「國父」的稱謂正式確定則是在抗戰期間民國29年（1940年）4月，國民政府下令尊崇孫中山爲「國父」。由此可以看到時間上與上舉之一例稱孫中山爲「國父」確有受到美國的影響。反之，在宗族論裡祖是遠遠高於父，也正因此，在日本天照大

255 David Armitage, *The Declaration of Independence: A Global History, Cambridge*（Massachusetts: Harvard University Press, 2007）, pp. 103-138.

256 前面馬基維利強調羅馬的開國時「不仰賴（dipendenza）他人，有自由的開始」，即是所謂的「新羅馬自由觀」。這點取自斯金納在劍橋某一堂演講。

257 美國尊稱建國諸位人士「建國國父」（founding fathers），依據R.B. Bernstein的研究，他發現founding fathers一詞出現晚於大家一般的認知，最早見於1916年俄亥俄州參議院議員沃倫·哈定（Warren Harding）的演講稿中，之後哈定陸陸續續用了幾次，到了1921年哈定的總統就職典禮演講中又提到「建國國父」，遂迅速廣爲流行。見R.B. Bernstein, *The Founding Fathers Reconsidered*,（New York: Oxford University Press, 2009）, pp. 3-5.

258 李恭忠，〈孫中山崇拜與民國政治文化〉，《二十一世紀》86：12（香港，2004），頁106-107，

神不是天父，而是天祖。

五、結語——作為「葵花寶典」的「東亞民族主義」

那麼，「東亞民族主義」或東亞型的民族主義的到底是什麼類型的民族主義與對民族主義的研究的啓發何在呢？由於本文限於篇幅，尚未對「民」一字在宋明以來的演變做詳細的交代，對國家一詞亦未深入討論，故仍然很難提出一個完整無缺的理論，只能暫時就本文已經觸及到的部分稍微衍生議論。東亞民族主義與民族觀當然不是「市民或公民的（civic）民族主義」，其實，亦非「族群（ethnic）民族主義」，而是「國家（statist）民族主義」。如果同意本文對東亞民族主義的論證，東亞民族主義則是一種世俗化宗統君統合一大宗制的實現擴大，那就須認識世俗化宗統君統合一大宗制的論述乃是極其「政治的」，更是贊翼國家的一種「統治技術」（governmentality）。世俗化宗統君統合一大宗制宗族論的終極目的，乃在鞏固政治權力，因爲，大宗制的宗族論在周代本來就是與政治（國家）緊密結合，這點是毫無爭議的。

族譜或系譜的編纂是要有位者才能進行，通常是「宗子」或其「代理人」，誰進族譜誰不能進族譜，到最後是政治權力（宗子）決定的，特別是在大宗制之下，理論上，同族之內只有一個人能決定，同族之內的人事皆有宗子一個人管。舉一個簡單的例子，爲何臺灣人需要日後成爲法律上定義的中國人，而東南亞的華人不需要也不准許，[259]就證明血緣本身不足以決定政治／民族身份。在東亞民族主義

259 莊國土、劉文正，《東亞華人社會的形成和發展：華商網絡、移民與一體化趨勢》（廈門：廈門大學出版社，2009），第7章，〈東南亞華人社會

下大宗的代理人——宗子就是國家，不然有黃帝的後代代理嗎？同理，韓國，北朝鮮也沒有找出／製造出檀君之後裔領導民族，越南也無此事，即使日本天皇名義上是宗子，實際上，則是其代理人——日本政府。東亞各國全部都由國家爲民族／宗族的代理人／宗子。

而大宗制的權力來自「始祖」，其權力無遠弗屆，百世不移。大宗制的宗族想像是抽象的，需要學習與信仰，非與生俱來的。這種群體想像需要經由一個祭祀塑造群體的皈依情感，建構一個共同的歷史神話／迷思，才能超越個人當下的利害關係，而以素不謀面的陌生人認定爲自己同族的親人，促使自己與實際上爲陌生人感同身受。因此，沒有意外，大小宗的宗族論與擬親屬關係在宋代以來的中國社會早已經成爲社會團體人際關係慣用的組成原理與方法，連接沒有眞正血緣關係的陌生人。適値再度面對外來的挑戰衝擊，在一手擁有船堅砲利，一手握著十字架的西方列強入侵之際，這樣富有宗教情緒的始祖崇拜與宗統君統合一的大宗宗族想像，於是迅速政治化擴大到更大的共同體想像、是以水到渠成轉化爲「民族」的想像。這亦是今天東亞諸國的關於國家與「民族」的論述，仍舊充斥著世俗化的儒家大宗宗法思考模式與語言。

小宗制的宗族論則否。小宗制促使宗族一直自我分散，財產在諸子平分的原理下一直分化，資本難以集中，在這種情況沒有一個人可以決定其他同族不同家人的事情，所以，社會裡不容易有世家大族。

的轉型與中國僑務政策的變化〉，頁232-256。日本的情況亦同，小熊英二指出日本人的「境界」——誰是日本人，到最後是國家決定，而且界定常常有變化，而絕非所謂「單一民族論」界定。見小熊英二，《日本人の境界——沖縄・アイヌ・台湾・朝鮮　植民地支配から復帰運動まで》（東京：新曜社，1998），特別是〈序章〉，頁3-15。

這在行郡縣制的宋元明清皇權眼裡是不具有威脅的社會力量，所以社倉、義學、編家譜等都不會成爲威脅皇權政治的勢力，還會能替朝廷分擔照顧管理百姓。小宗制以五世以內近親血緣爲主富有親情溫情的倫理道德與家庭關係是一種去政治（de-politicized）的、非政治（apolitical）的宗族論，一個服膺國家權力、難以抗拒中央集權的一種有時限非永久的（impermanent, non-perpetual）社會組織，一種缺乏法人性格的中間團體。小宗制父祖的權力是近距離的，具體而直接，往往「人亡政息」，及世而終。小宗制的宗族／族群想像建立在可能互相認識範圍的前提上，一個極度受到時空限制的共同體想像，因此無法擴大到所有與自己有血緣關係的同族人，更遑論涵蓋一國之內所有或大部分的人。一旦大宗制宗族論轉化／世俗化爲民族論以後，無論集權或追求自由平等的民族主義國家，卻又需要近似小宗的家庭形態，一個比以前小宗制宗族範圍更小的家庭關係，這就是一夫一妻上下兩代組成的核心家庭形態（nuclear family）。

中國、朝鮮、越南在20世紀以前，是一個大宗的族領導其他百姓各小宗的族組成之政體，日本則是一大堆的大宗家族聯合政體。這兩種組織人民的典範皆無法應對來自西方的挑戰，前一種則是一盤散沙，後一種則是山頭林立，皆於事無補，會澤正志齋把這點看得最清清楚楚，沒有任何猶豫，沒有任何妄想。所以，他要想像出一種新的典範，強化政治／國家對人民的組織／控制，使得日本可以有效迎接即將到來的西方侵略。他也從封建郡縣之爭看到任何政體制度都不重要，也就是黑貓白貓都可，重點便是如何重新「組織」、「控制」、「改造」人民以對付解決外患。於是，他擷取國學派的論述與濫觴於《公羊傳》的宗統君統合一大宗制宗族論，創造出一個超越實存的國體，一個所有人皆爲同一族的理論原型。這是一個徹徹底底的政治思想，一個冷靜的利害計算，一種國家的理性（ragion di stato/raison d'etre）。這就是東亞型民族主義基礎與原型。從這個原型發展出兩個政治過程，一個則是大宗制宗族論演變為民族論與民族主義，國家以此組織人民，同時另一個過程則是國家推動小宗制宗族的縮小簡單化，形成國家之下有無數的核心小家庭。這些無數的小家庭就是服從大宗宗子——國家的新小宗家庭（核心家庭）。

建立在世俗化大宗制宗族論的東亞民族主義，在系譜／族譜的建構過程為了凸顯己國的「創建」與「正當性」源自有「始祖」的「民族」，所以需要將許多不符合這個「民族」論述的歷史與文化否定、遺忘或篡改。這在日本江戶時期國學派的論述中已經提供了兩個後來常見於其他東亞民族主義（自我）否定的模式。其一，「反中國」，這裡有好幾個層次的「中國」，有歷史、文化、儒家、當今的「中國」等等。這裡的「中國」並不需要逼眞符實，而且常常是誇大失眞，甚至是捏造的中國形象，總之是雞蛋裡挑骨頭，「中國」在此只是一個稻草人，一個邪惡的符號，一個需要推倒的對象；其二，建構一個本土文化的論述，本土文化據說是原始的，聲音先於漢字的，自然的，純潔的等等優美善良的特質，可是歷史上卻又飽受到中國文化的污染，極需除魅。這兩點緊緊相扣，相互聲援。只是問題在東亞各國包括中國本身，所謂本土文化在歷史上又與中國的種種面向難分難解，更何況在此一反中國的本土文化論述興起時，其時代背景，正是中國文化，特別是以漢字、漢文、漢詩與宋明儒學等等在各國最普遍最深入社會的時候。這樣的論述於是就非常有選擇性的挑選、刪除、捏造、遺忘歷史，需要處處否定閃避己國過往的種種，才能譜寫出一個源自始祖、一個先於中國影響的本土／一國／民族論述，這樣的論述才可以主導政治化的大宗制宗族——「民族」系譜敘述。

這個否定或自我否定一旦政治化以後，便容易轉爲政治運動與政治改革，乃至政治革命的莫大動力。否定的力道亦是政治意志張力的呈現。否定的歷史時間越早，後來訴諸政治行動時，否定的力道越是溫和或受到其他因素的制約越大。反之，否定的歷史時間越晚，否定的內容會越徹底，範圍越廣。政治改革越順利，否定的力道與範圍亦會越有限。政治受挫越大，否定越激烈越全盤。否定與自我更生是關聯的，惟有自我否定，才有自我更生。日本的自我否定早，政治改革也相對順利成功，因此，自我否定很快的就停頓或與原來的社會文化妥協。再以漢字爲例，明治時期的文部省大臣森有禮，主張廢除漢字以及推行一些西化政策，最後在明治憲法公布的那一天（1889年2月11日）被一位國粹主義者用日本菜刀砍死。日本至今使用漢字，二戰前日本漢字未曾簡化，亦無羅馬拼音化。之後漢字在二戰後的簡化相當有限，而且公用漢字使用字數一直增加。雖然近年來有些對漢字挑戰的本土文化論述戰略偶爾現身，比如日本本來常用漢字「生產」或「製造」，不過從1997-98以來日本政府通商產業省僞造一個大和語「ものづくり」（monozukuri），霎時之間，在日本政府的推動下與媒體的配合，變得幾乎無所不在，還有設立一所大學叫「ものづくり大學」。[260]然而即使在安倍晉三上臺後，右翼民族主義人士在日本政壇掌權，這個僞造大和語與其所代表的產業政策的風潮，卻已經不復十年前的風光，連安倍政府也不再提及。

從中國的我手寫我口，簡化漢字到本來欲行而後作廢的漢字羅馬拼音化，越南的國語運動（Quốc Ngữ，羅馬拼音化卻叫國語，不就

260 蔡孟翰，〈物造神話論：一個被加工出來的製造業意識形態〉，《日本學刊》2（北京，2007），頁123-132。

大有玄機嗎），到韓國、北朝鮮的廢漢字，用諺文（諺文是舊名，現代則用한글發音hangul，沒有漢字，是「純」韓語），都足以證明自我否定的時間越晚，政治改革挫折越大，自我否定即越徹底越全盤。此外這些種種的現象都仍是東亞民族主義裡頭，國學派的本土原始語言論思路下衍生的劇本台詞，並非別出心裁。東亞各國的反中國言論亦是源自東亞民族主義中日本的反／脫中國中心論，讀來大同小異，連近年臺灣民族主義的中國批判，也多爲拾人牙慧，人云亦云，陳腔濫調。[261]雖說，東亞民族主義最後成於日本，可是日本對此態度向來十分複雜矛盾，明治以來反對其中某些主張從未間斷或某些很中國的制度從未受到質疑，如日本以年號紀元與引進明清一個皇帝一個年號的規矩至今屹立不搖。[262]

中國、日本、朝鮮，越南的民族主義當然仍各有不同之處，不同之處也絕非皆可以本文所提出的理論完全顧及，這並非本文所視而不見的，但是本文認爲唯有先求找到其共同之處，才能更妥善的解釋安排其相異處。希望本文已勾勒出東亞民族主義共同的輪廓，對其中細節涉足尚淺，對某些歷史敘述尚需補強證據，不過希望已經能因指見月。如稍微整理本文對東亞民族主義內容的描述，即可察覺直到今日東亞各國很多民族主義的論述、心態與性質，仍然沒有離開東亞民族

261 江户時期的度會常彰（1665-1752）在以漢文書寫的《神道辨明》一書，有段幾乎可說是眾多反中國言論的原型（prototype），他說：「學者生日本地，啜日本泉，不辨内外，不分親疏，言此國則蔽美而露惡，動呼東夷，言彼國則隱惡而揚善，稱曰中華，曰中國，曰中原，曰中土。」他接著譴責這些日本人爲：「乃形貌者日本，而心者西土人。」轉引自里見岸雄，《國體論史》（東京：展轉社，2007），上，頁554-555。

262 日本每年2月11日爲建國紀念日，就是紀念神武天皇開國的節日，戰前這個節日也叫紀元紀念日。

主義的範疇，也就是孫悟空跳不開如來佛的手掌心一般。雖然，在1920年代以後，東亞各國之間，漸行漸遠；中國的民族主義受到美國，德國，蘇聯的影響，越南接受法國的薰陶也愈來愈深，同時亦越來越像一個「東南亞」國家，基督教在朝鮮勢力也逐漸散播，成爲韓國戰後一股巨大的社會主流。另一方面，日本民族主義越走越偏激（丸山眞男稱之超國家主義），直欲達成八紘一宇，一種最猙獰的帝國主義，對美國珍珠港性突襲之際，還借天皇的名義，發送敕文給正準備偷襲珍珠港的帝國海軍以鼓舞士氣，文中襲取諸葛亮〈出師表〉之語氣文意自比，以小搏大，悲壯不已，亦相當有自知之明。[263]儘管如此，在各國史料面前，在政治思想史這個層次，本文闡抉的東亞國家民族主義，亦即是政治化宗統君統合一大宗制宗族之民族主義，依舊可能是理解近一百多年來東亞政治與東亞各國的民族主義的共同與差異最有效力的一個理論。

東亞政治思想史與更廣義的思想史文化史，從宋代以來發展的線索不少，在中國、朝鮮、日本、越南、琉球五國各有精彩的展開，猶如七寶樓台，玲瓏滿目，目接不暇。最後由宗族論脫穎而出，雖不令人意外，但亦足以唏噓，因爲從宗族論走到東亞民族主義後，東亞各國都歷經不同程度的自我否定與相互否定，受難越深，革命越激烈，受挫越大，否定越徹底。東亞民族主義在這激動苦難的年代，遂成爲保國保種的必勝秘笈，然而，此秘笈竟有如金庸《笑傲江湖》裡的《葵花寶典》——「欲練成，先自宮」。於是，東亞各國便在「東方不

263 筆者於2013年5月與普林斯頓大學伊斯蘭思想史專家Michael Cook教授夫婦參觀東京靖國神社的遊就館時看到的，只是這裡展出的理由是要強調日本攻擊美國是萬不得已的苦澀抉擇。此外很令人深思的是遊就館的「遊就」一詞出於《荀子．勸學篇》「君子居必擇鄉，遊必就士」。

敗」與「岳不群」兩個人格間飄擺不定，裝模作樣，相互嘲諷，相互助紂爲虐。可惜自宮以後，雖然猶如再生，時亦勢不可擋，不過自我生成能力已去，只能借他人所生爲己生或到處認養，這便是「東亞民族主義」與現代東亞政治最大弔詭與荒誕。杜甫在安史之亂後寫了「國破山河在，城春草木深」，現在換的是「國在山河破，城冬不見日」。是爲誌。

後記：此論文在日本與臺灣兩地四個先後不同的場次發表，感謝其中三位評審人米原謙、辻本雅史、沈松僑細心的閱讀與諸多十分有益的建議批評。同時致意兩位匿名評審人的鞭策，使得拙文在審查後的修改，格外努力而所改觀。首先值得一提的是2012年1月應米原謙的邀請到「東亞民族主義研究會」上，才開始認眞構思執筆。之後，又在關西大學少數族群研究中心2012年3月的年度會議發表。爾後，在2013年5月經藍弘岳邀請到臺北開會，引介辻本雅史爲評論人，對本文的批評與指導有極大的助益，特別是提醒筆者最好詳細討論會澤正志齋的《新論》，使得全文現在論點較爲首尾一貫，補上一個大漏洞。最後2013年11月由中研院政治思想研究中心諸位師友盛情邀請參與《民主與國族主義》學術研討會，給予筆者一個機會，將原來日語的論文稿，重寫爲中文，期間陳宜中的支持令人感銘。此外，藍弘岳、高貴禮（Gregory Noble）、蕭高彥、渡邊浩、蔡英文、安武眞隆、郭秋永、高全喜、李強與葉鵬飛亦提出一些中肯的建議，在此一併致上謝意。最後，《思想史》編輯助理林慧芬與曾婉甄在春節前勤奮校稿，使得拙文整齊可觀而不至於狼狽，於此附記。此研究初期的經費來自關西大學少數族群研究中心「日本文科省私立大學戰略研究經費」項目，借此特別鳴謝。所有文責，當然皆歸筆者。

From Lineage to Nation:
The Emergence and Nature of East Asian Nationalism

Mon-Han Tsai

Abstract

In this paper, I first ask if there is a commonly shared EA nationalism or several types of nationalisms in East Asia. I proceed to tackle the origins and uses of minzu/minzoku (nation民族). Afterwards, I place the discussion of lineage (宗族) in the context of fengjian/hoken (封建) and junxian/gunken (郡縣) and follows how it evolves from Song China, through late Ming and early Qing China, and how it continues in Tokugawa Japan.

The development in Japan reaches the definitive breakthrough in the *Shinron* of Aizawa Seishisai with his ingenious synthesis of Ito Togai's neutral, comparativist view on hoken/gunken, and the mythical/historical narrative of the nativists as represented by Motoori Norinaga (without adopting their view on language and aesthetics).

Aizawa singlehandedly produces the nearly finished template for East Asian nationalism when he conceives kokutai above hoken/gunken, and a new Japan led by the descendants of Japan's (not yet Japanese) progenitor-Amaterasu-a new manifestation of the main branch lineage system (大宗制).

Aizawa's formulation was updated with Western political and legal terminologies by Hozumi Yatsuka in his constitutional theory in the 1890's. He thus popularizes the use of minzoku (nation) further and brought the notion to the forefront of political and legal thinking in Japan and elsewhere in East Asia.

I compare the progenitor in East Asian political thought and its equivalent in Europe. In *Patriarcha*. Filmer develops his absolutist theory of the state based on the idea of Adam as the progenitor. The alternative version is based on the founding of Rome with Romulus as its progenitor or founding father. Through Livy, Machiavelli centers his discussion of the prince on Romulus in his *Discourse* and in turn, this influences Harrington, Rousseau and the American Revolution.

Finally, I examine the politics of East Asian nationalism based on the main branch lineage discourse, and conclude that EA nationalism is neither civic nor ethnic nationalism; it is a statist nationalism.

Keywords: Nationalism, Lineage, Fengjian, Great Descent-line, Zhu Xi, Zhang Zai, Aizawa Seishisai, Hozumi Yatsuka, Kokutai, Political Thought

徵引文獻

一、傳統文獻

內藤湖南，《內藤湖南漢詩文集》，廣西：廣西師範大學出版社，2009。
太宰春台，《春台先生紫芝園稿》（宝暦二年刊），東京：ぺりかん社，1986。
文部省，《国体の本義》，東京：文部省，1937。
方苞，《方苞集》，下，上海：上海古籍出版社，2012。
木崎愛吉、賴成一共編，《賴山陽全書》，東京：國書刊行會，1983［1932］。
毛亨注，鄭玄箋，《毛詩傳箋》，收入《漢魏古注十三經 附四書章句集注》，上，北京：中華書局，1998。
公羊高撰，何休注，《春秋公羊傳》收於《漢魏古注十三經 附四書章句集注》，下，北京：中華書局，1998。
王夫之，〈黃書〉，收入《梨洲船山五書》，臺北：世界書局，1988［1656］。
王國維，《王國維手定 觀堂集林》，杭州：浙江教育出版社，2014。
王弼著，樓宇烈校釋，《王弼集》，北京：中華書局，1980。
司馬遷，《史記》，北京：中華書局，1982。
伊藤東涯，《制度通》，京都：中文出版社，1993。
伊藤東涯，《周易經翼通解》收於《漢文大系16・周易・傳習錄》，臺北：新文豐，1978。
朱熹著，黎靖德編，《朱子語錄》，北京：中華書局，1994。
____、呂祖謙編纂，《近思錄》，臺北：金楓出版，1987［1176］。
左丘明撰，杜預注，《春秋經傳集解（左傳）》收於《漢魏古注十三經 附四書章句集注》，下，北京：中華書局，1998。
吳宣德、宗韻編，《明人譜牒序跋輯略》，上海：上海古籍出版社，2013。
吳時任，《春秋管見》，收入北京大學儒藏編纂與研究中心編，《儒藏 精華編越南之部一冊》，北京，北京大學出版社，2013。
吳兢撰，謝保成集校，《貞觀政要集校》，北京：中華書局，2003。
阮文超，《方亭隨筆錄》，臺北：國立臺灣大學出版中心，2013。
柳宗元撰，楊家駱主編，《柳河東全集》，上冊，臺北：世界書局，1999。
孫中山，《三民主義》，臺北：三民書局，1965［1924］。
孫希旦，《禮記集解》，北京：中華書局，1989。
班固著，陳立注，《白虎通疏證》，北京：中華書局，1994。
馬瑞辰，《毛詩傳箋通釋》，北京：中華書局，1989。

桂馥，《說文解字義證》，濟南：齊魯書社，1987。
淩廷堪，《禮經釋例》，臺北：中央研究院中國文哲研究所，2012。
張載，《張載集》，北京：中華書局，1978。
梁啓超，《先秦政治思想史》，長沙：嶽麓書社，2010。
章太炎，《章氏叢書》，下，臺北：世界書局，1982。
陳子龍著，王英志輯校，《陳子龍全集》，北京：人民文學出版社，2011。
陳荊和編校，《大越史記全書》，東京：東京大學東洋文化研究所，1986，校合本。
馮桂芬，《校邠廬抗議》，鄭州：中州古籍出版社，1998。
會澤正志齋，《新論》，安政四年（1857）和本（線裝）版。
__________著，名越時正編，《會澤正志齋文稿》，東京：國書刊行會，2002。
萬斯大撰，溫顯貴校注，《經學五書》，上海：華東師範大學出版社，2012。
廖平，《穀梁古義疏》，北京 中華書局，2012。
德川齊昭，《弘道館記》，收入《日本思想大系53・水戶學》，東京：岩波書店，1973。
劉師培撰，李妙根編，《劉師培辛亥前文選》，北京：三聯書店，1998。
穗積八束，《憲法大意》，日本：穗積八束博士遺稿憲政大意發行所，1917［1896］。
______，〈憲法の精神〉，收入長尾龍一編，《穗積八束集》，東京：信山社，2001［1900］。
鄭玄注，《禮記》，收入《漢魏古注十三經 附四書章句集注》，上，北京：中華書局，1998。
____注，賈公彥疏，《儀禮注疏》，上海：上海古籍出版社，2008。
錢謙益，《牧齋有學集》，上海：上海古籍出版社，1996。
蘇洵，《嘉佑集》，收入《三蘇全集》，上，京都：中文出版社，1986。
顧炎武，《日知錄》，臺北：世界書局，1991。
______，《顧亭林詩文集》，香港：中華書局，1976，港版。
穀梁赤撰，範寧注，《春秋穀梁傳》，收於《漢魏古注十三經 附四書章句集注》，下，北京：中華書局，1998。
Campbell, Gordon. *The Holly Bible, King James* version. Oxford: Oxford University Press, 2010［1611］.
Filmer, Robert. *Patriarcha and Other Writings*. Cambridge: Cambridge University Press, 1991.
Harrington, James. J.G.A. Pocock ed., *The Commonwealth of Oceana and A System of Politics*. Cambridge: Cambridge University Press, 1992.

Livy, *The Early History of Rome*. New York: Penguin Classics, 1960.

Machiavelli, Niccolò. translated with an introduction and notes by Julia Conaway Bondanella and Peter Bondanella, *Discourses on Livy*. Oxford: Oxford University Press, 1997.

Plutarch, *Parallel Lives in Complete Works of Plutarch*. Delphi Classics, 2013.

二、近人論著

三谷博，《明治維新を考える》，東京：岩波書店，2012。

上里隆史，《琉日戦争一六〇九——島津氏の琉球侵攻》，沖縄：ボーダーインク，2009。

丸山眞男，《日本政治思想史研究》，東京：東京大學出版會，1999［1952］。

________，《忠誠と反逆——転形期日本の精神史的位相》，東京：筑摩書房，1992。

________，《現代政治の思想と行動》，東京：未来社，2006。

大庭脩，《徳川吉宗と康熙帝——鎖国化での日中交流》，東京：大修館書店，1999。

子安宣邦，《日本ナショナリズムの解読》，東京：白澤社，2009。

小倉紀蔵，《朱子学化する日本近代》，藤原書店，2012。

小島毅，《宋学の形成と展開》，東京：創文社，1999。

_______，《増補 靖國史觀——日本思想を読みなおす》，東京：筑摩書房 2014

小森陽一，《日本語の近代》，東京：岩波書店，2000。

小熊英二，《日本人の境界——沖縄・アイヌ・台湾・朝鮮　植民地支配から復帰運動まで》，東京：新曜社，1998。

山田賢，〈「宗族」から「民族」へ——近代中国における「国民国家」と忠誠のゆくえ〉，收入久留島浩、趙景達編，《国民国家の比較史》，東京：有志舎，2010，頁115-136。

山室信一，《思想課題としてのアジア——基軸・連鎖・投企》，東京：岩波書店，2001。

井上寿一、波多野澄雄、酒井哲哉、国分良成、大芝亮編，《日本の外交 第3巻—外交思想》，東京：岩波書店，2013。

今井昭夫，〈二〇世紀初頭のベトナムにおける開明的儒学者たちの国民国家構想〉，收入久留島浩、趙景達編，《アジアの国民国家構想——近代への投企と葛藤》，東京：青木書店，2008，頁149-188。

王汎森，《權力的毛細管作用——清代的思想，學術與心態》，臺北：聯經出版公司，2013。
木村淳也，〈琉球史書の特質と問題——東アジア国際関係を軸として〉，收入堀池信夫，增尾伸一郎，松崎哲之編，《交響する東方の知——漢文文化圏の輪郭》，東京：明治書院，2014，頁161-192。
王明珂，〈論攀附：近代炎黃子孫國族建構的古代基礎〉，《中央研究院歷史語言研究所集刊》，73：3（臺北，2002），頁1-42。
王建文，《奉天承運——古代中國的「國家」概念及其正當性基礎》，臺北：東大圖書，1995。
王柯，《20世紀中国の国家建設と「民族」》，東京：東京大学出版会，2006。
方維規，〈論近代思想史上的民族，Nation與中國〉，《21世紀》，4（香港，2002），頁33-43。
田世民〈水戶藩の儒禮受容——喪祭儀略を中心に〉，《京都大學大學院教育學研究科紀要》53（京都，2007），頁137-149。
石塚正英、柴田隆行監修，《哲學・思想翻譯語事典》（增補版），東京：論創社，2013。
名越時正，《水户藩弘道館とその教育》，茨城：茨城縣教師會，1972。
安田浩，《近代天皇制国家の歴史的位置——普遍性と特殊性を読みとく視座》，東京：大月書店，2011。
米原謙，《日本政治思想》，東京：ミネルヴァ書房，2007。
______、金鳳珍、區建英，《東アジアのナショナリズムと近代——なぜ対立するのか》，大阪：大阪大学出版会，2011。
辻本雅史，《近世教育思想史の研究——日本における「公教育」思想の源流——》，京都：思文閣出版，1990。
________，《思想と教育のメディア史——近世日本の知の伝達》，東京：ぺりかん社，2011。
何炳棣，《思想制度史論》，臺北：聯經出版公司，2013。
余英時，《中國思想傳統的現代詮釋》，臺北：聯經出版公司，1987。
吳偉明，〈日本德川前期吳太伯論的思想史意義〉，《新史學》，25：3（臺北，2014），頁143-170。
呂妙芬，《孝治天下：《孝經》與近世中國的政治與文化》，臺北：聯經出版公司，2011。
金觀濤、劉青峰，《觀念史研究——中國現代重要政治術語的形成》，北京：法律出版社，2009。
尾藤正英，《日本の国家主義——「国体」思想の形成》，東京：岩波書局，2014。
李恭忠，〈孫中山崇拜與民國政治文化〉，《二十一世紀》86：12（香港，

2004），頁101-111。

李隆獻，〈復仇觀的省察與詮釋——以《春秋》三傳爲重心〉，《臺大中文學報》，22：6（臺北，2005），頁99-150。

杜正勝，《古代社會與國家》，臺北：允晨文化，1992。

沈松僑，〈我以我血薦軒轅——黃帝神話與晚清的國族建構〉，《臺灣社會研究》，28：12（臺北，1997），頁1-77。

______，〈近代中國民族主義的發展：兼論民族主義的兩個問題〉，收入林毓生主編，《公民社會基本觀念》下卷，臺北：中央研究院人文社會研究中心，2014，頁547-608。

赤嶺守，《琉球王國》，東京：講談社，2004。

邢義田，《天下一家：皇帝、官僚與社會》，北京：中華書局，2011。

裡見岸雄，《國體論史》，上，東京：展轉社，2007。

東（宮沢）より子，〈宣長神学のコスモロジー：「国」概念の発見〉，《下関女子短期大学紀要》，14：15（山口，1996），頁1-13。

林來梵，〈國體概念史〉，《中國社會科學》，3（北京，2013），頁65-84。

河野有理編，《近代日本政治思想史——荻生徂徠から網野善彦まで》，京都：ナカニシヤ出版，2014。

苅部直、黒住眞、佐藤弘夫、末木文美士、田尻祐一郎編，《日本思想史講座4-近代》，東京：ぺりかん社，2013。

邸永君，〈「民族」一詞見於《南齊書》〉，《民族研究》3（北京，2004），http://big.hi138.com/wenxueyishu/hanyuwenxue/200808/72386.asp#.VOKgELv9mpo（2015/2/15）。

金觀濤、劉青峰，《觀念史研究——中國現代重要政治術語的形成》，北京：法律出版社，2009。

長尾龍一，《日本國家思想史研究》，東京：創文社，1982。

前田勉，《兵学と朱子学・蘭学・国学——近代日本思想史の構図》，平凡社，2006。

星山京子，〈後期水户學と近代——會澤正志齋を中心に〉，《大航海》，67（東京：2008），頁58-65。

孫隆基，〈清季民族主義與黃帝崇拜之發明〉，《歷史研究》，3（北京：2000），http://www.douban.com/note/223028101/（2015-02-16）。

宮崎市定，《アジア史概説》，東京：中公文庫，1987。

高山大毅，〈「遅れてきた「古学」者——会沢正志斎の位置」〉，《日本思想史》，79・［特集］儒教の解釈学的可能性（東京：2012），頁113-132。

常建華，〈明代宗族祠廟禮制及其演變〉，《南開學報》，3（天津：2001），頁64-66。

眞壁仁，《德川後期の学問と政治——昌平坂学問所儒者と幕末外交変容》，名古屋：名古屋大学出版会，2007。
莊國土、劉文正《東亞華人社會的形成和發展：華商網絡、移民與一體化趨勢》，廈門：廈門大學出版社，2009。
許倬雲，《我者與他者——中國歷史上的內外分際》，臺北：時報出版，2009。
張壽安，《禮學考證的思想活力》，臺北：中央研究院近代史研究所，2001，第3章〈「爲人後」：清儒論君統之獨立〉，頁215-335。
渡辺浩，《東アジアの王権と思想》，東京：東京大学出版会，1997。
______，《近世日本社会と宋学》，東京：東京大学出版会，1985。
黃克武，〈從追求正道到認同國族：明末至清末中國公私觀念的重整〉，收入黃克武、張哲嘉主編，《公與私：近代中國個體與群體之重建》，臺北：中央研究院近代史研究所，2000。
楊念群，《何處是江南？清朝正統觀的確立與士林精神的異變》，北京：三聯書店，2010。
溝口雄三、丸山松幸、池田知久，《中國思想文化事典》，東京：東京大學出版會，2001。
福島正夫，《日本資本主義と家》，東京：東京大学出版会，1967。
蔡孟翰，〈物造神話論——一個被加工出來的製造業意識形態〉，《日本學刊》，2007：2（北京，2007），頁123-132。
蔡英文，〈民族主義、人民主權與西方現代性〉，收入林毓生主編，《公民社會基本觀念》，上卷，臺北：中央研究院人文社會研究中心，2014，頁27-66。
鄧小南，《祖宗之法——北宋前期政治述略》，北京：三聯書店，2006。
蕭高彥，《西方共和主義思想史論》，臺北：聯經出版公司，2013。
藍弘嶽，〈「神州」、「中國」、「帝國」——會澤正志齋的國家想像與十九世紀日本之亞洲論述〉，《新史學》，22：3（臺北，2011），頁71-112。
瀨谷義彥、今井三郎、尾藤正英，《日本思想大系53．水戸学》，東京：岩波書店，1973。
羅志田，《民族主義與近代中國思想》，臺北：東大圖書公司，1998。
藤井隆，〈政体論から「開明専制論」を読む〉，《修道法学》34：2（広島，2012），頁25-81。
藤田寛，《近世後期政治史と対外関係》，東京：東京大学出版会，2005。
龔鵬程，《江西詩社宗派研究》，臺北：文史哲出版社，1983。
______，《思想と文化》，臺北：業強出版社，1986。
Anderson, Benedict. *Imagined Communities: Reflections on the Origin and Spread of Nationalism*. (Revised Edition), London: Verso., 1991.

Armitage, David. *The Declaration of Independence: A Global History*. Cambridge. Massachusetts: Harvard University Press, 2007.

Bernstein, R.B. *The Founding Fathers Reconsidered*. New York: Oxford University Press, 2009.

Breuilly, John. *Nationalism and the State* (second edition). Manchester: Manchester University Press, 1993.

Burke, Peter. "Nationalisms and Vernaculars, 1500-1800", in John Breuilly ed., *The Oxford Handbook of the History of Nationalism*. Oxford: Oxford University Press, 2013.

Burns, Susan L. *Before the Nation: Kokugaku and the Imagining of Community in Early Modern Japan*. Durham: Duke University Press, 2003.

Robert Carroll, *The Bible*, *King James* version, (Oxford: Oxford University Press, 1997 [1611]), pp.1-64.

Ch'en, Paul Heng-chao. *The Formation of the Early Meiji Legal Order: The Japanese Code of the 1871 and its Chinese Foundation*. New York: Oxford University Press, 1981.

Chow, Kai-Wing. *The Rise of Confucian Ritualism in Late imperial China: Ethics, Classics, and Lineage Discourse*. California: Stanford University Press, 1994.

Chow, Kai-wing. (周啓榮), and Kevin M. Doak and Poshek Fu, eds., *Constructing Nationhood in Modern East Asia*. Michigan: The University of Michigan Press, 2001.

Dikotter, Frank. *The Discourse of Race in Modern China*. Hong Kong: Hong Kong University Press, 1992.

ed., *The Construction of Racial Identities in China and Japan*. London: Hurst & Company, 1997.

Duara, Prasenjit. *Rescuing History from the Nation: Questioning Narratives of Modern China*. Chicago: The University of Chicago Press, 1995.

Dunn, John. *Western Political Theory in the Face of the Future*. (Canto Edition) Cambridge: Cambridge University Press, 1993.

Ferguson, Niall. *The War of the World: History's Age of Hatred*. London: Allen Lane, 2006.

Gat, Azar. *Nations: The Long History and Deep Roots of Political Ethnicity and Nationalism*. Cambridge: Cambridge University Press, 2013.

Gellner, Ernest. *Nations and Nationalism*. Oxford: Blackwell, 1983.

Hobsbawm, Eric. *Nations and Nationalism since 1780: Programme, Myth, Reality*. Cambridge: Cambridge University Press (Canto), 1991.

Koschmann, J. Victor. *The Mito Ideology: Discourse, Reform, and Insurrection in Late Tokugawa Japan*, 1790-1864. Berkeley: University of California Press, 1987.

Laslett, Peter. ed., *Two Treatises of Government*, by John Locke. Cambridge: Cambridge University Press, 1988.

Levenson, Joseph R. *Confucius China and Its Modern Fate: A Trilogy*. Berkeley: University of California Press, 1965.

Liah, Greenfeld. *Nationalism: Five Roads to Modernity*. Massachusetts: Harvard University Press, 1992.

Minear, Richard H. *Japanese Tradition and Western Law: Emperor, State, and Law in the Thought of Hozumi Yatsuka*, Cambridge Massachusetts: Harvard University Press, 1970.

Reid, Anthony. *Imperial Alchemy: Nationalism and Political Identity in Southeast Asia.* Cambridge: Cambridge University Press, 2009.

Rozman, Gilbert. ed. *East Asian National Identities: Common Roots and Chinese Exceptionalism.* California: Stanford University Press, 2012.

Schmid, Andre. *Korea Between Empires*, 1815-1919. New York: Columbia University Press, 2002.

Schmitt, Carl. trans by George Schwab, *Political Theology: Four Chapters on the Concept of Sovereignty*. Chicago: University of Chicago Press, 2005.

Shin, Gi-Wook. *Ethnic Nationalism in Korea: Genealogy, Politics, and Legacy.* California: Stanford University Press, 2006.

Skinner, Quentin. "A Genealogy of the Modern State," *Proceedings of the British Academy*, 162 (2009), pp. 325-370.

Smith, Anthony D. *The Cultural Foundations of Nations: Hierarchy, Covenant, and Republics*. Oxford: Blackwell Publishing, 2008.

Smith, Anthony D. *The Nation in History:Historiographical Debates about Ethnicity and Nationalism.* Cambridge: Polity Press, 2000.

Strauss, Leo. *Natural Right and History* (paperback edition). Chicago: University of Chicago Press, 1965.

Taylor, Keith Weller. *The Birth of Vietnam.* Berkeley: University of California Press, 1983.

郝時遠，〈中文民族一詞源流考辨〉，2010年1月20日發布，共識網：http://www.21ccom.net/plus/wapview.php?aid=2812（2015/2/16）。

中華民國總統府官網：http://www.president.gov.tw/Default.aspx?tabid=131&itemid=30931&rmid=514（2015/2/16）。

【論著】

Revisiting Mou Tsung-san's Idea of Moral Religion:

A Dialogue with Hegel and T. H. Green

Roy Tseng（曾國祥）

Roy Tseng is Professor of Political Theory at National Sun Yat-Sen University. He specializes in political philosophy and the history of political thought. Professor Tseng is the author of *The Sceptical Idealist: Michael Oakeshott as a Critic of the Enlightenment* (2003) and *Subject and Reason: a Conservative Interpretation of Liberalism* (2009, in Chinese), and is the editor-in-chief of *Societas: A Journal for Philosophical Study of Public Affairs.*

Revisiting Mou Tsung-san's Idea of Moral Religion:
A Dialogue with Hegel and T. H. Green

Roy Tseng
Professor of Political Theory, National Sun Yat-sen University

Abstract

Consideration of the Confucian notion of moral religion has a long history, but while I am appreciative of the fruits of previous studies, here I am concerned specifically with a reconstruction of Mou Tsung-san's idea of moral religion through a potential dialogue with Hegel and T. H. Green. More precisely, my aims in this paper are twofold: First, I am trying to highlight the three main aspects of the idea of moral religion in the thought of Hegel and Green: the disapproval of the orthodox Christian view that God is external to humanity; a reinterpretation of the attributes of God through internalization; and the moral ideal of self-realization as the fulfillment of one's inner morality through communicating with the way in which God works in history. Second, I am arguing that Mou Tsung-san's renovation of Confucian moral religion is intensely indebted to Hegel; and consequently that his re-examination of the ethical personality in Confucian thought bears a remarkable resemblance to Green's idea of self-realization. Seen in this light, a far-reaching dialogue between Neo-Confucianism and British Idealism, which promotes a certain form of "perfectionist liberalism," can help to answer the question of how and in what sense Confucianism can accommodate liberal values.

Keywords: Mou Tsung-san, Hegel, T. H. Green, Moral Religion, the Authentic Self, Self-Realization

I. Preface

One of the major themes underpinning the rebirth of Neo-Confucianism in the modern epoch has been an attempt to reformulate the religious aspect of Chinese culture.[1] For instance, the centrality of moral religion in Confucianism was greatly emphasized in the famous "Manifesto for a Reappraisal of Sinology and Reconstruction of Chinese Culture" (1958), the authors of which included the four leading Neo-Confucians T'ang Chün-i (1909-1978), Carsun Chang (1887-1967), Mou Tsung-san (1909-1995), and Hsü Fu-kuan (1903-1982):

> Chinese culture arose out of the extension of primordial religious passion to ethical moral principles and to daily living. For this reason, although its religious aspects have not been developed it is yet pervaded by such sentiments, and hence is quite different from occidental atheism. To comprehend this, it is necessary to discuss the doctrine of "*hsin-hsing*" [the concentration of the mind on an exhaustive study of the nature of the universe], which is a study of the basis of ethics and forms the nucleus of Chinese thoughts and is the source of all theories of the "conformity of heaven and man in virtue." Yet this is what is most neglected and misunderstood by

1 For a particulrarly notable work on this topic, see Tu Wei-ming, *Centrality and Commonality: An Essay on Confucian Religiousness* (Albany: State University of New York Press, 1989).

Sinologues.[2]

In my view, there are at least three indispensible ingredients for making the Confucian notion of moral religion intelligible. First, according to Confucianism, there is no arbitrary division between morality and religion; in the deepest sense moral consciousness is dependent on religious consciousness, which offers an objective "moral source" and the highest "moral ideal" for human action. That said, seen from the perspective of moral religion, the ethical course of learning to be fully human is predicated on "the idea of *homo religiosus*, which is an ontological assertion about human nature." [3] In sharp contrast to modern secular systems of morality, such as mainstream liberalism, existentialism, and post-modernism, the constellation of moral religion in Confucian thought contains a cluster of comprehensive metaphysical viewpoints about the creation of the world, the first principles of morals, the nature of man, and, perhaps, the meaning of human history.

Second, the *religiousness* of Confucianism does not point to the rituals, institutions, and authorities of a conventional religion; rather, "religiousness" here means the pathway for man to fulfill his spiritual life. That is to say, Confucianism as a moral religion is a "religion without Church;" what makes it a "religion" is not "ecclesiastical" aspects that would concern a "theologian," but the true meaning of being a man, which concerns a "philosopher." In this regard, it is not surprising that a pivotally

---

2 Quoted in Liu Shu-hsien, *Essentials of Contemporary Neo-Confucian Philosophy*（Westport, Connecticut: Praeger, 2003）, p. 35.

3 Tu, *Centrality and Commonality*, p. 116.

important principle in Confucianism is *T'ien-jen-ho-i* (the conformity of Heaven and man in virtue, or Heaven and humanity in union), which entails the anthropocosmic view that "to fully express our humanity, we must engage in a dialogue with Heaven because human nature, as conferred by Heaven, realizes itself not by departing from its source but by returning to it." [4] In short, an internalized conception of Heaven, and its transcendent meaning for completing humanity, lies at the heart of Confucian moral religion.

Third, given the ultimate guiding force of *T'ien-jen-ho-i*, it follows that the moral ideal that characterizes Confucianism is closely related to a profound understanding of the fulfillment of self-realization. More precisely, this has played an essential role in formulating the moral relation of man to Heaven in Confucianism. In the most accepted tradition of Confucius and Mencius, this relationship is described in the doctrine of "*hsin-hsing*," that is, a theory of human mind (heart) and human nature that denotes "inner morality" or "the inwardness of morality." In brief, the moral ideal that Confucianism proposes involves an inner process of "ultimate self-transformation" that leads toward the actualization of the "authentic self." [5]

Whilst the three key features of moral religion may represent a general moral picture of Confucianism, Mou Tsung-san's influential elucidation on

---

4 Ibid., p. 102.

5 See esp. Tu Wei-ming, *Confucian Thought: Selfhood as Creative Transformation* (Albany: State University of New York Press, 1985); Tu Wei-ming, *Centrality and Commonality*.

these topics is what concerns me in this essay. Here I have several purposes: First and foremost, despite Mou's reputation for reconstructing a moral metaphysics based on a critical reading of Kant's transcendental philosophy,[6] it remains the case that some crucial aspects of Mou's academic enterprise are greatly indebted to Hegel, and that its "ultimate objective, which somewhat echoes that of Western post-Kantian philosophy, is to demonstrate the limits of Kant and what the contribution of Chinese thought may be to surpass him." [7] More exactly, while Mou

6 For a critical introduction to Mou's moral metaphysics, see Sebastien Billioud, *Thinking Through Confucian Modernity: A Study of Mou Zongsan's Moral Metaphysics* (Leiden: Brill, 2012); N. Serina Chan, *The Thought of Mou Zongsan* (Leiden: Brill, 2011), Chapters 4-6.

7 Billioud, *Thinking Through Confucian Modernity*, pp. 9-10; see also Stephan Schmidt, "Mou Zongsan, Hegel, and Kant: The Quest for Confucian Modernity," *Philosophy East and West* 61(2): 278. Put briefly, Mou believes that Kant's philosophy, representing the highest peak of Western philosophy, could be very beneficial, on several grounds, in shedding light on traits of Chinese philosophy. First, Mou claims that Kantian moral autonomy strikingly parallels the notion of moral subjectivity implicit in ancient Confucianism, especially the tradition of interpreting *hsin-hsing* from Mencius to the Lu-Wang School of Sung-Ming Confucianism. Second, while Kant denies the existence of what Mou calls "intellectual intuition" in grasping the thing-in-itself, the thread running through the main streams of Chinese philosophy, including Confucianism, Taoism, and Buddhism, consists of their total affirmation of "intellectual intuition," particularly in pursuing what are referred to as the profound "wisdom of life" concerns. Third, there appears, for Mou, a serious limitation in Kant's moral philosophy, namely that his transcendental deduction simply treats free will as a "postulate" of practical reason. This falls short of establishing a deep-rooted moral metaphysics, particularly with regard to concerns about the meaning of human life, concerns that are indeed central to Chinese philosophy. Fourth, it follows for Mou that the growth of a

intentionally reads Kant's idea of autonomy into Mencius and the Lu-Wang School of Sung-Ming Neo-Confucianism, so as to erect the Western-view-based ethical principle of Confucianism in a time when Chinese culture is facing the crisis of meaning, it is Hegel's dialectical philosophy that enables Mou to turn the ethos of Chinese philosophy into a "universal ethics," enriching the deep meaning of a human being for all human beings. The vital point here is that, for Neo-Confucians such as Mou, there is a profound potential value linkage between the Chinese and Western worlds in terms of the spirituality that is embedded in humanity.

Instead of fleshing out Mou's moral and political thinking in a full sense, it is sufficient to point out here only that apart from the Hegelian idea of the "self-negation of inner moral consciousness," which is central to Mou's work, Mou is also receptive to Hegel's theological understanding of history as the realization of human freedom, to the Hegelian principle of embodiment, or the particular principle of individuality or subjectivity,[8]

---

wide-ranging concept of humanity must be predicated upon an attempt to overcome the Kantian bifurcated worlds of noumena and phenomena. This entails accepting that the task, which is most apposite for Chinese philosophers, at present, is to foster a fusion of horizons, by linking the "wisdom of life" debate embedded in Chinese philosophy with the achievements of democracy and science implemented within Western modernity.

8 "For Hegel, reality (*Wirklichkeit*) in its full sense requires the cooperation of two principles, namely the universal principle of the idea and the particular principle of individuality or subjectivity. Without the latter, no progress is possible, because only the individual subject can provide the kind of opposite (*Gegensatz*) without which there is no vehicle for the idea to become real. Freedom, for instance, is one of Hegel's more concrete names for the idea that evolves in history, but without human beings who strive to be free and who

making human action meaningful in history, and to Hegel's attempt to transcend Kant's skeptical definition of human reason in respect to the bifurcated world and the unknown of the thing-in-itself.[9] Regarding moral religion in particular, Hegel's immanent theology actually provides Mou with "a prominent Western voice lending critical support for the inner sageliness of human beings, a main theme of Mou's moral metaphysics;" [10] in fact, I take it that precisely thanks to the influence of Hegel, Mou's reading of Christianity reaffirms "Kant's many seemingly passing and unimportant remarks on religion in the first *Critique*." [11] In short, the presence of the Hegelian way of thinking did not prevent Mou from taking Kant's scheme as his pathway to reach out through a "unique" system of moral metaphysics across cultures; on the contrary, it makes a great addition to our understanding of Mou's momentous contributions to the creative transformation of Confucianism in modern times.

Moreover, in this sense, it is instructive to compare Mou with T. H. Green in relation to moral religion. Just as in the work of Green, who tries to bring together Kant's transcendental subject and Hegel's immanent God

---

establish institutions meant to secure their freedom, the idea of freedom lacks reality and remains abstract. The principle of individuality manifests itself as the particular will of human beings who make freedom their purpose and set out to put it into practice." Schmidt, "Mou Zongsan, Hegel, and Kant," pp. 280-281.

9 For an insightful account of Hegel's influence on Mou, see Chan, *The Thought of Mou Zongsan*, Chapter, 3; Schmidt, "Mou Zongsan, Hegel, and Kant," pp. 279-286.

10 Chan, *The Thought of Mou Zongsan*, p. 95.

11 Schmidt, "Mou Zongsan, Hegel, and Kant," p. 278.

in establishing his own idea of eternal consciousness, it is widely agreed that the notion of moral subjectivity in Confucianism is a blend of transcendence and immanence.[12] By exploring the philosophical similarities between Mou and Green, I shall be able to make the claim that, despite the fact that recent scholarship has largely directed attention to the connection between the Confucian self and the Kantian self, the Confucian self is, on the whole, far closer to Hegelian self-realization than to Kantian self-determination.

Finally, provided that there are salient affinities between Green and Mou in terms of moral religion, the ethics of self-realization, the idea of historical subjectivity, the notion of personalism as opposed to (atomist) individualism, and so on, it is my conviction that a far-reaching dialogue between Neo-Confucianism and British Idealism can help to "liberalize" Confucianism. This could be achieved through encouraging a re-appreciation of the values of perfectionist liberalism and ethical democracy on the one hand, and "broadening" the cultural horizons of Idealism on the other.

II. Hegel: The Reconciliation of God and Humanity

Let me begin with a brief examination of Hegel's philosophical

---

12 As T'ang Chün-i writes in his Preface to *Chung-Kuo Wen-Hua Chih Ching-Shen Chia-Chih* (The Spiritual Values of the Chinese Culture), "Now I realize that every person has a moral self or a mind-substance, which is both immanent and transcendent." Quoted in Liu, *Essentials of Contemporary Neo-Confucian Philosophy*, p. 91.

reflection on Christianity. Overall, what is essential to Hegel's philosophical enterprise is a self-awareness of the growing sense of alienation and estrangement in human feeling, caused, among other factors, by the snapping of the bonds between man and God. As Hegel stated, "our religion wishes to educate men to be the citizens of heaven who always look on high, and this makes them strangers to human feeling." [13]

1. Rethinking Christianity

In fact, in his search for "a purely moral religion," [14] Hegel's early writings displayed his aversion to the orthodox doctrines of Christianity. For example, in "The Positivity of the Christian Religion," Hegel comes to challenge Christian authorities on two main counts: his Romantic love for

13 Quoted in Raymond Plant, *Hegel on Religion and Philosophy* (London: Phoenix, 1997), pp. 13-14.

14 To quote Hegel, "[Jesus] was the teacher of a purely moral religion, not a positive one. Miracles and so forth were not intended to be the basis of doctrines, for these cannot rest on observed facts; those striking phenomena were perhaps simply meant to awaken the attention of a people deaf to morality. On this view, many ideas of his contemporaries, e.g., their expectations of a Messiah, their representation of immortality under the symbol of resurrection, their ascription of serious and incurable diseases to the agency of a powerful evil being, etc., were simply *used* by Jesus, partly because they stand in no immediate connection with morality, partly with a view to attaching a nobler meaning to them; as contemporary ideas they do not belong to the content of a religion, because any such content must be eternal and unalterable." G. W. F. Hegel, *Early Theological Writings*, trans. T. M. Knox (Philadelphia: University of Pennsylvania Press, 1971), p. 71.

Greek "folk religion," whose ultimate truth was beauty, and his early devotion to Kantian ethical thinking in favor of autonomy and rationality. Although a "deep sympathy for the doctrine of the Gospel" as a resolution for his "inner struggle" is present in "The Spirit of Christianity and Its Fate," [15] Hegel describes the tragedy of Christianity by remarking that:

> In all the forms of the Christian religion which have been developed in the advancing fate of the ages, there lies this fundamental characteristic opposition in the divine which is supposed to be present in consciousness only, never in life. ...... Between these extremes of the multiple or diminished consciousness of friendship, hate, or indifference toward the world, between these extremes which occur within the opposition between God and the world, between divine and life, the Christian church has oscillated to and fro, but it is contrary to its essential character to find peace in a non-personal living beauty. And it is its fate that church and state, worship and life, piety and virtue, spiritually and worldly action, can never

---

15 Put simplyly, since "the moral principle of the Gospel is charity, or love, and love is the beauty of the heart, a spiritual beauty which combines the Greek Soul and Kant's Moral Reason," it appears to Hegel that the possibility of bringing together God and the world, the divine and human life, may lie in the ultimate truth of "moral beauty" that appears in the Gospel. Richard Kroner, "Introduction: Hegel's Philosophical Development," in Hegel, *Early Theological Writings*, p. 9. In this regard, the spirit of Jesus can be understood as "a spirit raised above morality," and "the opposition of duty to inclination has found its unification in the modifications of love, i.e., in the virtues." Hegel, *Early Theological Writings*, p. 212, 225.

dissolve into one.[16]

What Hegel complains about here are the "extremes which occur within the opposition between God and the world, between divine and life." As might be expected, this not only reiterates St. Paul's identification of the Christian as "a pilgrim in a foreign land," but also anticipates Hegel's later famous expression of "unhappy consciousness" in his *Phenomenology of Spirit*. In Hegel's statement, passing through ancient Stoicism and Skepticism, the self-consciousness emerging in the Christian spirit is so indifferent to human life that, although one is free in the "beyond," he is restricted in this world, as the "beyond" is "something that cannot be found." [17]As a result of this, the Christian is supposed to live in neither world and can never feel "at home." On this account, I think Judith Shklar is correct in remarking that "Hegel had a very deep sense of the enduring wounds that the 'unhappy consciousness' had inflicted on the European spirit," and that "there was one element in Kant's moral theory that Hegel hated even more than its passivity: its vestigial Christianity and craving for a 'beyond'." [18]

Although it seems that Hegel never changed his mind about the failure of the orthodox doctrine of an externalized God, that is, to treat God as

---

16 Hegel, *Early Theological Writings*, p. 301.

17 G. W. F. Hegel, *Phenomenology of Spirit*, trans. A. V. Miller（Oxford: Oxford University Press, 1977）, p. 131.

18 Judith N. Shklar, *Freedom and Independence: A Study of the Political Ideas of Hegel's 'Phenomenology of Mind'*（Cambridge: Cambridge University Press, 1976）, p. 30, 184.

something out there to be reached, there is a turn to philosophy in *Phenomenology of Spirit*. In other words, while Hegel continues to describe religion on rational grounds,[19] *Phenomenology of Spirit* finally offers a *philosophical* transformation of Christianity that could bring about a reconciliation of God and humanity.[20] The crucial point here is that Hegel does not reject Christianity entirely, but that he only accepts a kind of Christianity that has been "systematically reinterpreted to be a vehicle of his own philosophy." [21] Seen in this light, "what is at issue is the consciousness of absolute reconciliation," "a new consciousness of humanity or a new religion," that accounts for the "consciousness of a reconciliation of humanity with God." [22] It is exactly in this sense that Raymond Plant argues:

> For Hegel, therefore, the philosophy of religion is not just a specific branch of philosophy dealing with a specific set of intellectual problems within religion. It is much more profound

---

19 As Charles Taylor (quoting H. S. Harris) points out, Hegel rests his hope of "new religion" on the following three rational goals: that "its doctrine must be grounded in universal reason;" that "fancy, heart and sensibility must not thereby go empty away;" and consequently that "it must be so constituted that all the needs of life and the public affairs of the sate are tied in with it." Charles Taylor, *Hegel* (Cambridge: Cambridge University Press, 1975), p. 55.

20 Indeed, there are transitions in some important works such as *The Earliest System-Programme of German Idealism* and *The Difference between Fichte's and Schelling's System of Philosophy*.

21 Taylor, *Hegel*, p. 102.

22 G. W. F. Hegel, *Lectures on the Philosophy of Religion*, One-Volume Edition, ed. Peter C. Hodgson, trans. R. F. Brown et al. (Berkeley: University of California Press, 1988), p. 459.

> and pervasive than that. The Christian religion, properly understood, provides us with an integrated account of human existence both historically and in the modern world. It is for Hegel the basis for a new humanity when it is philosophically transcribed and comprehended.[23]

Indeed, what Plant says here stands for the paradigmatic example of moral religion that I am seeking in this essay: namely, that morality and religion are inseparable. In the case of Hegel (as well as Green), however, it should be remembered that this does not necessarily imply that philosophy and religion are identical:

> [Religion] is the consciousness of absolute truth in the way that it occurs for all human beings. Thus it is found in the form of representation. Philosophy has the same content, the truth; it is the spirit of the world generally and not the particular spirit. Philosophy does nothing but transform our representations into concepts. The content remains always the same.[24]

2. The Self-Positing God

To understand Hegel's religious thought completely, one must therefore consider his philosophy. However, space does not permit me to introduce Hegelian dialectics in detail. Instead, I only intend to remark that the aim of his dialectics is to demonstrate how different stages of

---

23 Plant, *Hegel on Philosophy and Religion*, p. 50.

24 Hegel, *Lectures on the Philosophy of Religion*, p. 78.

consciousness proceed from a lower level to a higher level as the "contradiction" in the former is unveiled;[25] and that dialectics always involve an "inner process" of the subject's self-development. Further, for Hegel "the Absolute, what is ultimately real, or what is at the foundation of everything, is subject," [26] and the process of the unfolding of the Absolute "is the process of its own becoming, the circle that presupposes its end as its goal, having its end as its beginning, and only by being worked out to be its end, it is actual." [27]

In this context, we should note that, for Hegel, the inner process of the development of the mind is *ensured* "because there is something analogous to the action of God united with human life and history whose action is the basis for the rationality of the process." [28] More precisely, according to Hegel, the rational necessity of the inner process is made certain because "God, as a conscious being, has this inner necessity, as all conscious

---

25 The dialectical movement involves what Hegel calls *Aufhebung*, meaning that while the defects and contradictions of the previous modes of knowledge are "annulled" and "cancelled," their partial truths are "preserved" and "enhanced" by being incorporated into a richer mode. Thus, the "reconciliation" (*Versohnung*) between God and humanity implies that "the two terms remain, but that their opposition is overcome;" for the unity that is achieved in reconciliation does not really "abolish" the dualism between man and God, but just provides for a richer form of understanding, in which the elements of what preceded it are both "annulled and preserved" (*Aufhebung*). Taylor, *Hegel*, pp. 49-50.

26 Ibid., p. 104. As Hegel put it, "substance is in itself or implicitly Subject, all content is its own reflection into itself." Hegel, *Phenomenology of Spirit*, p. 33.

27 Hegel, *Phenomenology of Spirit*, p. 10.

28 Plant, *Hegel on Philosophy and Religion*, p. 26.

beings do, to externalize himself in nature and in human life – that is to say in otherness – and through this process of externalization to come to full consciousness." [29] As Hegel puts it elsewhere: "The divine Idea is just this: to disclose itself, to posit the Other outside itself and to take it back again into itself in order to be subjectivity and spirit." [30]

In this reading, I think that Charles Taylor's argument is plausible in following Hegel's use of the term "posit" (*setzen*) to identify his concept of God as the "self-posting God," who eternally makes the conditions of his own existence," and who is "the subject of the rational necessity which manifests itself in the world." [31] More precisely,

> Like the theist view, he [Hegel] wants to see the world as designed, as existing in order to fulfill a certain prospectus, the requirements of the embodiment for *Geist*. But like the naturalistic, he cannot allow a God who could design this world from outside, who could exist before and independently of the world. His idea is therefore that of a God who eternally makes the conditions of his own existence.[32]

Here, we are arriving at the core of Hegel's "new religion," in which it is posited that God not only internalizes within human mind, but also manifests in nature and history. In this sense, nature and history are,

---

29 Ibid., p. 32.

30 G. W. F. Hegel, *The Philosophy of Nature*, ed. M. J. Petry (London: George Allen and Unwin, 1970), Vol. 1, p. 205.

31 Taylor, *Hegel*, p. 102.

32 Ibid., p. 101.

therefore, not in conflict, but they are just the essence of God embodied in different forms. Regarding the creation of the world, Hegel makes it clear that:

> Nature is the Son of God, not as the Son however, but as abiding in otherness, in which the divine idea is alienated from love and held fast for a moment. Nature is self-alienated spirit; spirit, a bacchantic good innocent of restraint and reflection has merely been let loose into it; in nature, the unity of the Notion conceals itself.[33]

On the other hand, he also describes the "incarnation" of God in the embodied Christ as a historical truth.

> In order for it [this divine-human unity] to become a certainty for humanity, God had to appear in the world in the flesh [cf. John: 1:14]. The necessity that God [has] appeared in the world in the flesh is an essential characteristics – a necessity deduction from what has been said previously, demonstrated by it – for only in this way can it become a certainty for humanity; only in this way is it truth in the form of certainty.[34]

3. The Realization of Self-Knowledge

There are two crucial points that can be derived from the above discussion. First, since God or the Spirit, as a conscious being, must

33 Hegel, *The Philosophy of Nature*, p. 205.

34 Hegel, *Lectures on the Philosophy of Religion*, p. 455.

externalize itself in otherness, "an understanding of the 'other' in which God is embodied, namely the world of nature and human history in its manifold forms, is itself a study of God." [35] To quote Hegel, "God can be known or cognized, for it is God's nature to reveal himself, to be manifest." [36]

Second, the principle of embodiment indicates that consciousness is not isolated, that it always involves encounter with otherness, and that it requires recognition by what one is not. Therefore, it follows that the dialectical process of the development of self-consciousness is one in which subject comes to realize the Absolute by *historically* engaging with otherness to bring together nature, history and all human knowledge under the name of the ultimate truth, that is, God. Indeed, it is only at the last stage of the development of self-consciousness that the ultimate reconciliation of God and humanity will become apparent to the philosophical mind as the Absolute Knowing. Thus, at the very end of *Phenomenology of Spirit* Hegel writes that:

> The *goal*, Absolute Knowing, or Spirit that knows itself as Spirit, has for its path the recollection of the Spirit as they are in themselves and as they accomplish the organization of their realm. Their preservation, regarded from the side of their free existence appearing in the form of contingent, is History; but regarded from the side of their [philosophically] comprehended

35 Plant, *Hegel on Philosophy and Religion*, p. 33.

36 Quoted in ibid., p. 33.

> organization, it is the Science of Knowing in the sphere of appearance: the two together, comprehended History, form alike the inwardizing and the Calvary of Absolute Spirit, the actuality, truth, and certainty of his throne, without which he would lifeless and alone.[37]

All this reaffirms that, for Hegel, freedom and reason can only be actualized and grasped in history, that the human mind must be historically conditioned, and that human practices always entail historical consciousness. Compared with Kantian *Moralität*, as a result, Hegelian *Sittlichkeit* suggests that "morality cannot be achieved by individuals, but only by an entire community or mankind as a whole, living in a wholly uncoercive, loving 'ethical commonwealth' for which [the] Lawgiver alone legislates."[38]

And so, according to Taylor, Kantian self-determination, based on "the conception of a noumenal agent,"[39] is understood as a form of "disengaged subjectivity," meaning that moral conduct is to act "from duty" by the guidance of "reason," irrespective of any desire and inclination and regardless of any culture and history, whereas Hegelian self-realization provides "one of the most profound and far reaching attempts to work out a vision of embodied subjectivity, of thought and freedom emerging from the stream of life, finding expression in the forms

37 Hegel, *Phenomenology of Spirit*, p. 493.

38 Shklar, *Freedom and Independence*, p. 185.

39 Charles Taylor, *Sources of the Self: The Making of Modern Identity* (Cambridge: Cambridge University Press, 1989), p. 367.

of social existence, and discovering themselves in relation to nature and history." [40]

III. Green: The Humanistic Calling for God

The religious thought of British Idealism was greatly influenced by Hegel. For our purposes, it is sufficient only to examine the Hegelian aspects of Green's idea of moral religion by bringing the following three issues into consideration: Green's criticisms of Catholicism, Green's notion of the eternal consciousness, and the Christian self appearing in his writings.[41]

1. Criticisms of Catholicism

Paralleling Hegel's disapproval of the Christian religion with respect to "unhappy consciousness," Green criticizes Catholicism for falling to acknowledge the proper relation between God and man as it asserts "the opposition between the inward and outward, between reason and authority,

40 Taylor: *Hegel*, p. 571; see also Charles Taylor, *Hegel and Modern Society* (Cambridge: Cambridge University Press, 1979), p. 168.

41 "Green's metaphysical doctrine of the reproduction of the eternal consciousness within the individual consciousness," as Andrew Vincent rightly argues, is "reliant upon the background of a Hegelian theology," and owes a great deal to German Hegelian theologist, Friedrich Christian Bauer. Andrew Vincent, "T. H. Green: Citizenship as Political and Metaphysical," in David Boucher and Andrew Vincent, *British Idealism and Political Theory* (Edinburgh: Edinburgh University Press, 2000), p. 38.

between the spirit and the flesh, between individual and the world of settled right." [42] In Green's mind, the major problem with Catholicism is that, over time, it has developed into a "Christianity of ordinances," [43] a "dogmatic theology," falling short of the "immediate consciousness" of a genuine religion or the "intuition" of the divine.[44] It therefore comes as no surprise that like Hegel, Green holds that Lutheran Protestantism, understood as a form of "revealed religion," has shed "inward light" upon the new Protestant subject by appealing to "justification by faith" and "the right of private judgment," [45] and that the Reformation has effectively had a positive impact upon the European Spirit, enabling it to move toward the reunification of humanity and God. According to Green, having "opened a breach in the substantial unity of Christendom," [46] the Reformation spread the fresh idea of autonomous consciousness over humanity, calling for a humanistic re-understanding of the connection between God and man. This is a "calling" that requires serious philosophical scrutiny, because when the new Protestant subject is "released from the dogma of the church," it is likely that "he will make a dogma of his own." [47] In this sense, it can be

42 T. H. Green, "Four Lectures on the English Revolution," in *Works of Thomas Hill Green*, ed. R. L. Nettleship, Vol. III (London: Longmans, Green, and Co, 1888), p. 281.

43 Ibid., p. 279; Cf. Vincent, "T. H. Green: Citizenship as Political and Metaphysical," p. 33, 37.

44 T. H. Green, "Essay on Christian Dogma," in *Works* III, p. 164.

45 Green, "Essay on Christian Dogma," p. 182; "Four Lectures on the English Revolution," p. 280, 282.

46 Green, "Four Lectures on the English Revolution," p. 279.

47 Green, "Essay on Christian Dogma," p. 182.

said that the "calling" is nothing but a rational expectation for the advent of a "true philosophy." As Andrew Vincent eloquently articulates,

> For Green, religion should neither try to place itself above secular authorities, nor fix God's presence into symbolic sacraments. The only hope, for Green, is a consciousness which moves beyond this dualism, one which "laboriously thoughtful" and apprehends (what we call) God in the rational educated consciousness of humanity. The aim of such an essentially Protestant philosophy would be "Christian citizenship" and because not claiming to be special or exceptional or miraculous, will do more for mankind than its "Catholic" form, hampered by false antagonism.[48]

Moreover, remaining alone Hegel's lines, Green firmly argues that, "all that was essential in Christianity was capable of being restated in terms of a rationally organized scheme of thought." [49] In fact, for Green, "philosophy does but interpret, with full consciousness and in system, the powers already working in the spiritual life of mankind." [50] That said, like Hegel, Green argues that a new religion can be developed, which is able to generate a true integration of human ethical personality within a community. "Christian dogma, then, must be retained in its completeness,

---

48 Vincent, "T. H. Green: Citizenship as Political and Metaphysical," p. 34.

49 Bernard M. G. Reardon, "T. H. Green as a Theologian," in T*he Philosophy of T. H. Green*, ed. Andrew Vincent（Aldershot: Gower Publishing Co. Ltd. 1986）, p. 41.

50 T. H. Green, "Popular Philosophy in Its Relation to Life," in *Works* III, p. 93.

but it must be transformed into a philosophy." [51] As Green's former pupil Arnold Toynbee puts it, "Other thinkers have assailed the orthodox foundations of religion to overthrow it. Mr. Green assailed it to save it." [52]

Following Hegel, then, Green sees one of major tasks of philosophy as re-articulating the religiousness in Christianity in a rational way. In reviewing J. Caird's "Introduction to Philosophy of Religion," Green remarks that:

> That there is one spiritual self conscious being, of which all that is real is the activity and the expression; that we are related to this spiritual being, not merely as parts of the world which is its expression, but as partakers in some inchoate measure of the self consciousness through which it at once constitutes and distinguishes itself from the world; that this participation is *the source of morality and religion*; this we take to be the vital truth which Hegel had to teach.[53]

In short, influenced by Hegel, Green's ethics is also embroiled in a form of moral religion, as religion was seen to be "giving expression to God in the moral life." [54]

---

51 Green, "Essay on Christian Dogma," p. 182.

52 Quoted in Andrew Vincent and Raymond Plant, *Philosophy, Politics and Citizenship* (Oxford: Basil Blackwell, 1984), p. 9.

53 T. H. Green, "Review of J. Caird: 'Introduction to the Philosophy of Religion," in *Works* III, p. 146.

54 Vincent and Plant, *Philosophy, Politics and Citizenship*, p. 16.

2. The Eternal Consciousness

For Green, the religiousness under discussion is nothing less than the "eternal consciousness," expressing a philosophical appreciation of God, the divine, or the infinite as an idea of reason and morality.[55] In "Fragment of an Address on the Text 'The World is Nigh Thee'," Green writes that:

> It has been sometimes remarked that if all the New Testament had been lost to us except some half-dozen texts, the essence of Christianity would have been preserved in these, so that out of them everything in it that is of permanent moral value might have been developed; and if there can be an essence within the essence of Christianity, it is the thought embodied in the text I have read; the thought of God, not as "far off" but "nigh" , not as a master but as a father, not as a terrible outward power, forcing us we know not whither, but as one of whom we may say that we are reason of his reason and spirit of his spirit; who lives in our moral life, and for whom we live in living for the brethren, even as in so living we live freely, because in obedience to a spirit which is our self; in communication with whom we triumph over death, and have assurance of eternal

55 In general, "the Hegelian element of Green's metaphysics is that the eternal consciousness, which is the self-organizing principle at the heart of his system, gradually realizes itself through the 'society' of finite individuals." Jeremy Dunham et al., *Idealism: The History of a Philosophy* (Durham: Acumen, 2001), p. 167.

life.[56]

Seen in this light, when Green says that "God has died and been buried, and risen again, and realized himself in all the particulars of a moral life," [57] and that "if Christ dies for all, all died in him: all were buried in his grave to be all made alive in his resurrection," [58] he is clearly saying that the basis of our moral life is predicated on a rational understanding of the eternal consciousness of God embedded in us. Thus, sticking to Hegel's conception of an immanent God and the principle of embodiment, Green also understands the meaning of incarnation from a moral point of view throughout. Indeed, for Green, "Christ is realized in moral action" ; "the incarnation of Christ *is* a moral idea implanted in the consciousness of the radically free subject." [59] In brief, Green retains Hegel's insight that the way to discover the divine is within man himself; for Christ has become the "necessary determination of the eternal subject, the objectification by this subject of himself in the world of nature and humanity." [60]

Now, it has become plain that Christ, as an idea of rationality and morality internalized within the human mind, actually speaks for man's

---

56 T. H. Green, "Fragment of an Address on the Text 'The World is Nigh Thee'," in *Works* III, p. 221.

57 Green, " Essay on Christian Dogma," p. 184.

58 T. H. Green, "The Witness of God," in *Works* III, p. 233.

59 Andrew Vincent, "T. H. Green and the Religion of Citizenship," in *The Philosophy of T. G. Green*, p. 54; " T. H. Green: Citizenship as Political and Metaphysical," p. 38.

60 Green, "Essay on Christian Dogma," p. 183.

own "true self," [61] that is, the moral ideal to be sought in a course of action. To quote Green,

> There is a conception to which every one who thinks about himself as a moral agent almost instinctively finds himself resorting, the conception variously expressed as that of the "better," the "higher," the "true" self. This conception, I believe, points the way to that true interpretation of our moral nature, which is also the only source of a true theology.[62]

It follows that the central theme of Green's moral religion holds the view that "Christ is the eternal act of God, perpetually re-enacted in individual human lives" [63] as they struggle to realize their own true selves. In other words, for Green,

> Christ is what all humans are in potentiality. The Christ figure is thus part of the eternal objectification of God in the world. This, for Green, is the root Christian idea. Religion becomes active

---

61 The attempt to treat the true self as divine and rational is quite common to many British Idealists. For example, A. C. Bradley writes that "the stirring of religion is the feeling that my only true self in the end is God, to be a pulse-beat of his infinite life, to feel and know that I am that and nothing but that, and that this horrible core of selfishness in my heart, that parts me from him, is not there in his eyes at all." A. C. Bradley, *Ideals of Religion* (Gifford Lectures, 1907) (London: Macmillan, 1940), p. 242. On the other hand, John Stuart Mackenzie argues that the "true self is what is perhaps best described as the *rational* self. It is the universe that we occupy in our moments of deepest wisdom and insight." J. S. Mackenzie, *A Manual of Ethics* (London: W. B. Clive, 1890; 4th edition. 1901), p. 148.

62 Green, "Fragment of an Address on the Text 'The World is Nigh Thee'," p. 223.

63 Vincent, "T. H. Green: Citizenship as Political and Metaphysical," p. 38.

morality. This is the substance to the radically free subject, the Christian citizen.[64]

To sum up what we have discovered so far, although, unlike Bradley, Green does not directly employ a dialectical method to establish his ethics, he clearly sets out to adopt Hegel's theology concerning moral issues. No matter how far Green was influenced by Kant regarding the idea of free will, his moral theory undeniably presents a typical Hegelian form of moral religion. Put succinctly, whereas for Kant religion is "an appendix to the ethical personality," and the philosophy of religion eventually becomes "an adjunct to moral philosophy," [65] Green follows Hegel's footsteps in seeing the philosophy of religion as "more profound and pervasive than that." The Christian religion, for Green, as for Hegel, is "the basis for a new humanity when it is philosophically transcribed and comprehended." In short, Green sees God as "immanent in individuals and in history" ;[66] that is to say, "immanent in the total structure of human experience, including science, history, and social and political life." [67]

3. The True Self

Having touched on Green's external consciousness, we are now in a better position to examine his discussion on the moral ideal of self-

---

64 Ibid.

65 Ibid., p. 40.

66 David O. Brink, "Editor's Introduction" to T. H. Green, *Prolegomena to Ethics* (Oxford: Oxford University Press, 2003), p. xviii.

67 Andrew Vincent, "Introduction" to *The Philosophy of T. H. Green*, p. 4.

realization. In what follows, with the aim of this study in mind, I shall clarify Green's idea of self-realization by briefly discussing Kant.

My argument so far has implied that it is only through a Hegelian reading of the eternal consciousness, allowing anything but distinctions between God and man, nature and morality, fact and value, phenomena and noumena, etc., that we can make real sense of Green's rejection of Kant's bifurcation in the first book of *Prolegomena to Ethics*. For Green, "there is but a single order of reality, nature, man and God being essentially one." [68] However, this is not to say that Green is entirely indifferent to Kant's transcendental philosophy. In fact, Green's idea of free subject and his theory of knowledge and experience owes a great deal to Kant.

Briefly, what underlines Kant's transcendental argument is the view that the task of a philosopher is to discover the *postulates* or *conditions* that make knowledge and morality possible in the first place. As J. G. Murphy comments,

> A transcendental argument or deduction, it will be recalled, proceeds from experience to a discovery of those conditions making this experience possible. It discovers presuppositions or necessary conditions for intelligibility... [Similarly, in morality] we do not discover that freedom is a value by inductive argument. We do not note that people say things like "Freedom is a good thing" with great frequency. Rather, we see that unless

68 Reardon, "Green as a Theologian," p. 41.

> freedom is *presupposed* as a basic value, much of our ordinary moral talk – that which it is the business of the moral philosopher to analyze – would not make sense, would not be intelligible.[69]

This suggests that one of the main tasks of Kant's *Critique of Pure Reason*, as is well known, is to pose a critique "of the faculty of reason in general, in respect of all knowledge after which it may strive independently of all experience." [70] Indeed, Kant's epistemology addresses the point that the knowing subject goes before the object, and that the ability to experience is prior to what is experienced.

Parallel to Kant's transcendental argument, Green argues in *Prolegomena to Ethics* that, since the motive for human action is not merely "felt desire," but "conceived desire," there must therefore be a self-distinguishing subject who is able to conceive and think. In other words, since "all desire is the act of a subject which thinks in desiring, all thought the act of a subject which desires in thinking," [71] it follows that subject precedes desire. And thus, it is not surprising that, following Kant, Green also calls the ability of the subject to conceive and think "the will," viz. "free-cause." [72] "The will is simply the man. Any act of will is the

---

69 J. G. Murphy, *Kant: Philosophy of Right*, 2nd edition (Macon: Mercer University Press, 1994), p. 32.

70 I. Kant, *Critique of Pure Reason*, trans. N. K. Smith (London: Macmillan, 1993), p. 9.

71 T. H. Green, *Prolegomena to Ethics*, ed. David, O. Brink (Oxford: Oxford University Press, 2003), p. 155.

72 Ibid., p. 85.

expression of the man as he at the time is." [73]

More to the point, analogous to Kant's transcendental unity of apperception, in which he argues that the world of experience is the result of an expanded and unified application of *a priori* forms and categories (objective reference) working on what is given, Green, too, adopts a unifying eternal subject. For Green, the self is related to a unity of relations by means of which we come to comprehend the world, which in turn implies an eternal consciousness that transcends individuals as particulars. "Human action is only explicable by the action of an eternal consciousness, which uses them as its organs and reproduces itself through them." [74] As a result, it seems that Green's eternal consciousness, the Absolute, embraces both transcendence and immanence, resulting in criticism from David Brink, who asserts that, for the sake of clarification, "Green must choose whether the Absolute is transcendent or immanent." [75]

From the standpoint I am taking, however, it is exactly the fact that the two fundamental meanings of eternal consciousness coexist in Green's thought that interests me the most in this essay. As has been indicated, the most distinctive characteristic of Confucian moral subjectivity is also a combination of transcendence and immanence, which can be more compatibly reconstructed in terms of Hegelian moral religion than *solely* in terms of a Kantian transcendental argument. Before turning to examine the idea of moral religion in Confucianism, I shall now try to show how it

73 Ibid., p. 173.

74 Ibid., p. 93.

75 Brink, "Editor's Introduction," p. xxviii.

is possible to accommodate both transcendence and immanence in Green's idea of self-realization, from a Hegelian viewpoint of moral religion.

To start with, in contrast with Kant's skeptical attitude toward metaphysics, we should remember that Green's inherent concern about moral religion obviously signifies that "he is essentially a religious philosopher" [76] with a resolute hope in metaphysics. Consequently, if it is true that God is the "ideal self" for the individual to re-enact within his mind, it seems to me equally sufficient to argue that the transcendental feature of eternal consciousness in Green's thinking subject not only denotes "what is already within me" before the world makes any sense to me, but, more importantly, it also implies the *spiritual breaking-through* of the self to reach out to the "ideal self" *above* me.

Second, it also follows that, in Green's thought, the eternal consciousness does not simply stand for the *postulates* of the existence of God. Far from the Kantian use of the term, Green's eternal consciousness argues for the real embodiment of God within me at various degrees. In Kant's examination, since God, the soul and the world are neither spatial nor temporal – no one can conceive anything that is outside of time and space – they are thus merely *things-in-themselves*, which are inaccessible to my subjectivity. Therefore, it is completely useless to employ a subjective category regarding understanding transcendental experience: that is, to employ causality to prove the existence of God. This is why Kant tries to show that traditional metaphysics leads to insoluble

76 Vincent, "T. H. Green: Citizenship as Political and Metaphysical," p. 53.

"antinomies," in which no progress is made compared to physical science. However, although the themes of traditional metaphysics have nothing to do with real science, for Kant they remain as matters of faith: "I had therefore to remove *knowledge* in order to make way for *belief*." [77] By claiming this, Kant leaves us with a bifurcated world: the physical world and the world of freedom (or in later versions, Nature and History).

In contrast with Kant's bifurcated world, Green never treated the existence of God, the immortality of soul and the free will as *things-in-themselves*. In a personal letter to Scott Holland, Green explained that his philosophical conclusions overall are "the inevitable result of thinking together God, the world and the history of man." [78] The crucial point here is that Green is an advocate of Absolute Idealism, caring about the real existence and true actualization of the eternal subject, rather than of Subjective Idealism, simply being interested in the transcendent conditions of genuine knowledge.

In the sphere of morality, the subject-matter of *Prolegomena to Ethics*, the key thread running through Green's work is as follows: given the necessary existence of the knowing subject and its will to conceive desire that initiates action, it follows that the satisfaction of an action, namely good, must be the actual realization of the capacities and potentialities of the self within community, rather than the exercise of the free will as a postulate. That is to say, for Green, the moral import of human action lies

77 Kant, *Critique of Pure Reason*, Preface.

78 Quoted in Vincent, "T. H. Green: Citizenship as Political and Metaphysical," p. 53.

in the idea of good located in the development of the process of self-realization, and, consequently, the degree of good is dependent on how great the capacities and potentialities of the self are to be realized in that action. In short, self-realization is "the realization of the capacities of the human soul" or "the perfecting of man" in history.[79]

Here we can see the communitarian facet of Green's discussion of the moral self.[80] Put briefly, since the human world, as we have seen, is an unfolding of the eternal act of God, the world that we inhabit is a world of the rationalization of divinity. To realize one's own "ideal self," a person must at the same time internalize the "common norms" within an integrated community, starting from family and social relationships, through civil society, to the state. In political terms, this means that the aim of the state is to promote the actualization of real freedom, that is, the full accomplishment of self-realization.

This is not the place to explore Green's political thought with regard

79 Green, *Prolegomena to Ethics*, p. 336.

80 As in Confucianism, there is also a tendency to emphasize the social dimension of the moral self in British Idealism. For example, F. H. Bradley famously articulated that "the 'individual' apart from the community is an abstraction. It is not anything real and hence not anything that we can realize, however much we may wish to do so. We have seen that I am myself by sharing with others, by including in my essence relations to them, the relations of the social state. If I wish to realize my true being, I must therefore realize something beyond my being as a mere this or that; for my true being has in it a life which is not the life of any mere particular, and so must be called a universal life. What is it then that I am to realize? We have said it in 'my station and its duties'." Bradley, *Ethical Studies*, p. 173.

to his perfectionist liberalism. Instead, we will now observe two more philosophically important features of his idea of self-realization. On the one hand, just as with contemporary thinkers such as Charles Taylor and Alasdair MacIntyre, the communitarian dimension of Green's thought still emphasizes the value of the individual, or the idea of freedom or autonomy (in the broader sense). As Green puts it, "no one can convey a good character to another." "Everyone must make his character for himself." [81]

On the other hand, it is worth mentioning that, while Hegel seems to have thought that the Absolute or God has achieved full realization in his own time, Green, under the influence of F. C. Baur, rather holds that "the self-realization of God is never a finished process." [82] To quote Green himself:

> The revelation therefore is not made in a day, or a generation, or a century. The divine mind touches, modifies, becomes the mind of mind, through a process which mere intellectual conception is only the beginning but of which the gradual complement is an unexhausted series of spiritual discipline through all the agencies of social life.[83]

However, this does not affect the fact that Green essentially follows Hegel's endorsement that full self-realization can only take place within an integrated community. At root, the center of Green's moral thinking is Hegelian *Sittlichkeit* rather than Kantian *Moralitate*. Moral action, Green

---

81 Green, *Prolegomena to Ethics*, p. 401.

82 Vincent and Plant, *Philosophy, Politics and Citizenship*, p. 12.

83 Green, "The Witness of God," p. 239.

insists, is "the expression of man's character as it reacts upon and responds to given circumstances." [84]

IV. Confucian Religiousness: A Hegelian Reconstruction

Thus far, we have unveiled the three main aspects of the idea of moral religion in the thought of Hegel and Green: the disapproval of the orthodox Christian view that God is external; a reinterpretation of the attributes of God through internalization; and the moral ideal of self-realization as the fulfillment of one's inner morality through communicating with the way in which God works in history. In this section, I want to argue that Mou Tsung-san's reconstruction of Confucian moral religion is intensely indebted to Hegel; and consequently that his reexamination of ethical personality in Confucian thought bears a remarkable resemblance to Green's idea of self-realization.

1. What Is Wrong with Christianity?

When Mou states that, "whoever wants to provide a positive account and affirmation for moral religion, will adopt the position of Idealism in philosophy," [85] he is self-consciously referring to the Hegelian revision of Christianity. In rethinking the problem of the relation between God and man in the West, Mou also publicly acknowledges Hegel's contribution

---

84 Green, *Prolegomena to Ethics*, p. 120.

85 Mou Tsung-san, *Sheng-Ming Te Hsüeh-Wen* (The Learning of Life) (Taipei: San-Min Shu-Chü, 1970), p. 82.

toward developing a humanistic version of Christianity.[86] As he remarks,

> The modern spirit of the west has forgotten about God and its transcendent medieval ideals and made its own social culture incarnate and immanent. This has had a humbling and alleviating affect on Christianity. While this could reflect an insufficiency or decline in the West's religious spirit, it also enables a greater unity between Heaven and man through *chien-hsing chin-hsing*, so revitalizing the West's religious spirit and launching a new transformation. Hegel's *Philosophy of History* is an attempt to demonstrate this change by verifying the embodiment of God in a secular world from the perspective of historical development. This is the only way that we can find a solution to the way things are in this world.[87]

It seems fair to indicate that Mou is interested in Christianity for two reasons: to examine the weakness of Western civilization, and to highlight the peculiarity of Chinese civilization. In Mou's terminology, the sharp distinction between orthodox Christianity and Confucianism can be singled out in terms of *li-chiao* ("distant religion") and *yuan-chiao* ("complete religion"). While following the Hegelian viewpoint, Mou sees the conventional Christian religion as based on the externalization of God, but the spirit of Confucianism as entirely humanistic. He remarks that:

> The life of Christ aimed to give up all things in reality, even to

86 Mou Tsung-san, *Tao-Te Te Li-Hsiang-Chu-I* (Moral Idealism) (Taipei: Hsüeh-Sheng Shu-Chü, 1959), pp. 183-185.

87 Mou, *Sheng-Ming Te Hsüeh-Wen*, p. 222.

> sacrifice his own life, in order to return to God. By returning to God his religious spirit proved that only the true God is the pure absolute, above man. In this sense, the religion created by Christ is non-humanistic or trans-humanistic. Despite this, he reveals a criterion of truth, which has become the criterion of human activity and formed the cultural system of Western Christianity throughout its development. In his religion, he does not aim to pursue the union of God and man or instill a moral subjectivity that can relate man to God. This is the spirit of a two-bladed knife [representing two separate worlds], so I refer to it as a remote religion.[88]

In contrast, as Mou continues, what is central to Confucianism is a form of "complete religion," emphasizing "intellectual intuition" and "concrete completeness." More precisely, the religiousness of Confucianism consists in the belief that "humanity forms an inseparable unity with Heaven, earth, and the myriad things, its sensibility is in principle all-embracing;" and thus, "in a deeper sense, self-knowledge is neither 'knowing that' nor 'knowing how'; it is, in essence, an objectless awareness, a realization of human possibility of 'intellectual intuition'." [89] Seen in this light, as in all other organized religions, "transcendence" is crucially important in Confucianism. However, more analogous to Hegel and Green than to orthodox Christianity, the "transcendence" at stake is not meant to signify

88 Mou, *Tao-Te Te Li-Hsiang-Chu-I*, p. 159.

89 Tu, *Confucian Thought*, p. 20.

the externalization of God, but the perfecting of man, the true self, as God or Heaven has bestowed within the mind. In short, Confucian religiousness clearly implies "the ethical personality of holiness." [90]

I shall return to the ideas of Heaven and self-realization in Confucian thought shortly. For now, we must note that this does not mean that man arrives fully formed with this "intellectual intuition" and "concrete completeness;" but rather, it is only through a lifelong effort in the thorny and arduous practice of the ethical life that the full potentialities of human nature can be actualized. This explains why, instead of the Gospels and the Messiah, the core of Confucianism contains the rich teachings of *kung-fu*, meaning the continual practices of the perfecting of a great man.

Therefore, in answering the disputed question about whether Confucianism is a religion, Mou's insights, which have continued to influence future generations of Neo-Confucians,[91] are as follows: in terms of "institutions," it is true that Confucianism has never developed into an organized setting of religious rituals; in terms of "principle," however, Confucianism is "highly religious," and represents "an extremely complete

90 Mou, *Tao-Te Te Li-Hsiang-Chu-I*, p. 43.

91 It is interesting to note that influenced by Mou's ethico-spiritual approach to Confucianism, the two prominent scholars from the "third generation" of Neo-Confucianism, namely Liu Shu-hsien and Tu Wei-ming, have tried to re-create an even more comprehensive framework of "universal ethics," aiming to promote Confucianism as "a spiritual resource for living in the contemporary world and for the formulation of a universal spiritual world creed" (Chan, *The Thought of Mou Zongsan*, p. 285), without discarding Catholicism, Judaism, or Islamism.

spirit of religion." [92] In other words, Mou thinks that, "although China has never come up with a religion such as Christianity, the most spectacular and complete moral consciousness, moral spirit or the state of moral affairs, is already represented by Confucianism." [93] Based on the moral ideal of *jen* (humanity, benevolence) and the central thinking about *hsin-hsing* (human mind and human nature) and *Tao* (the Way of Heaven), Confucianism has achieved a complete "pathway to spirit life," [94] gradually reaching toward the unity of Heaven and man in virtue. In short, Confucianism, properly understood, is a comprehensive form of moral religion, containing the moral "basis of ordinary life" and the spiritual "motif of cultural creation." [95]

2. The Internalization of Heaven

By disclosing the religiousness of Confucianism from a Hegelian viewpoint, Mou is also making explicit its humanistic implications; indeed, the moral religion in his mind is one "upon which human dignity is based, and from which human value stems." [96] Therefore, it comes as no surprise that Mou's statements about *T'ien-jen-ho-i*, paralleling Hegel and Green, show us a further demonstration of the internalization of Heaven in

---

92 Mou Tsung-san, *Chung-Kuo Che-Hsüeh Te T'e-Chih* (The Features of Chinese Philosophy) (Taipei: Hsüeh-Sheng Shu-Chü, 1963), p. 138.

93 Mou, *Sheng-Ming Te Hsüeh-Wen*, pp. 32-33.

94 Mou, *Tao-Te Te Li-Hsiang-Chu-I*, pp. 125-141.

95 Ibid., p. 259.

96 Ibid., p. 152.

Confucian thought.

To realize the interrelationship between Heaven and man, Mou actually traces the origins of the idea of Heaven back to an older tradition in Chinese culture. In that tradition, as Mou maintains, Heaven is understood in terms of *ching* (esteem). "In esteem, our subjectivity does not face toward God; what we do is not self-negation, but self-affirmation." [97] That is to say, in sharp contrast to original sin and the fall, when the mind is full of *ching*, the more we come to know about Heaven, the more we will come to realize the holiness and completeness that we already have within our subjectivity. In fact, for Mou, the very idea of "intellectual intuition" running through Chinese culture (including Confucianism, Taoism, and Buddhism) can be characterized in terms of three assertions: the mental activity of *self-affirmation*; the fact that the ability to conduct this self-affirmation can be seen as *moral ability*; and that this ability is the infinite and *absolute universal*.[98]

Confucian moral religion certainly takes as its point of departure the idea that humanity or human nature is deeply rooted in Heaven, rather than opposed to it. To quote the first sentence of *Chung-Yung* (*the Doctrine of Mean*): "Human nature is what Heaven imparts." Further, as Mou accurately argues, we can only truly appreciate "inner morality" as being nothing but the "universal reason regulated by humanity in harmony with

97 Mou, *Chung-Kuo Che-Hsüeh Te T'e-Chih*, p. 23.

98 Mou Tsung-San, *Chih Te Chih-Chiao Yu Chung-Kuo Che-Hsüeh*（Intellectual Intuition and Chinese Philosophy）（Taipei: Shang-Wu Shu-Chü, 1971）, pp. 196-199.

divinity," [99] if we view the framework of Confucianism from a perspective of moral religion. Therefore, Confucius's highest virtue of *jen* (humanity, benevolence) or Mencius's four germs: *jen*, *i* (righteousness), *li* (the rituals), *chih* (wisdom), are just different expressions of the universal reason within us: the universal moral ability to undertake self-affirmation endowed by Heaven. For this reason, Mou is likely to identify Confucianism as a form of "rational Idealism" or "idealistic rationalism," in Western philosophical terms.

In accordance with "rational Idealism," (or I would say Absolute Idealism), there is another sense in which Mou deliberately employs Hegel's philosophy of religion to reconstruct the idea of Heaven and man in union. In Hegel's terminology, as Mou reminds us, the idea of Heaven and man in union actually stands perfectly for the "Real Unification" of subjectivity and objectivity, that is, the actualization of "Real Reality." [100] In other words, the Confucian way of grasping Heaven and man in union is reminiscent of Hegel's Absolute Spirit. Thus it comes as no surprise that for Mou the idea of "inner-holiness" in Confucianism, which represents the capability of grasping "the heavenly, sagely or enlightened way," is equivalent to that of "knowing God" inwardly in the Hegelian revision of Christianity; as Mou articulates, Hegel's "learning is an understanding that attains an all-encompassing utter clarity of the development and realization

99 Mou Tsung-san, *Li-Shih Che-Hsüeh* (Philosophy of History) (Taipei: Hsüeh-Sheng Shu-Chü, 1955), p. 371. Cf. *Tao-Te Te Li-Hsiang-Chu-I*, p. 5; *Sheng-Ming Te Hsüeh-Wen*, p. 237.

100 Mou, *Chung-Kuo Che-Hsüeh Te T'e-Chih*, p. 55.

of the mind and human nature," which in turn is advantageous for acknowledging Kant's "self-imposed barrier to metaphysical insight with his epistemology." [101]

Thus seen, the development of "inner morality" or the "inwardness of *jen* and *i*" simply signifies what Hegel has called the inner process of self-consciousness, whereas the objectification and externalization of *jen* and *i* denotes how subjective spirit develops into objective spirit. As Chung-ying Cheng puts it,

> *Jen* is the beginning and the end of a full process of humanizing a human person or, for that matter, a process of human perfecting. *Jen* is also such a process of continuing achievement and effort toward the end of humanization and perfection.[102]

In Mou's phrase, then, "Confucius's *jen* and *i* are not only related to morals, but also to their objective realization;" "every institution is but the objectification of Reason, the expression of objective spirit." [103] In short, the key notion of *jen* in the Confucian *Analects* is equal to Absolute Reason in Hegel's philosophy.[104]

At this point, it is interesting to note that just as Hegel's Absolute Reason seeks the unification of any possible divisions, the term *jen* in Confucianism literally means "humanity" as a whole. According to Wing-

---

101 Chan, *The Thought of Mou Zongsan*, pp. 106-107.

102 Chung-ying Cheng, *New Dimensions of Confucian and Neo-Confucian Philosophy*（Albany: State University of New York Press, 1991）, p. 298.

103 Mou, *Tao-Te Te Li-Hsiang-Chu-I* , p. 5.

104 Mou, *Sheng-Ming Te Hsüeh-Wen*, p. 181, 183, 193.

tsit Chan's prevailing definition, *jen* leads to general virtue "which is basic, universal and the source of all specific virtues," although Confucius "never defined it." [105] Furthermore, in Mou's interpretation, *jen* is not simply the highest virtue, the perfecting of man, or the ideal self; it also implies the moral capacity and potentiality that are within us.

In the latter usage, *jen* has two general features, namely, *chüeh* (awareness) and *chien* (constancy). While *chueh* means the self-awareness of moral heart, "only when one acquires awareness, he will gain the heart of four germs;" *chien* demands that one should "abide by the constancy of the Way of Heaven" so as to unify humanity and Heaven in virtue.[106] In this regard, the general picture of Confucius's moral thinking can be seen as his own personal struggle in seeking ethical personality, that is, *hsia-hsüeh* ("learning from what is around me," mainly history and rites) and *shang-ta* ("getting through to what is to up above," [107] i.e. Heaven).

Put clearly, in parallel with the internalization and externalization of the Absolute Knowing, Mou gives two similar meanings to *jen* through his Hegelian reading of Confucianism. In his expression, *jen i kan-t'ung wei hsing, i jun-wu wei jun* ("the nature of *jen* is the all-embracing sensibility, while its function is to nurture the myriad things.")[108] Through the *kung-*

---

105 Wing-tsit Chan, "Chinese and Western Interpretations of Jen (Humanity)," *Journal of Chinese Philosophy* 2 (1975), p. 109.

106 Mou, *Chung-Kuo Che-Hsüeh Te T'e-Chih*, p. 43. See also, *Tao-Te Te Li-Hsiang-Chu-I*, pp. 14-15, 24.

107 The *Analects*, 14: 23.

108 Mou, *Li-Shih Che-Hsüeh*, p. 178.

fu (practice) of putting *jen* into action, the moral sources within my heart can therefore be reverberated with the Way of Heaven. Therefore, he argues that *jen*, just like Hegel's Absolute Spirit, can be well understood as the "real life," the "real substance," the "real subjectivity," or the "real self" in the deepest moral sense.[109]

In Hegelian theology, as we have seen, one of the most significant consequences stemming from the immanence of God is the corresponding inward tendency to reinterpret the incarnation of Christ. In contemporary Neo-Confucianism, there is also an inclination to universalize the spirituality of the ethical life of Confucius. To quote T'ang Chün-i, another leading Neo-Confucian, "the life of Confucius is the stage of the incarnation of Chinese culture." [110] In a similar way, Mou argues that Confucius and Mencius should not be treated simply as philosophers according to the Western standard; far from it, their endeavors to conduct a meaningful ethical life manifest concrete and real models of realizing the Way of Heaven. Put clearly,

> The *jen-t'i* (the substance of *jen*) in Confucius is the greatest fulfillment of *jen-t'i*. The book of *Ch'un-ch'iu* (the historical work he revised) is full of strict *i* (righteousness), and compassionate *jen*. This is impossible unless one has sympathy for the whole universe. And so, the expressions of Confucius

---

109 Mou, *Tao-Te Te Li-Hsiang-Chu-I*, p. 41, 44. See also, Mou Tsung-san, *Chung-Kuo Che-Hsüeh Shih-Chiu-Chiang* (Nineteen Lectures on Chinese Philosophy)(Taipei: Hsüeh-Sheng Shu-Chü, 1983), p. 80.

110 Quoted in Mou, *Li-Shih Che-Hsüeh*, Appendix1, p. 15.

> reflect his cultural life and ideals, which in turn symbolize the perfection of *jen-lun* (ethical life), and the paradigm of *jen-lun*. In other words, his life as a whole represents (Chinese) cultural life, and his sayings as a whole represent (Chinese) cultural ideals, which (through historical practice) have transformed into the personality of *te-hui* (virtues and wisdoms) as a whole.[111]

3. The Authentic Self

In summary, the notion of *jen* in the *Analects* and the recreation of Mencius's "four germs" can generally be seen to have established the "real subjectivity" or the "moral subjectivity" of Confucianism.[112] "Since Confucius and Mencius represent the orthodoxy of Chinese Confucianism, the stress on subjectivity is central to the great tradition of Chinese thought. Therefore, Chinese intellectual thought can be generally described as *hsin-hsing chih hsueh* ('the theory of the mind and human nature')." [113]

In this sense, the moral outlook of Confucianism, for the most part, can be outlined in terms of Mencius's famous mottos about *chin-hsin* ("for a person to give full realization to his heart"), *chih-hsing* ("for a person to understand his own nature"), *chih-t'ien* ("to know Heaven"). To quote from *Mencius*,

> Mencius said, "For a man to give full realization to his heart is

111 Ibid., p. 98.

112 Mou, *Chung-Kuo Che-Hsüeh Te T'e-Chih*, p. 92.

113 Ibid., p. 92.

for him to understand his own nature, and a man who knows his own nature will know Heaven. By returning his heart and nurturing his nature he is serving Heaven. Whether he is going to die young or to live to a ripe old age makes no difference to his steadfastness of purpose. It is through awaiting whatever is to befall him with a perfected character that he stands firm in his proper destiny." [114]

Accordingly, there are several things that can be said about the similarity of the moral ideal of self-realization in Confucianism and in Hegelianism, especially in Green's version.[115] First, the moral agency of Confucianism is similar to that of Green in the sense that the fundamental basis of morality is predicated on a quasi-Kantian subjectivity that is endowed with certain moral ability and potentiality. In the *Analects*,

The master said, "Is *jen* really far away? No sooner do I desire

114 *Mencius*, 7A:1.

115 Here, it can be argued that the idea of self-realization so understood has a trace of Aristotelian usage, and consequently that the dialogue between Hegel, Green, and Mou will turn out to be an interlocuion between Aristotelianism and Confuciusism, just as the virtue aproach is. However, given that the ultimate objective of Mou's moral metaphysics, echoing that of post-Kantian philosophy, is an attempt to "demonstrate the limits of Kant and what the contribution of Chinese thought may be to surpass him," I believe that my discussion of self-realization in Confucianism actually reopens a door for incorporating the idea of perfectionism into the outlook of Mou's Neo-Confucian "universal ethics." Based on what has been said in this paper, it is my next task to reassess Mou's contribution to the idea of moral practice within the context of perfectionist ethics.

> it than it is here." [116]
>
> The master said, "It is Man who is capable of broadening the Way. It is not the Way that is capable of broadening Man." [117]

Mencius states that:

> Benevolence (humanity), righteousness, the rites, and wisdom are not welded on to me from the outside; *they are in me originally*. And a different view is simply due to want of reflection. Hence it is said, "Seek and you will find them. Neglect and you will lose them." [118]

However, we have pointed out that Confucian subjectivity contains both transcendence and immanence; *jen* and "four germs" are not only inherent in man, but they also serve as transcendental principles leading to the perfecting of man. "*Jen*," as Chung-ying Cheng argues, "is rooted in one's very nature and being;" however, "it is a need to transcend oneself to a higher level of universality and spirituality and to a larger extension of the human interrelationship in well-being and unity at the same time." [119]

Second, as in Green, the pursuit of self-realization in Mencius's wing of Confucianism is to bring out the best of "what is in me originally," that is, to realize one's moral capacities and potentialities. Here, it is worth noticing that, again as with Green's scholarship, a lot of effort has been put

---

116 *The Analects*, 7:30.

117 *The Analects*, 15:29.

118 *Mencius*, 6A:4.

119 Chung-ying Cheng, *New Dimensions of Confucian and Neo-Confucian Philosophy*, p. 298.

into considering the connection between Mencius and Kant regarding transcendental feature of moral subjectivity. The most salient *differentia* between Kant and Mencius is that, while for Kant, our inner moral ability in terms of free will is taken as a *postulate* which makes moral activity possible, for Mencius, as for Green, freedom is not just a *thing-in-itself*, but it is what is *actually* exercised in our action: the *actualization* of one's moral capacities and potentialities in concrete circumstances. "*Jen*-transcendence is always accompanied by *jen*-extension." [120]

Third, Confucianism in general would agree with Green's argument that "everyone must make his character for himself." Indeed, it has been widely agreed that Confucianism is, above all, an ethics of self-edification; for Confucians, one has to seek the inward light of morality by his own effort. One of Mou's most well-known pupils, the former Harvard professor Tu Wei-ming, when trying to sketch the rationale for self-realization in East Asian civilization, offers a twofold approach, as follows:[121]

(1) Each human being has sufficient internal resources for ultimate self-transformation; we can become a sage, a Buddha, or a true person through our self-effort because sageliness, buddhahood, or

120 Ibid., p. 298.

121 Tu, *Confucian Thought*, p. 8. In a similar manner, Stephen Angle points out that the core meaning of contemporary Neo-Confucianism "should be centered around the ideal of all individuals developing their capacities for virtue—ultimately aiming at sagehood—through their relationships with one another and with their environment." Stephen C. Angle, *Contemporary Confucian Political Philosophy* (Cambridge: Polity, 2012), pp. 1-2.

the *Tao* is inherent in our human nature.

(2) The path to the highest good, to *nirvana*, or to oneness with the *Tao* is long and strenuous.

Fourth, while Tu's first argument matches perfectly with the Hegelian meaning of self-realization, his second point reflects to a great extent the difficulty of moral practice according to Green. In Green's mind, as has been indicated, man is not created with all of his capacities and potentialities; but rather he must strive for their full development through history in which God is immanent. By the same token, Confucius and Mencius are modest about the true realization of the ideal self. Further, just as Green sees the self-realization of God in human history as an unfinished process, under no circumstance does Confucianism believe that the actualization of Heaven can be exhausted. As Mou puts it, what Confucius and Mencius have done is "to realize that which Heaven has unveiled in *hsin*, in *jen*, in morality, this is not to say that they can actualize the whole meaning or the infinite mystery in a complete sense." [122]

Finally, echoing Hegel's *Sittlichkeit*, the teachings of Confucianism encourage people to find self-realization in the activities, institutions and relationships within their own society. As Mou articulates,

> According to Confucian doctrines, there is no isolated virtue, because *jen* and *i* cannot exist in the individual independently… Why is this so? This is because the virtues of *jen* and *i* must be objectified in the world of humanity; and their objectification

122 Mou, *Chung-Kuo Che-Hsüeh Te T'e-Chih*, p. 138.

even should spread over the whole of Heaven, earth and all things. This is why Wang Yang-ming (1472-1529) says that "the great man thinks of Heaven, earth and the myriad things as oneness." In a similar way, Ch'eng Ming-tao (1032-1085) remarks that "the person of *jen* is related to Heaven, earth and the myriad things in oneness." This is completely in accordance with the idea of *ch'eng-chi ch'eng-wu* (the completion of the self necessitates that of things) in the *Doctrine of Mean*, meaning that since "*Ch'eng-chi* is jen, *ch'eng-wu* is wisdom," what is implied *ch'eng-chi ch'eng-wu* is "the Way of unifying inwardness and outwardness." This also reflects Mencius's teaching that: "All the ten thousand things are there in me. There is no greater joy for me than to find, on self-examination, that I am true to myself." [123] In Confucian doctrines, the only way to accomplish virtues is by reaching this completeness and fullness. [124]

4. Personalism and the Ethics of Self-Realization

To conclude, I argue that post-Kantian Western moral philosophy, including Kantianism, Utilitarianism, and the Hegelian critics of Kant, take autonomy, freedom, independence, free will, and the like to be the cardinal condition of human conduct. Therefore, it may be appropriate to

123 *Mencius*, 7A: 4.
124 Mou, *Sheng-Ming Te Hsüeh-Wen*, p. 43.

describe "human dignity" as the Western "overlapping consensus" on common humanity. Even so, there are two relevant but not identical idioms of "human dignity" that have hovered over the modern history of Western moral thinking, which can be framed as the Kantian notion of self-determination or self-responsibility, and the Hegelian notion of self-realization or self-fulfillment.

Now, based on what has been said, it seems to me that the moral ideal of self-realization as the actualization of the authentic self in Confucianism can be much better reconstructed in terms of Hegelian self-realization related to the immanent vision of "moral religion" than in terms of Kantian self-determination related to the transcendental project about "metaphysics of morals." To make it clearer, though it should be remembered that granting Mou's "moral metaphysics" is based on his lifelong engagement with Kant's philosophy, it nonetheless departs from Kant's "metaphysics of morals" in a pivotally crucial way: while for Kant morals are the object of his transcendental enquiry, which is designed to discover the rational conditions of our moral action, the focus of attention in Mou's "moral metaphysics" is "the universe in its metaphysical dimension," and thus morals are at once pointing to "the practical approach toward the actualization in our lives and through our deeds (including emotions and intentions) of the ultimate (metaphysical, cosmological, ontological) reality shared by both the universe and by our nature." [125]

In fact, the idea of the authentic self, as expressed in this essay,

125 Billioud, *Thinking Through Confucian Modernity*, p. 21.

reiterates what William Theodore de Bary has referred to as "personalism in Confucianism" from a different angle. As de Bary states:

> When Western notions of liberalism and individualism reached East Asia in the nineteenth century, they had no precise equivalents in Chinese or Japanese parlance, and neologisms had to be invented for them. *Ko-jen chu-i* (Jap. *Kojin shugi*), the term devised for "individualism," emphasized the discrete or isolated individual. This contrasts with Confucian personalism referred to in my earlier lectures, which conceived of the person as a member of the larger human body, never abstracted from society but always living in a dynamic relation to others, to a biological and historical continuum, and to the organic process of the Way.[126]

V. Conclusion

All this, of course, does not mean that there are no significant differences between Mou's Neo-Confucianism, and Hegel's and Green's Absolute Idealism. For our purposes, there are at least two matters that need to be noted. First, for Mou, the fundamental dissimilarity between Western thinkers and Chinese writers is that, while the former are "philosophers" in pursuit of knowledge, the latter the "saints" full of wisdom. Therefore, Western philosophers often fall victim to the positivity,

---

126 Wm Theodore de Bary, *The Liberal Tradition in China* (NY: Columbia University Press, 1983), p. 43.

encouraged by Confucius, Mencius and Sung-Ming Confucians, that sees "All-Under-Heaven" as the content of their personal responsibility, and treats what they learn as the guiding principles of personal, political, and social practices." [127] In other words, Confucianism has a *specific* view about "the unification of practice and theory," insisting that "practice is always the practice of theory." [128] I said "specific," because, unlike mainstream Western philosophy in general, there is no "pure theoretical metaphysics" in Chinese thinking.

Thus, in addition to launching a criticism of Kant for his treatment of freedom as a postulate, Mou also expresses a deep reservation about Hegel's dialectic "being detached from praxis." [129] Putting aside the issue of whether Mou has done justice to Hegel, here I just want to remark that although the spiritual legacy of Mou's philosophical enterprise, as I have shown, can be much better re-appreciated and re-evaluated when he is regarded as a post-Kantian critic of Kant's philosophy rather than as a fervent admirer of Kant, and to give substance to his "moral metaphysics," we must delve into his discussions of "intellectual intuition," the ultimate

---

127 Mou, *Tao-Te Te Li-Hsiang-Chu-I*, p. 22; see also pp. 158-159.

128 Ibid., p. 39.

129 Chan, *The Thought of Mou Zongsan*, p. 109. Here is Chan's important quotation from *Sheng-Ming Te Hsüeh-Wen*: "Hegel's great Logic was erected without a basis. He cut off the background of 'the display of spirit in human praxis' and without any basis adopted a bare 'Absolute' as the starting point of his dialectical development, and this dialectical development began with 'the Absolute itself' in the medium of pure thought and pure reason and unfolded paradoxically to the end. In this way, he deduced all the categories. This is actually a paradox of thought itself and is an unnecessary grand trick."

"perfect" teaching, the "two-door mind" paradigm, and the notion of "moral praxis" in detail. Because of space, however, I will have to leave these issues for another study.

Furthermore, unlike Absolute Idealism in particular, "intellectual intuition" *always* takes the form of self-affirmation, regardless of the process of self-negation. For this very reason, the problems of the dualism of subjectivity and objectivity have never occurred to the Chinese Spirit. Accordingly, although Mou would strongly rebuff Hegel's Eurocentric opinion that "Cicero gives us *De Officiis*, a book of moral teaching more comprehensive and better than all the books of Confucius," that "for their reputation it would have been better had they never been translated," [130] he does not completely deny another notorious comment that Hegel makes about China in his *Lectures on the Philosophy of World History*: "the Orientals do not yet know that the spirit or man as such is free in himself." [131]

On the one hand, because the universal subjectivity in China has never undergone the process of self-negation, Hegel seems to have been correct in observing that no clear consciousness of individual freedom was alive in ancient China; that only one person, the Emperor himself, was free in political terms. By contrast, as Mou notices, in spite of "the enduring wounds that the 'unhappy consciousness' had inflicted on the European

130 G. W. F. Hegel, *Lectures on the History of Philosophy*, trans. E. S. Haldane (Lincoln: University of Nebraska Press, 1995), Vol. 1, p. 121.

131 G. W. F. Hegel, *Lectures on the Philosophy of World History, Introduction: Reason in History*, trans. H. B. Nisbet (Cambridge: Cambridge University Press, 1975), p. 54.

spirit," the appearance of Christianity as a self-negation of self-consciousness has brought out the free subject, which in turn has helped take shape the formulation of Western modern politics in favor of individual freedom and democracy: "Only with the coming of Christianity, Hegel maintains, did people come to recognize that all human beings are in principle free because all are equal in the eyes of God." [132] It is exactly in this Hegelian background that Mou makes his famous statement that, from the perspective of the philosophy of history, the Chinese Spirit must summit to the process of self-negation to establish its own democracy. In other words, the political failure of Confucianism in the modern time consists in the fact that, without going through the *differentiation* of individual consciousness, its moral ideal has never objectified itself through the personal life to the public domain, through the realization of the authentic self to the establishment of the legitimacy of political authority. In short, in Confucian terminology, *nei-shen* ("inner-holiness") has never really extended to and stretched out the *wai-wang* ("outer-kingliness").

On the other hand, however, to say that China does not foster individual freedom is not to say that the rationality in China is static. In truth, it has embodied itself in a specific way that is different from Western history: "intellectual intuition" always involves an ethical personality of holiness, a self-affirmation of the *holistic embodiment* of Heaven. If it is

---

132 Stephen Houlgate, *An Introduction to Hegel: Freedom, Truth and History* (Oxford: Blackwell, 1995), p. 13.

true that for Hegel and Green to cure the malaise of fragments in human feelings, the Western Spirit has to call for the reconciliation of God and humanity – a spiritual idea that is in essence compatible with Confucianism – then, it seems fair for Liang Sou-ming (1893-1988) to say that Chinese culture is, in fact, a "premature version of rationality."

重訪牟宗三的道德宗教理念：與黑格爾和格林的對話

曾國祥
中山大學政治所教授

摘要

學界有關儒家道德宗教觀念的探究已有很長一段歷史。先前研究成果誠然令人欽佩，此文特別關注的問題則是如何通過與黑格爾和格林的對話，來重建牟宗三的道德宗教理念。本文主要目標有二：首先，我將試著揭露構成黑格爾與格林之道德宗教思想的三個基本觀點：對正統基督教主張上帝外在於人類世界之看法的否決、從內在化的角度重新界定上帝屬性、將自我實現的道德理想理解成個人之內在道德在歷史中的客觀實現。其次，我將接著指出，牟宗三活化儒家道德宗教的基本構想，其實深受黑格爾的啓發；也因此，他對儒家思想中的倫理人格的解釋，十分類似於格林著稱的自我實現倫理。由此觀之，開啓新儒家與提倡「圓善論自由主義」的英國觀念論之間的廣泛對話，將有助於我們反思儒家與自由民主價值的相容問題。

關鍵詞：牟宗三、黑格爾、格林、道德宗教、真實自我、自我實現

【論著】

How Democratic were British Politics from the Wilkesites to the Chartists (1760s-1840s)?

Harry T. Dickinson

Having served the professorship, presidency of learn societies and educational committees for more than forty years in the Great Britain, USA, Europe and Asia, Harry T. Dickinson is now Emeritus Professor of British history at the University of Edinburgh. He is the author and editor for many books, including *The Politics of People in Eighteenth-Century Britain* (New York, 1993), *Caricatures and the Constitution, 1760-1832* (Cambridge, 1986), *Liberty and Property: Political Ideology in Eighteenth-Century Britain* (London, 1977), and *Ireland in the Age of Revolution 1760-1805*, 6 vols. 2013 (Editor).

How Democratic were British Politics from the Wilkesites to the Chartists (1760s-1840s)?

Harry T. Dickinson
University of Edinburgh

Abstract

This article suggests that Britain experienced efforts at a democratic revolution in the later eighteenth and earlier nineteenth centuries just as much as France or the USA. British radicals over these decades engaged in an intense ideological campaign to defend civil liberties, promote active political rights and to advocate greater economic equality. They also engaged in major political campaigns to extend the franchise to more Britons, but did not often attack monarchy or aristocracy. Some radicals did propose ways to improve the economic conditions of the poor masses. While impressive, neither the ideological campaign in support of greater liberty nor the political efforts to achieve a fairer and more democratic society achieved complete success. This does not mean however that British political culture was not more democratic by the mid-nineteenth century than it had been a century before. To appreciate Britain's more open and participatory culture by the mid-nineteenth century it is necessary to look at such activities and developments as popular involvement in elections, urban expansion, the growth of a free press, wider literacy, the expansion of voluntary associations, and the frequency of public meetings and popular disturbances.

Keywords: radicalism, ancient constitution, natural rights, economic equality, parliamentary reform, electioneering, urban expansion, press freedom, voluntary associations, popular disturbances.

I

The Ideological Defence of Liberty

The political rights and liberties of human beings can be divided into three categories. There is what can be termed negative freedom, that is, the right of all people in a state to be free from tyrannical and arbitrary power and to possess the constitutional right to defend their life, liberty and possessions by appeals to civil liberties that are universal and indefeasible except when lost through criminal or subversive behaviour. There is the positive freedom of the active political right of all people to engage freely and constitutionally in a range of political activities, including the right to choose representatives who can limit the actions of the government and can call the executive to account. Finally, there is the recognition that civil liberties cannot be defended nor positive rights exercised effectively in societies where vast amounts of wealth are controlled by a very small minority and the great majority of people are economically and socially dependent on this very prosperous elite.

In Britain, by the later eighteenth century, the ideological defence of negative freedom was widely accepted and deeply entrenched among the propertied elite as well as among the middling and lower orders. Although in practice, power was sometimes abused and civil liberties were occasionally curtailed, the vast majority of politicians and political commentators were critical of absolute and arbitrary power, cherished the rule of law, and defended the rights of all people to a range of civil liberties. Even conservative thinkers, such as William Blackstone and

Edmund Burke, never offered an ideological challenge to the benefits of limited government, the rule of law or the universal possession of such civil liberties as equality before the law, liberty of conscience, and the right to freedom of expression, free association or free movement.[1] In times of crisis, these liberties might be infringed, but this was still largely done through constitutional actions and laws, which were temporary in their application. There was certainly no sustained campaign to suggest that such civil liberties should be permanently abolished. With some justice the British people could claim to be freeborn citizens living under the rule of law in a free society.

On the other hand, Britain in the later eighteenth century was undoubtedly governed by a minority of propertied men who dominated the executive, judicial and legislative functions of government. The belief that active political rights should be possessed only by a minority of propertied men, who were educated, leisured and independent, was deeply entrenched and widely held. The majority of Britons were seen as poor, ignorant, unstable and dependent. Hence, they could not be trusted with an active role in deciding who should govern, what laws should be made or what policies should be pursued. British radicals who wished to challenge such an exclusive view of political rights and who wished to widen the political system developed a number of ideological justifications for their demands, not all of which were fully democratic.

---

1 William Blackstone, *Commentaries on the Laws of England* (4 vols. Oxford, 1765), i, 29; Edmund Burke, *Reflections on the Revolution in France*, ed. Conor Cruise O'Brien (Harmondsworth, 1968), p. 149.

Some supporters of the campaign to widen active participation in British politics appealed to an ideology that has been called Classical Republicanism or Civic Humanism.[2] These men believed that an active role in politics, including electing representatives to the House of Commons, should be exercised only by those who owned sufficient property to make them independent of other men and to enable them to have sufficient knowledge of the world in order to cast their votes wisely. They were convinced, however, that men could possess other forms of property than landed estates and hence they wished to extend active citizenship to men whose wealth was based on commerce, industry, finance and income made from the learned professions and who paid sufficient taxes to make a real contribution to government and society. They resented the undue influence of the crown and the aristocratic landed elite and believed that a wider propertied interest deserved to be allowed to play an active role in the political life of the nation.

Many more British radicals in the later eighteenth century appealed to the notion that Britain possessed an ancient constitution that had existed since before the Anglo-Saxons came to Britain in the fifth century AD.[3] Relying on a false but strongly held reading of English history, they convinced themselves that England had possessed a parliament in the

---

2 J. G. A. Pocock has done most to explore this ideology. See, in particular, *The Machiavellian Moment* (Princeton, NJ, 1975), chaps. 12-14.

3 See H. T. Dickinson, *Liberty and Property: Political Ideology in Eighteenth-Century Britain* (London, 1978), pp. 62-65, 77-83, 186-87, and 298-300.

distant past and that in Anglo-Saxon times all men had possessed the right to vote and to take an active role in the decision-making processes of the English state until an absolute monarchy had been imposed by force as a result of the Norman Conquest of 1066.[4] They interpreted all English history from that date as a constant struggle by the people to limit the power of the monarch and to recover their lost rights, including the right to elect representatives to the House of Commons. The Glorious Revolution of 1688-89 had finally ended the threat of absolute and arbitrary monarchy, but it had not eliminated the excessive political influence of crown and aristocratic patronage and corruption that could be removed only by restoring the right to vote to all adult males.

More radical, though not necessarily more popular, was the ideological appeal to universal and imprescriptible natural rights. As early as the late seventeenth century John Locke had maintained in his *Second Treatise of Government* that God had bestowed on all men the right to possess and defend their right to life, liberty and property, that the only legitimate form of civil government was based on an original contract, achieved by the consent of the sovereign people, and that the sovereign people had the right to resist a government that betrayed its trust.[5] This political ideology did not lead Locke, however, to attack the parliamentary system of his own day (which was clearly dominated by a narrow landed elite) or to

4 See Christopher Hill, 'The Norman Yoke', in *idem*, *Puritanism and Revolution* (London, 1958), pp. 50-122.

5 Julian H. Franklin, *John Locke and the Theory of Sovereignty* (Cambridge, 1978); and Richard Tuck, *Natural Rights Theories* (Cambridge, 1979), ch. 8.

campaign for a major extension of the franchise.[6] A century later, however, a significant and growing number of influential radicals, including Richard Price and Thomas Paine, had come to recognise the historical flaws in the appeal to the ancient constitution and had begun to develop a more liberal and common sense interpretation of Locke's notion of natural rights, popular sovereignty, and government by consent. Their arguments were given greater appeal because they could enlist Protestant Dissenters who used natural rights arguments to campaign for greater religious equality and recruit enlightened thinkers who were stressing the virtues of natural, primitive man and were confident that a reliance on human reason could advance the prospect of unlimited future progress.[7] The theory of natural rights attacked an hereditary monarchy and aristocracy, proposed to give all men the right to vote for their representatives in the legislature, and stressed that sovereignty lay with the people not only when civil government was first erected (as John Locke

6 Richard Ashcraft, *Revolutionary Politics and Locke's 'Two Treatises of Government'* (Princeton, NJ, 1986), pp. 521-89; A. John Simmons, *The Lockean Theory of Rights* (Princeton, NJ, 1992), pp. 68-102; and Ruth W. Grant, *John Locke's Liberalism* (Chicago, 1987), pp. 64-98.

7 Russell E. Richey, 'The Origins of British Radicalism: The Changing Rationale for Dissent', *Eighteenth-Century Studies*, 7 (1973-74), pp. 179-92; Richard Price, *Observations on Reversionary Payments* (London, 1771), p. 275; *idem*, *A Review of the Principal Questions and Difficulties in Morals* (London, 1769), p. 345; Joseph Priestley, *An Essay on the First Principles of Government*, pp. 3-8, 127-91; J.B. Bury, *The Idea of Progress* (London, 1920), pp. 217-37; and David Spadafora, *The Idea of Progress in Eighteenth-Century Britain* (New Haven, CT, 1990).

had claimed), but throughout the entire existence of civil government.[8]

This radical appeal to natural rights remained very influential in Britain into the early decades of the nineteenth century, but it began to come under attack from rival ideologies that stressed other ways of justifying and promoting human freedom. Jeremy Bentham and his utilitarian disciples argued that the claim that God had created all men equal and had granted all men the same imprescriptible natural rights was simply unprovable. Instead, the Benthamites advanced a utilitarian ideology based on the claim that governments should be judged on their consequences, and hence on their utility. This was best measured by calculating how well any government served the interests of the people as a whole and therefore produced 'the greatest happiness of the greatest number'. Bentham maintained that all men were equal only in the sense that each man was the best judge of his own interest and hence the people aggregated together must be the best judge of the public interest. As far as possible, governments should leave individuals to pursue their own best interests, but, in order to ensure that when it did need to act the government served the public interest, then all men should be granted an active role in choosing the representatives sitting in the sovereign legislature and in holding their government to account.[9]

---

8 H. T. Dickinson, *Liberty and Property*, pp. 65-72, 79-89, 126-28, 197-205, 215-29, 232-63; and H. T. Dickinson, *The Politics of the People in Eighteenth-Century Britain* (Basingstoke, 1995), chap. 5.

9 See Mary P. Mack, *Jeremy Bentham: An Odyssey of Ideas 1748-1792* (London, 1962), pp. 409-66; Philip Schofield, *Utility and Democracy: The Politi-*

Most of the adherents of the natural rights and utilitarian ideologies regarded a tyrannical and oppressive political system as one in which the government interfered excessively and arbitrarily in the individual's life, liberty and economic activities. They complained that the great majority of the population could not control such government actions as foreign wars and high taxation that helped to keep most people in poverty. It was therefore the poor's lack of political power that kept them in poverty. Hence, political reforms alone would help the mass of the population to improve their economic circumstances. By the 1820s, however, with the advance of industrialisation, urbanisation and capitalism, a small number of thinkers, usually referred to as proto-socialists or utopian socialists, such as Robert Owen, Thomas Hodgskin and John Gray, began to argue that it was the economic structure of society that kept the lower orders poor and hence politically weak. In an industrial and capitalist society a minority of men who possessed enormous wealth were able to hold the mass of the population in economic subjection, as wage slaves compelled to accept the poor rewards offered for their labour by their capitalist

---

cal Thought of Jeremy Bentham (Oxford, 2006); Ross Harrison, *Bentham* (London, 1983), chaps. 4, 7-9; and James Steintrager, *Bentham* (London, 1977), chaps. 4-5. For his disciples, see John Plamenatz, *Man and Society* (2 vols. London, 1963). ii, chap. 1; *idem*, *The English Utilitarians* (2nd edn., Oxford, 1958); Elie Halévy, *The Growth of Philosophic Radicalism* (London, 1972), Part I, chap. 3, Part II, chaps. 1 and 3; Joseph Hamburger, *Intellectuals in Politics: John Stuart Mill and the Philosophic Radicals* (New Haven, CT, 1965); and William Thomas, *The Philosophic Radicals* (Oxford, 1979), chaps. 1-4.

masters. People held in such economic subjection could not be free even if they were actually enfranchised. Their economic weakness would inevitably lead them to vote as their masters dictated. This would therefore result in a political system that increasingly entrenched the power of capitalist employers. The mass of the people could therefore be active in politics in ways that served their interests only if they were first freed from economic oppression. Democracy was impossible in a society where there were such enormous disparities in wealth and hence in political power, however widely the parliamentary franchise was distributed.[10]

The reliance of British radicals on different political ideologies indicated their intellectual vitality, but it also created divisions that prevented them reaching the same conclusions and agreeing to work together towards a genuine democracy. The Classical Republicans could

---

10 John Plamenatz, *Man and Society,* ii, chap. 2; J. R. Dinwiddy, 'Charles Hall, Early Socialist', *International Review of Social History*, 21 (1976), 256-76; R. K. P. Pankhurst, *William Thompson* (London, 1954); Elie Halévy, *Thomas Hodgskin* (London, 1956); David Stack, *Nature and Artifice: The Life and Thought of Thomas Hodgskin, 1787-1869* (Woodbridge, 1998); Jamie Bronstein, *John Francis Bray: Transatlantic Radical* (Pontypool, 2009); H. L. Beales, *The Early English Socialists* (London, 1933); G. D. H. Cole, *A History of Socialist Thought* (2 vols., London, 1953), ii, chaps. 3 and 9-12; Gregory Claeys, *Machinery, Money and the Millenium: From Moral Economy to Socialism, 1815-1860* (Cambridge, 1987); *idem*, *Citizens and Saints: Politics and anti-politics in early British socialism* (Cambridge, 1989), chaps. 1, 5-7; William Stafford, *Socialism, radicalism and nostalgia: Social criticism in Britain, 1775-1830*; Keith Taylor, *The Political Ideas of the Utopian Socialists* (London, 1982); Noel W. Thompson, *The People's Science: The popular political economy of exploitation and crisis 1816-34* (Cambridge, 1984); and *idem*, *The Real Rights of Man* (London, 1998)

justify their efforts to widen the franchise to a larger and more diverse body of property owners, but they could not justify granting the franchise to the poor masses. Appeals to the ancient constitution were weakened by advances in historical scholarship that undermined the claim that all men had been able to vote for the national legislature in the Anglo-Saxon past. Benthamite utilitarianism appealed more to middle-class intellectuals than to the lower orders, and it was more concerned with honest and effective government than with encouraging the masses to participate in national politics. Stress was placed on the rule of law to protect life and property and to avert anarchy. The early socialists alienated middle-class property-owners, threatened to promote unrealistic demands by the labouring poor, and thought the struggle for political democracy was a secondary concern. It was natural rights ideology that most excited popular demands for radical political reforms, but, unfortunately for its advocates, it was based on assumptions that could not be proved and that aroused the most intense hostility from the defenders of the established political and social order. Moreover, as we shall see, there were definite limits to the political reforms advanced by the majority of even the most committed natural rights advocates.

II

Proposals to widen the political nation

The earlier eighteenth century witnessed a growing trend towards an aristocratic interpretation of Britain's unwritten constitution and the firm entrenchment of the conviction that sovereignty lay with the combined legislature of the King, the House of Lords and the House of Commons. These developments did excite fears that the independence of parliament would be undermined and the civil liberties of the people would be subverted. To weaken crown patronage and aristocratic influence over the composition of the House of Commons campaigns were waged by critics of oligarchy to reduce the number of royal officials, placemen and pensioners in the parliament, to increase the frequency of general elections, to make electoral bribery a punishable offence, to redistribute parliamentary constituencies from small boroughs to the counties and to London and some larger towns, and to advise voters to elect men who would remain independent of the executive and serve the interests of their constituents. Little or no effort was made, however, to press for a significant widening of the franchise before the 1760s and 1770s.

The political debates raised by ministerial instability in the 1760s and by the American crisis did much to encourage an interest in a radical reform of the electoral system. The American colonists reminded many Britons of the important connection between taxation and representation. In his famous pamphlet, *Take Your Choice!*, published in 1776, John Cartwright developed the connection between taxation and representation and concluded that, since all adult males contributed to the public purse by paying a wide range of indirect taxes, they ought to be represented in the House of Commons. He believed that representation ought to be attached to the person and not to the property of a man. Poverty was no justification for stripping a man of his natural right to vote for those who would represent his interests in the House of Commons.[11] Other radicals soon shared this opinion and also agreed with Thomas Paine when he maintained: 'The right of voting for representatives, is the primary right by which other rights are protected. To take away this right, is to reduce man to a state of slavery, for slavery consists in being subject to the will of another, and he that has not a vote in the election of representatives is in this case'.[12]

By 1780, the advanced radicals in the Westminster Association had developed an extensive programme of demands for electoral reform that became known as the Six Points of Parliamentary Reform: namely, universal manhood suffrage, equal electoral districts, annual parliaments, the secret ballot, the abolition of property qualifications for Members of Parliament and the payment of MPs.[13] This radical programme was adopted by a succession of radical protest campaigns: by the Society for Constitutional Information in the 1780s, the London Corresponding Society in the 1790s and in the Chartist petitions of the 1830s and 1840s. We need to remember, however, that not all radicals adopted this programme and that some prominent radicals were not entirely convinced that all adult males should enjoy equal political influence. Obadiah Hulme

---

11 John Cartwright, *Take Your Choice!* (London, 1776), pp. 19-22.

12 Thomas Paine, 'Dissertation on the First Principles of Government' (1795), in *The Complete Writings of Thomas Paine*, ed. Philip S. Foner (2 vols. New York, 1945), ii, 579.

13 *Report of the Subcommittee of Westminster, 27 May 1780* (London, 1780), also published in The *Works of John Jebb*, ed. John Disney (3 vols. London, 1787), iii, 403-23.

and James Burgh wished to see the franchise extended only to those householders who paid local rates and other specified taxes.[14] Richard Price was conscious that many men were too poor, ignorant and dependent to be trusted with the franchise. He believed that the franchise should be restricted to men who had a certain level of education and enjoyed a measure of economic security.[15] Joseph Priestley maintained that the right to vote should be annexed to educational qualifications of some kind.[16]

It is also clear that these radicals expected that those who would be enfranchised even under the six points of parliamentary reform would elect men of superior education and greater wealth. They had no wish to see poor men enter the House of Commons. James Burgh, Richard Price and Joseph Priestley all made this clear. James Mackintosh expected the enfranchised masses to 'value the superiority of enlightened men' and 'to retain a sufficient consciousness of ignorance to preclude rebellion against their dictates'.[17] John Cartwright, despite his advocacy for adult male suffrage, expected the voters to elect men of birth and status to the House

---

14 [Obadiah Hulme,] *An Historical Essay on the English Constitution* (London, 1771), pp. 76, 153-54: and James Burgh, *Political Disquisitions* (3 vols. London, 1774), i, 26-28, 36-38, 51-54, 87-94, 106-27.

15 H.T. Dickinson, 'Richard Price on Reason and Revolution' in *Religious Identities in Britain, 1660-1832*, ed. William Gibson and Robert G. Ingram (Aldershot, 2005), pp. 231-54.

16 Joseph Priestley, *Lectures on History and General Policy* (3rd edn. Philadelphia, 1803), pp. 116-18; and Margaret Canovan, 'Paternalistic Liberalism: Joseph Priestley on Rank and Inequality', *Enlightenment and Dissent*, 2 (1983), 23-37.

17 James Mackintosh, *Vindiciae Gallicae* (London, 1791), pp. 365-66.

of Commons and he referred to MPs as an 'elective aristocracy'.[18] John Thelwall never expected the poor to become sufficiently qualified to enter the House of Commons or to hold high office. Instead, he expected the lower orders to follow the lead of enlightened men from the middling ranks of society.[19] The same attitude can be attributed to Henry Hunt, William Cobbett and Feargus O'Connor in the earlier nineteenth century.

The majority of leading radical propagandists, moreover, stopped short of advocating the vote for women. They regarded women as dependent on their male fathers or husbands and as incapable of exercising the political rights of a fully independent citizen. Adult females were often regarded as the mere appendages of men and as existing on the same level as children or domestic servants. John Cartwright argued that women had no right to elect representatives to Parliament because they were disqualified by nature from serving in government or acting as the military defenders of their country.[20] Thomas Spence was prepared to let women participate in parliamentary elections, but not to take an active role in the legislature or the executive because of the weakness of the female sex.[21] Even Mary Wollstonecraft, the leading female radical of late eighteenth-

---

18 John Cartwright, *The Commonwealth in Danger* (London, 1795), p. 163.

19 John Thelwall, *The Natural and Constitutional Rights of Britons to Annual Parliaments, Universal Suffrage and the Freedom of Popular Association* (London, 1795), pp. 46-48.

20 John Cartwright, *An Appeal, Civil and Military, on the Subject of the English Constitution* (London, 1799), p. 17.

21 *The Political Works of Thomas Spence*, ed. H. T. Dickinson (Newcastle-upon-Tyne, 1982), pp. xiv-xv, 62-63, and 107.

century Britain and a vigorous campaigner for improvements in the social status and economic condition of women, did not actively campaign for the political rights of women because they still remained in a position of subordination and dependence that rendered them unfit at present to play an active role in politics. Although she hinted that she might campaign for the political rights of women at some future date, 'for I really think that women ought to have representatives instead of being arbitrarily governed without having any direct share allowed them in the deliberations of government',[22] she never, in fact, did so. James Mill, a leading Benthamite, in his famous essay on 'Government' in a supplement to the 5th edition of the *Encyclopaedia Britannica* in 1820, explicitly rejected the claim that women should be granted the parliamentary vote.[23] Even the Chartists of the 1830s and 1840s, who sometimes pressed for improved education, better employment and equal pay for women and who accepted the support of many distinct female Chartist organisations, were generally lukewarm in their support of the female suffrage.[24] The great national

22 Mary Wollstonecraft, *A Vindication of the Rights of Woman*, ed. Miriam Kramnick (1792; Harmondsworth, 1985), p. 260.

23 Mill's essay has been reprinted in *Utilitarian Logic and Politics*, ed. Jack Lively and John Rees (Oxford, 1978), pp. 53-95. His rejection of the vote for women, on the grounds that their fathers or husbands represented their interests, is presented on p. 79. In 1869 Mill's more famous son, John Stuart Mill, produced a major ideological case for the rights of women, when he wrote *The Subjection of Women* (London, 1869).

24 On the Chartist views on women in politics, see, David Jones, 'Women and Chartism', *History*, 68 (1983), 1-21; and Dorothy Thompson, *The Chartists* (London, 1984), pp. 120-51.

Chartist petitions only campaigned for the vote for adult males. William Lovett claimed that the demand to give the parliamentary vote to women was initially supported by the Chartists, but this demand was left out of the Charter petitions in case it retarded the campaign for universal male suffrage.[25] Feargus O'Connor, a leading Chartist, opposed giving the vote to women because it might lead to political disputes within the family.[26] John Watkins and R.J. Richardson were both prepared to support giving the vote to adult unmarried women and to widows, but not to married women because they too wanted to avoid political disputes between husbands and wives.[27]

None the less, while granting the parliamentary vote to women never became a major demand of the radical writers and activists in the later eighteenth or earlier nineteenth centuries, it is important to recognise that the ideological case for enfranchising women was in fact well made by a few radicals. A small number of commentators could not see why stupid men deserved political rights and intelligent women did not. They insisted that women were as capable as men of exercising the vote and even sitting in the legislature or serving in government. As early as the 1790s, George Phillips, Thomas Cooper, and an anonymous contributor to *The Cabinet*,

---

25 William Lovett, *Life and Struggles of William Lovett* (1876; London, 1967), p. 141.

26 *The Northern Star*, 1 July 1843.

27 John Watkins, 'Address to the Women of England' in the *English Chartist Circular*, volume I, number 13 (April 1841); and R.J. Richardson, 'The Rights of Women' (1840) in *The Early English Chartists*, ed. Dorothy Thompson (London, 1971), pp. 115-127.

published in Norwich, argued unequivocally for adult female suffrage and even for the right of women to sit in parliament and to hold executive office. They did, however, acknowledge, that there was little support among their fellow male radicals for such reforms.[28] Jeremy Bentham at first denied women's claim to the franchise, but he later changed his mind. When he did advocate the vote for women, he accepted that women might be as intelligent as men, that both sexes could be distracted by domestic duties, and that women might legitimately have different interests to their fathers or husbands.[29] By far the fullest and most influential ideological case for the political rights of women, however, was published by William Thompson in 1825. This was his *Appeal of One-Half of the Human Race, Women, against the Pretensions of the Other Half, Men, to retain them in Political, and thence in Civil and Domestic Slavery*.[30]

Another major limitation on the democratic aims of the radicals in the later eighteenth and earlier nineteenth centuries was their failure to advocate the abolition of monarchy and aristocracy. Fearful perhaps of being charged with treason and recognising that they might lose support if

---

28 George Phillips, *The Necessity of a Speedy and Effectual Reform of Parliament* (Manchester, 1792), p. 12 note; H. M. Ellis, 'Thomas Cooper: A Survey of His Life. Part I: England, 1759-1794', *South Atlantic Quarterly*, 19 (1927), 38; and *The Cabinet* (3 vols. Norwich, 1795), i, 178-184 and ii, 42-48.

29 Philip Schofield, *Utility and Democracy*, pp. 85-86, 90-91, and 149-150.

30 William Thompson, *Appeal of One-Half of the Human Race, Women, against the Pretensions of the Other Half, Men, to retain them in Political, and thence in Civil and Domestic Slavery* (London, 1825). Richard Pankhurst has edited a modern edition of this work (London, 1983).

they did so, many radicals, including John Cartwright and Richard Price, explicitly denied that they wished to undermine monarchical government or planned to abolish aristocratic privileges.[31] A few radicals, however, were prepared to launch a forthright attack on aristocratic government and hereditary privilege. They argued that titles, honours and inherited privileges should not be tolerated in a society that desired to treat all men as political equals. Neither monarchy nor the House of Lords could be defended on any rational principle and hence they should be cast aside in the march of progress. John Oswald bitterly attacked all hereditary distinctions and concluded that: 'In a free state, there can be but one class of men, which is that of citizen; as there is but one will, which is that of the people'.[32] Jeremy Bentham admired aspects of the American republic and advocated the abolition of the monarchy and the House of Lords, but he did not develop his arguments into a well-developed case.[33] Thomas Paine was without doubt the most determined and clearest advocate of a democratic republic. In his view, there could be no justice in a political system that tried to create hereditary legislators out of a tiny minority of the population. The House of Lords was accountable to nobody and hence was not to be trusted by anybody. The idea of an hereditary legislator was

---

31 John Cartwright, *The Commonwealth in Danger* (London, 1795), pp. xxv, ci-cii; Richard Price, *Political Writings*, ed. D.O. Thomas (Cambridge, 1991), p. 165, n. 19; and, for Price, D.O. Thomas, 'Neither republican nor democrat', *The Price-Priestley Newsletter*, 1 (1977), 49-60.

32 John Oswald, *Review of the Constitution of Great Britain* (3rd edn. London, 1793), p. 12.

33 Philip Schofield, *Utility and Democracy*, pp. 248, 347-348.

as foolish a notion as an hereditary judge, an hereditary mathematician or an hereditary poet. A free people would never freely and willingly set up a monarchy nor approve of an hereditary aristocracy. These institutions, no matter how long they had existed in England, could have been established only by force or fraud, at the expense of the political rights and liberties of the vast majority of the people. The present mixed and balanced constitution in Britain was therefore corrupt, expensive and unjust and it ought to be totally abolished and a better political system created to replace it.[34] Richard Carlile supported Paine's radical attack on the monarchy and the aristocracy in his periodical, *The Republican*, which he launched in August 1817.[35] The Chartists believed in human equality and rejected hereditary political privileges, but they did not openly or often advocate republicanism until the movement was in decline. Peter McDouall was in a distinct minority when he offered some criticism of monarchy and aristocracy in his *Chartist and Republican Journal* in 1841, and it was not until 1850 that George Julian Harney began his *Red Republican* journal and not until 1855 that W. J. Linton published his twenty *Republican Tracts* that launched more substantial attacks on hereditary political power.[36]

---

34 Thomas Paine, *Rights of Man*, pp. 102-106, 144-145, 148, 152-153, 162-166, 186-187, 200, 206, and 220-204.

35 James A. Epstein, *Radical Expression: Political Language, Ritual, and Symbol in England, 1790-1850* (Oxford, 1994), pp. 100-146; and Joel H. Wiener, *Radicalism and free thought in nineteenth-century Britain: The Life of Richard Carlile* (London, 1983).

36 On later popular republicanism in Britain, see Antony Taylor, 'Republicanism

While very few radicals indeed wished to abolish monarchy and aristocracy, some radicals were very well aware that parliamentary reform would not create a democratic society so long as wealth was so badly distributed and a small minority of wealthy men controlled the economic, social and hence political lives of the mass of the labouring poor. They disagreed however on how best to tackle this problem. Many undoubtedly hoped that cheap government, a pacific foreign policy and low taxes would improve the economic lot of the lower orders, but few advised on ways to go beyond this. Many radicals were fearful of suggesting any attack on private property or any policy of redistributing wealth by force. A radical political meeting in Sheffield resolved in 1794: 'We are not speaking of that visionary equality of property, the practical exertion of which would desolate the world and re-plunge it into the darkest and wildest barbarism.'[37] Jeremy Bentham proclaimed: 'Equality in property is destructive of the very principle of subsistence: it cuts up society by the roots. No body would labour if no one were secure of the fruits of his labour'.[38] Thomas Paine, however, in the very successful second volume of his *Rights of Man* (1792), did put forward several proposals for the

---

reappraised: anti-monarchism and the English radical tradition, 1850-1972', in *Re-reading the Constitution: New narratives in the political history of England's long nineteenth century*, ed. James Vernon (Cambridge, 1996), pp. 154-178.

37 *The Parliamentary History of England*, ed. William Cobbett (36 vols. London, 1806-20), xxxi, col. 738.

38 Quoted in Mary P. Mack, *Jeremy Bentham: An Odyssey of Ideas 1748-179*, p. 464.

alleviation of poverty, including old age pensions, family allowances and maternity benefits. In a later pamphlet, *Agrarian Justice* (1797), Paine suggested that the landed property of the rich should be taxed so that enough revenue could be raised to give every man the sum of £15 when he reached the age of 21 and a pension of £10 per annum from the age of 50.

A handful of Paine's contemporaries went beyond his proposals, which merely sought the alleviation of the worst consequences of poverty. They demanded a major redistribution of wealth. William Ogilvie wanted to grant farms to the poor created out of wasteland, forests and crown lands.[39] William Godwin even wished to see the elimination of private property altogether, but he opposed forcible confiscation and hoped that the rich could be persuaded by rational arguments to give up their excessive and unjust wealth.[40] A more revolutionary scheme for redistributing wealth among the whole population was put forward by Thomas Spence in the late eighteenth century. Convinced that political rights alone, however extensive, could never prevent the rich from oppressing the poor, he wanted to place what he regarded as the real source of all power – the land – into the hands of all citizens. He argued that the real rights of man must be grounded in economic not just in political power: 'the question is … no longer about what form of government is most favourable to liberty … but which system of society is most favourable to existence and capable of delivering us from the deadly

39 William Ogilvie, *Essay on the Right of Property in Land* (London, 1782).

40 William Godwin, *Enquiry concerning Political Justice*, II, pp. 423-477.

mischief of great accumulations of wealth which enables a few unfeeling monsters to starve whole nations'.[41] Spence's famous Land Plan, explained and defended in most of his writings, did not advocate the nationalisation of the land so that it could be placed under the control of the central government. Instead, he wanted all the inhabitants of each parish in the country to form themselves into local democratically elected parochial corporations that would own and control all the land and other natural resources (such as rivers and mines) within each parish boundary. The land and natural resources would be rented out with the agreement of the parish corporation to the highest bidders, who would be allowed to farm the land and exploit the natural resources at a profit after paying the agreed rent, but the land and natural resources would be leased and not privately owned. The rent that was paid would be used to pay for the building of parish houses, bridges, roads, schools, libraries, meeting halls, hospitals, etc for the benefit of all parishioners. The rich would not be deprived of their personal possessions in this new society and men of industry and talent who rented out the land and natural resources might be able to run them at a profit. These men might be richer than the less industrious and talented, but under Spence's Land Plan there would be no fabulously rich men and no destitute poor. Real political democracy would be able to flourish because there would be no economic oppression by the rich and no economic enslavement of the poor.[42]

---

41 *The Political Works of Thomas Spence*, ed. H.T. Dickinson, p. 92.

42 See *ibid*., pp. xii-xiii and many of Spence's pamphlets printed in this book and illustrating his famous Land Plan.

Spence influenced radical writers such as Richard Carlile well into the nineteenth century and his Land Plan even influenced the Chartist efforts to create small farms for the people.[43] The Chartist movement, however, despite attracting greater support than any other reform campaign before 1850, was preoccupied with achieving political reforms rather than economic change. As Gareth Stedman Jones has persuasively argued, Chartists advocated a political programme of reforms because they believed that the economic distress of the poor had political causes rather than economic causes. For many Chartists, it was the unequal distribution of political power that resulted in a minority of rich men oppressing the poor majority in Britain.[44] Even Bronterre O'Brien, who cared deeply about the economic plight of the poor, observed:

> Knaves will tell you that it is because you have no property, you are unrepresented. I tell you the contrary, it is because you are unrepresented that you have no property … your poverty is the result not the cause of your being unrepresented.[45]

O'Brien, however, and Ernest Jones and George Julian Harney,[46] did

---

43 Malcolm Chase, *The People's Farm: English Radical Agrarianism 1775-1840* (Oxford, 1988), pp. 121-189; and Alice Mary Hadfield, *The Chartist Land Company* (Newton Abbot, 1970).

44 Gareth Stedman Jones, *Languages of Class* (Cambridge, 1983), pp. 90-178.

45 Quoted in Alfred Plummer, *Bronterre: A Political Biography of Bronterre O'Brien, 1804-1864* (London, 1971), pp. 177-178.

46 *Ernest Jones: Chartist*, ed. John Saville, (London, 1952); Miles Taylor, *Ernest Jones, Chartism and the Romance of Politics 1819-1869* (Oxford, 2003); and A.R. Schoyen, *The Chartist Challenge: A portrait of George Julian Harney* (London, 1958).

seek to unite the Chartist political programme with demands for economic reforms. In their view, Chartism needed to have an economic programme as well as political objectives and should be socialist as well as democratic. Jones and Harney became increasingly socialist as they looked to state ownership of land, productive resources and the means of exchange in order to improve the plight of the labouring masses.[47]

These Chartists, however, tended to turn to socialism largely *after* the failure of the last great Chartist petition in 1848. Earlier than this, a few men, such as Charles Hall, Robert Owen, William Thompson, Thomas Hodgskin, John Gray and John Francis Bray, did insist that the re-ordering of economic relations and the more equal distribution of wealth should take precedence over parliamentary reform if a genuinely freer and truly fairer society was ever to be created in Britain. John Francis Bray was convinced that the labourers were robbed of at least two-thirds of their wages, and he too wanted the means of production to pass from the hands of the few into the hands of society at large. He did not believe that political reforms alone could right this injustice:

> Some men, when they speak of equal rights, mean thereby simply that there should be universal suffrage, vote by ballot, and free admission to Parliament; while others, advancing rather nearer to first principles, call for the complete subversion of the monarchy and the establishment of a nation. ... But an examination of the subject will convince us, that if the working

47 Noel Thompson, *The Real Rights of Man* (London, 1998), chap. 9.

> classes of the United Kingdom should obtain any or all of the political changes just mentioned, they would remain in almost the same condition of poverty and ignorance and misery as they are at present.[48]

These early socialist writers all believed that it was the control of the means of production, not the right to vote, that conferred real power and the labouring poor would not improve their lot until they could exercise control over the economy of Britain. Working-class ownership and regulation of the means of production were the best means of creating a really just and democratic society. Labour must be freed from the oppressive control of capital and from the powerful administrative machinery of government that existed simply to benefit the rich and entrench poverty, exploitation and inequality. These early socialist writers were too optimistic, even unrealistic about how a society of social and economic equals could be created and organised. They believed that economic oppression would be eliminated when all men understood their real rights in an industrial economy and when they understood that the means of production needed to be properly regulated. They were confident that knowledge and education, of the kind produced in their own economic tracts, would teach the poor how to transform the means of production and re-shape economic, social and ultimately political relations.[49]

48 John Francis Bray, *Labour's Wrongs and Labour's Remedy*, p. 17.

49 See the works cited in note 10, above.

III

Promoting popular participation and a democratic culture

By the mid-nineteenth century British political theorists, propagandists and activists had developed a variety of ideological justifications in support of radical versions of civil liberties, political rights and economic freedom. They had also devised political programmes that advocated major revisions of the electoral system that would produce a democratically chosen House of Commons. Careful examination of these ideologies and reform programmes shows that they were not entirely democratic and that only limited progress had been made towards establishing a democratic political system in Britain. If we widen our investigation, however, to appreciate the political actions of the later eighteenth and earlier nineteenth centuries, we can appreciate the many different ways in which large numbers of Britons actively participated in a wide range of political activities of some kind or other. If we also explore the political culture of these decades we can discover a host of ways in which Britons took active steps to shape and control their lives rather than remain passive victims or recipients of decisions taken by their social superiors.

Britain did not experience a violent political revolution over these decades (though of course Ireland did). There were a few revolutionary plots and violent conspiracies and a few small and ineffective groups did arm themselves and plan insurrections,[50] but the vast majority of Britons

---

50 See, for example, Roger Wells, *Insurrection: The British Experience, 1795-1803* (Gloucester, 1983); John Stanhope, *The Cato Street Conspiracy* (Lon-

advocating reform sought to achieve their aims by peaceful and constitutional means. They preferred to exploit the opportunities provided by frequent parliamentary elections, demographic changes, urbanisation, and a flourishing press to establish a host of clubs, nationwide associations and pressure groups to achieve political changes; to create friendly societies and cooperative ventures to improve their economic conditions; and frequently to take to the streets in large numbers to safeguard their livelihoods and their civil liberties.

By the later eighteenth century about 400,000 adult males had the right to vote in parliamentary elections. This figure had more than doubled by the mid-nineteenth century. Elections were quite frequent occurrences and they engendered considerable political excitement and popular participation, particularly in the larger constituencies. It is a mistake to conclude that the voters were entirely subservient to their social superiors. The elite had to manage the voters and to make considerable efforts to secure their support at the polls in the counties and the larger boroughs. The electors were canvassed and courted, treated and flattered. Parliamentary patrons and candidates had to spend considerable amounts of time, energy and money in order to canvass the electors and make sure they turned up to vote. They were expected to deploy their economic resources, social status and political influence to assist the voters they hoped to court. They were expected to spend money in their constituencies

don, 1962); Peter B. Ellis and Seumas Mac A'Ghobhainn, *The Scottish insurrection of 1820* (2nd edn. Edinburgh, 2001); and David Jones, *The Last Rising: The Newport Insurrection of 1839* (Oxford, 1998).

for the benefit of local merchants, tradesmen and innkeepers, to contribute generously to the erection of public buildings and creation of local amenities, and to reduce or forego rents and distribute charity when times were hard. When called upon, they were expected to use their influence to help their constituents secure minor government posts and small contracts, to secure leases to land and property, and to gain access to local schools, hospitals, asylums and workhouses. The voters also expected to be transported to the polls, which could be some distance away, and to be compensated for any expenses incurred or income lost by bothering to cast their votes. Wise patrons and candidates did not seek to bully or bribe outright their constituents, but endeavoured to handle them with great care and tact. Any MP, who failed to do so, might well find it difficult to retain the loyalty of his constituents at the next election. Moreover, contested elections, especially in the larger constituencies, could last for several days and could generate considerable excitement since voting was by voice in open spaces and hence the state of the polls was public knowledge as the electioneering progressed. Elections thus became very public spectacles at which unenfranchised spectators could congregate in large numbers and participate in what could become emotionally charged theatrical events. Candidates could tour the constituencies before, during and after the polling. Proceedings could be enlivened with music, effigies, volleys of gunfire, firework displays, bonfires, and bell ringing – as well as being accompanied by a great deal of eating, drinking, merriment and even violence. As a form of street theatre, parliamentary elections drew many non-voters into participating in the crowds on the streets, the audiences at speeches, the processions to the polls and the celebrations organised by the victors. Nearly all electors cherished their right to vote and many non-voters enjoyed playing some active role in parliamentary elections. Most voters were not servile dependants and a great many non-voters were not content to be passive bystanders.[51]

Over these decades the population of Great Britain more than doubled and an increasing proportion of this population lived in towns. It was in the towns, and especially in the large towns, that popular politics flourished most vigorously and most persistently.[52] Britain was one of the most urbanised countries in the world by 1760 and was even more urbanised by the mid nineteenth century. London was the largest city in Europe, reached a population of about one million by 1801 and was well

51 H.T. Dickinson, *The Politics of the People*, chap. 1; Frank O'Gorman, *Voters, Patrons and Parties: The Unreformed Electorate of Hanoverian England, 1734-1832* (Oxford, 1989); and David Eastwood, 'Contesting the politics of deference, 1820-1860', in *Party, state and society: electoral behaviour in Britain since 1820*, ed. Jon Lawrence and Miles Taylor (Aldershot, 1997), pp. 27-49.

52 H.T. Dickinson, *The Politics of the People*, chap. 3; David Eastwood, *Government and Community in the English Provinces, 1700-1870* (Basingstoke, 1997), chap. 3; P.J. Corfield, *The Impact of English Towns 1700-1800* (Oxford, 1982), chaps. 8-9; James Walvin, *English Urban Life 1776-1851* (London, 1984), chap. 7; Rosemary Sweet, *The English Town 1680-1840: Government, Society and Culture* (Harlow, 1999), chaps. 4-5; and *idem*, 'Corrupt and corporate bodies: attitudes to corruption in eighteenth-century and early nineteenth-century towns', in *Corruption in urban politics and society: Britain 1780-1950*, ed. James R. Moore and John Smith (Aldershot, 2007), pp. 41-56.

over two million by 1850. By the latter date, Britain had four other towns with over a quarter of a million inhabitants, another four with over 100,000, and several dozen other towns had over 20,000 inhabitants. Britain was rapidly becoming the most urbanised country in the world. Political leadership in these towns was largely provided by the middle classes, who sometimes made up a quarter or a third of the inhabitants, but the poor could be so numerous that their interests could also not be ignored. Urban communities were the centres of economic growth, social mobility, religious tensions and popular disturbances. Literacy rates were always higher in urban areas and the larger towns were centres of a thriving press. In over two-thirds of the boroughs the town councils were dominated by the wealthier inhabitants, who could serve on the council for life. In the more 'open' boroughs, which included London itself, all the freemen could vote for the members of the town corporation. Civic activities in the towns were increasingly national rather than local in focus and scope. Many townspeople across Britain joined in fast days and thanksgiving days, in celebrations of military and naval victories, and in marking such royal occasions as the recovery of George III from serious illness in 1789, the beginning of his fiftieth jubilee year in October 1809 or the centenary of the Hanoverian succession in 1814.[53]

---

53 See, for example, *Britain and the French Revolution, 1789-1815*, ed. H.T. Dickinson (Basingstoke, 1989), p. 113; *Jubilee Jottings: The Jubilee of George the Third*, ed. Thomas Preston (London, 1887); and Linda Colley, 'The Apotheosis of George III: Loyalty, Royalty and the British Nation 1760-1820', *Past and Present*, 102 (1984), 94-129.

No matter how the town was governed and the corporation was chosen, the governing elite almost always faced challenges to their authority from a broad body of citizens whenever the corporation abused its powers. London was regularly the scene of political disputes about the internal affairs of the city that involved many thousands of its citizens. Most other large towns frequently saw the decisions taken by the town corporation challenged by large numbers of citizens. There were disputes about parliamentary elections, the choice of local officials, the creation of new freemen, access to local charities and amenities and the raising of local rates and taxes. In addition to many dozens of town corporations experiencing local disputes over political decision-making, from the later eighteenth century onwards hundreds of new statutory authorities were established to deal with the town planning problems faced by rapidly growing urban communities. There were statutory bodies created to maintain harbours, docks, bridges, canals, markets and burial grounds. Even more important were statutory authorities to establish workhouses and turnpike trusts, and improvement commissions to deal with the lighting, paving, cleaning and policing of the streets. Large numbers of ordinary rate-paying householders were involved in these authorities. As new statutory authorities and improvement commissions were established, so disputes multiplied over the decisions to erect, staff and finance them. Attacks on town and parish oligarchies and the misuse of their funds multiplied and campaigns were mounted to open up the ways in which town councils and parish vestries were chosen. The Vestries Act of 1831 recognised the right of women ratepayers to vote in parochial elections and allowed the electors to opt for the secret ballot.[54] The Municipal Reform Act of 1835 was a major step in making town corporations more open and more accountable to local rate-paying householders.[55]

Pre-publication press censorship had ended in England as early as 1695 and thereafter the press in Britain became an increasingly effective way of providing a large proportion of the British people with political news and with the means to publicise their own political views.[56] The size and spread of the British press grew enormously in the later eighteenth and earlier nineteenth centuries. Newspapers were largely town based, but successful efforts were made to distribute them to surrounding rural areas. By 1760 London already had about ten newspapers, there were newspapers in about thirty other towns, and the annual sales of newspapers had reached seven million copies. By 1800 the annual sales had reached sixteen millions. By 1830 there were nearly 200 local newspapers published in every town of significance in Britain, with large towns being served by more than one newspaper. These newspapers were full of political information and political views, much of it about national politics.

54 James Vernon, *Politics and the People: A study in English political culture, c. 1815-1867* (Cambridge, 1993), pp. 17, 19-20.

55 *Ibid.*, pp. 20, 25; Rosemary Sweet, *The English Town 1680-1840*, pp. 152-61; and G.B.A.M. Finlayson, 'The politics of municipal reform 1835', *English Historical Review*, 81 (1966), 673-92.

56 Jeremy Black, *The English Press in the Eighteenth Century* (London, 1987); Hannah Barker, *Newspapers, Politics, and Public Opinion in late Eighteenth-Century England* (Oxford, 1998); Marcus Wood, *Radical Satire and Print Culture 1790-1822* (Oxford, 1994); and A. Aspinall, *Politics and the Press, c. 1780-1850* (London, 1949).

Almost every important government decision, legislative action or parliamentary debate received some coverage in both the London and the provincial press. The British people were undoubtedly the best politically informed nation on earth in the earlier nineteenth century. The press was an essential support of an open political system, a vital safeguard of civil liberties, and a means of disseminating criticisms of government actions and publicising ways of coordinating campaigns to reform the political system.

The political press extended far beyond the weekly or daily newspapers. There were numerous political magazines, and hundreds of political books, pamphlets and satirical political prints were published every year.[57] Radicals and reformers exploited the press to a remarkable extent, despite government attempts to control the press by stamp duties and prosecutions for seditious libel. Thomas Paine's pamphlets were distributed in their tens of thousands and so were radical serial publications such as William Cobbett's *Political Register* (which sold one million copies in the first six months of its existence in 1818-19), Bronterre O'Brien's *Poor Man's Guardian* (which sold about 16,000 copies every issue in the early 1830s) and Feargus O'Connor's *Northern Star* (which averaged about 36,000 sales every week from 1839).[58] Most radical

57 On satirical prints, see H.T. Dickinson, *Caricatures and the Constitution 1760-1832* (Cambridge, 1985); and Diana Donald, *The Age of Caricature: Satirical Prints in the Reign of George III* (New Haven, CT, 1996).

58 Lynne Lemrow, 'William Cobbett's Journalism for the Lower Orders', *Victorian Periodicals Review*, 15 (1982), 11-20; John Stevenson, 'William Cobbett:

newspapers were unstamped, and hence illegal, but, at times of intense political excitement, they outsold all the legitimate papers in the country. In 1858, parliament finally abandoned attempts to control the press by taxation.[59]

In most towns the middle and lower classes increasingly organised themselves into a whole variety of clubs and societies that provided social, educational and economic benefits for their members. Most of these voluntary associations were organised by their urban middle and lower class members, not by the aristocratic, rural elite. The members made their own rules, controlled entry, appointed their own officials (such as a president, secretary and treasurer), raised financial subscriptions, acted in their meetings in an open and democratic manner, and offered support to one another.[60] There were clubs and societies to promote knowledge and education, reading and debating, as well as Sunday schools, night schools, mechanics' institutes, reading rooms, and improvement societies to

---

Patriot or Briton', *Transactions of the Royal Historical Society*, 6th series, 6 (1996), 123-36; Kevin Gilmartin, *Print Politics: The Press and Radical Opposition in Early Nineteenth-Century England* (Cambridge, 1996); Patricia Hollis, *The Pauper Press: A Study in Working-Class Radicalism of the 1830s* (Oxford, 1970); and *Papers for the People: A Study of the Chartist Press*, ed. Joan Allen and Owen R. Ashton (London, 1995).

59 William H. Wickwar, *The Struggle for the Freedom of the Press 1819-1832* (London, 1928); and Joel H. Wiener, *The War of the Unstamped* (Ithaca, NY, 1969).

60 H.T. Dickinson, *The Politics of the People*, chap. 2; and Peter Clark, *British Clubs and Societies 1580-1800: The Origins of an Associational World* (Oxford, 2000), chaps. 3-7

promote literacy, thrift and temperance among the urban poor.[61] There were also associations to protect the economic interests of both employers and workers. Many associations of employers, particularly those engaged in the textile, metal and pottery industries, formed highly effective organisations in order to lobby government and petition parliament to protect their economic interests.[62] The landed elite might dominate the government and parliament, but neither institution could afford to ignore the welfare of the commercial, financial and industrial sectors of society. Such self-protecting activities extended well beyond the middling orders. There were a few cooperative village communities where families shared possessions and worked together as a social and economic unit and a few labour exchanges where skilled workers could exchange the products they had made.[63] Over seventy thousand men contributed to the Chartist Land Plan in an attempt to return to a more independent life on the land.[64] The most popular and widespread associations involving the working classes were the Friendly Societies, established by workers themselves, who collected small weekly subscriptions in order to insure their members against sickness, unemployment, old age and the consequences of

---

61 Emma Griffin, *Liberty's Dawn: A People's History of the Industrial Revolution* (London, 2013), pp. 165-185.

62 H.T. Dickinson, *The Politics of the People*, pp. 56-92.

63 R.G. Garnett, *Cooperation and the Owenite socialist communities in Britain 1825-45* (Manchester, 1972).

64 Alice Mary Hadfield, *The Chartist Land Company* (Newton Abbot, 1970); and Malcolm Chase, *The People's Farm: English Radical Agrarianism , 1775-1840* (Oxford, 1988).

premature death. As early as 1815 these Friendly Societies had enrolled nearly one million members, including significant numbers of women.[65] They grew strongly after that until perhaps a third of working families had established some kind of insurance against sickness, unemployment, and the death of their principal wage earner. British workers also learned to protect their economic interests and to bring pressure upon their employers by joining workers' combinations and trade unions. Trade unions composed of skilled workers in particular were widespread by the late eighteenth century. Although these workers' combinations were made illegal by parliament between 1800 and 1825 this legislation did not prevent skilled workers forming local trade unions. In 1815, for example, it has been estimated that there were about half a million trade unionists. After 1825, when their activities were legalised, numbers increased dramatically.[66] Strikes were common throughout this whole period, and by the 1830s efforts were being made to form nationwide trade unions and

---

65 Simon Cordery, *British Friendly Societies 1750-1914* (Basingstoke, 2003); P.H.J.H. Gosden, *The Friendly Societies in England, 1815-75* (Manchester, 1961); Peter Clark, *British Clubs and Societies 1580-1800*, chap. 10; and Martin Gorsky, 'The growth and distribution of English friendly societies in the early nineteenth century', *Economic History Review*, 2nd series, 51 (1998), 489-511.

66 C. R. Dobson, *Masters and Journeymen: A Prehistory of Industrial Relations 1717-1800* (London, 1980); Iorwerth J. Prothero, *Artisans and Politics in early nineteenth-century London* (London, 1979); A. E. Musson, *British Trade Unions 1800-1875* (London, 1972); R.G. Kirby and A. E. Musson, *Voice of the People: John Doherty, Trade Unionist, Radical and Factory Reformer, 1798-1854* (Manchester, 1975); and Malcolm Chase, *Early Trade Unionism: Fraternity, skill and the politics of labour* (Aldershot, 2000).

some militants were even contemplating a general strike.[67]

These voluntary associations were political in that their members endeavoured to exercise power over their own lives and their own economic interests by cooperating together and seeking to achieve unity and a common sense of identity.[68] While the majority of Britons might be excluded from the government and parliament, they lived in a society in which the state increasingly pursued laissez-faire policies, which left the majority of the population to their own devices. British people were left free to take actions on their own initiative in order to protect and extend their own social and economic interests. Sometimes, however, in order to achieve their own social and economic objectives, these voluntary organisations had to engage in political activities. In order to bring pressure to bear upon the national or local government and upon parliament many pressure groups, particularly those dominated by the urban middle classes, learned to use very sophisticated techniques. They established local and sometimes national committees in order to coordinate their activities, which could involve printing propaganda, holding celebratory dinners and public meetings, organising speeches, lecture tours, and petitions, hiring lawyers to draft legislation, lobbying peers and MPs, and sending expert witnesses to give evidence before parliamentary committees. Some pressure group campaigns were remarkably sophisticated and were organised on a massive scale, drawing in support

67 Mick Jenkins, *The General Strike of 1842* (London, 1980).

68 R. J. Morris, 'Voluntary Societies and British Urban Elites, 1780-1850: An Analysis', *The Historical Journal*, 26 (1983), 95-118.

from very large numbers from both the middling and lower orders. Among the most famous were the campaigns against Roman Catholic relief in 1779-80 and in 1829,[69] the campaigns against the slave trade, especially in the years 1788-92, the popular movement to abolish slavery in the colonies in the early 1830s,[70] and the successful Anti-Corn Law League of 1839 to 1846.[71] There were also a very large number of significant, though smaller and less well-organised campaigns in support of temperance, moral reform, factory reforms, poor law reforms, educational reforms, and for or against particular legislative measures being debated by parliament.

Easily the largest voluntary movement during these decades was the Volunteer corps, approved by the government and parliament and raised to defend Britain from a French invasion and to maintain internal law and order should an invasion stimulate domestic insurrection. When, in 1794, the government asked for volunteers to enlist in a civilian defence force, which was not under military control, the results were astounding. By

---

69 Christopher Hibbert, *King Mob: The Story of Lord George Gordon and the Riots of 1780* (London, 1959); and Peter Jupp, *British Politics on the Eve of Reform: The Duke of Wellington's Administration 1828-30* (Basingstoke, 1998), pp. 372-75.

70 Seymour Drescher, *Capitalism and Antislavery: British Mobilization in Comparative Perspective* (Basingstoke, 1986); J.R. Oldfield, *Popular Politics and British Anti-Slavery: The Mobilisation of public opinion against the slave trade 1787-1807* (Manchester, 1995); and James Walvin, *England, Slavery and Freedom, 1776-1838* (Basingstoke, 1986).

71 Norman McCord, *The Anti-Corn Law League* (2nd edn. London, 1968); and Paul A. Pickering and Alex Tyrrell, *The People's Bread: A history of the Anti-Corn Law League* (Leicester, 2000).

1797 some 51,000 men had enlisted. This number more than doubled by the end of 1798 and rose to over 380,000 by 1804. Outside the ranks of the Volunteers corps a great many organisers, subscribers and supporters, including some female committees helped to provide the poorer Volunteers with uniforms, equipment and other material benefits. Although the Volunteers genuinely wished to resist a French invasion, they were not necessarily supporters of the government's war policies and nor were they a loyalist police force anxious to crush any radical political activity.[72] It is true that a minority of yeoman cavalry corps, officered by country gentlemen and recruited from their tenants, servants and labourers, were ready to resist political changes, which they feared were influenced by French revolutionary principles. A large majority of Volunteers, however, served in infantry corps and these were mainly raised in towns, were officered by middle-class men from rich merchants to humble shopkeepers and tradesmen, and were recruited from their employees. The governing elite at national and county level failed to exercise strict control over the appointment of officers in these urban corps and the officers themselves found that their authority was limited by elected committees, which included rank and file Volunteers. These committees could accept or reject potential officers and private men, could decide what uniforms should be worn and how subscriptions should be spent, and could decide what punishments could be inflicted on offenders. All Volunteers were also free

72 J. R. Western advanced this argument in 'The Volunteer Movement as an Anti-Revolutionary Force, 1793-1801', *English Historical Review*, 71 (1956), 603-614, but later and more detailed research has refuted his claim.

to resign at any time. Some contemporaries expressed alarm at the arming of the middling and lower classes and even noted that some radicals were enlisting to gain access to arms and to experience military training. Their fears were confirmed when a number of Volunteer corps refused to act against crowd disturbances, especially against food rioters. The government recognised these fears, but retained the Volunteers so long as there was a serious threat of a French invasion. From 1808, however, the government established a Local Militia force, raised by balloting men of military age, which, unlike the Volunteers, was placed under central government and military control. Thereafter, the number of Volunteers was steadily reduced and all the infantry corps were disbanded at the end of the war in 1814.[73] Some yeoman cavalry corps were retained because they were more under aristocratic control and were more loyalist in their political attitudes. They were sometimes employed against popular crowd demonstrations, killing fifteen and injuring several hundred in St Peter's Fields in Manchester in August 1819, for example.[74]

A growing number of clubs and societies in the later eighteenth and earlier nineteenth centuries served a directly political purpose,

---

73 J. E. Cookson, 'The English Volunteer Movement of the French Wars, 1793-1815: Some Contexts', *The Historical Journal*, 32 (1989), 867-891; Austin Gee, *The British Volunteer Movement 1794-1814* (Oxford, 2003); and *Resisting Napoleon: The British response to the threat of invasion 1797-1815*, ed. Mark Philp (Aldershot, 2006).

74 Donald Read, *Peterloo: The 'massacre' and its background* (Manchester, 1973); and Robert Reid, *The Peterloo Massacre* (London, 1989).

campaigning for parliamentary reform.[75] From the Constitutional Societies and the Societies for the Supporters of the Bill of Rights in the 1760s and 1770s, through such societies as the Yorkshire Association of the 1780s, the London Corresponding Society of the 1790s, the Hampden Clubs of the 1810s, the Political Unions of the late 1820s and early 1830s, and the numerous Chartist Societies of the later 1830s and 1840s, many tens of thousands of British radicals involved themselves in nationwide campaigns for parliamentary reform. Often the lead was taken by a particular club or association, but it endeavoured to enlist support from similar organisations across the country in support of nationwide petitioning campaigns and national conventions. Over 60,000 men signed political petitions in the late 1760s and early 1780s; in 1817, over 700 parliamentary reform

---

75 There is a vast literature on the campaigns for parliamentary reform from the 1760s to the 1840s. See, in particular, John Cannon, *Parliamentary Reform, 1640-1832* (Cambridge, 1973); Ian R. Christie, *Wilkes, Wyvill and Reform: the parliamentary reform movement in British politics, 1760-1785* (London, 1962); Eugene Charlton Black, *The Association: British Extraparliamentary Political Organization 1769-1793*; *The French Revolution and British popular politics*, ed. Mark Philp (Cambridge, 1991); E. P. Thompson, *The Making of the English Working Class* (revised edn. Harmondsworth, 1968); H. T. Dickinson, *British Radicalism and the French Revolution 1789-1815* (Oxford, 1985); Peter Spence, *The Birth of Romantic Radicalism: War, popular political English Radical reformism, 1800-1815* (Aldershot, 1996); Carlos Flick, *The Birmingham Political Union and the Movement for Reform in Britain 1830-1839* (Hamden, CT, 1978); Nancy D. LaPotin, *Political Unions, Popular Politics and the Great Reform Act of 1832* (Basingstoke, 1999); *The People's Charter: Democratic Agitation in Early Victorian Britain*, ed. Stephen Roberts (London, 2003); Dorothy Thompson, *The Chartists* (London, 1984); and Malcolm Chase, *Chartism : A New History* (Manchester, 2007).

petitions with several hundred thousand signatures were sent to parliament from all over Britain; and the famous Chartist petitions were supported by over one million signatures in 1839 and over three million in 1842, while over two million men signed the 1848 petition, if not the 5,700,000 that its supporters claimed. Efforts were made in the early 1780s, early 1790s, in 1816, in the late 1820s and early 1830s, and, by the Chartists in 1839, 1842 and 1849, to establish national conventions of delegates from a wide range of political clubs and societies. The National Charter Association, which was established in Manchester in 1840, had linked some 400 local clubs with about 50,000 members by 1842. Popular political campaigns did not always focus on political reforms; they also sought to resist progressive changes. Very large numbers of Britons were active in nationwide campaigns to oppose Catholic reform in 1778-80 and in 1828-29,[76] and to suppress radical activities in the early 1790s.[77]

Popular political movements tried to make their activities and their cause enjoyable, exciting and inspirational. They shared in debating, listened to readings, speeches, and music, participated in dinners, feasts and tea parties, built bonfires and set off fireworks, engaged in marches

---

76 See note 69 above.

77 H. T. Dickinson, 'Popular conservatism and militant loyalism, 1789-1815', in *Britain and the French Revolution, 1789-1815*, ed. H. T. Dickinson (Basingstoke, 1989), pp. 103-125; *idem*, 'Popular loyalism in the 1790s', in the *Transformation of Political Culture: England and Germany in the late Eighteenth Century*, ed. Eckhart Hellmuth (Oxford, 1990), pp. 503-533; and Jennifer Mori, 'Languages of Loyalism: Patriotism, Nationhood and the State in the 1790s', *English Historical Review*, 118 (2003), 33-59.

and processions, produced and distributed propaganda, canvassed signatures on petitions, drank toasts, and took part in plays, dances, and sports, and attended Sunday or evening schools. At times they organised huge public rallies in the open air, as in London in 1795, Manchester in 1819, Birmingham in 1831, and Kennington in 1848, and recruited tens of thousands of supporters to march through the streets. Popular radical meetings and protests were the chief leisure activities of many people and they offered a political education to a great many more. They bound men together in fellowship and mutual support, and sometimes enlisted women too. They helped to promote a common sense of purpose, and by the Chartist era they were even developing a sense of class-consciousness among many tens of thousands of industrial workers.

The vast majority of radicals and popular political activists used constitutional means and peaceful tactics in order to achieve their political aims in the later eighteenth and earlier nineteenth centuries. They tried to justify their activities by appeals to traditional rights and to both past and recent history, even when they were essentially motivated by natural rights ideology. They referred to the Norman yoke and the Glorious Revolution, and they gave toasts to past heroes and martyrs such as Algernon Sidney, John Hampden and John Locke and to modern heroes such as Charles James Fox, Tom Paine, Henry Hunt, and Feargus O'Connor. Some caused more alarm by using a variety of radical signs and symbols, wearing caps of liberty, planting liberty trees, flying the tricolour, and singing the *Ça Ira*. While eschewing violent revolution, they asserted their right to take control of their local streets by marches and open-air gatherings and, when unable to protect their rights by constitutional means, they claimed the right to intimidate their oppressors by sheer numbers. In the late eighteenth and earlier nineteenth centuries there were quite simply thousands of street protests and crowd disturbances which often descended into violent riots. These occurred in both urban and rural areas and in every part of Great Britain.[78] The most frequent and widespread popular protests into the early nineteenth century were caused by the shortage and consequent high price of food. The largest and most violent riots occurred in London in early June 1780 when tens of thousands of Gordon rioters ran amok until large numbers were shot or arrested by the regular army.[79] The most serious and widespread industrial disorders occurred in 1811-13, when Luddite textile workers in the East Midlands, West Yorkshire and South Lancashire smashed many machines and attacked other property in order to preserve their skills and to force their employers to improve their wages and working conditions. It took thousands of troops and hundreds

---

78 See, for example, John Stevenson, *Popular Disturbances in England 1700-1832* (2nd edn. London, 1992); Nicholas Rogers, *Crowds, Culture and Politics in Georgian Britain* (Oxford, 1998); H.T. Dickinson, *The Politics of the People*, chap. 4; John Bohstedt, *Riots and Community Politics in England and Wales 1790-1810* (Cambridge, MA, 1983); and Adrian Randall, *Riotous Assemblies: Popular Protest in Hanoverian England* (Oxford, 2006).

79 Christopher Hibbert, *King Mob: The Story of Lord George Gordon and the Riots of 1780* (London, 1959); *The Gordon Riots: Politics, Culture and Insurrection in late eighteenth-century Britain*, ed. Ian Haywood and John Seed (Cambridge, 2012); and Robert Kent Donovan, *No popery and radicalism: opposition to Roman Catholic relief in Scotland, 1778-1782* (New York, 1987).

of arrests to restore order and even these determined efforts did not completely prevent future outbreaks of a similar kind.[80] Rural disorder on an alarming scale occurred in 1830-31, when very large numbers of agricultural labourers and village craftsmen took part in hundreds of violent protests across the counties of southern England, from Kent and Norfolk in the east to Wiltshire in the west. These protests were caused by the widespread distress resulting from enclosures, food shortages, low wages, high rents and church tithes, reduced poor relief, and the introduction of threshing machines, which reduced winter employment. Nearly two thousand arrests were made and severe punishment was meted out to over one thousand protesters.[81]

In some years – throughout the 1790s, 1811-13, 1816-19, the early 1830s and 1839-42 – popular riots were so numerous, widespread and threatening that the governing elite genuinely feared mass insurrection and violent revolution, even though modern historians are less convinced that there was ever such a threat.[82] There is very little evidence, however, to

---

80 See, in particular, Malcolm I. Thomis, *The Luddites: Machine Breaking in Regency England* (Newton Abbot, 1970); and Eric Hobsbawm, 'The Machine Breakers', *Past and Present*, 1 (Feb. 1952), 57-70.

81 E. J. Hobsbawm and G. Rudé, *Captain Swing* (revised edn. London, 1973); 'Captain Swing Reconsidered', ed. Steve Poole and Andrew Spicer, in *Southern History*, 32 (2010); Carl J. Griffin, 'The Violent Captain Swing?', *Past and Present*, 209 (2010), 140-180; and Carl J. Griffin, *The Rural War: Captain Swing and the Politics of Protest* (Manchester, 2012).

82 E. P. Thompson in his famous study, *The Making of the English Working Class* (new edn. London, 1991), discussed occasions when he thought revolution was a distinct possibility. His claims have been supported by Roger Wells in

suggest that these protests aimed to promote radical political changes. On the other hand, it is a mistake to regard them as mindless reactions to economic misery. A great deal of modern research into popular disturbances during these decades has clearly demonstrated that the protesters resorted to acts of intimidation and physical violence as a last resort in an effort to bring pressure to bear on their rulers, employers and grasping merchants, who were artificially increasing the price of food, undermining their wages, working conditions and practices, and attacking their traditional rights, customs and privileges. They freely followed leaders from their own communities and often combined effectively to pursue their objectives in a rational and disciplined fashion. Even though they could not elect representatives to parliament, they possessed a strong sense of what was fair and just, and they were fully conscious of their rights as freeborn Britons.[83] Since the authorities could call upon large numbers of regular troops, militiamen and Volunteers only during the French wars and there were no professional police forces before 1829 (and such forces existed in only a few big cities before the mid-nineteenth

Insurrection: The British Experience 1795-1803 (Gloucester, 1983), but they have been challenged by Malcolm I. Thomis and Peter Holt, *Threats of Revolution in Britain, 1789-1848* (London, 1977).

83 E.P. Thompson, in 'The Moral Economy of the English Crowd in the Eighteenth Century', *Past and Present*, 50 (Feb. 1971), 76-136, did much to demonstrate the moral sense of those engaged in popular crowd disturbances. More resent research has refined some of his arguments (see note 78 above), but no modern scholar has challenged his primary claim that most rioters were not simply acting in a mindless fashion because of their miserable economic circumstances.

century), the governing elite often had to make concessions, such as amending the laws of the country or deciding not to impose those that remained on the statute book. Employers had to bow more often to the demands of militant workers. There is much evidence to show that the British governing elite and a wide range of employers recognised the limits of their ability to dictate and control the political culture of the country and the material rewards of the lower orders. Radical ideology and radical political movements failed to democratise the political system in these decades, but the determined efforts of the middling and lower orders ensured that Britain was the most open society in Europe and hence it was possible for very large numbers of men to take part in a wide variety of political activities should they have the desire, determination and courage to do so. Very large numbers of unenfranchised men in the middling and lower orders of British society undoubtedly possessed and exercised these qualities in the later eighteenth and earlier nineteenth centuries.

英國政治有多民主（1760s-1840s）？

Harry T. Dickinson

摘要

此文論證，在十八世紀末與十九世紀初，英國與法國、美國一樣，都有促成民主革命的嘗試與作爲。英國激進派在這幾十年間積極介入緊張的意識形態活動，意欲確保公民自由、提升政治參與權、提倡更廣義的經濟平等權。他們也投入於重要的政治活動，意欲擴大英國群眾的選舉權，卻不必攻擊王室與貴族。有些激進派的確爲貧窮群眾提出改善方案。雖然上述活動都令人印象深刻，但是，無論是爲爭取更大自由的意識形態活動，或是爲了達到更公平或更民主的政治作爲，都未能得到完整成果。這並非意指，十八世紀中葉的英國政治文化的民主程度與百年之前一無差別。但唯有觀察其選舉的群眾參與、都會化、出版自由的提升、識字率的增加、民間社團的成長、群眾集會、抗議的頻率等等各方面的活動與發展，吾人才能眞正體會英國十八世紀中葉更開放、更具參與度的文化。

關鍵詞：激進主義、古憲法、自然權利、經濟平等、國會改革、選舉權推廣、都會化、出版自由、自由結社、群衆動亂

【研究討論】

近代早期歐洲思想史中的曼德維爾

陳禹仲

牛津大學歷史學博士生。研究興趣爲歐洲政治思想史、近代早期歐洲思想史、啓蒙思想史與史學史，目前研究主題爲喬治・柏克萊與十八世紀歐洲思想風貌。

近代早期歐洲思想史中的曼德維爾

摘要

本文是對十八世紀思想家伯納德·曼德維爾（Bernard Mandeville, 1670-1733）的研究討論，藉由梳理歐美學界到目前爲止對曼德維爾的研究，爲中文讀者引介這名被啓蒙哲士如大衛·休謨（David Hume, 1711-1776）、尚－賈克·盧梭（Jean-Jacques Rousseau, 1712-1778）、亞當·斯密（Adam Smith, 1723-1790）與伊曼紐·康德（Immanuel Kant, 1724-1804）重視與批評的思想家。本文指出，當代思想史對曼德維爾的研究，著重在其經濟與社會思想對十八世紀文人的影響。經濟與社會固然是曼德維爾關懷的重要課題，然而，曼德維爾著作的多面性，如他應用醫學理論、哲學論述、以及自然哲學來建構自己的社會理論，仍然有待更進一步的研究，而這樣的研究，也能有助於思想史家掌握十八世紀思想文化，各種知識領域交錯的多面與複雜。除此之外，本文尚有另一個目的，即希望能透過文獻回顧，反思近年思想史家對於「歷史」的理解，並強調專題討論不應只是引介既有的研究著作，而要能有效地反問史家書寫歷史時，對自身研究本質的認識。

關鍵詞：伯納德·曼德維爾、十八世紀辯論、近代早期歐洲思想史、專題討論、歷史、過往

I

當代歐洲思想史研究的一大特色，在於強調解釋歷史文本時，必須要重建文本書寫時的思想文化，如此方能有效「解釋」作者書寫時的意圖。[1]如斯取徑所提出的問題，並非是如何「詮釋」文本的內容，而是作者書寫的目的爲何？作者書寫時預期的讀者爲誰？以及作者爲何採用文本所呈現的形式書寫？[2]文本的作者有如羅馬共和時期的雄辯家一般，採取各種論述模式以說服聽眾讀者、勸服論敵。事實上，近代早期歐洲的文人也確實甚爲熟悉羅馬共和時期關於辯術修辭的論著，並時時援引作爲著書立說時的思想資源。[3]依此而論，書寫文本實質上一種政治行爲，而作者則無疑是政治行爲的能動者，試圖透過書寫文字的權力說服受眾。

歷史學術書寫的背後也存在著如此的權力關係，歷史學者不僅是史料發聲的媒介，也絕非只是透過史料，試圖重建一個與現代時空相

1 關於「詮釋」(interpret) 文本與「解釋」(explain) 文本的差異，可參見：Quentin Skinner, *Forensic Shakespeare* (Oxford: Oxford University Press, 2014), pp. 2-3.

2 Quentin Skinner, "Motives, intentions and interpretation", in Idem., *Visions of Politics, Vol. I, Regarding Method* (Cambridge: Cambridge University Press, 2012), pp. 90-102.

3 對修辭學於近代早期歐洲思想文化的論著甚多，於此僅列幾本較爲經典的著作：Paul Oskar Kristeller, *Renaissance Thought and the Arts: Collected Essays* (Princeton: Princeton University Press, 1990, the expanded edition), pp. 228-246; Markku Peltonen *Classical Humanism and Republicanism in English Political Thought 1570-1640* (Cambridge: Cambridge University Press, 1995), pp. 18-53; Quentin Skinner, *Reason and Rhetoric in the Philosophy of Hobbes* (Cambridge: Cambridge University Press, 1996), pp. 19-211.

距甚遠的環境結構，史家在有心無意間，會使歷史著作成爲說服讀者的工具，史家撰寫史著也因此必然是一種政治行爲。[4]例如，政治思想史家的著作，可以借由重建政治哲學文本如洛克《政府論次講》（*The Second Treatise of Government*）書寫時的思維脈絡，以駁斥當代政治哲學對於洛克《政府論》乃是爲1688年革命辯護而作的迷思。[5]職是之故，史家在閱讀同儕歷史著作時，也當要關注史著書成時的學術文化，如此或能認識不同史家研究時的意圖，以及研究所企求的目的，而最有效的方式，也許是耙梳史著的史學史。

史學史在歐美歷史學已是行之有年的領域，而更能令史家反思其研究本質的，或許是一種史學的思想史（the intellectual history of historiography），探討史家書寫歷史時，對「歷史」的理解與想像，同時也討論史家所處的文化如何看待「歷史」。[6]歷史書寫做爲一種在一定時間軸度裡，描繪人類行爲事件與自然環境變遷等消逝現象的論述，體現的是書寫者對不同時間區段下，不同空間中各種活動的認知。不同的歷史書寫，也因此反應了不同書寫者，對過往時間所俱意義的認識。[7]在這樣的關懷下，史家面對不同年代與領域的歷史書寫

4 Cf. J. G. A. Pocock, "The historian as political actor in polity, society and academy", in Idem., *Political Thought and History: Essays on Theory and Method*（Cambridge: Cambridge University Press, 2009）, pp. 217-238.

5 Peter Laslett, "Introduction" to John Locke, *Two Treatises of Government*, ed. Peter Laslett（Cambridge: Cambridge University Press, 1988, reprinted edition）, pp. 3-126.

6 近年來最具代表性的論著，當是：J. G. A. Pocock, *Barbarism and Religion, 6 Vols*.（Cambridge: Cambridge University Press, Vol. I - Vol. V 1999-2010, Vol. VI 2015 forthcoming）.

7 Cf. Reinhart Koselleck, "Time and history", in Idem., *The Practice of Conceptual History: Timing History, Spacing Concepts*（Stanford: Stanford

時，或許易於反思史著可能隱含，屬於不同史家的「歷史」的概念。而在不同歷史研究的領域裡，著重探究概念與論述的思想史，尤當如此。

作爲一篇研究討論，本文的目的有二。首先，藉討論歐美思想史對十七世紀末十八世紀初思想家伯那德・曼德維爾（Bernard Mandeville, 1670-1733）的討論，引介予中文讀者這名被大衛・休謨（David Hume, 1711-1776）、尚一賈克・盧梭（Jean-Jacques Rousseau, 1712-1778）、亞當・斯密（Adam Smith, 1723-1790）與伊曼紐・康德（Immanuel Kant, 1724-1804）等啓蒙哲士熱議的思想家。另一方面，本文希望能夠透過此研究討論，梳理二十世紀後半葉以來，歐美思想史研究取徑的變遷，並進而從此提供不同研究取徑，對十七世紀末十八世紀初那段時間，思想文化所俱意義的不同理解。

II

約翰・波考克(J. G. A. Pocock)在其研究十七、十八世紀歐洲政治思想的經典《馬基維利的時刻》（*The Machiavellian Moment*）裡論道，十八世紀的歐洲，有一場「介於美德與激情，土地與商業，共和與帝國，價值與歷史」之間的「十八世紀辯論」（Eighteenth-Century Debate）。[8]同樣地，馬爾康・傑克（Malcolm Jack）也在其著作《敗落

University Press, 2002), pp. 100-114; Idem., "History, histories, and formal time structure", in Idem., *Future Past: On the Semantics of Historical Time* (Columbia: Columbia University Press, 2004), pp. 93-105; Idem., "Representation, event, and structure", in Ibid., pp. 105-114.

8 J. G. A. Pocock, *The Machiavellian Moment: Florentine Political Thought and the Atlantic Republican Tradition* (Princeton: Princeton University Press,

與進程》（*Corruption & Progress*）裡提及：「（歐洲思想家們）一方面珍視隨著商業生活進展而來的種種好處，另一方面卻又深爲物質富裕逐漸凌駕於道德操守的現象所困擾。」[9]

歐洲思想家在十七世紀末十八世紀初，面臨了物質經濟逐漸繁榮，但美德觀念逐漸淡薄的兩難。一般認爲，這個物質與美德相衝突的困境，是歐洲商業社會逐漸興起所造成。商業社會的興起使得包含法國、荷蘭共和國與英國等地的西北部歐洲社會，在物質生活上逐步富裕，社會大眾的關注也漸次較著重世俗生活的物質享樂。如何積聚財富，並進一步以此財富換取物質享樂，成爲處於商業社會裡人們的一大根本關懷。

之所以有此物質發展與美德消退的兩難，是因爲不論積聚財富還是物質享樂，兩者都與歐洲當時的美德觀念相背離，甚至被時人斥爲罪惡。在這個背景之下，商業社會所帶來的物質繁華要如何與歐洲既有的美德傳統共存，便成爲困擾當時思想家的課題。環繞著這個課題，思想家們各自對商業社會提出不同的詮釋。有的思想家認爲，物質的繁華不但不會腐化美德，還使人類比諸過往更爲文明。休謨便曾

1975), 462. "…between virtue and passion, land and commerce, republic and empire, value and history". Cf. Christopher J. Berry, *The Idea of Luxury: A Conceptual and Historical Investigation* (Cambridge: Cambridge University Press, 1994), pp. 126-176; Cf. Istvan Hont, "Needs and Justice in the Wealth of Nations", in Idem. *Jealousy of Trade: International Competition and the Nation-State in Historical Perspective* (Cambridge, Mass.: Belknap Press of Harvard University Press, 2010), pp. 389-443.

9 Malcolm Jack, *Corruption & Progress: The Eighteenth-Century Debate* (New York: AMS Press, 1989), p. 1. "…on the one hand, they valued the advantages that the growth of commercial life brought with it; on the other , they were disturbed by the effects of increased material wealth upon moral well-being".

論及，任何國家與其人民的生活幸福與否，都與商業發展脫離不了關係。[10]也有思想家抱持反對的立場，認爲商業社會的物質發展，使人類亦趨沉淪，如盧梭（Jean-Jacque Rousseau, 1712-1778）即表明，商業將使人喪失其之所以爲人的一切本質，淪爲喪失人性，純粹受享樂慾望驅使的奴隸，甚至，當人類開始擁有私有財產的概念後，便是人類遭受奴役的開始。[11]

在這些思想家中，旅居倫敦的荷蘭醫生曼德維爾在思考「物質－美德」兩難時，提出一種在時人眼中既新奇又挑釁的觀點。他於其最惹人非議的著作《蜜蜂的寓言》（*The Fable of the Bees*，以下簡稱《寓言》）裡表明，所有人最卑劣的惡行，最終都會在某方面爲社會帶來好處。這是曼德維爾對十八世紀辯論的回應。他那「私惡公益」（Private Vices, Public Benefits）的主張，暗示了個人私惡其實有惠於公眾利益。這使他受到如喬治．柏克萊（George Berkeley, 1685-1753）和法蘭西斯．哈奇森（Francis Hutcheson, 1694-1746）等思想家批評。甚至，曼德維爾還因此被倫敦的密德塞克斯(Middlesex)大法官起訴，並以「倡議奢侈、貪婪、傲慢，以及諸多罪惡」的罪名求處死刑。[12]然而，十八世紀中後期的思想家們，如休謨與斯密等，皆

10 David Hume, *Essays: Moral, Political and Literary*, ed. Eugene F. Miller (Indianapolis: Liberty Fund, 1987), pp. 253-267.

11 Jean-Jacques Rousseau, *Discourse on the Origin and the Foundations of Inequality Among Men*, in Idem., *The Discourses and Other Ealy Political Writings*, ed. Victor Gourevitch (Cambridge: Cambridge University Press, 1997), pp. 113-188.

12 Bernard Mandeville, *The Fable of the Bee, or Private Vices, Publick Benefits, Vol. I*, ed. F. B. Kaye (Indianapolis: Liberty Fund, 1988. Reprinted.), p. 385. "…recommend luxury, avarice, pride, and all kind of vices, as being necessary to public welfare".

在一定程度上接受了曼德維爾的想法。[13]

曼德維爾在十八世紀初期的英格蘭，可謂惡名昭彰。他的著作，被視爲支持商業社會、倡議物質文明、誘使美德腐化最有力的舵手。他被視爲與馬基維利（Niccolò Machiavelli, 1469-1527）、湯瑪斯・霍布斯（Thomas Hobbes, 1588-1679）與約翰・托蘭（John Toland, 1670-1722）等人齊名，鼓吹罪惡與無神論的作家。[14]儘管如此，曼德維爾的《寓言》卻仍舊是十八世紀英格蘭最爲暢銷的書籍之一，而十八世紀歐洲思想家在辯證商業優劣時，也難免將曼德維爾所勾勒的商業社會圖像納入討論。由此看來，曼德維爾著作對十八世紀文人社群的衝擊不可謂不小，而這或許也正是歐美思想史家對曼德維爾產生興趣的原因。然而，當代學者對曼德維爾的興趣，並非始自歷史學。

III

或許是因爲休謨與斯密在論證自己的政治經濟學思想時，回應了曼德維爾論點的緣故，當代學界討論曼德維爾論著時，聚焦點往往是曼德維爾對商業與經濟的析論。於1924年隻手重新整理曼德維爾手

13　十八世紀思想家們對曼德維爾批評與討論，詳見：Thomas A. Horne, *The Social Thought of Bernard Mandeville: Virtue and Commerce in Early Eighteenth-Century England*（New York: Columbia University Press, 1978）, pp. 76-95；關於曼德維爾對休謨與亞當斯密的影響，後人論著甚多，近年最具代表性的著作或爲：Pierre Force, *Self-Interest Before Adam Smith: A Genealogy of Economic Science*（Cambridge: Cambridge University Press, 2003）.

14　Cf. John Wesley, *The Journal of the Reverend John Wesley, Vol. I*（New York: 1837）, p. 600; John Brown, "Honour, A Poem", in Robert Dodsley ed., *A Collection of Poems in Six Volumes, Vol. III*（London, 1782）, p. 335.

稿與著作的弗里德里希・凱伊（F. B. Kaye, 1892-1930），在其所編纂的《寓言》導論裡提及，曼德維爾思想影響後是最為深遠的，當是的經濟理論。[15]凱伊指出，曼德維爾對奢侈消費的正面論述，以及他對人性與市場經濟的洞見，皆成為後世經濟理論的重要論據資源，包含亞當斯密的《國富論》（*An Inquiry Into the Nature and Causes of the Wealth of Nations*, 1776）。不僅於此，凱伊強調，曼德維爾在《寓言》所提倡的，無疑便是十九二十世紀歐洲主流的自由放任理論。[16]從這個層面來說，曼德維爾實際上是歐洲啓蒙期間最為重要的思想家之一，甚至，就對後人的影響而言，綜觀十八世紀能夠比《寓言》更加重要的英語著作，定然屈指可數。

凱伊對曼德維爾的重視點起了英語文學界對十八世紀初英語論著的興趣，但比起曼德維爾，英語文學學者更為注重的，是與曼德維爾同時活躍的喬納森・史威夫特（Jonathan Swift, 1667-1745）與丹尼爾・狄福（Daniel Defoe, 1684-1731）等人。[17]英語文學學界對曼德維爾的討論，要待到1970年，曼德維爾三百歲冥誕時，才出現較為系統地試圖全面重新討論曼德維爾著作的研究，其成果為一本於1975年出版，名為《曼德維爾研究》（*Mandeville Studies*）的論文集。該文集討論了曼德維爾著作的許多面向，例如宗教、道德與政治等主題，但更著重於曼德維爾與同時代文人如狄福的關係，以及曼德維爾

15 Kaye, "Introduction" to Mandeville, *Fable of the Bees, Vol. I*, pp. cxxxiv-cxlvi.

16 Ibid., p. cxxxix.

17 Irwin Primer ed., *Mandeville Studies: New Explorations in the Art and Thought of Dr. Bernard Mandeville (1670-1733)* (Hague: Martinus Nijhoff, 1975), pp. vii-viii.

諷諭文學的書寫風格。[18]歐洲思想史學者對曼德維爾的討論，可能與凱伊對曼德維爾經濟理論的高度評論更有關聯，特別是凱伊編纂《寓言》約莫五十年後，對曼德維爾思想創見的回應。

諾貝爾經濟學獎得主海耶克（F. A. Hayek, 1899-1992）於1966年，在英國國家學術院(British Academy)受邀演講，主題是「一個偉大的心靈」（Lecture on a Master Mind）。海耶克演講的主題正是曼德維爾，在其中，海耶克強調，曼德維爾對商業社會的觀察，啓迪了包含休謨與斯密等重要經濟學人的理論，他因此將曼德維爾放置於現代經濟思想發展史的最前緣。海耶克認爲，雖然曼德維爾並未提出任何具體的社會與經濟學理論，但曼德維爾對商業社會有「自發性秩序」（spontaneous order）的討論，卻直接反映了商業社會的本質，而「自發性秩序」也成爲後人經濟理論的基礎。[19]換句話說，對海耶克而言，儘管曼德維爾不若休謨與史密斯等人有完善的思想理論建構，但曼德維爾對商業社會的論述，卻是後人之所以能夠發揚他們自由經濟思想的前提。在演講的最後，海耶克將曼德維爾與達爾文（Charles Darwin, 1809-1882）並列，認爲兩人皆以驚世駭俗的方式，引領人類的智識心靈進化。

凱伊與海耶克此般將曼德維爾與人類經濟行爲與經濟理論關聯討論的作法，反映了一種思考過往意義的圖像。人類現代的種種，必然有其過往爲因，而過往事件的意義，便在於其如何參與塑成現代的形態。曼德維爾的論著之所以重要，在於他啓迪了斯密與休謨，在於他

18 Ibid., esp. pp. 98-211.

19 Reprinted as: F.A. Hayek, "Dr. Bernard Mandeville（1670-1733）", in Idem., *The Trend of Economic Thinking: Essays on Political Economists and Economic History*（Indianapolis: Liberty Fund, 1991）, pp. 79-100.

提出了自由放任理論的雛形，在於他以邁向「現代」的概念衝擊了既有的框架。這種對過去的認識，如同麥克·奧克夏（Michael Oakeshott, 1901-1990）所言，是一種「實用過往」（practical past），其所理解的歷史，是以現代所有的現象爲本，探求這個「現代」於過往中存在的痕跡，以求理解這個「現代」的「歷史」。「歷史」在這種意義下，便成爲對「現代」有用的過往。[20]

如此思考「歷史」與「過往」的圖像，也體現在其他曼德維爾研究上。例如，法國人類學家路易·杜蒙（Louis Dumont, 1911-1988）在《從曼德維爾到馬克思》（*From Mandeville to Marx*）一書裡，指陳曼德維爾是第一個將美德哲學與經濟分析合一而論的思想家，而這種融美德哲學與經濟分析的經濟思想，延續到史密斯等人的政治經濟學體系。[21]此外，如安·若特（Anne Metter Hjort）的〈曼德維爾的矛盾現代性〉（"Mandeville's Ambivalent Modernity", 1991）和亞歷山大·比克（Alexander Bick）的〈曼德維爾與荷蘭經濟〉（"Bernard Mandeville and the Economy of Dutch", 2008）等文，都分別討論曼德維爾對現代性論述與市場經濟理論的貢獻。[22]

當代史學著作中，將曼德維爾視爲十八世紀歐洲思潮轉變，擺脫古典通往現代的要角，最具代表性的著作，當是湯馬斯·霍恩

20 Michael Oakeshott, *Three Essays on History*, in Idem., *On History and Other Essays* (Indianapolis: Liberty Fund, 1999, reprinted), pp. 38-48.

21 Louis Dumont, *From Mandeville to Marx: The Genesis and Triumph of Economic Ideology* (Chicago: University of Chicago Press, 1977).

22 Anne Mette Hjort, "Mandeville's Ambivalent Modernity", *MLN*, 106:5 (Dec., 1991): pp. 951-966; Alexander Bick, "Bernard Mandeville and the Economy of the Dutch", *Erasmus Journal for Philosophy and Economics*, 1:1 (Autumn, 2008): pp. 87-106.

（Thomas A. Horne）《伯納德・曼德維爾的社會思想》（*The Social Thought of Bernard Mandeville*）一書。霍恩認爲，曼德維爾的思想承襲了十七世紀以降，法國輝格諾派（Huguenot）道德哲學家們對美德（virtue）的懷疑論。十七世紀後期，輝格諾派在宗教迫害下逃離法國旅居荷蘭，也將他們對人性的論述帶到當時的荷蘭共和國。曼德維爾也因此得以近距離接觸到這些道德哲學家，如尙・楓丹（Jean de La Fontaine, 1621-1695）與皮耶・貝爾（Pierre Bayle, 1647-1706）等人的論著。事實上，於鹿特丹（Rotterdam）成長的曼德維爾，很可能親炙當時旅居鹿特丹的貝爾的課堂。[23]

霍恩認爲，輝格諾道德哲學家很大程度上接受了詹森派（Jansenism）對人性的悲觀見解。詹森派對人性的看法是，自從人類受了誘惑被逐出伊甸園後，人性便只剩下傾向不斷地背叛上帝、自甘墮落的一面。輝格諾哲學家承襲了這樣的看法，認爲人的天性既無理性也無道德感，而是一味地受自然慾望的激情（passions）所操縱，而所有的激情中，自私地只喜愛自己（self-love）是激情最強力的展現。霍恩進而指出，近乎相同的人性論述在曼德維爾身上也表露無遺，只是曼德維爾更進一步的陳述了人性天生的激情與社會之間的關係：人性利己的天性激情會有利於社會公共利益。[24]這是曼德維爾的創見，也是海耶克說曼德維爾發現社會「自發性秩序」的原因，也是

23 E. D. James, “Fiath, sincerity and morality: Mandeville and Bayle”, in Irwin ed., *Mandeville Studies*, pp. 43-65; Cf. Wiep van Bunge, “The presence of Bayle in the Dutch Republic”, in Wiep van Bunge and Hans Bots eds., *Pierre Bayle (1647-1706), Le Philosophe De Rotterdam: Philosophy, Religion and Reception, Selected Papers of the Tercentenary Conference Held at Rotterdam, 7-8 December 2006* (Leiden: Brill, 2008), pp. 197-216, esp. pp. 203-204.

24 Horne, *The Social Thought of Mandeville*, pp. 19-31.

曼德維爾思想之所以影響後世思想家的主因。霍恩也因此將曼德維爾視爲十八世紀歐洲思潮轉折的重要推手。[25]

IV

相比上述的「歷史」視域，當代歐洲思想史家，或許更熟悉另一種看待「歷史」的方式，其對「過往」的理解，較近似於奧克夏所言的「歷史過往」（historical past），即已然消逝於現代，只能藉由蛛絲馬跡重新挖掘的現象。[26]「歷史」正是這種消逝過往所構成，「歷史」也因此成爲「我們所失去的世界」（the worlds we have lost）。[27] 這樣的歷史思維認爲，今人所閱讀的思想文本，正是消逝過往遺留至現代的殘簡，要能正確地理解文本作者書寫文本的動機，以及採用某種形式進行書寫的目的，皆必須要透過謹慎地重構文本內容文字所屬的，已然亡佚的語言世界。[28] 而在成功地重構那些過往語言世界後，我們或

---

25 對霍恩此論的質疑，可見：J. G. A. Pocock, "Authority and property: The question of liberal origins", in Idem., *Virtue, Commerce, and History: Essays on Political Thought and History, Chiefly in the Eighteenth Century* (Cambridge: Cambridge University Press, 1985), pp. 51-71.

26 Oakeshott, *Three Essays*, in Idem., *On History*, pp. 8-11, 51-65.

27 Cf. J. G. A. Pocock, "Present at the creation: With Laslett to the lost worlds", *International Journal of Public Affairs* 2 (2006): 7-17.

28 此處的「語言」，並非指英語、法語等語言，而是人們在論述單一課題時所採用的議論方式，其中包含了使用某些詞彙時特殊的意義，以及文句結構的安排等。本文此後使用「語言」一詞時，都將採取此意。見：Pocock, "The reconstruction of discourse: Towards the historiography of political thought", in Idem., *Political Thought and History*, pp. 67-86; Idem. "The concept of a language and the métier d'historien: some considerations on practice"', in Ibid., pp. 87-105; Cf. Koselleck, "Begriffsgeschichte and social history", in Idem., *Future Past*, pp. 75-92.

可了解文本中的文句段落，在那個世界裡所擁有的意涵，再進而由此意涵正確地理解文本的意思。[29]如此的思維十分重視文本與書寫脈絡的關聯，因此又被稱爲「脈絡主義」（contextualism）。尤於提倡必須在書寫脈絡中閱讀文本的學者多與劍橋大學有關，強調脈絡的思想史取徑也往往被冠以「劍橋學派」（the Cambridge School）之名，儘管亦有不少身處劍橋的思想史家反對此學派的存在。[30]

脈絡史學最具代表的著作是名爲Ideas in Context的叢書。該叢書自1984年創立迄今，以出版逾百本的思想史專著，近一期的《觀念史期刊》（*Journal of the History of Ideas*）亦爲了紀念此里程碑，特別專號討論此書系的貢獻。[31]書寫時段橫跨希臘古典到廿世紀中葉，主題也包羅萬象，從數學理論、醫學論述到法學著作皆有名篇。[32]然而，該書系最著重的，仍舊是近代早期歐洲的政治論述，而這也明顯

---

29 J. G. A. Pocock, "Languages and their implications: The transformation of the study of political thought", in Idem., *Politics, Language, and Time: Essays on Political Thought and History*（Chicago: Chicago University Press, 1989）; Skinner, "Interpretation and the understanding of speech acts", in Idem., *Visions of Politics, Vol. I, pp. 103-127.*

30 前年不幸過世的史家宏特（Istvan Hont, 1947-2013）便曾在哈佛大學的演講中反對劍橋學派一詞。Istvan Hont, "Rousseau and Smith: A conversation with Istvant Hont", https://www.youtube.com/watch?v=v83Zh2IenM4（影片由CESHarvard於2011年8月11日上傳。）

31 Journal of the History of Ideas, "Ideas in Context series, Cambridge University Press", *Journal of the History of Ideas*, 75:4（Oct., 2014）: pp. 651-695.

32 Cf. Reviel Netz, *The Shaping of Deduction in Greek Mathematics: A Study in Cognitive History*（Cambridge: Cambridge University Press, 1999）; Ian Maclean, *Logics, Signs and Nature in the Renaissance: The Case of Learned Medicine*（Cambridge: Cambridge University Press, 2002）; T. J. Hochstrasser, Natural Law Theories in the Early Enlightenment（Cambridge: Cambridge University Press, 2006）.

反應在書系早期的出版專著上。[33]

莫瑞斯・高史密斯（Maurice M. Goldsmith）於1985年出版的《私惡，公益》（*Private Vices, Public Benefits*），是Ideas in Context書系的第三本著作，其論旨將曼德維爾的《寓言》一書，置於英格蘭自1688年革命以來，輝格（Whig）與托瑞（Tory）兩黨政治辯論的語言脈絡中，檢視曼德維爾的書寫目的，並重新解釋英格蘭政黨政治初期的辯論課題。[34]高史密斯指陳，對私利與公益的討論，早在曼德維爾之前，就已在英格蘭議會政治辯論裡行之有年，是以商業活動爲本的輝格紳士，與以土地產出爲業的托利貴族間，批判彼此階級形象與意識形態的辯論。這樣的論辯傳統，加上商業社會興起後，對於個人幸福追求的重視，是形塑曼德維爾思想的兩大脈絡。

高史密斯在分析曼德維爾生活時英格蘭的政治思想背景，以及該背景與曼德維爾思想的關連後指出，曼德維爾把私利公益辯論與個人幸福聯合後，產生了他自己的觀點，即個人自私地各自追求自我幸福的同時，也爲社會帶來了經濟與生活上的繁榮，這也是商業社會的根本，個人爲了追求私欲的滿足進行各種貿易行爲，這種貿易行爲將使社會整體更爲富足。高史密斯認爲，曼德維爾此舉，是同時爲十八世紀初期執政的輝格黨與1688年北渡的荷蘭王室辯護，概因當時輿論與托利黨政治論述對兩者的批評，皆著眼於兩者過度重視商業，並強調商業行爲中，人性自私的一面，將使社會腐敗沉淪。[35]值得一提的

33 Journal of the History of Ideas, "Ideas in Context at 100: Introduction", *Journal of the History of Ideas*, 75:4 (Oct., 2014): pp. 651-652.

34 M. M. Goldsmith, *Private Vices, Public Benefits: Bernard Mandeville's Social and Political Thought* (Cambridge: Cambridge University Press, 1985).

35 Ibid., pp. 78-159.

是，高史密斯對曼德維爾的觀察，與凱伊和海耶克等人相似，在強調曼德維爾思想重要之處時，他特別指出曼德維爾「私惡公益」的想法，可以被視爲現代資本主義最原初的提倡者之一。[36]

相較於高史密斯對政治辯論的興趣，同樣出版於Ideas in Context書系的《啓蒙的寓言》（*The Enlightenment's Fable*），對曼德維爾的寫作，有更爲細緻的討論。[37]《啓蒙的寓言》的作者愛德華・杭德（Edward J. Hundert）認爲，曼德維爾思想活動的目的，是爲了向世人提倡一個屬於商業社會，不受基督信仰道德規範所束縛的社會理論，同時提供一個對人類社會起源的解釋。在建構如此理論時，曼德維爾觸及了許多啓蒙時期歐洲思想文化的重要課題，例如：人性論、社會起源、政治權力的歸屬、人類宗教信仰的起源，以及何謂「進步」與「幸福」的生活。曼德維爾對這些課題的見解，使他成爲許多啓蒙文人寫作時無可迴避的討論對象，但對杭德而言，曼德維爾思想的精彩之處，不在於他對後世有多深遠的影響，而在於他吸收消化了許多十七世紀文人辯論的哲學語言，並於自己的著作中鎔鑄成一種新的論述語言，此一新的語言也成爲啓蒙文人思考社會問題時的資源。[38]例如，曼德維爾沿用了「激情」（passion）一字在十七世紀論述語言裡，描寫人性中與「理智」（reason）對立的情緒，卻在論及社會起源時，扭轉了十七世紀語言中，認爲「激情」將對人體與社會造成傷害，唯有「理智」克制才有益於個人與群體的概念，反而強調人類克制己身欲望，並非出於「理智」明白欲望傷身，而是出於想要獲取同

36 Ibid., pp. 123-142.

37 E.J. Hundert, *The Enlightenment's Fable: Bernard Mandeville and the Discovery of Society*（Cambridge: Cambridge University Press, 1994）.

38 Ibid., 219-236.

儕讚揚的榮譽，換句話說，人類之所以克制欲望，也是渴求名欲的「激情」所致。[39]

不同於之前的論著，杭德並未特別突顯曼德維爾與前人的差異，他更著重於曼德維爾人類社會起源的論點，如何成爲啓蒙哲士反思人類文明進程的要素。與十七世紀慣常的契約論不同，曼德維爾認爲，人類文明的發展，並不會因爲個人發自意願，突然訂定契約後，便從自然狀態演進至政治社會。相反地，政治社會是由緩慢、漸進的歷史進程，逐步發展而來。[40]由於在自然狀態下，人類可能會面臨到諸多災厄，爲了延續生存，人類逐漸聚居，進而逐步有了文明發展。這與人性嚮往更好的生活息息相關，而爲了達到這個目標，人們會盡可能的滿足自己的一切欲求，以讓自己過得更爲舒適安逸。曼德維爾認爲，唯有在一個以商業爲主的社會，方能避免人類爲了各自的利益爭相奪鬥，其原因在於商業社會下的人們，可以透過各種貿易行爲滿足自身的欲望，並在滿足自身欲望的同時，也提供他人滿足其欲望的資源，這也正是「私惡公益」的要旨。[41]曼德維爾將人類社會的起源與社會中個人的種種良善行爲，訴諸於人性「激情」對於享樂的趨性，並強調這樣的社會觀，遠比基督信仰道德論述裡的人性論與社會觀更爲眞實。杭德指出，正因爲這種融貫十七世紀哲學語言發展出的社會論述，使啓蒙哲人如孔狄拉（Étienne Bonnot de Condillac, 1714-1780）與盧梭等人皆爲之煩擾，進而著述抨擊，然而，儘管盧梭等人反對曼

39 Ibid., pp. 23-61.

40 Bernard Mandeville, *A Search into the Nature of Society*, in Idem., *The Fable of the Bees*, ed. Kaye, pp. 323-369.

41 Idem., *The Fable of the Bees, or Private Vices, Publick Benefits, Vol. II*, ed. F. B. Kaye (Indianapolis: Liberty Fund, 1988), pp. 266-357.

德維爾的觀點，卻又不得不採那曼德維爾對商業與人性欲求的討論。[42]杭德以爲，這種面對曼德維爾論著的矛盾態度，正是人類在商業蓬勃且物質享樂發達的社會裡，面對欲望與道德時的兩難抉擇。因此，十八世紀文人面對曼德維爾的掙扎，也正是人類文明現代性的掙扎。[43]

杭德對曼德維爾的討論，聚焦於啓蒙哲士對曼德維爾理論的正反辯言，約翰・羅伯森（John Robertson在）《啓蒙例證》（*The Case for the Enlightenment*）一書裡，則更加強調了曼德維爾與「啓蒙運動」的關係。[44]羅伯森反對近年歷史學對「啓蒙運動」的反思，強調「啓蒙」作爲一個思想潮流，並不會因爲思想家居住地域的差異，而有「多種啓蒙」（multiple enlightenments）存在。他舉拿坡里（Naples）與蘇格蘭（Scotland）的思想社群爲例，指出分處歐洲地緣南北兩極的文人社群，閱讀同樣的論著，探討同樣的課題，並提出各自對如何幫助人類社會進展的看法，由此可見，十八世紀的歐洲文人，其思想活動其實是跨越國別地域的。羅伯森同意強納森・伊斯瑞爾（Jonathan Israel），認爲啓蒙運動是十七十八世紀歐洲思想社群共享的思潮，其共同的思辨課題是人類社會如何邁入文明的進程。[45]然而，與伊斯瑞爾相反，羅伯森認爲眞正的「啓蒙運動」，要待到1750年以後，歐洲文人開始大量論述人類社會進程，並強調政治經濟學之

42 Hundert, *Enlightenment's Fable*, pp. 62-115.

43 Ibid., p. 15.

44 John Robertson, *The Case for the Enlightenment: Scotland and Naples 1680-1760*（Cambridge: Cambridge University Press, 2005）.

45 Ibid., pp. 1-51; Cf. Jonathan Israel, *Radical Enlightenment: Philosophy and the Making of Modernity 1650-1750*（Oxford: Oxford University Press, 2001）, pp. 3-22.

於文明進展的重要後，才正式展開。[46]

羅伯森論述的啓蒙文人，有共同的思想資源，即貝爾的著作。在拿坡里，貝爾對基督信仰的嘲諷，引起如維柯（Giambattista Vico, 1668-1744）等人的回覆，並進而成就拿坡里思想社群對人類社會的反思。[47]而在蘇格蘭，貝爾的著作則在曼德維爾的文字中重生。曼德維爾對宗教的嘲諷，認爲基督信仰的道德規範只是權謀方便的治術，目的是爲了滿足教會的私欲，比貝爾更直接地挑戰了教會的權威。更重要的是，曼德維爾在《寓言》的第二冊裡，對人類社會起源，以及宗教如何出現於人類社會的描述，從根本處否定了基督信仰與人類文明開展的關係，眞正有助於文明進程的，是對商業社會的理解。《寓言》第二部寫道，人類唯有在追求共同的利益，或面臨共同的危險時，才可能放下自私本性，共同生活。這是人類社會構成的根本原因，但這樣的社會結構並不穩固，一旦共同的利益或敵人消失，社會也將瓦解。能夠使社會長久存在的原因，是一群「精明政治家」（skillful politician）的存在，這群精明政治家操弄人類的名譽的渴望，強調克制欲望是一種無上美德，也因此使人類開始逐步克己，基督信仰的道德規範，也是在這樣的狀態下產生。[48]然而，這樣穩固的社會，卻仍不足以擁有文明，文明必須建立在所有人皆能滿足欲求，享受物質安樂上，也因此，文明的要素不在於道德約束，而在商貿行爲。曼德維爾的這個觀點，也深刻反映在十八世紀中葉，思想社群對人類宗教概念起源與政治經濟學的興趣上，其中最顯著的人物，即是

46 Robertson, *The Case for the Enlightenment*, pp. 377-405.

47 Ibid., pp. 201-255.

48 Mandeville, *The Fable of the Bees, Vol. II*, ed. Kaye, pp. 148-265.

休謨。[49]

高史密斯、杭德與羅伯森的專著，分別將曼德維爾的思想至於不同的書寫脈絡討論，這也體現了脈絡史學在研究取徑的關懷，即避免目的論式地解釋歷史文本，避免將「過去」視爲一種「實用過往」。這三本著作，並未如凱伊、海耶克與霍恩等人一般，特別強調曼德維爾對「現代」現象的貢獻，但這三本著作在論及曼德維爾思想的意義時，仍就難免將其重建的「歷史過往」投射至「現代」關懷，因此高史密斯會強調，曼德維爾點出了商業資本主義社會的原則，儘管他並沒有商業資本主義的概念。同樣的，杭德也指出，十八世紀文人閱讀曼德維爾所感受到的掙扎，是一種「現代」對個人欲望與道德的掙扎，甚至暗指二十世紀經濟學家對資本主義的種種質疑，皆因爲經濟學家爲曾好好閱讀曼德維爾之故。[50]羅伯森雖然未認爲曼德維爾爲「現代」的思維奠定基礎，卻將曼德維爾視爲「啓蒙運動」於英倫三島發跡的重要人物，而「啓蒙運動」正是「過往」與「現代」的過渡。要言之，脈絡史學對曼德維爾的討論，雖然未因爲曼德維爾著作這個「過往」，視爲資本主義這個「現代」的「歷史」，卻仍然將此種「過往」與「現代」相結。兩者的差別，只在「實用過往」從「現代」的現象出發，書寫構成「現代」現象的「歷史」。「歷史過往」仰賴「過往」於「現代」的殘留，視圖重建「過往」的世界，而後反思此「現代」理解此失落「過往」後，對「現代」現象可能的「未來」貢獻。

這種連結「過往」與「現代」的方式，與脈絡史學對「歷史」的

49 Robertson, *The Case for the Enlightenment*, pp. 261-283.

50 Hundert, *The Enlightenment's Fable*, pp. 247-249.

理解有關。雖然脈絡史學對「過往」的理解，與奧克夏對「歷史過往」的論述相仿，但兩者對「歷史」的認知卻有不小的差異。奧克夏所說的「歷史」，即是「過往」所屬，遺失於「現代」的世界。歷史學家的工作，僅要重建如此的世界即可，無需討論「過往」對「現代」現象的貢獻，更無需討論「過往」對「未來」可能的幫助。[51]但脈絡史學對這樣的「歷史」頗感懷疑。例如，波考克認爲，歷史學家重建「過往」世界的同時，也是在「現代」進行書寫，史家書寫「歷史」的方式會觀係到史家的「現代」對「過往」的認知，並可能由此影響對「現代」的理解，在時間恆動的原則下，對「現代」的理解，則很可能反應於「現代」現象在「未來」的開展。由此看來，於「現代」重建「過往」，都將難免影響「現代」的「未來」。[52]脈絡史學理論的主要提倡者昆廷．史基納(Quentin Skinner)也有類似，卻更簡潔的看法。他認爲，對消逝「過往」的認知，能爲「現代」的種種困境，提供另一種思考「未來」的可能。[53]

除此之外，脈絡史學對語言的重視，使脈絡史家的思想史研究，往往著重於論述語言的變遷，尤其是從「過往」到「現代」的語言轉化時期，換句話說，脈絡史學著作的一大特色，在探討「過往」如何逐漸成爲失落的「過往」。史基納最著名的論著，即在強調近代歐洲早期的政治語言，在十七世紀中葉時，經歷了自以羅馬共和（The Roman Republic）爲理想的共和論述，轉化爲強調政治體爲一虛擬人

51 Oakeshott, *Three Essays on History*, in Idem., *On History*, pp. 65-104.

52 Cf. Pocock, “Time, institutions and action: and essay on traditions and their understanding”, in Idem., *Political Thought and History*, pp. 187-217.

53 Quentin Skinner, *Liberty before Liberalism*（Cambridge: Cambridge University Press, 1998）, pp. 101-120.

格的語言，共和論述在此後逐漸成爲「過往」。史基納認爲，霍布斯正是這個語言轉換過程的主角。[54]波考克對語言轉變的理解，較史基納爲後，他認爲，轉變的過程與商業社會興起息息相關。由於社會文化的變動，使新的論述語法與詞彙開始同既有的語言相融，並從此衍生出一種新的語言。「十八世紀辯論」正是這樣的語言轉變時期。[55]前文所提及，脈絡史學對曼德維爾的研究，也都呼應了這樣的脈絡。高史密斯認爲曼德維爾爲1688年革命與輝格黨政權的辯護，轉化了英格蘭原有議會辯論的語言，在其中鎔鑄了對商業與「私惡公益」的討論，也因此將經濟面向帶入政治語言中。杭德則認爲曼德維爾對社會起源的見解，是啓蒙哲士辯論商業社會的個人在欲望與道德兩難時，不可或缺的論述資源，而這和曼德維爾轉化十七世紀道德哲學語言，用以形塑其自身的社會理論息息相關。羅伯森則認爲曼德維爾的著作再現了貝爾的思想，其對社會起源與宗教起源的討論，是啓蒙論述思考人類文明進成中不可或缺的一環。簡言之，脈絡史學觀下的曼德維爾，是歐洲語言轉換從「過往」過渡至「現代」的重要成員，而這歸因於他對商業的重視，以及對宗教道德的嘲諷。

V

上兩節分別論述兩種歷史觀對曼德維爾的討論，一者著重其經濟

54 Idem., “From the state of princes to the person of the state”, in Idem., *Visions of Politics, Vol. II, Renaissance Virtues* (Cambridge: Cambridge University Press, 2002), pp. 368-413.

55 Pocock, *Machiavellian Moment*, pp. 423-505; Cf. Idem., “Authority and property: The question of liberal origins”, in Idem., *Virtue, Commerce, and History*, pp. 51-71.

思想，從資本主義發展的角度談論曼德維爾，認爲他是資本主義最早的提倡者。一者則從重建十八世紀的語言脈絡出發，強調曼德維爾對商業社會的論述，是近代早期歐洲語言轉換時的要角。史學界對曼德維爾的討論當然不僅於此，近年來有更多學者，試圖將曼德維爾視爲某一歷史現象的一員，而非憑一己之力扭轉思維模式的哲人。例如，巴克－班菲爾（G. J. Barker-Benfield）便認爲，曼德維爾與十八世紀初英格蘭文人針對禮儀（manner）與美德的辯論，是商業逐漸興起後，崇尚古典男性魁武美德，擔憂商業將使男子女性化的文人，與支持商業，並在一定程度上同情女性社會地位的曼德維爾間的爭論。[56] 班菲爾的著作試圖探討十九世紀文學對「感性」（sensibility）的想像從何而來，曼德維爾與十八世紀初的辯論，便只是「感性」發展這個現象的一幕，但影響「感性」論述最深遠的，當還是十八世紀女性作家的書寫。如此歷史書寫對曼德維爾研究衝擊最深者，則是哈洛德．庫克（Harold J. Cook）的專著與論文。

庫克的研究主旨在探討十七世紀末十八世紀初，荷蘭共和國的醫學文化與理論，在其專著中，也探討了荷蘭的醫學知識如何成爲當地文人的論著資源，而他認爲，在荷蘭受訓成爲醫師的曼德維爾也深受當時的醫學理論影響。庫克強調，荷蘭醫學界自十七世紀末期開始，普遍認爲醫學不僅僅是在治癒病患的生理病痛，同時也是在診視人性，以祈能救治人類自被逐出伊甸園後墮落的靈魂的原因。[57] 曼德維

56 G. J. Barker-Benfield, *The Culture of Sensibility: Sex and Society in Eighteenth-Century Britain* (Chicago: University of Chicago Press, 1992), pp. 37-134.

57 Harold J. Cook, *Matters of Exchange: Commerce, Medicine, and Science in the Dutch Golden Age* (New Heaven: Yale University Press, 2007), pp. 378-409.

爾的社會論述，與此息息相關，例如，荷蘭當時的醫學思想傾向於導引病人的病癥，而非以藥物強行壓制，這種觀念便便體現在曼德維爾與同時思想家的差異上。當時的思想家普遍認爲，唯有壓抑個人享樂的慾望，才能使國民免於耽溺於聲色享樂，也才能使國家免於沉淪在奢華享受之中。曼德維爾社會理論中的政治家卻沒有提倡美德教化，相反地，他們順應著人民的私欲需求，並技巧性地使滿足這種需求的行爲轉化爲對公共國家有利的消費。[58]

庫克所論的曼德維爾，是荷蘭醫學理論影響文人社群的重要範例，但曼德維爾的文人生涯始於其遷居倫敦之後，其所使用的語言、論述內容、辯論對象與討論主題皆以英格蘭社會中的現象爲主。就此而言，曼德維爾雖然生於荷蘭，其文人生涯與論著內容卻皆屬於英格蘭思想文化的一環。荷蘭醫學理論對曼德維爾爲英語讀者書寫英格蘭事物的影響，以及曼德維爾如何使用醫學語言進行社會論述，仍需要更細緻的分析。安．湯姆森（Ann Thomson）近年對十七十八世紀歐洲自然哲學語言與宗教辯論交織的分析，或許可爲此提供一種研究可能。[59]

班菲爾與庫克的曼德維爾，呈現與前兩節所述著作非常不同的面貌，曼德維爾只是史家記述歷史現象中的一部份。班菲爾追索「感性」這個概念與詞彙出現的歷史，庫克則探討全球經濟與歐洲醫學發展的關係。近年思想史對曼德維爾的討論，則重新審思曼德維爾於思想傳統中的定位。克里斯多福．布魯克（Christopher Brooke）在探討

---

58 Harold J. Cook, "Bernard Mandeville and the therapy of 'the Clever Politician'", *Journal of the History of Ideas*, 60:1 (Jan, 1999): pp. 101-24

59 Ann Thomson, *Bodies of Thought: Science, Religion, and the Soul in the Early Enlightenment* (Oxford: Oxford University Press, 2008), esp. pp. 29-134.

斯多葛哲學人性論，於近代早期歐洲道德論述的轉化時，指陳曼德維爾所反對的並不單僅是基督信仰的道德原則，而是斯多葛哲學對理智的崇尚，曼德維爾對第三任沙福茨伯里伯爵（Anthony Ashley Cooper, 3rd Earl of Shaftesbury, 1671-1713）的批判，也源於此。[60]

這些著作也各自表現了史家對於「歷史」與「過往」的看法。班菲爾致力於發掘文字書寫的歷史中，女性的活動與其所扮演的腳色。這樣的「歷史」直接呼應二十世紀後半，反省傳統歐洲史學過度聚焦白種男性的問題，重構女性的「歷史」與「過往」，因此有直接的「現代」政治目的。[61]庫克的書寫則要強調全球貿易與文化交流，對歐洲思想文化的衝擊，他試圖重構的「歷史」，是一種地域文化與全球化互動的歷史，其結果是地域文化在全球化經濟活動中，發展出一套似乎適用於全球的醫學理論，他探討的「過往」，是一種「現代」的起源。[62]相比於此，布魯克對近代早期歐洲使用斯多葛語言辯論的討論，似乎更近似奧克夏所言的「歷史事件」，他並爲強調「過往」與「現代」的關聯，而旨在考掘「現代」對「過往」認知中遺漏的部分，即斯多葛哲學人性論對近代早期歐洲政治語言的重要性。儘管對「過往」與「歷史」的看法殊異，三人著作的共通點，在於曼德維爾只是「過往」的一部份，而非「過往」與「現代」的橋梁。

---

60 Christopher Brooke, *Philosophic Pride: Stoicism and Political Thought from Lipsius to Rousseau*（Princeton: Princeton University Press, 2012）, pp. 153-159.

61 Cf. Dena Goodman, *The Republic of Letters: A Cultural History of the French Enlightenment*（Ithaca: Cornell University Press, 1996）, pp. 1-11, 233-280dj.

62 Cook, *Matters of Exchange*, pp. 410-416.

VI

曼德維爾在歐洲思想史已然是十八世紀最重要的思想家之一，對曼德維爾的討論，無論是專著論文或是文中章節，都已甚繁。當此之時，何以還需要特別爲文談論曼德維爾研究？

曼德維爾的背景，使他熟悉近代早期歐洲的醫學與自然哲學語言，他對諷諭文學的翻譯，與他擅長應用十七十八世紀歐洲諷諭文學體裁也或有關連，同時，他也是文人俱樂部的成員，也是名多產的輿論作家，此外，他對哲學的興趣，反映在他的閱讀上。要言之，曼德維爾擁有極爲豐富的思想資源，供他著書立說之用，這也許解釋了他爲何能談論諸多乍看之下並無關連的主題。曼德維爾廣博的書寫，也是他批評者甚多的原因，而爲數甚多的批評，也成爲史家一窺十八世紀思想辯論的極佳材料。無論史家如何看待「過往」與「歷史」，「過往」的既定事實，即是曼德維爾實爲十八世紀歐洲文人辯論時，最常被提及的名字之一。回顧到目前爲止對曼德維爾的研究，除了可以幫助思想史家掌握思想史對十八世紀思想社群的討論外，也能從中發現十八世紀思想史尚待探討的面向。就曼德維爾所處的十八世紀早期而言，有兩個仍待探討的主題，而這兩個主題也都與曼德維爾息息相關：十八世紀文人使用了何種知識語言參與宗教辯論、以及醫學與自然哲學知識如何在辯論中被應用。這兩個主題的研究，都將有助於史家了解不同領域的知識，如何在同樣的語言場域(linguistic sphere)中交織，並進而認識十八世紀思想脈絡的多面與複雜。

十七世紀末十八世紀初曾被史家視爲歐洲宗教世俗化的時段。[63]

---

63 Paul Hazard, *The Crisis of the European Mind 1680-1715* (New York: New York Review of Books, 2013, Grafton Edition). Cf. Jonathan Israel,

然而，近幾年對十八世紀歐洲思想文化的研究，已經指出宗教仍是當時許多文人思考寫作時，最爲關切的課題，宗教辯論也是十八世紀歐洲思想活動的重要面相。[64]宗教辯論的論述形式，也包含了從教會史重新審視教會權力來源、考據聖經論述挑戰教會教條、比較不同宗教於人類歷史中發展的軌跡，進而探討基督信仰是否眞爲神聖等不同課題，而這之中，最容易引發爭論的，則是援引各種哲學傳統詮釋基督信仰的道德語言，曼德維爾利用輝格諾派對「激情」的討論，以人類渴求名譽的「激情」來解釋律己的道德行爲，便是此中一例。曼德維爾此番論述，已然受到學界討論，但更值得注意的，是曼德維爾討論人類宗教性時，對人類宗教與基督信仰的看法。

曼德爲爾在探討人類爲何會有宗教信仰時，強調恐懼是導致人類崇仰自然界無形力量的原因，人類的宗教性因此與社會性相同，皆是天性的「激情」導致。就此而言，歐洲的基督信仰，與世界各地的宗教相比，並未有特別突出之處，甚至，基督信仰與舉世宗教無異，皆

Enlightenment Contested: Philosophy, Modernity, and the Emancipation of Man 1670-1752 (Oxford: Oxford University Press, 2006), pp. 63-222; Anthony Pagden, *The Enlightenment and Why It Still Matters* (Oxford: Oxford University Press, 2013), pp. 19-124.

64 Cf. J. C. D. Clark, *English Society 1688-1832: Ideology, Social Structure and Political Practice During the Ancien Regime* (Cambridge: Cambridge University Press, 1985); J. A. I. Champion, *The Pillars of Priestcraft Shaken: The Church of England and Its Enemies 1660-1730* (Cambridge: Cambridge University Press, 1992); Roger D. Lund ed., *The Margins of Orthodoxy: Heterodox Writing and Cultural Response 1660-1750* (Cambridge: Cambridge University Press, 1995); J. G. A. Pocock, *Barbarism and Religion, Vol. V, Religion: The First Triumph* (Cambridge: Cambridge University Press, 2010); Sarah Mortimer and John Robertson eds., *The Intellectual Consequences of Religious Heterodoxy, 1660-1750* (Leiden: Brill, 2014).

只是「精明政治家」爲了社會安定而發明的治術而已。[65]曼德維爾對此論述時，應用了許多同時期的知識語言，例如，他檢視人類爲何有宗教信仰時，採取了十七世紀文人討論此課題時，常用的論證形式，即從人性分析著手，進而檢視人類何以有宗教信仰。[66]他的觀點，則呼應了霍布斯等人，皆強調「激情」對人類宗教性的意義，以此說明基督信仰與其他信仰相較，並未特別神聖。[67]在援用哲學語言外，他轉向十八世紀的歷史語言，論述宗教信仰如何在人類社會發展，從實例中強調基督信仰亦只是人類宗教史的一環。[68]

曼德維爾融貫哲學語言與歷史語言辯證基督信仰神聖性的作法，絕非孤例，喬治・柏克萊在爲基督信仰辯護時，亦從人性論與自然哲學對物質的討論著手，融合哲學與自然哲學知識，試圖藉由反對物質實存以證明上帝的存在，並強調人類之所以受物質存在假象欺瞞，是受到人性自傲的影響，而忽略了自然界原本的無形力量。[69]十八世紀

65　Mandeville, *Fable of the Bees, Vol. II*, ed. Kaye, pp. 203-224.

66　Cf. John Locke, *An Essay Concerning Human Understanding*, Ed. Peter H. Nidditch (Oxford: Clarendon Press, 1985, reprinted), pp. 525-651; Benedict de Spinoza, *The Ethics: Demonstrated in Geometric Order and Divided into Five Parts...etc.*, in Idem. *A Spinoza Reader: The Ethics and Other Works*, ed. Edwin Curley (Princeton: Princeton University Press, 1994), pp. 85-152.

67　Thomas Hobbes, *Leviathan*, in Idem., *The Clarendon Edition of the Works of Thomas Hobbes, Vol. IV: Leviathan: The English and Latin Text* (*i*), ed. Noel Malcolm (Oxford: Clarendon Press, 2012), pp. 164-187.

68　Cf. Bernard Picart, *The Ceremonies and Religious Customs of the Various Nations of the Known World... etc., 7 Vols*. (London: Claude du Bosc, 1733-1739).

69　George Berkeley, *A Treatise Concerning the Principles of Human Knowledge,* in Idem., *The Works of George Berkeley, Bishop of Cloyne, Vol. II*, eds. A. A. Luce and T. E. Jessop (Edinburgh: Thomas Nelson and Sons Ltd., 1949), pp. 25-113.

對知識領域的界定並未如當待如此分隔，文人著書立說時援引各種知識領域作爲論證工具，並非罕見。曼德維爾如何轉化哲學、歷史學、宗教著作與政治論述等知識，成就其對人類宗教性的討論，以及批判曼德維爾的文人如柏克萊等人，又如何轉化其各自所擁有的思想資源，參與辯論，值得更進一步的研究，對不同領域的知識，如何交織於宗教辯論文本的研究，也能爲史家提供一幅更深刻的十八世紀宗教辯論圖像。

如此研究也能強調過往十八世紀歐洲思想史研究中，較易被忽略的面向，即自然哲學與醫學知識，如何在道德、社會、神學乃至政治經濟學辯論上被使用。[70]如前段所述，十八世紀宗教辯論的課題之一，在於無形力量是否存在，這將直接牽涉到上帝是否存在的問題。十八世紀文人對此的討論，往往涉及對物質與靈魂等觀念的探討，他們也因此碰觸解剖學與實驗科學的知識，以利於形塑自己的論點。除了宗教討論外，時人對社會文明進展的辯論，也往往因爲著重對人性的探討，而與這些自然哲學知識相連。

曼德維爾對剖析人性時，有意識地稱之爲「心性的解剖」（the anatomy of the mind），希望從近代早期歐洲醫學對心理疾病的認識，探討人類天性爲何的哲學課題，包含人類的欲望如何產生，以及理性如何思考等等。[71]借用解剖學語言談論人性中的「激情」與「理性」，

---

70 洛伊．波特（Roy Porter, 1946-2002）的遺作，與近年安．湯姆森的著作，是少數有注意此面向的研究。見：Roy Porter, *Flesh in the Age of Reason: How the Enlightenment Transformed the Way We See Our Bodies and Souls*（London: Penguin, 2004）; Thomson, *Bodies of Thought.*

71 Bernard Mandeville, *A Treatise of the Hypochondriack and Hysterick Passions, Vulgarly Call'd the Hypo in Men and Vapours in Women, in Which the Symptoms, Causes, and Cure of Those Diseases are Set Forth after a*

同樣也是十七十八世紀歐洲文人慣用的論述形式，狄卡兒（René Descartes, 1596-1650）便認爲，人體一切行爲，包含思考，皆源於心臟的脈動促使血液循環，人類感知外界事物與思辯的能力，也不過是血液循環造成的現象而已。[72]醫學與自然哲學語言被應用於十八世紀思想辯論，還有另一個著名的例子，即對人類爲何有語言能力的辯論。[73]包含曼德維爾在內，十七十八世紀歐洲文人認爲，語言是人類社會構成最主要的因素之一，因爲唯有透過語言，方能有交換意見，並商談合作的可能。正因如此，語言成了辯論的重要主題，其所注重者，在於符號與其所指涉的事物存在間，是否存在落差。[74]這樣的討論，往往導向探討語言所代表的物質，是否眞實存在，自然哲學關於物質存在的論述，便成爲思想社群論證時的必要工具。[75]要言之，醫學論述與自然哲學語言，是十八世紀思想家辯論時慣常挪用的論述資源，對當時文人如何於辯論時使用此類知識，思想史學者卻較少關注

Method Merely New... etc.（London, 1711）, pp. 124-161.

72 René Descartes, *Description of the Human Body and of All its Functions, Both Those Which Do Not in Any Way Depend on the Soul, and Those Which Do, and Including the Chief Cause of the Formation of the Parts of the Body*, in John Cottingham, Robert Stoothoff, and Dugald Murdoch trans., *The Philosophical Writing of Descartes, Vol. I*（Cambridge: Cambridge University Press, 1985. Hereafter *Descartes I*）, pp. 314-324, esp. pp. 316-319; Idem., *Principles of Philosophy*, in Ibid., pp. 279-284; Idem., *The Passions of the Soul*, in Ibid., pp. 335-338.

73 本段的語言一詞，意思與本文其他段落的「語言」不同，並非指進行論述的形式，而是人類言語的能力。

74 Cf. Locke, *Essay*, pp. 402-524; Berkeley, *Principles*, in *Works II*, pp. 33-41; Rousseau, *Second Discourse*, in Idem., *The Discourses and Other Writings*, ed. Gourevitch, pp. 144-152.

75 Cf. Avi Lifschitz, *Language & Enlightenment: The Berlin Debates of the Eighteenth Century*（Oxford: Oxford University Press, 2012）, pp. 39-64.

如此重要的面向。身爲醫生，同時又積極參與論戰，並成爲後人論爭對象的曼德維爾，會是思想史研究這個主題，一個非常適宜的切入點。研討曼德維爾如何轉化醫學與自然哲學語言，論證人性、檢視社會、探究文明進程，也將更有助思想史家理解十八世紀思想文化裡，各種知識語言錯綜交織的複雜性與多面性。

除卻回顧近代早期歐洲思想史對曼德維爾的研究外，本文另一個目的，是希望透過此研究討論，指出史家著作與史家「歷史」理解的關係。從這個角度看來，本文實可以說是一種「視史學著作爲呈現史家『歷史』概念的一種思想史」（reading historiography as an intellectual history of representing historians' conceptions of History）的案例。理解書寫者如何認識「歷史」，對理解該書寫者所著的歷史書寫，有著關鍵且切要的意義，畢竟，史家對「過往」的重構，往往與史家如何理解「過往」密切相關。彼得・告許（Peter Ghosh）在其去年的著作裡便指出，唯有深思馬克斯・韋伯（Max Weber, 1864-1920）對「歷史」的理解，方能詳實地體會其《新教倫理與資本主義精神》（*Protestant Ethics and the Spirit of Capitalism*）的關懷。[76]事實上，本文所討論關於曼德維爾的著作，也都體現了史家對「過往」的不同理解，如何反應在史家所重構的曼德維爾的「歷史」上。就此而言，史家對不同「歷史」觀的嗅覺，對其如何反思自身所書寫的「歷史」，實有莫大幫助。

研究討論與研究回顧在今日專業史學訓練裡，已是不可或缺的一環。研究生在眞的開始研究自己的課題前，往往必須要交出一份份量

76 Peter Ghosh, *Max Weber and the Protestant Ethic: Twin Histories* (Oxford: Oxford University Press, 2014), pp. 43-44, 223-228, 388-390.

十足的研究回顧，以顯示其對自己研究主題的熟稔，學者出版專書著作時，也難免要於導論中回顧過往研究，以強調自己的著作可以有何等的學術貢獻。研究回顧自然有其意義，但其意義不當只限於展現研究者對自身領域的熟悉程度，而是令研究者於過程中省思過往著作裡，史家如何重構不同的「歷史」，這些「歷史」與史家的史觀有何關係，以及研究者自身即將或正在書寫的「歷史」，又帶有什麼樣的意涵。近年對歐美學界對思想史的反省之一，在於思想史家似乎不甚願意批判性地反省自身研究的本質，學者往往強調要反對目的論式的觀念史，說明自己的研究要將觀念書寫置回其歷史脈絡，檢視觀念在這個「過往」中的面貌，如此方能有效解釋文本。然而，如此聲明的學者，卻鮮少反省這種書寫文本「過往」脈絡的「歷史」，無疑也是出自學者自身對「過往」與「歷史」的想像。就此而言，脈絡史學與目的式觀念史的差異，只是不同的「現代」視野，對「過往」與「歷史」的認知差別而已。在人文學逐漸式微的今日，批判性的研究討論與回顧，或許可以提醒思想史家乃至歷史學者，在研究論著的同時，也能有意識地反思自身研究的本質，並思考對「歷史」的認知與對「過往」的重構，是否有更多可能。[77]

77 Cf. Peter Gordon, "Contextualism and criticism in the history of ideas", in Darrin M. McMahon and Samuel Moyn eds., *Rethinking Modern European Intellectual History* (Oxford: Oxford University Press, 2014), pp. 32-55; Jan-Werner Müller, "On conceptual history", in Ibid., pp. 74-93; Samuel Moyn, "Imaginary intellectual history", in Ibid., pp. 112-130.

Economy and Society in Early Modern European Intellectual History:
Aspects of Mandeville

Alvin Chen

Abstract

This article reviews the scholarship on Bernard Mandeville (1670-1733), an Anglo-Dutch physician and literatus whose narratives on commercial society provoked a series of debates in Enlightenment Europe. Intellectual historians have focused on two themes in Mandeville's thought: the impact of Mandeville's economic writings on the laissez-faire theory, and the argumentation for Mandevillian sociability. Whilst these themes are certainly critical to Mandeville's social theory, more profound, even elusive, aspects of Mandeville's works have been somewhat neglected; that is, the ways in which Mandeville employed multiple languages from branches of knowledge such as medicine, philosophy, and natural philosophy in developing his conceptions of the nature of society. This review suggests that research exploring the interrelations among these languages would shed light on our understanding of the multiplicity and complexity of the eighteenth-century European intellectual landscape. As well, this review also shows how reading historiography as a sort of intellectual history reveals historians' conceptions of history and the past. In this case, review articles are less a genre of academic historical writing demonstrating historians' knowledge of the field in question than they are a presentation historians' awareness of the nature of their practices.

Keywords: Bernard Mandeville, eighteenth-century debates, early modern European intellectual history, review articles, history and past

參考書目

史料

Berkeley, George, *The Works of George Berkeley Bishops of Cloyne* 9 Vols., ed. A. A. Luce and T. E. Jessop. Edinburgh: Thomas Nelson and Sons Ltd., 1948-1957.

Brown, John, "Honour, A Poem", in Robert Dodsley ed., *A Collection of Poems in Six Volumes, Vol. III*. London, 1782.

Descartes, René, *The Philosophical Writing of Descartes, Vol. I*, trans. John Cottingham, Robert Stoothoff, and Dugald Murdoch. Cambridge: Cambridge University Press, 1985.

Dodsley, Robert ed., *A Collection of Poems in Six Volumes, Vol. III*. London, 1782.

Hobbes, Thomas, *Leviathan*, in Idem., *The Clarendon Edition of the Works of Thomas Hobbes, Vol. IV: Leviathan: The English and Latin Text (i)*, ed. Noel Malcolm. Oxford: Clarendon Press, 2012.

Hume, David, *Essays: Moral, Political and Literary*, ed. Eugene F. Miller. Indianapolis: Liberty Fund, 1987.

Locke, John, *An Essay Concerning Human Understanding*, ed. Peter H. Nidditch. Oxford: Clarendon Press, 1975.

______, *Two Treatises of Government,* ed. Peter Laslett. Cambridge: Cambridge University Press, 1988, reprinted edition.

Mandeville, Bernard, *A Treatise of the Hypochondriack and Hysterick Passions, Vulgarly Call'd the Hypo in Men and Vapours in Women, in Which the Symptoms, Causes, and Cure of Those Diseases are Set Forth after a Method Merely New... etc.*. London, 1711.

______, *The Fable of the Bees, or Private Vices, Public Benefits,* 2 Vols., ed. F. B. Kaye. Oxford: Clarendon Press, 1924; reprinted Indianapolis: Liberty Fund, 1988.

Picart, Bernard, *The Ceremonies and Religious Customs of the Various Nations of the Known World... etc., 7 Vols.*. London: Claude du Bosc, 1733-1739.

Rousseau, Jean-Jacques, *The Discourses and Other Ealy Political Writings*, ed. Victor Gourevitch. Cambridge: Cambridge University Press, 1997.

Spinoza, Benedict de, *A Spinoza Reader: The Ethics and Other Works*, ed. Edwin

Curley. Princeton: Princeton University Press, 1994.
Wesley, John, *The Journal of the Reverend John Wesley, Vol. I.* New York: 1837.

二手研究

Barker-Benfield, G. J., *The Culture of Sensibility: Sex and Society in Eighteenth-Century Britain.* Chicago: University of Chicago Press, 1992.

Bick, Alexander, "Bernard Mandeville and the Economy of the Dutch", *Erasmus Journal for Philosophy and Economics*, 1:1（Autumn, 2008）, pp. 87-106

Berry, Christopher J., *The Idea of Luxury: A Conceptual and Historical Investigation*. Cambridge: Cambridge University Press, 1994.

Brooke, Christopher, *Philosophic Pride: Stoicism and Political Thought from Lipsius to Rousseau*. Princeton: Princeton University Press, 2012.

Bunge, Wiep van, and Bots, Hans eds., *Pierre Bayle (1647-1706), Le Philosophe De Rotterdam: Philosophy, Religion and Reception, Selected Papers of the Tercentenary Conference Held at Rotterdam, 7-8 December 2006*. Leiden: Brill, 2008.

Bunge, Wiep van, "The presence of Bayle in the Dutch Republic", in van Bunge and Bots eds., *Pierre Bayle*, pp. 197-216.

Champion, J. A. I., *The Pillars of Priestcraft Shaken: The Church of England and Its Enemies 1660-1730*. Cambridge: Cambridge University Press, 1992.

Clark, J. C. D., *English Society 1688-1832: Ideology, Social Structure and Political Practice During the Ancien Regime*. Cambridge: Cambridge University Press, 1985.

Cook, Harold J., *Matters of Exchange: Commerce, Medicine, and Science in the Dutch Golden Age*. New Haven: Yale University Press, 2007.

______, "Bernard Mandeville and the therapy of 'the Clever Politician'", *Journal of the History of Ideas*, 60:1（Jan., 1999）, pp. 101-24

Dumont, Louis, *From Mandeville to Marx: The Genesis and Triumph of Economic Ideology*. Chicago: University of Chicago Press, 1977.

Ghogh, Peter, *Max Weber and the Protestant Ethic: Twin Histories*. Oxford: Oxford University Press, 2014.

Goldsmith, M. M., *Private Vices, Public Benefits: Bernard Mandeville's Social and Political Thought*. Cambridge: Cambridge University Press, 1985.

Goodman, Dena, *The Republic of Letters: A Cultural History of the French Enlightenment*. Ithaca: Cornell University Press, 1996.

Gorden, Peter E., "Contextualism and criticism in the history of ideas", in Darrin M. McMahon and Samuel Moyn (eds.), *Rethinking Modern European Intellectual History*, pp. 32-55

Force, Pierre, *Self-Interest Before Adam Smith: A Genealogy of Economic Science*. Cambridge: Cambridge University Press, 2003.

Hayek, F. A., *The Trend of Economic Thinking: Essays on Political Economists and Economic History*. Indianapolis: Liberty Fund, 1991.

Hazard, Paul, *The Crisis of the European Mind 1680-1715*. New York: New York Review of Books, 2013, Grafton Edition.

Hochstrasser, T. J., *Natural Law Theories in the Early Enlightenment*. Cambridge: Cambridge University Press, 2006.

Hont, Istvan, *Jealousy of Trade: International Competition and the Nation-State in Historical Perspective*. Cambridge, Mass.: Belknap Press of Harvard University Press, 2010.

Horne, Thomas A., *The Social Thought of Bernard Mandeville: Virtue and Commerce in Early Eighteenth-Century England*. New York: Columbia University Press, 1978.

Hundert, E. J., *The Enlightenment's Fable: Bernard Mandeville and the Discovery of Society*. Cambridge: Cambridge University Press, 2005.

Israel, Jonathan, *Radical Enlightenment: Philosophy and the Making of Modernity*. Oxford: Oxford University Press, 2002.

______, *Enlightenment Contested: Philosophy, Modernity, and the Emancipation of Man 1670-1752*. Oxford: Oxford University Press, 2006.

Jack, Malcolm, *Corruption & Progress: The Eighteenth-Century Debate*. New York: AMS Press, 1989.

James, E. D., "Fiath, sincerity and morality: Mandeville and Bayle", in Irwin ed., *Mandeville Studies*, pp. 43-65

Journal of the History of Ideas, "Ideas in Context series, Cambridge University Press", *Journal of the History of Ideas*, 75:4 (Oct., 2014), pp. 651-695

Koselleck, Reinhart, *The Practice of Conceptual History: Timing History, Spacing Concepts*. Stanford: Stanford University Press, 2002.

______, *Future Past: On the Semantics of Historical Time*, trans. Keith Tribe. New York: Columbia University Press, 2004.

Kristeller, Paul Oskar, *Renaissance Thought and the Arts: Collected Essays*. Princeton: Princeton University Press, 1990, expanded edition.

Laslett, Peter, "Introduction" to Locke, *Two Treatises of Government*, ed. Laslett.

Cambridge: Cambridge University Press, 1988, reprinted edition.

Lifschitz, Avi, *Language & Enlightenment: The Berlin Debates of the Eighteenth Century.* Oxford: Oxford University Press, 2012.

Lund, Roger D., *The Margins of Orthodoxy: Heterodox Writing and Cultural Response 1660-1750*. Cambridge: Cambridge University Press, 1995.

Maclean, Ian, *Logic, Signs and Nature in the Renaissance: The Case of Learned Medicine*. Cambridge: Cambridge University Press, 2002.

McMahon, Darrin M., and Moyn, Samuel (eds.), *Rethinking Modern European Intellectual History*. Oxford: Oxford University Press, 2014.

Mortimer, Sarah, and Robertson, John eds., *The Intellectual Consequences of Religious Heterodoxy, 1660-1750*. Leiden: Brill, 2014.

Moyn, Samuel, "Imaginary intellectual history" , in Darrin M. McMahon and Samuel Moyn (eds.), *Rethinking Modern European Intellectual History*, pp. 112-130

Müller, Jan-Werner, "On conceptual history", in Darrin M. McMahon and Samuel Moyn (eds.), *Rethinking Modern European Intellectual History*, pp. 74-93

Netz, Reviel, *The Shaping of Deduction in Greek Mathematics: A Study in Cognitive History*. Cambridge: Cambridge University Press, 1999.

Oakeshott, Michael, *Three Essays on History*, in Idem., *On History and Other Essays*. Indianapolis: Liberty Fund, 1999, reprinted.

Peltonen, Markku, *Classical Humanism and Republicanism in English Political Thought 1570-1640*. Cambridge: Cambridge University Press, 1995.

Pocock, J. G. A., *The Machiavellian Moment: Florentine Political Thought and the Atlantic Republican Tradition*. Princeton: Princeton University Press, 1975.

______, *Virtue, Commerce, and History: Essays on Political Thought and History, Chiefly in the Eighteenth Century*. Cambridge: Cambridge University Press, 1985.

______, *Politics, Language, and Time: Essays on Political Thought and History*. Chicago: Chicago University Press, 1989.

______, "Present at the creation: With Laslett to the lost worlds", *International Journal of Public Affairs* 2 (2006), pp. 7-17

______, *Political Thought and History: Essays on Theory and Method.* Cambridge: Cambridge University Press, 2009.

______, *Barbarism and Religion, Vol. V, Religion: The First Triumph*. Cambridge: Cambridge University Press, 2010.

Porter, Roy, *Flesh in the Age of Reason: How the Enlightenment Transformed the*

Way We See Our Bodies and Souls. London: Penguin, 2004.

Primer, Irwin ed., *Mandeville Studies: New Explorations in the Art and Thought of Dr. Bernard Mandeville (1670-1733)*. Hague: Martinus Nijhoff, 1975.

Robertson, John, *The Case for the Enlightenment: Scotland and Naples 1680-1760*. Cambridge: Cambridge University Press, 2005.

Skinner, Quentin, *Reason and Rhetoric in the Philosophy of Hobbes*. Cambridge: Cambridge University Press, 1996.

_______, *Liberty before Liberalism*. Cambridge: Cambridge University Press, 1996.

_______, *Visions of Politics, Vol. I: Regarding Method*. Cambridge: Cambridge University Press, 2002.

_______, *Visions of Politics, Vol. II: Renaissance Virtues*. Cambridge: Cambridge University Press, 2002.

_______, *Forensic Shakespeare*. Oxford: Oxford University Press, 2014.

Thomson, Ann, *Bodies of Thought: Science, Religion, and the Soul in the Early Enlightenment*. Oxford: Oxford University Press, 2008.

網路資料

Hont, Istvan, "Rousseau and Smith: A conversation with Istvant Hont", https://www.youtube.com/watch?v=v83Zh2IenM4影片由CESHarvard於2011年8月11日上傳。

【書評】

評李淑珍《安身立命——現代華人公私領域的探索與重建》

楊貞德

中央研究院中國文哲研究所研究員

李淑珍《安身立命——現代華人公私領域的探索與重建》，臺北：聯經出版事業公司，2013。452頁。

晚清以降的中國知識分子試圖從方方面面解讀與因應來自西方的現代性（modernity）衝擊。這一現代性內涵強大的解構力，挾帝國勢力向非西方世界的擴張，更帶來變動不已的物質和精神世界，造成中國政治、社會與文化上的多重危機。中國知識分子因此所遭逢的難局，不僅是外在世界的崩解，而且是內在心靈的惶惑。他們因爲傳統政治、社會和文化秩序的解體，而得以脫除既有的桎梏，並在中外文明的交會中看見更多重建秩序的可能，但也因此必須負起更大的責任，設法在急遽變動與重估一切價值的世界中，爲自己安身立命。無論發於自願抑或環境使然，樂觀奮發抑或悲觀直視，積極行動抑或消極不爲，中國知識分子不得不有所抉擇。這些抉擇影響所及，除了一己的性命之外，還可能涉及國家政治、社會和文化的走向，乃至於昔日友人、同志、鄰居與鄉親的命運。

學界早已注意近代中國相關於生命意義的探尋及其重要性，針對知識分子與近代中國的倫理和價值危機、甚或自殺現象的討論，不一而足。以思想史研究爲例，張灝於1987年以英文出版、目前已見中文譯本的《危機中的中國知識分子：尋求秩序與意義，1890-1911》一書，[1]首先直接且明白地揭示這一議題，就康有爲（1858-1927）、譚嗣同（1865-1898）、章太炎（1869-1936）、劉師培（1884-1919）四人的思想內涵，討論晚清知識分子共同面臨的「迷失」難局；亦即：「對傳統道德價值產生懷疑」、「對苦難、死亡、命運等存在困境感到

1　Chang Hao, *Chinese Intellectuals in Crisis: Search for Order and Meaning, 1890-1911* (Berkeley: University of California Press, 1987)；張灝著、高立克、王躍譯、毛小林校譯，《危機中的中國知識份子：尋求秩序與意義，1890-1911》（北京：新星出版社，2006）。

焦慮」，與傳統形上世界觀的傾頹。[2]另如，王汎森與賀照田分別就青年的疑慮，解說這一危機在新文化運動以降（二十、三十年代）和後革命時期（1980年代初）的面貌。[3]李淑珍於2013年出版的《安身立命——現代華人公私領域的探索與重建》一書，則再度以個別知識分子爲對象，並且標舉「安身立命」一詞，回溯晚清及至於八十年代期間思想界面對意義危機的方式及其意涵。

《安身立命》一書探討「在驚濤駭浪的20世紀，華人知識分子如何苦苦掙扎，在私領域及公領域尋找『安身立命』之道」（頁1）。全書分爲九章，文字流暢、綱目井然。書中主要說明梁啓超（1873-1929）、李叔同（1880-1942）、林語堂（1895-1976）、徐復觀（1904-1982）等四位近代名人在公私領域求索「安身立命」的經驗和過程，藉由他們「特別廣闊的視野、不尋常的敏銳感受、格外深刻的反省能力、和幸運保存下來的豐富文本」，反映大時代中知識精英安頓精神和追尋價值的努力（頁9、10、59）。下文即分列「安身立命」與「命自我作」兩部分，引介本書要旨及其相關問題。

（一）安身立命

《安身立命》一書既有具體歷史的描述，也有時代風潮的評議。第1章〈導論〉以言簡意賅的方式，指出全書主旨與特色。首先，本書十分重視歷史研究的脈絡化，開宗明義以「『歷史三峽』中的『大

2 轉引自李淑珍：《安身立命——現代華人公私領域的探索與重建》，頁5。

3 王汎森，〈「煩悶」的本質是什麼——「主義」與中國近代私人領域的政治化〉，《思想史》，1（臺北，2013），頁85-137；賀照田，〈從精神史看當代史〉，《思想》，5（臺北，2007），頁219-230。

我』與『小我』」（頁1），標誌出近代中國知識分子所處「天翻地覆」的歷史情境，「小我」在其中的流離，以及將一己安頓於「大我」中的意圖和挫折。第二，書中肯定儒學的現代意義。儒家思想於近代中國的命運是功是過，於中國的現代化是爲助力或阻力？這兩項極具爭議性的問題早在清末出現，於今因爲中國大陸對於儒家的興趣，以及西方現代性所帶來的問題，再度引起諸多討論。作者主張儒家於今仍「相當具有啓發性，特別是可以對西方啓蒙式『現代性』提出反省與針砭」（頁15）。第三，作者強調史學承先啓後的現實意義，刻意採取不盡符合學界主流和常規的作法——包含「選題疏闊」，側重知識精英在智性、德性與靈性的表現；帶有強烈的文學性，「寓含明顯的價值意識」（頁17）——力圖以淺顯、感性的文字出入於宏觀與微觀的敘述，以期建立專業史學和大眾閱讀之間的橋樑，促成過去、現在與未來之間的對話（頁18-20）。就這一層面而言，全書也是作者追求生命意義的體現。

第2章至第5章分別記敘梁啓超等人的生命「實踐」（而不只是思想論述），並在個人故事中尋繹超乎個人的意義，藉以討論重大的歷史問題和當前的現實關注。第2章〈私領域中的梁啓超——兩性關係與家族倫理的轉型〉，旨在理解梁啓超的實際生活，作爲梁啓超在公領域所引起爭議的參考，以及思索近百年來中國私領域所見變化的意義（頁28-29）。梁啓超以帶著感情的筆鋒，帶動近代中國思想的重大變化。本章著重他較少引起注意的私生活，敘說他家族本位的親子和兩性關係——爲人子謹守舊倫理，爲人夫視妻妾爲功能（而非靈魂）上的伴侶，爲人父則既親密又偏心。從這一角度看，「他的『社群主義』色彩，遠比『自由主義』色彩來得濃厚」顯得更容易理解，但也留下私領域要如何配合重建公領域的問題（頁52-53）。文中另亦藉由徐志摩再婚一事，映照出梁啓超與時代的距離，與預示家族社會解體、個人在私領域中享有自由和不確定性的時刻就要到來。

第3章〈從李叔同到釋弘一——意義危機時代的信仰歷程〉，記敘浪漫才子李叔同皈依佛門的戲劇性轉變，並梳理「李叔同爲何出家」和「弘一是否證道解脫」兩件公案，藉以探詢儒家和佛教在意義危機時代所提供的資源及其限制。作者取美國哲學家詹姆斯（William James, 1842-1910）所謂「生病的靈魂」一說，標誌李叔同一生不斷追尋、創造自我的變化，以對於「美」和「無常」的敏銳感受，作爲他種種變動中的基調。根據書中所述，李叔同無法藉由自幼修習的儒學或之後在中西藝術上的深厚造詣，有效解決國家和家庭問題、或者回應個人存在的焦慮；他在「無常感及罪業感的雙重驅迫下，點點滴滴因緣積聚」，皈依佛門（頁97），但仍仰賴某些儒家（和道家）因素，面對群己和修身的問題，直到晚年「才找到與自己、與世界和平相處的方式」（頁117）。文末比較李叔同和其他中國知識分子意圖救世而讓自我縮減或消解於大我之中的取向（頁110），表示：以左翼革命的路徑爲對比，弘一所走的道路雖然孤獨，卻「閃著幽光，隱隱通向天際」（頁130）。

第4章〈論林語堂的改宗經驗——東西信仰的個人抉擇〉，同樣帶著深厚的傳記色彩，記敘林語堂一生曲折的變化。作者從林語堂引起正反不同評價，與他以「一團矛盾」自我描述說起。文中記敘林語堂出身閩南基督教家庭，除了基督教教義之外，深爲西方文明（包含科學理性和日常生活）所吸引，曾經有意投身神職。不過，對於教義的質疑、對於中國文化的接觸和欣賞、缺乏原罪感等等因素，使他暫時離開了教會。此後歐美遊學四年的經驗和刺激，使林語堂又一次重新評價中國文化，曾經主張「精神歐化」和激進政治，但不久就改

「以性靈文學逃避〔國內的〕政治壓力」，「以老莊曠逸對治西方現代資本主義、工業文明」形成的牢籠（頁178）。林語堂最終回到「包含有力量及光的明朗」的基督教（頁189），但這並未使他達觀以對晚年失女之痛和一己生命的消殞。本章最後指出：林語堂的世俗性生命情調最接近現代人，而他走不出困境的狀況，「也讓同爲凡人的我們感同身受」（頁202）。

接下來的第5至第7章，皆以徐復觀爲主題，其中原因除了作者對徐復觀比較熟悉與「他的生命幅度、關懷層面特別寬廣」（頁10）之外，或者也因於他與「臺灣」和「儒學」這兩項作者極爲關注的議題有密切的關係。第5章〈徐復觀在臺灣——兩岸文化的激盪與交融〉，從1949年臺海兩岸人民困頓的生活說起，取1949年後流亡「外省知識分子」在臺灣的三個陣營，以及臺灣與中華文化和西方文化互動的歷史過程爲脈絡，觀察徐復觀在其中的位置。全文以不小的篇幅談論臺灣的過去，並以徐復觀的多變和不變，說明「外省知識分子對戰後臺灣文化影響的複雜性，遠遠超出『白色恐怖』、『經濟奇蹟』之外」，仍有待深入探索（頁248）。文中的徐復觀盱衡時局，試圖在政治和文化的夾縫中找到出路。他同情社會主義，但無法原諒共產黨土改的殘暴，感激蔣中正（1887-1975）的知遇，但對國民黨高層的腐化深感痛心（頁207）；主張中體西用，希望「透過對中國傳統的重新詮釋」，「彌補『西化』『現代化』之不足」（頁243）。作者感慨徐復觀走過的道路已經「荒草沒膝」，但也認爲：「只要有人繼續走，未必不能盼到柳暗花明」（頁248）。

第6、第7兩章討論徐復觀曾經參與的論戰，論辯性高於故事性，涉及中西政治和藝術的多層次辨析；文中的提問和詮釋透露出作者看待歷史人物時的縝密心思和同情理解。第6章〈《民主評論》的民主想像——儒家／民主的多重詮釋〉，梳理徐復觀創辦和主持《民主評論》（1949-1966）的過程，與他和新儒家陣營的內部爭議；目的在於理解1949年後港臺的「文化保守主義」和徐復觀思想在爭辯中發展的過程，並就21世紀初的時空條件衡量這些爭議的價值（頁251）。文中所梳理的爭議有二。一是徐復觀與錢穆（1895-1990）針對解讀歷史的方式、「傳統中國有無專制」、傳統中國士人的性格，與「現代中國是否需要民主」等議題的論辯。徐復觀重視史家的時代意識和理學基底（頁272-273）；他區分文化和歷史，認同先秦和漢宋的「典範儒家」，抨擊中國傳統專制政治，並意圖結合儒家與民主，使民主政治獲得更高的根據、儒家思想得其眞正客觀的構造（頁277）。然而，徐復觀面對民主的立場不無曖昧之處（頁297）。他和唐君毅（1909-1978）、牟宗三（1909-1995）與勞思光（1927-2012）等人，另就民主的性質和學術與政治之間應有關係展開爭議。徐復觀這時強調，民主只是政治的形式，可以容納不同的內容，毋須以學術或道德理想統攝或奠基；學術與政治各有其領域，修己的境界可以無限上提，治人則要重視「常民」、以百姓的基本生存爲依歸（頁291）。作者在「結論」中檢視徐復觀的看法於當前臺海兩岸的意涵，並主張「仍有必要踵繼徐復觀的腳蹤，繼續探究儒家文化與民主制度的磨合關係」（頁302）。

第7章〈徐復觀論現代藝術——藝術、政治與人性〉，討論徐復觀於1961年夏天質疑現代藝術的意義，進而與臺灣現代畫壇展開的論戰。作者分別從五十、六十年代臺灣文藝青年轉向「現代主義」的情境，臺灣美術史的脈絡，與徐復觀的思想「內在理路」，檢討論戰中的重要議題，特別是徐復觀何以有「現代藝術爲共產世界開路」的說法。根據文中所述，徐復觀係以儒家人性論爲基礎，秉美善合一的美學思想，抨擊破壞自然形象的現代抽象繪畫和文學；他認爲：現代藝術「反理性、反人性精神」，「把世界放逐於個人精神之外」、「把自己幽囚於窄迫幽黯的牢籠中」，「既否定德性，又否定知性；既不承接傳統，也開不出未來」，恰爲同樣反人性的共產主義開路（頁349、353、354）。作者指出徐復觀對於現代藝術的理解有其限制，但也表示：他背後所關注的不過是個「把人當人看」的世界罷了（頁359）。

第8章〈全球化的我在哪裡？——儒家人格主義在全球化時代的意義〉，反思近代西方和華人世界的發展，論及現代世界的特徵與學界關於中國是否有個人主義的不同意見。文中以現代世界的認同危機爲脈絡、近代西方個人主義爲對照，就儒家「人格主義」（personalism）」解說儒家在近代中國的命運與再起的契機。作者認爲：儒家人格主義以強烈的自我觀念——亦即：「既是一切人際關係的核心，又是精神發展的動態過程」（頁365）——與人倫關係，成就「人生意義不假外求」的人生觀；在近代中國「個人主義」（自由主義）和集體主義（社會主義）兩相攻詰之下，已經難以爲繼。然而，面對今日更單一、也更破碎的世界，面對資本主義的財富追求和網路虛擬世界的人際關係，儒家人格主義中修身、成德的人生目的，與樂天之命、不誠無物等等原則，實有相當大的啓發性和可能性（頁399）。作者坦承儒家「要在現代繼續發生意義」，還要面對許多課題；注意到人格主義的限制（頁400-401），但也強調：「沒有『人的理想』作爲價值標竿，也很難成就美好的人間秩序」（頁404）。

第9章〈結論〉回顧前列各章所討論的民國／臺灣經驗，對其他華人地區的參考價值。這些具有參考性的觀察，包含：家族瓦解後公私領域產生變化，及至於在全球化世界中，留下「個人」面對龐大的

「世界」，留下「無家可歸的失根感和自我認同的危機」（頁409）。這時，儒家思想儘管喪失指導政治、人生的權威地位，其人文性格仍然在私領域中發生作用，在公領域中仍可透過教育有所貢獻。例如：「儒家對政治人物的道德要求，儒家二千餘年來累積的政治智慧，以及以儒家倫理爲核心的社會是非共識」，都是穩定華人民主的重要文化資產。儘管如此，作者表示：安身立命是永恆的問題，所謂「現代華人公私領域的探索與重建」的成果，「最多也只能是暫時性的」（頁417）。

（二）命自我作

本書討論近代中國的意義危機，梳理知識分子在生活和思想上面對自我與世界的過程及其難局。作者自云本書以「現代華人世界」爲題，但只談及大陸和臺灣的部分時刻；「希望未來能有機會補足這些缺失」（頁19），「希望喚起大家對這些議題更多的討論」（頁406）。就這一部分，本書雖然不曾納入相關於移民、女性和左翼知識分子的探究，卻也提供了新的思考方向與參照——亦即：以「安身立命」爲主軸，透過生活的歷程，檢視這些群體中個別人物對於生命意義的追求。

事實上，書中論及的內容已經相當豐富，可以分由不同的方向閱讀、把握和評述；史學的性質（史學脈絡化的必要和作爲人文學科的任務，與不同歷史詮釋與研究取徑的異同），現代性的面貌，近代中國思想上生活、藝術（含文學）與政治之間的糾結，中西文化的互動、衝撞與抉擇，臺灣的歷史和前景（包含外省知識分子曾有的努力及其作用，與邁向自由民主的過程和有待面對的問題），對於梁啓超等四人言行的具體觀察和詮釋等等議題，皆可爲例。在此將僅就安身立命這一主題，綜合討論本書的特徵、貢獻，與可以繼續開拓的方向。

一言以蔽之，本書十分清楚地顯現出近代中國知識分子尋求「安身立命」過程中，「命自我作」的歷史和生命處境。就近代中國知識分子採用的表述語詞與作者所關心的儒家思想而言，本書以「安身立命」爲題毋寧是最爲貼切的選擇。另若就書中所描繪的歷史現象而言，則「命自我作」一詞恰可標誌全書所示：個人在現代世界中尋求生命意義，所面臨既是機會、也是失落的弔詭情境，與身陷其中必須自作決定的層層挑戰。下文即分別說明書中所見「命自我作」所意涵的多元和開放性、個人性，在實踐中融小我於大我的取向，以及循此開出的議題。

「命自我作」一詞借自書中所見袁了凡（1533-1606）「命自我作，福自己求」的說法（頁87），不過在此意指現代沒有所謂「正確」答案的多元和開放性選擇，更多於傳統語境所著重的：告誡人們善惡有報、積善求福，或者考驗個人是否能夠堅持意志，走上特定的道路。書中記敘梁啓超等人或者輾轉於家庭、藝術、政治或宗教等等不同的領域中探求／實踐生命的意義，或者在不同人際關係、藝術流派、政治主張、或宗教信仰中選擇與詮釋，俾以掙脫個人面對生和死的疑惑與困境。林語堂的個人主義和徐復觀的自由民主信念，明白透露出：他們不僅意識到、而且明白肯定這般多元和開放的走向。本書作者相關於儒家的討論，更進一步彰顯出「命自我作」的多元和開放性意涵；她如同徐復觀般主張重振儒家，但比徐復觀更爲認同多元的走向，明白表示儒家只是面對問題時「眾多『可能答案』中的一個選項」（頁417）。

多元和開放性所內涵的解放和選擇機會，不必然帶來快樂無憂的過程或結果。本書不僅重視個人「改宗」的現象，承認安身立命只有「暫時」的答案（頁416-417、388-390），更清楚展現出：隨著機會而來的頻繁變化，需要以不斷的思想和行動相因應。李叔同在勸朋友信仰宗教時，具體表述了面對意義危機的困境；他說：「耶、佛、伊」都行，以「求精神上的安樂」（頁92、121）。即使在皈依宗教後，李叔同也無法掙脫個人面對自我和世界的拉扯；林語堂仍難脫面對基督教義肯與不肯的依違；徐復觀更意圖評議與重建儒家，在參與論戰中持續地自我省思。這些痛苦的掙扎與他們的人格和識見有密切的連繫，也充分反映出他們內心的「個人主義」傾向。

「命自我作」的最大問題性，或即在於它的「個人主義」意涵；這也是本書多所著墨、但仍可再加補充和開展的重要議題。「個人主義」一詞有很大的歧義性和爭議性（參見第8章）：在此主要意指：個人在多元與開放的情境下，自己尋找、判斷和決定生命的意義。用林語堂的話表述，也就是：「在這種對最高貴眞理〔意指宗教〕的探索，每一個人都必須遵由他自己的途徑，而這些途徑是人各不同的。……各人必然有各人不同的路」。[4]本書作者也簡潔有力地指出：「『全球化的我』究竟在哪裡？——朋友：除了你自己，還有誰能找到答案？」（頁404）弔詭的是，強調個人自決的「命自我作」，卻經常帶來投向大我、乃至於質疑和否定個人小我的結果。

現代「命自我作」的一大難題在於：面對可變的自我和多變的世界，個人難以只是憑藉一己之力，解答對於生命意義的質疑；愈多選

4 林語堂著、胡簪雲譯，《信仰之旅：論東西方的哲學與宗教（新版）》（臺北：道聲出版社，1992），頁13。

擇的機會很可能只是使得問題更加地棘手。從20世紀以降的人類經驗和相關反思看來，個別的「小我」回應這一難題的方式，往往是走向社群（community）性「大我」——特別是國家和宗教——甚者反爲大我所吞噬。以近代中國爲例，學界早已指出：晚清以降的知識分子總是意圖將小我融入大我之中，並且在所謂啓蒙與救亡的兩難中向救亡的一面傾斜，促成了國家主義的高張和異化。本書如同既有研究般重視梁啓超等人將小我安置於大我中的安排，但涉及更多、更爲糾結的面相。書中突顯的大我，有國家、民族、藝術，還有宗教。其中相關於宗教性、「個人」和儒家命運的討論，與現代生活尤其關係密切。

在宗教性部分，本書以深入的洞察力，選擇李叔同等人作爲討論的對象，並以包含出世和入世的「宗教」視野指出：李叔同、林語堂最後分別轉向佛教與基督教，徐復觀則堅守儒家，追求此世的「天人合一」。書中相關於宗教的討論，或者因於作者所選擇的筆法、或者因於史料的限制，比較著重具體的事件和影響，而略於討論相關於「宗教性」的形上和神聖層面。書中記敘李叔同如何「大大提升淨土的境界」與面對死亡，但略於解說他根據佛典相關於生死、宇宙實相的詮釋；指出林語堂以自然爲善的來源，敬畏生命，視宗教爲「高級的理性」、是個人「和上帝之間的事」（頁187、200），討論他對於原罪說的保留，但略於闡釋他如何把握與上帝的關係，如何同時以理性與直覺詮釋宗教；論及徐復觀以「人性主義」體現儒家的宗教性，但略於解說他對於「宗教性」和儒家性命觀的詮釋。

換言之，李叔同、林語堂和徐復觀如何看待「宗教」和「宗教性」，以及彼此間的異同，仍有待更詳細的討論。他們三人皆具敏銳的心靈和洞識，但選取不同安頓身心的處所；探討他們對於「宗教」

和「宗教性」曾有的思索，將有助於深化對於現代生命意義危機和佛、耶、儒三教所可能提供資源的認識。不僅如此，相較於二十世紀許多全然融入大我的小我，李叔同等三人都認同大我（包含國家與宗教）、但並未以既定的大我爲絕對認同或效忠的對象，而是力守個人的獨立性。他們都主張也支持救國，但是並未因此主張國家至上；林語堂更因此遭受不同世代的批評。李叔同皈依佛教後依舊徘徊在孤守自我和利他濟世之間；林語堂強調個人對於生命意義的探索，是段踽踽獨行的過程，明白挑戰神學和基督教會；徐復觀則企圖分疏儒家的長短，在同樣肯定儒家的保守主義陣營中堅持己見。他們的努力彰顯出小我與大我之間互相支撐、同時互相抗衡的張力。其間，他們如何看待不同的大我？如何以宗教性的關注反思國家的需求與要求？究竟是他們的個人主義影響了對於大我的理解？還是他們對於「信仰」和「宗教性」的把握和詮釋，強化他們固守個人獨立判斷的意志？凡此糾結儘管不易釐清，卻值得進一步思考。

另如，現代「命自我作」肯定個人自作抉擇的個人主義，這可能走向推崇「超人」，乃至於因此蔑視或唾棄他人不作選擇或作出不同的選擇；也可能走向看重和體諒「個人」（包含自己和他人）的平等相待。兩者之中，李叔同等人顯得比較傾向於後者。或是源於儒家文化氛圍的薰陶，或是基於佛教、基督教和儒家的教誨，或是因於個人性格和知識的特徵？他們各以不同的方式關注無聲的他人。李叔同「但願眾生得離苦」（頁106）。林語堂明言「個人便是人生的最後事實」，視極端的個人主義者爲「獨裁的暴君最可怕的敵人」（頁136）。徐復觀主張盡心於自己該做的事，「便是把握到了最高的價值」（頁396）；他在戰爭中看見「純樸無知的鄉農村嫗」、「天眞無邪的少女青年」「一夜之間，變成待罪的羔羊」（頁205-207），在政治上重視民意的向背。李叔同、林語堂和徐復觀三人對於自我的堅持和對於他人的關注，雖然並未帶出有系統的個人主義論述，卻在他們「命自我作」的主張和實踐中添加了人道主義的色彩，並形成一種對於大我的警戒；使他們在投入大我的同時，更容易察覺、並試圖抗拒大我對於小我（不只是自己而且是其他「個人」）的侵軋。本書清楚討論他們三人在動盪世界中的濟世和避世選擇，爲進而檢視李叔同、林語堂和徐復觀思所「宗教」與「個人」的方式有何特徵、異同，及其歷史和現實的意涵，提供了堅實的基礎。

本書所彰顯現代「命自我作」所涉及的另一難題是：在多元和開放的社會中，「個人」如何面對自己所從出的文化？書中並未正面回答這一去脈絡的問題，而是以儒家現代命運——更確切地說，是「華人的當代處境」（頁402）——的討論，清楚反映出這一問題的重要性和複雜性。徐復觀和本書作者都強調儒家是華人的文化資源，但都無意採取相對主義或「認同政治」的立場，堅持「我（們）的」就是「正確」或「眞的」。他們分疏儒家與現代社會相合與相悖的成分，並試圖說明先前飽受抨擊、現在顯得與生活毫不相干的儒家，之所以仍然值得重視。對於「儒家有何現代意義？」這一在近代中國思想史上以不同面貌重複出現的問題，本書除了藉由對於歷史人物的觀察和反思，說明儒家在公私領域得以扮演的角色之外，並且更清楚地指出儒家在多元社會中的位置。作者坦承儒家在現代世界中只是眾多選項之一，更明白表示儒家所能提供的價值觀，「不一定要通過儒家教養才能建立」（頁306）。（果眞如此，則儒家是否必要？）她慶幸生逢「把儒家當作『問題』的時代」（頁417），「正好可以促使它反省經典原意，擺脫歷史糾葛」，從王官學還原爲百家學，回歸到教育的領域（頁15）。（這時，儒家是否如何能在自由競爭的平台上獲得足夠的青睞，成爲現實生活中倫理道德的重要資源？）本書是作者努力將儒家帶回教育的見證；最後，她以儒者「帶著『盡人事而聽天命』的坦然，繼續知其不可而爲的志業，「在廣宇長宙中」安身立命（頁417），結束本書。

整體而言，如同作者所說，本書的目的不在提供動盪世界中安身立命的典範和解答，而是彰顯爲求安身立命曾有的思索、抉擇，與留下的問題。無論就理解個人在現代社會中的處境、把握近代中國思想史的脈動，或展望儒家如何在現代安身立命而言，本書都很值得一讀。

《思想史》稿約

1. 舉凡歷史上有關思想、概念、價值、理念、文化創造及其反思、甚至對制度設計、音樂、藝術作品、工藝器具等之歷史理解與詮釋，都在歡迎之列。
2. 發表園地全面公開，竭誠歡迎海內外學者賜稿。
3. 本學報爲半年刊，每年三月及九月出版，歡迎隨時賜稿。來稿將由本學報編輯委員會初審後，再送交至少二位專家學者評審。評審人寫出審稿意見書後，再由編委會逐一討論是否採用。審查採雙匿名方式，作者與評審人之姓名互不透露。
4. 本學報兼收中（繁或簡體）英文稿，來稿請務必按照本刊〈撰稿格式〉寫作。中文論文以二萬至四萬字爲原則，英文論文以十五頁至四十頁打字稿爲原則，格式請參考 *Modern Intellectual History*。其他各類文稿，中文請勿超過一萬字，英文請勿超過十五頁。特約稿件則不在此限。
5. 請勿一稿兩投。來稿以未曾發表者爲限，會議論文請查明該會議無出版論文集計畫。本學報當儘速通知作者審查結果，然恕不退還來稿。
6. 論文中牽涉版權部分（如圖片及較長之引文），請事先取得原作者或出版者書面同意，本學報不負版權責任。
7. 來稿刊出之後，不付稿酬，一律贈送作者抽印本30本、當期學報2本。

8. 來稿請務必包含中英文篇名、投稿者之中英文姓名。論著稿請附中、英文提要各約五百字、中英文關鍵詞至多五個；中文書評請加附該書作者及書名之英譯。
9. 來稿請用眞實姓名，並附工作單位、職稱、通訊地址、電話、電子郵件信箱地址與傳眞號碼。
10. 投稿及聯絡電子郵件帳號：intellectual.history2013@gmail.com。

《思想史》撰稿格式

（2013/08修訂）

1. 橫式（由左至右）寫作。
2. 請用新式標點符號。「 」用於平常引號，『 』用於引號內之引號；《 》用於書名，〈 〉用於論文及篇名；英文書名用Italic；論文篇名用“ ”；古籍之書名與篇名連用時，可省略篇名符號，如《史記・刺客列傳》。
3. 獨立引文每行低三格（楷書）；不必加引號。
4. 年代、計數，請使用阿拉伯數字。
5. 圖表照片請注明資料來源，並以阿拉伯數字編號，引用時請注明編號，勿使用“如前圖”、“見右表”等表示方法。
6. 請勿使用：“同上”、“同前引書”、“同前書”、“同前揭書”、“同注幾引書”，“ibid.,”“Op. cit.,”“loc. cit.,”“idem”等。
7. 引用專書或論文，請依序注明作者、書名（或篇名）、出版項。
   A. 中日文專書：作者，《書名》（出版地：出版者，年份），頁碼。
      如：余英時，《中國文化史通釋》（香港：牛津大學出版社，2010），頁1-12。
      如：林毓生，〈史華慈思想史學的意義〉，收入許紀霖等編，《史華慈論中國》（北京：新星出版社，2006），頁237-246。
   B. 引用原版或影印版古籍，請注明版本與卷頁。

如：王鳴盛，《十七史商榷》（臺北：樂天出版社，1972），卷12，頁1。

如：王道，《王文定公遺書》（明萬曆己酉朱延禧南京刊本，臺北國家圖書館藏），卷1，頁2a。

C. 引用叢書古籍：作者，《書名》，收入《叢書名》冊數（出版地：出版者，年份），卷數，〈篇名〉，頁碼。

如：袁甫，《蒙齋集》，收入《景印文淵閣四庫全書》第1175冊（臺北：臺灣商務印書館，1983），卷5，〈論史宅之奏〉，頁11a。

D. 中日韓文論文：作者，〈篇名〉，《期刊名稱》，卷：期（出版地，年份），頁碼。

如：王德權，〈「核心集團與核心區」理論的檢討〉，《政治大學歷史學報》，25（臺北，2006），頁147-176，引自頁147-151。

如：桑兵，〈民國學界的老輩〉，《歷史研究》，2005：6（北京，2005），頁3-24，引自頁3-4。

E. 西文專書：作者—書名—出版地點—出版公司—出版年分。

如：Samuel P. Huntington, *Political Order in Changing Societies* (New Haven: Yale University Press, 1968), pp. 102-103.

F. 西文論文：作者—篇名—期刊卷期—年月—頁碼。

如：Hoyt Tillman, "A New Direction in Confucian Scholarship: Approaches to Examining the Differences between Neo-Confucianism and Tao-hsüeh," *Philosophy East and West*, 42:3 (July 1992), pp. 455-474.

G. 報紙：〈標題〉—《報紙名稱》（出版地）—年月日—版頁。

〈要聞：副總統嚴禁祕密結社之條件〉，《時報》（上海），2922號，1912年8月4日，3版。

"Auditorium to Present Special Holiday Program," *The China Press* (Shanghai), 4 Jul. 1930, p. 7.

H. 網路資源：作者—《網頁標題》—《網站發行機構／網站名》—發行日期／最後更新日期—網址（查詢日期）。

倪孟安等，〈學人專訪：司徒琳教授訪談錄〉，《明清研究通迅》第5期，發行日期2010/03/15，http://mingching.sinica.edu.tw/newsletter/005/interview-lynn.htm (2013/07/30)。

8. 本刊之漢字拼音方式，以尊重作者所使用者爲原則。
9. 本刊爲雙匿名審稿制，故來稿不可有「拙作」一類可使審查者得知作者身分的敘述。

《思想史》購買與訂閱辦法

（2014/3/31修訂）

一、零售價格：每冊新臺幣480元。主要經銷處：聯經出版公司官網、門市與全省各大實體書店、網路書店。

二、國內訂閱(全年二冊／3、9月出版)：
機關訂戶，新臺幣960元；個人訂戶，新臺幣760元；學生訂戶，新臺幣720元。郵政劃撥帳戶「聯經出版公司」，帳號01005593。

三、海外訂閱(全年二冊／3、9月出版)：

港澳／大陸地區——航空每年訂費NT$2200元（US$78），
海運每年訂費1972元（US$70)

亞洲／大洋洲地區—航空每年訂費NT$2342元（US$82），
海運每年訂費2086元（US$74）

歐美／非洲地區——航空每年訂費NT$2542元（US$90），
海運每年訂費2086元（US$74）

若需掛號，全年另加US$5

請將費用以美金即期支票寄至：

臺北市大安區新生南路三段94號1樓　聯經出版公司

1F., No.94, Sec. 3, Xinsheng S. Rd., Da'an Dist., Taipei City 106, Taiwan (R.O.C.)

TEL：886-2-23620308

Subscription

A. List price: (surface postage included)

Hong Kong, Macao, China US$70 per issue; Asia, Oceania, America, Europe, Australia and Other Areas US$74. (Add US$5 for registered mail)

B. List price: (air mail)

Hong Kong, Macao, China: US$78 per issue; Asia and Oceania Areas US$82 per issue;

America, Europe, Australia and Other Areas: US$90. (Add US$5 for registered mail)

C. Subscription Rate: (2 issues per year)

Please pay by money order made payable to:

Thoughts History, 1F., No.94, Sec. 3, Xinsheng S. Rd., Taipei City 106, Taiwan (R.O.C.)

E-mail：lkstore2@udngroup.com

TEL：886-2-23620308

FAX：886-2-23620137

聯經出版事業公司

《思想史》期刊　信用卡訂閱單

訂購人姓名：______________________

訂購日期：______年______月______日

信用卡別：□VISA CARD　□MASTER CARD

信用卡號：________________（卡片背面簽名欄後三碼）______必填

信用卡有效期限：______月______年

信用卡簽名：________________________（與信用卡上簽名同）

聯絡電話：日(O)：________________　夜(H)：________________

傳眞號碼：________________________

聯絡地址：____

訂購金額：NT$______________________元整

發票：□二聯式　□三聯式

統一編號：______________________________

發票抬頭：______________________________

◎若收件人或收件地不同時，請另加塡！

收件人姓名：□同上__________________________□先生　□小姐

收件人地址：□同上____

收件人電話：□同上　日(O)：_____________　夜(H)：____________

※茲訂購下列書籍，帳款由本人信用卡帳戶支付

訂閱書名	年／期數	寄送	掛號	金額
《思想史》	訂閱____年	□航空 □海運	□是 □否	NT$

訂閱單塡妥後

1. 直接傳眞FAX：886-2-23620137
2. 寄臺北市大安區新生南路三段94號1樓　聯經出版公司 收

   TEL：886-2-23620308

思想史
思想史 4

2015年3月初版　　定價：新臺幣480元

編　著　思想史編委會
發行人　林載爵

出版者　聯經出版事業股份有限公司
地址　台北市基隆路一段180號4樓
編輯部地址　台北市基隆路一段180號4樓
叢書主編電話　(02)87876242轉225
台北聯經書房　台北市新生南路三段94號
電話　(02)23620308
台中分公司　台中市北區崇德路一段198號
暨門市電話：(04)22312023
台中電子信箱　e-mail：linking2@ms42.hinet.net
郵政劃撥帳戶第0100559-3號
郵撥電話　(02)23620308
印刷者　世和印製企業有限公司
總經銷　聯合發行股份有限公司
發行所　新北市新店區寶橋路235巷6弄6號2樓
電話　(02)29178022

叢書編輯　陳逸達
封面設計　沈佳德

行政院新聞局出版事業登記證局版臺業字第0130號

本書如有缺頁，破損，倒裝請寄回台北聯經書房更換。　ISBN 978-957-08-4558-7 (平裝)
聯經網址：www.linkingbooks.com.tw
電子信箱：linking@udngroup.com

國家圖書館出版品預行編目資料

思想史 4 /思想史編委會編著．初版．臺北市．聯經．
2015年3月（民104年）．344面．14.8×21公分
（思想史：4）
ISBN 978-957-08-45589-7（第4冊：平裝）

1.思想史 2.文集

110.7 104005956